# Advanced Missiology

"Nehrbass and company tackle multiple missiological big questions with adroitness and nuance in this ambitious text. Rather than focusing on what missiologists believe and use, they give us glimpses into how said missiologists utilized their own disciplinary frameworks as launching pads to engage God's mission. From where I sit, this is the best available examination of ideas and practices that currently drive the discipline of evangelical missiology.... This is a perfect book for those who want an overarching view of contemporary missiology from an evangelical vantage."
—SCOTT MOREAU, Academic Dean, Wheaton College Graduate School

"Nehrbass has succeeded in writing a thorough and comprehensive volume that addresses key issues facing missiology, both historically and in the present era of change.... This book will be useful to all those who are learning about, or are currently engaged in, the missions enterprise."
—STEPHEN A. CLARK, Professor of Intercultural Studies, Moody Bible Institute

"Having been frustrated by the scarcity of textbooks in missiological research methodology during my past twenty-four years of teaching at the doctoral level, I am glad that this book can fill that void. It is an outstanding text due to its comprehensive coverage, including both historical heritage and contemporary development."
—ENOCH WAN, Director of Doctor of Missiology and EdD Programs, Western Seminary

# Advanced Missiology

How to Study Missions in Credible and Useful Ways

Kenneth Nehrbass

CASCADE *Books* • Eugene, Oregon

ADVANCED MISSIOLOGY
How to Study Missions in Credible and Useful Ways

Copyright © 2021 Kenneth Nehrbass. All rights reserved. Except for brief quotations in critical publications or reviews, no part of this book may be reproduced in any manner without prior written permission from the publisher. Write: Permissions, Wipf and Stock Publishers, 199 W. 8th Ave., Suite 3, Eugene, OR 97401.

Cascade Books
An Imprint of Wipf and Stock Publishers
199 W. 8th Ave., Suite 3
Eugene, OR 97401

www.wipfandstock.com

PAPERBACK ISBN: 978-1-7252-7222-4
HARDCOVER ISBN: 978-1-7252-7223-1
EBOOK ISBN: 978-1-7252-7224-8

*Cataloguing-in-Publication data:*

Names: Nehrbass, Kenneth, author | Martinez, Julie, contributor | Burnett, Rebeca de la Torre, contributor | Dzubinski, Leanne, contributor.

Title: Advanced missiology : how to study missions in credible and useful ways / by Kenneth Nehrbass, with contributions by Julie Martinez, Rebeca de la Torre Burnett, and Leanne Dzubinski.

Description: Eugene, OR: Cascade Books, 2021 | Includes bibliographical references.

Identifiers: ISBN 978-1-7252-7222-4 (paperback) | ISBN 978-1-7252-7223-1 (hardcover) | ISBN 978-1-7252-7224-8 (ebook)

Subjects: LCSH: Missions—Theory.

Classification: BV2063 N44 2021 (print) | BV2063 (ebook)

Scripture quotations marked (NIV) are taken from the Holy Bible, New International Version®, NIV®. Copyright © 1973, 1978, 1984, 2011 by Biblica, Inc.™ Used by permission of Zondervan. All rights reserved worldwide. www.zondervan.com The "NIV" and "New International Version" are trademarks registered in the United States Patent and Trademark Office by Biblica, Inc.™

Scripture quotations marked (ESV) are from The Holy Bible, English Standard Version® (ESV®), copyright © 2001 by Crossway, a publishing ministry of Good News Publishers. Used by permission. All rights reserved.

Scripture quotations marked (NLT) are taken from the Holy Bible, New Living Translation, copyright ©1996, 2004, 2007, 2013 by Tyndale House Foundation. Used by permission of Tyndale House Publishers, Inc., Carol Stream, Illinois 60188. All rights reserved.

Scripture quotations marked "KJV" are taken from the Holy Bible, King James Version (Public Domain).

# Contents

Introduction  1

PART I: The Tributaries of Missiology

Chapter 1: Missiology Like a River  11
Chapter 2: ConnectingTheology to Cross-cultural Discipleship  35
Chapter 3: Connecting History to Cross-cultural Discipleship  71
Chapter 4: Connecting Anthropology to Cross-cultural Discipleship  99
Chapter 5: Connecting Intercultural Studies to Cross-cultural Discipleship  133
Chapter 6: Connecting Development Theory to Cross-cultural Discipleship (Julie Martinez with Kenneth Nehrbass)  151
Chapter 7: Connecting Education to Cross-cultural Discipleship (Rebeca Burnett and Leanne Dzubinski)  173

PART II: The Distributaries of Missiology

Chapter 8: Defining Cross-cultural Discipleship  197
Chapter 9: Seminal Theories of Cross-cultural Discipleship  206
Chapter 10: Seminal Models for Cross-cultural Discipleship  229
Chapter 11: The Future of Missiology  277

*Contributors' Biographies*  299
*Bibliography*  301

# Introduction

THE PURPOSE OF THIS book is to help you integrate multiple academic fields in order to increase your understanding of how Christianity spreads across cultures.

### By the end of this book

**You should know:**
- Major theorists and perspectives that have shaped the study of how Christianity spreads across cultures.
- Current and emerging global issues that impact missionary strategies.

**You should be able to:**
- Exegete Scripture for answers to tough questions about the way Christianity spreads across cultures.
- Exegete cultures so the gospel has a deep impact as you bring it across cultural boundaries.
- Increase your rapport with those across cultural boundaries.
- Apply culturally-relevant educational strategies to make disciples across cultures.
- Apply sustainable community development strategies which result in spiritual and physical transformation.
- Study missions in a way that is timely, credible, and useful.

**You should develop the following attitudes:**
- Curiosity about new academic fields that can help you understand how Christianity spreads across cultures.
- Conviction that a paramount goal of any academic study is to make disciples across cultures.

Missiology has become quite complex as it has incorporated numerous academic fields (e.g., theology, education, psychology, international development, and so on). While nobody could possibly become an expert in all these fields, those who desire to carry out credible and original studies of missions must be familiar with the people and ideas that have shaped missiology. They must also understand how these ideas actually impact missionary strategies. Regrettably, missiologists have not always explicitly connected their abstract theories to the task of making disciples across cultures. We have produced this book to address that gap between theory and practice. Each chapter shows how numerous theories, subfields, models, and strategies of missiology ultimately facilitate the Great Commission.

Since this book critically examines foundational missiological theories and models, it does not particularly serve as an *introduction* to missiology. A number of high-quality introductory texts are already available, including those written for a popular audience[1] as well as some seminal missiology texts.[2] Some recent introductions to missiology are fairly technical and original, including Bosch's discussion of the paradigms of mission,[3] and Tennent's missiology from a Trinitarian perspective.[4] Other introductions are written from a more denominational perspective[5] or from an ecumenical posture.[6] What we have found lacking is a book that shows how missiologists have actually generated academically credible theories that are useful for those missionary-practitioners who are making disciples across cultures.

While this is not an introductory text, readers will come across a number of widely circulated methods and theories of missions throughout the book, as we critically examine the ideas that have shaped missiology.

---

1. Goheen, *Introducing Christian Mission Today*; Moreau et al., *Introducing World Missions*.

2. Bavinck, *Introduction to the Science of Missions*; Pentecost, *Issues in Missiology*; Tippett, *Introduction to Missiology*; Verkuyl, *Contemporary Missiology*.

3. Bosch, *Transforming Mission*.

4. Tennent, *Invitation to World Missions*.

5. Terry et al., *Missiology*.

6. Verstraelen et al., *Missiology*.

## What to Expect from the Chapters

Chapter 1 challenges the conventional wisdom that missiology stands on three legs (theology, social sciences, and history). I suggest that the weaknesses of the "three-legged stool" compel us to develop a better model that demonstrates how the upsurge of interdisciplinarity has drastically expanded missiology to incorporate a widening set of disciplines. The model, "missiology like a river" serves as a guiding metaphor throughout the rest of the book. Readers should use the metaphor to recognize what "stream" of missiology they are comfortable swimming in, and the areas in which they have yet to get their feet wet. Hopefully the book will inspire you to dive in to the other currents of missiology with which you are less familiar.

In chapter 2, readers will come across the common missiological argument that a thread of mission(s) runs throughout the Bible.[7] But rather than simply recounting this compelling theory, I discuss its weaknesses and suggest an alternative approach toward missiological theology. This approach relies on examples of how missionary-theologians have tackled theological questions as they make disciples across cultures. Readers will learn to look to Scripture for answers to tough questions about the way Christianity spreads across cultures.

Likewise, instead of tracing the lives of canonical figures of mission history in chapter 3, as many introductions to the history of missions do, I have developed a missiological historiography that incorporates six criteria for examining history from a missiological perspective. I show how histories of missions can help us implement lessons from the past in our efforts to make disciples across cultures.

Again, rather than simply introducing the study of culture in chapter 4, I have examined how missiological anthropologists have actually used specific studies of social organization, mythology ritual, etc., to further missiological theories and strategies. You will learn to exegete cultures so the gospel can have a deep impact as you bring it across cultural boundaries.

Chapter 5 is unique because, even though many Christian universities place missions under the rubric of intercultural studies, almost no scholars have delineated what intercultural studies is actually comprised of. And few texts have explained how intercultural studies is distinct from anthropology. In this chapter, I outline the parameters of intercultural

---

7. Van Engen et al., *Announcing the Kingdom*; Wright, *Mission of God*.

studies and show how missiologists have made intercultural studies useful for making disciples across cultures.

In chapter 6, Julie Martinez and I discuss how theories of economic development impact missionary work. In the twentieth century, evangelicals had a difficult time balancing social action, on the one hand, and the mandate to teach about Jesus, on the other. The development of holistic (or integral) missions helped resolve that conflict. But the solutions related to hunger, oppression, health inequality, and other physical and social ills are still highly complicated. And missiologists are not agreed on the way to address these needs. The chapter should help readers to apply sustainable community development strategies which result in spiritual and physical transformation.

In chapter 7, educational missiologists Leanne Dzubinski and Rebeca Burnett describe how missiologists have incorporated theories from education—a less frequently studied tributary that informs our discipline. They discuss what missiologists have learned about formal and non-formal education as a missionary strategy throughout the world. This chapter should equip cross-cultural disciple-makers to "teach them all Jesus has commanded" by utilizing culturally relevant educational strategies.

In chapter 8, I define cross-cultural discipleship. Readers will critique multiplication models for evangelism and church planting.

In chapter 9, I introduce well-known models and theories that are idiosyncratic to the field of missiology. I show how missionary-practitioners have tested these models "on the ground"; and I bring out some of the deficiencies of these models.

Chapter 10 shows how the task of making disciples is connected to all sorts of things missionaries do, including church planting, teaching in higher education, teaching English as a second language, translating the Bible, and so on. Readers will not be engaged in all of these various efforts, but they should be able to draw from these various missionary strategies to ensure their own cross-cultural work holistically "teaches them to obey all that Jesus commanded."

Chapter 11 looks at global trends that will be shaping the mission field in the future. We need to know what issues have been addressed over the past decades, so we don't reinvent the wheel. Readers should identify missiological issues that have been neglected, or ones that have been saturated. We need to be aware of current pressing issues so our missionary methods stay relevant.

## Profiles of Missiologists

A unique feature of this book is the sidebars entitled "Missiologist Profiles." These are not profiles of famous missionaries; rather, they are appraisals of theoretical contributions by scholars (many of whom served for long periods as missionaries) who influenced the "science of missions." In compiling these profiles, I have included the educational background of these missiologists 1) in order to show the wide array of fields that have influenced missiology, and 2) because this information is, at times, not easily available in biographical sketches of missiologists. Some may wonder how I selected the men and women that end up in this "missiological hall of fame." I have had to rely on my own experience in missiology to develop a "canon" of important missiologists—but I also received feedback from missiologists across the country, regarding who should be on the list. I wish that the profiles represented more ethnic and gender diversity in the field; and I regret omitting many who did not "make the cut" in the list of profiles. Each semester I have my students suggest names of influential missiologists, and their own lists reveal that many more men and women have left a profound mark on the discipline.

## Defining Models and Theories

The way academics in any field make an impact on the world is by developing theories about the way the world works. Practitioners develop models for "best practices", sometimes by incorporating those theories, and sometimes in ignorance of those theories. The following chapters show how missiology makes use of theories and models from other disciplines like theology, anthropology, history, development, education, and intercultural studies.

For the sake of clarity, I will refer to theories as *descriptive* explanations of the way the world works. And models are *prescriptive* ways for doing things. Note that both models and theories may have titles, and they can both be expressed in propositional sentences. For example, the theory of "functional substitutes" was expressed with the proposition that if a newly Christian community omits a cultural practice, adherents will fill the void created by that omission with a substitute (see chapter 4).

The word "theory" is sometimes misunderstood to mean "an untested hypothesis." But in the social sciences (where missiology often occurs), theories are not hypotheses. Whereas hypotheses are articulated before research is carried out, theories in the social sciences are grounded in data that is gathered from the field. Hiebert defined theories as "limited, low-level systems of explanation that seek to answer specific questions about a narrow range of reality, using perceptions, concepts, notions, causation and the like."[8] These "systems of explanation" are discovered through prolonged study of people in their social contexts.

> **Theories** are *descriptive* explanations, grounded in data, of the way the world works.
>
> **Reductive theories** look for simple explanatory facts.
>
> **Categorizing theories** assign labels for the various viewpoints on an issue

The word "model" can also be confusing. Some people use "models" the way I use the word "theories" in this book. Geertz recognizes this ambiguity when he describes two types of models: models *of* and models *for*.[9] Models *of* are representations of how the world does work (that is, they are descriptive). For example, a model of a combustion engine shows how the cams and pistons and drive shaft work together. On the other hand, models *for* are prescriptive and pragmatic; they are road maps for how things should be done to reach certain ends. For example, Hiebert's critical contextualization[10] (described in chapter 9) is a model because it is prescriptive for how the church should contextualize the gospel. To avoid confusion, I only use the word "model" to refer to *prescriptive* ways for doing things.

## *Theories that Influence Missiology*

Hiebert noted that theories have been constructed in three ways: Early modernist theories were reductive, looking for the simplest explanatory "facts."[11] Malinowski's biological functionalism[12] (chapter 4) was a reductive theory, reducing all of human culture to seven

---

8. Hiebert, *Anthropological Reflections on Missiological Issues*, 35–37.
9. Geertz, *Interpretation of Cultures*, 93.
10. Hiebert, "Critical Contextualization."
11. Hiebert, *Gospel in Human Contexts*, 129–31.
12. Malinowski, *Scientific Theory of Culture and Other Essays*.

basic biological and psychological needs. Other theories are stratified, compartmentalizing aspects of human culture. For example, some Christians accept Christianity as a private matter for personal illumination, but turn to a materialistic worldview to explain scientific matters, and to a secular approach for public policy. Today, scholars have moved away from reductive theories; yet Christian thinkers are also unsatisfied with the compartmentalization that is endemic to stratified theories. So Hiebert advocated a third approach of building theories, called the systems approach. This approach recognizes that humans are impacted by multiple interacting systems: biology, economic, political, supernatural, etc. Each of these systems has only partial explanatory scope. For instance, people may convert to Christianity because the Holy Spirit tugs at them; but their conversion is also partly explained by their social networks, or the improvements they expect in their lives.

Researchers generate theories first by collecting data to answer a research question, and then by making sense of that data. Sometimes theories describe multiple viewpoints, experiences or attitudes of a certain group of people (e.g., female missionaries, or Muslim background believers, or missionary kids). These theories assign labels to a handful of categories which summarize the multiple perspectives and experiences. I refer to these theories as "categorizing theories." Below are some examples of categorizing theories that are discussed in this book:

1. Beliefs about the destiny of the un-evangelized can be categorized into three camps: Universalists, Inclusivists and Exclusivists (chapter 2).
2. Christian missionary efforts have gone through six paradigm shifts (chapter 3).
3. Societies can be divided into three taxa: tribal, peasant, and industrial (chapter 4).
4. Some societies are more hierarchal, some are more egalitarian (chapter 5).
5. Theories about community development focus on macro-economic level, eg., theory, or at the grassroots level, eg., transformational development (chapter 6).
6. Missionaries used formal and non-formal education to make disciples (chapter 7).

7. Responses to the gospel can be categorized in six ways, along a spectrum (chapter 9)

Sometimes theories try to explain a phenomenon or to make a statement about "the way things are," such as the following theories that will be discussed in this book:

1. Missionary activity is rooted in God's nature as a God who sends (chapter 2).
2. Female missionaries tend to have a relational-based missiology (chapter 3).
3. Myths are used as a means of social control (chapter 4).
4. Symptoms of culture shock include withdrawal and complaining about the host culture (chapter 5).
5. Wealth is created when entrepreneurs add value to material resources (chapter 6).
6. Teachers model their own spiritual lives to their students (chapter 7).
7. Western missionaries often ignored the role of demons, ghosts, and spirits; therefore, practitioners of folk religions continued shamanism, even after becoming Christianized (chapter 9).

*Models that Influence Missiology*

**Models** are *prescriptive* ways for doing things. They are "best practices" that emerge from empirical research.

Practitioner-scholars develop models to make academic theories useful in the real world. Such models are "best practices" that emerge from empirical research. Some examples of models are discussed in this book include:

1. The incarnation is a model for missionary activity; or the book of Acts as a normative model for church planting; or the "representational" model of evangelistic witness (chapter 2).

2. The history of missions should be studied in ways that reveal best practices for making disciples across cultures (chapter 3).

3. Missionaries should replace pagan rituals with "functional substitutes" (chapter 4).

4. Missionaries should know their role within the host culture, and should behave according to those roles (e.g., patron, or expert leader) (chapter 5).

5. Communities should participate at each stage in development projects (chapter 6).

6. Missionary training should involve experiential learning (chapter 7).

7. Missions should focus on the most unreached peoples of the world between 10 and 40 degrees north latitude (chapter 9).

8. Missionaries should start businesses that actually generate income, rather than using business as a "platform" for missions (chapter 10).

In addition to adopting theories from other disciplines, missiologists have generated many of their own theoretical explanations and models. Chapter 9 discusses widely distributed theories and models that were formulated specifically in the field of missiology.

Theories and models in any discipline have a sort of "half-life" and eventually may even become discredited.[13] Missiology is not immune to this—the models and theories in this book have all been contested; some theories and models have outlived their usefulness, while others have a longer "tail life."[14] Students of any discipline are not exempt from having to learn the genealogy of these theories. And in order to be conversant in missiology, one must be familiar with the development of thought in the fields on which missiology draws. Some theories and models reverberate for decades, and spawn new theories that are useful for the next generation of practitioner-scholars (I return to this point in chapter 11).

---

13. Arbesman, *Half-life of Facts*.
14. Nehrbass, "Half-life of Missiological Facts."

### "Move Into Action," Further Research, Reflection, and Review

Each chapter has action points, ideas for further research, as well as reflection and review questions.

It is my hope for this book that readers will gain tools to make their own mark on missiology, all for the sake of making disciples across cultures.

*Chapter 1*

# The Multiple Disciplines of Missiology[1]

SEVEN OF JESUS'S FRIENDS had been fishing all night, with nothing to show for their efforts. Perhaps the lake had been over-fished. Maybe the bait was old. Or the fish were too savvy for the strategies and methods that the disciples were using. Jesus told them to try it a new way—cast the net on the other side of the boat (John 21:6). Maybe Jesus's "new tactic" was anti-climactic; but the results were drastic! That's what missiology is supposed to do: inspire those of us who have always been fishing on one side of the boat to cast a net in a different way. Maybe that means learning new pedagogies, or studying cultural theory more, or revisiting missionary history, or learning from global theologies. This chapter outlines numerous ways you can start casting your net more broadly.

> **Chapter Goals**
>
> *Knowledge goals:*
>
> - Decide on the definition of missiology that you will use consistently.
> - Understand the role that theology plays in the study of missions, in relationship to all other academic fields.

---

1. This chapter has been modified from Nehrbass, "Does Missiology Have Three Legs to Stand On?"

*Action goals:*

- Recognize which field of study you are most likely to use to further understand how Christianity spreads across cultures.
- Recognize which field of study you need to pursue more, in order to further understand how Christianity spreads across cultures.

*Heart goals:*

- Commit not only to advancing the study of missions, but to completing the "feedback loop" by influencing the academic fields that shape missiology.

Below, I begin by briefly working out a definition of missiology; then I explore five limitations of the commonly promulgated "three-legged stool" metaphor, which errs in suggesting that the academic disciplines within missiology are static and finite in number, containing firm boundaries between each of them. It also erroneously implies that these disciplines exert a unidirectional influence on missiology. And while a stool has legs of equal length, scholars are not likely to ascribe equal prominence to each of the fields that influence missiology.

To better understand the role of interdisciplinarity within the study of Christian missions, I will suggest the image of missiology as a river. This dynamic and expanding metaphor remedies the limitations of an inert stool, and allows for a meta-theoretical framework for describing the fluid and expanding nature of the discipline. To develop this metaphor, I will discuss emerging theories of interdisciplinarity, which have received little notice from missiologists; and I will uncover some of the dangers of casting such a broad interdisciplinary net. I argue that it is not the use of theology, social sciences, and history that lends missiological significance to a study; instead, it is the use of an interdisciplinary approach for the sake of making disciples across cultures that describes how missiology is done (see below for a more expanded discussion on the definition of missiology). In critiquing metaphors of the discipline of missiology, I desire to help emerging scholars of Christian missions find where they best fit within the discipline. They should cast their net ever more broadly, while standing firmly in their own area of expertise.

## Defining Missiology

Just as a definition of "Christian missions" has been elusive and hotly contested over the years, scholars have had difficulty pinning down exactly what missiology is. As the study of Christian missions advances, it incorporates countless disciplines, ranging from biblical exegesis to cultural anthropology, to computational linguistics, to the use of psychology in member care and cultural adjustment, and so on. The advantage of this broad influence is that scholars of missions can draw on their diverse academic backgrounds and interests as they apply their understanding of the *missio Dei* to their contexts. However, the ever expanding net that missiologists cast may lead to the same problem that Stephen Neill warned about when it comes to defining missions: If everything is missiology, then nothing is missiology.[2] To avoid this crippling ambiguity, we must answer, *What is the nature of interdisciplinarity within missiology? What common denominator brings these disciplines together? How can an academician specialize, and yet be interdisciplinary at the same time? What is the relationship between academic theories of missions and the actual practice of Christian missions?* And at the very foundation of all these questions, we must settle on a definition of the discipline: *What is missiology?*

To define missiology, we may start with the definition offered by a scholar who has done more than any other to shape the discipline. Alan Tippett defined missiology as "the academic discipline or science which researches, records and applies data relating to the biblical origin, the history . . . the anthropological principles and techniques, and the theological base of the Christian mission."[3] Tippet's definition is an early instance of the trifecta of theology, anthropology and history, with theology made prominent. Missionary strategies (techniques) are also mentioned. We can also detect in Tippett's definition an earlier, more basic definition of missiology as simply "the science of Christian missions."

---

2. Neill, *Creative Tension*.
3. Tippett, "Missiology, A New Discipline", 26.

## Missiology

is the utilization of multiple academic disciplines to develop strategies for making disciples across cultures.

## A Missiologist

is someone whose primary work is to study the way Christianity spreads across cultural boundaries.

*Note that later in the book, I will give definitions of cross-cultural (chapter 5), missionary (chapter 8), and "making disciples" (chapter 8).*

 

While Tippett's definition is seminal, I suggest that it is unhelpful to leave the word "missionary" or "missions" undefined in a definition of missiology. Instead, we should aim to actually flesh out—concisely—the essence of these terms. While many definitions of Christian missions have been offered, for the sake of parsimony, I begin with Scherer's pithy definition as the church's endeavor to cross boundaries.[4] I maintain throughout this book that missiology is the use of academic disciplines to bring the church across cultural boundaries for the sake of making disciples.

This brings us to one other limitation in Tippett's definition: Missiology has moved far beyond the confining threefold taxonomy of theology, history, and the social sciences. So I would broaden a definition of missiology significantly to "the utilization of multiple academic disciplines to develop strategies for making disciples across cultures."

---

4. Scherer, "Missiology as a Discipline and What It Includes," 37.

## Profile of a Missiologist: Alan Tippett

### (1911–1988)

*Education: L.Th. Queens College, Melbourne; MA (social anthropology) Washington University; PhD (anthropology) University of Oregon*

*Occupation: Methodist Missionary; professor of missiology*

Alan and Edna Tippett served as missionaries for twenty years in Fiji, where Alan began a lifelong project of lobbying for the transfer of the colonial mission to indigenous leadership.[1]

Fuller School of World Mission professor Donald McGavran became aware of Tippett's missiological genius and invited him to teach at Fuller. Tippett brought an anthropological focus to McGavran's thoughts on church growth, and Tippett "helped shape a number of key concepts that became popular in missiological discourse. Among these included the concepts of functional substitutes, power encounter, people movements, and indigenous church."[2] Along with Paul Hiebert, Eugene Nida, and Louis Luzbetak, Tippett helped shape the budding field of missiological anthropology. Tippett explained, "Anthropology does not bring individuals to Christ, but it shows missionaries how they may be more effective and less of a hindrance in doing so."[3]

Tippett authored over 500 pieces, according to Caldwell's bibliography of Tippett, which lists his major missiological contributions in English.[4] Several of his books meticulously recorded themes from the Pacific, including the contribution of Pacific Islander evangelists[5] and the anthropology of Christianity in the Pacific.[6]

Charles Kraft eulogized Tippett as follows:

> Alan Tippett is considered by most missiologists as one of the two or three best in our generation in terms of his ability to comprehend and articulate (especially in writing) the intricate relationships between biblical, cultural, personal and strategic aspects of the Christian mission.[7]

---

[1] Kraft and Priest, "Who Was this Man?" 271.
[2] Whiteman, "Legacy of Alan R Tippett," 165.
[3] Tippett, *Introduction to Missiology*, 28.
[4] Caldwell, "Selected Missiological Works of Alan R. Tippett."
[5] Tippett, *People Movements in South Polynesia; Deep Sea Canoe.*
[6] Tippett, *Solomon Islands Christianity.*
[7] Kraft, "Tippett, Alan Richard (1911–1988)," 374.

## Depicting Missiology

Once we have a basic definition of missiology, we can begin searching for a metaphor that depicts how the study of Christian missions is actually done. Missiologists have typically organized the discipline around three intersecting academic fields: theology, history, and anthropology (or more broadly, the social sciences).[5] Some have likened missiology's dependence on three major disciplines to a stool that stands on three legs.[6] While the stool metaphor is helpful in naming the "big three" disciplines, it has numerous limitations.

To begin with, scholars of missions who have expertise in other areas like education[7] or mission strategy[8] argue that the stool actually stands on a fourth leg. However, it is debatable what exactly that fourth leg should be, since scholars are tempted to emphasize the importance of those disciplines in which they have extensive professional experience. And if we added more legs to the stool, Olson and Fanning's model of missiology would stand on five legs (which they call dimensions): history, theology, anthropology, demographics, and strategy.[9] How many more legs can be added to the stool before it becomes something else altogether? While we know that missiology is by nature interdisciplinary, we have had difficulty delineating the disciplines that are especially "in" or "out."

It is also difficult to find a metaphor that depicts how theory relates to practice in missiology. Justice Anderson's tripartite equation was reminiscent of the three-legged stool, but incorporated a space for strategy: The theology of mission plus the history of mission comprise a philosophy of mission (approaches) which will, in turn, lead to cross-cultural strategies.[10] Baker turned the three-legged stool metaphor on its figurative head by suggesting that the stool is inverted like a top: Theology, history, and anthropology are situated above the much more prominent part: the seat of the stool.[11] The seat, where these legs meet

---

5. Conn, *Eternal Word and Changing Worlds*; Tippett, *Introduction to Missiology*; Winter and Hawthorne, *Perspectives on the World Christian movement*, 27.

6. Steffen, "Missiology's Journey for Acceptance in the Educational World."

7. Langmead, "What is Missiology?"

8. Luzbetak, *Church and Cultures*.

9. Olson and Fanning, *What in the World is God Doing?*

10. J. Anderson, "Overview of Mission," 8.

11. Baker, "Missiology as an Interested Discipline."

up, is mission strategy. However, the more we tweak the stool metaphor to make it describe missiology, the more suspicious we become of its usefulness as a heuristic device.

Below, I will explore five limitations of the stool metaphor. The point is not so much to decry the metaphor itself, but to see how exposing these limitations can bring to light the true richness of the interdisciplinary nature of missiology.

## Limitation 1: Stool Legs Are Distinct, Static and Separate

A significant limitation of a stool metaphor is that furniture is solid, stationary, and unchanging. The legs of a stool are distinct, and do not touch each other. Reducing missiology to a short list of static disciplines creates artificial boundaries, and excludes other fields that are also influential. For example, the line between history and anthropology is often blurred in ethnographic studies, as a society's past tends to shape its cultural makeup. Or to take another example of these fuzzy boundaries between disciplines: No theology can be developed without a theory of humankind—that is, without combining theology and anthropology. Baker pointed out the fuzzy boundaries between disciplines in the study of Christian missions when he argued that history, theology, and anthropology are metonyms for the "continually expanding array of disciplines and sub-disciplines" such as ethnohistory, ethnotheology, and ethnodoxology.[12]

Missiology is not static; it has been shaped over the years by needs, trends, shifts, and paradigms. Rather than limit the academic disciplines that feed into the study of Christian missions, we need to emphasize the dynamic and expanding nature of missiology.

### Ethnotheology

is the study of beliefs held by a particular people. All theologies are actually ethnotheologies, though Westerners have often thought of ethnotheology as the study of beliefs held by Christians outside of the Western world.

---

12. Baker, "Missiology as an Interested Discipline," 18.

**Ethnodoxology**

is the study of worship practices (including music, dance, and visual arts) within a particular culture. Again, all doxologies are actually ethnodoxologies, though Westerners have often thought of ethnodoxology as the study of worship practices held by Christians outside of the Western world.

## Limitation 2: Stool Legs Are of Equal Length (or Prominence)

Now that the distinct lines between the stool's legs have been blurred, the length of each leg is also called into question. A stool fails if one of its legs is longer than the others. But missiologists recognize that the equal weight should not be given to each academic sub-field. What they do not agree on is *which* leg is prominent.

Most missiologists would agree that theology has a leg up on the other fields. Missiological anthropologist Paul Hiebert argued that missiology must be built on theology—but not just any theology; rather, it must embrace a theology that has mission at its core.[13] To keep theology prominent, Pentecost's image of missiology places theology at the hub of a wheel, and our various other academic pursuits are the spokes that stem out of the hub.[14] While some missiologists give prominence to theology, ironically, theology classes make up only a small percentage of the curriculum in schools of missions or intercultural studies. Bible and theology courses make up on average 21 percent of the required curriculum for doctoral degrees in missiology at six well-known Christian universities in the USA, with a minimum of 13 percent and maximum of 38 percent.[15]

Just as theologians would argue that the discipline should occupy a prominent role in the study of Christian missions, anthropologists are

---

13. Hiebert, "Social Sciences and Missions," 203.

14. Pentecost, *Issues in Missiology*, 16.

15. I compared the ratio of credits for courses that are overtly theological or biblical in nature to the total credits required for the DMiss (alternatively called the Doctor of Intercultural Studies) at the following six academic institutions: Biola (6 out of 40 credits), Grace Seminary (18 out of 48 credits), Western Seminary (9 out of 36 credits), Assemblies of God Theological Seminary (9 out of 38 credits), Southern Baptist Theological Seminary (6 out of 48 credits) and for the PhD in Missiology at Concordia Theological Seminary (15 out of 72 credits).

trying to secure their influence in missiology. Anthropology is in crisis in academia, and the role of anthropology in seminaries is increasingly contested, for fear that secular ideas about humanity from the social sciences will have a corrupting influence. And more broadly, "the social sciences, in the minds of many theologians, should not be allowed a dialogue partner role".[16]

Twenty years ago, Hesselgrave concluded that evangelical missiologists have a "fascination" with the social sciences as he compared the use of social sciences, theology and history in the conciliar *International Review of Missions* (IRM) to those in *Evangelical Missions Quarterly* (EMQ). Four percent of articles in IRM were historical, 15 percent were theological, and 1 percent were based on social sciences. In contrast, 1 percent of articles in EMQ used historical inquiry, 7 percent were theological in nature, and 6 percent relied on the social sciences.[17]

The role historians have to play in missiology is also ambiguous. Is the study of history an end in itself, or is it only useful insofar as it provides insights about failures, successes, and paradigm shifts in Christian missions? While evangelicals have not neglected theology, they have a short memory (they have neglected history) and have had what Corwin called a "love affair with [cultural] research and analysis."[18] With such an emphasis on research in the social sciences, some feared that missiology was actually becoming de-theologized.[19]

Interestingly, the origin of the "three-legged stool" analogy is related not only to interdisciplinarity but to questions about giving prominence to a specific discipline. Throughout the twentieth century, the metaphor of a three-legged stool was typically ascribed to Reformation leader Richard Hooker. Hooker developed an Anglican hermeneutic that leaned on Scripture, reason, and authority (or tradition):

> Be it in matter of the one kind or of the other, what Scripture doth plainly deliver, to that the first place both of credit and obedience is due, the next whereunto is whatsoever any man can necessarily conclude by force of reason; after this the Church succeedeth that which the church by her ecclesiastical authority shall probably think and define to be true or good,

---

16. Priest, "Value of Anthropology for Missiological Engagements," 30.
17. Hesselgrave, "Preface," 2.
18. Corwin, "Sociology and Missiology," 20.
19. McQuilkin, "Use and Misuse of the Social Sciences," 176.

must in congruity of reason overrule all other inferior judgments whatsoever.[20]

Some historical theologians challenge the notion that Hooker developed such a three-legged hermeneutic that would give Scripture, reason, and authority equal weight. Instead, Hooker and most other reformers envisioned a hierarchy or chain of command, with Scripture at the top. Reason and tradition are also essential for guiding our lives, but are subservient to Scripture.

Missiologists employ a similar chain of command for developing the study of Christian missions; but there is disagreement about what is at the top of the chain. The stool metaphor does not adequately capture the way in which disciplines are weighted or given prominence.

### Limitation 3: Stool Legs Do Not Represent a Recursive Process

Our understanding of missiology must also reflect the interplay between theory and practice. If we think of theory as legs on which to stand, or as ideas that funnel down to strategy, we fail to recognize the recursive interaction between theory and strategy. In reality, our theories are shaped by real experience; so there is, as Baker put it, a feedback loop.[21] The field experiences of missionaries are continually applied to missiology to refine theory and strategies. Missiologists pine for a scenario where the study of Christian missions not only stems from systematic theology, but also informs the work of theologians! And, in fact, some theologians have certainly been influenced by missiologists. New Testament scholars D. A. Carson and Andreas Köstenberger, and pastoral theologian John Piper are some examples. Timothy Tennent,[22] after Andrew Walls, has built a strong argument for the necessity of cross-cultural influence on every area of systematic theology. This feedback is especially helpful as missiologists can further the field of theology by distinguishing between cultural forms and underlying meanings.[23]

Missiology and anthropology are in a continual process of cross-pollination (to switch metaphors for a minute). At the end of the nineteenth century, Christian missions played a major part in forming

20. Hooker, *Of the Lawes of Ecclesiasticall Politie*, Book V, 23.
21. Baker, "Missiology as an Interested Discipline," 18.
22. Tennent, *Theology in the Context of World Christianity*.
23. Allison, "Contribution of Cultural Anthropology to Missiology," 38.

the discipline of anthropology. Whiteman has traced the contribution made to anthropological theory by missionaries like Robert Codrington, John Batchelor, Maurice Leenhardt, Henri Alexandre Junod, and William and Charlotte Wiser.[24] Missionaries provided data from all over the world on so-called primitive cultures, and they modeled high standards for ethnographic field methods.

The feedback loop can also be seen in the way missionaries provided data on the world's minority languages at a time when linguistics was becoming recognized as a science in its own right. Kenneth Pike, founder of the Summer Institute of Linguistics (SIL), was a formative linguist. Eugene Nida, from the United Bible Society (UBS), helped bring anthropology, linguistics, and Christian missions together.

Since this time, theories from anthropology, linguistics, pedagogy, and so on, have in turn influenced missiology. To take several examples, missiology incorporated the notion of functional substitutes from Malinowski's biological functionalism;[25] the orality movement gained steam from Walter Ong's seminal work on the subject;[26] Edward Hall's research from the Foreign Service Institute (FSI) shaped missionary cross-cultural training for decades.[27] Missiologists Lingenfelter's and Mayers's models of cross-cultural communication[28] drew on Kluckhohn and Strodtbeck's comparative study of cultural values;[29] and their grid-group model relied on work from anthropologist Mary Douglas.[30] And more recently, Livermore's application[31] of Cultural Intelligence (CQ) to short-term missions was borrowed from the business world.[32] (Note that each of these theories is discussed in subsequent chapters.)

In any interdisciplinary context, borrowing and modifying is a two-way process. It is as if theology, history, the social sciences, linguistics, etc., move forward alongside missiology; the more diffusion of ideas there is between the disciplines, the more they have in common. The

---

24. Whiteman, "Anthropology and Mission."
25. Malinowski, *Scientific Theory of Culture and Other Essays*.
26. Ong, *Orality and Literacy*.
27. Hall, *Silent Language; Beyond Culture; Hidden Dimension*.
28. Lingenfelter and Mayers, *Ministering Cross-culturally*.
29. Kluckhohn and Strodtbeck, *Variations in Value Orientations*.
30. Douglas, *Cultural Bias*.
31. Livermore, *Cultural Intelligence*.
32. Ng et al., "Cultural Intelligence."

stool metaphor, though, does not allow for the influence that one leg has on the other.

## Limitation 4: Missiology Is Not Done That Way

Additionally, while the "three leg" metaphor has become nearly canonical, it does not describe how missiology is actually done. Over twenty years ago, missiologists recognized that missiological training for the twenty-first century would certainly involve theology and the social sciences, but would also include studies from other areas like economics, poverty, urbanization, migration, globalization, and the breakdown of the family.[33] Pocock's list of sciences that are part of missiology included "anthropology, sociology, psychology, communications, linguistics, demography, geography and statistics."[34]

In fact, missiology has been branching beyond the "three big disciplines" for decades. For example, Anderson recognized the role that agriculture, education, medicine, and public health play in shaping the study of Christian missions.[35] Kraft's missiology leaned heavily on theology, history, and anthropology, but also drew from communication theory. Cross-cultural training relies on the psychology of cultural adjustment experienced by sojourners and immigrants. Research methods inevitably get into philosophy; evangelism relies on studies of world religions, pluralism, and epistemology. Business as Mission (BAM) relies on economics and social justice.[36] To mitigate the fault of the "three and only three disciplines" in the stool analogy, Tippett's organization of the study of Christian missions involved a Venn diagram with two dozen or so overlapping sub-disciplines (demographics, sociology, etc).[37]

The ever-widening pool of theory from which missiology draws can be seen in specific research projects. For example, Ott's recent article on biblical metaphors drew on (among others) biblical studies of atonement and ecclesiology, as well as the use of metaphor in higher education, the role of ontology in architecture, the use of symbol and ritual in culture, and

---

33. Steffen, "Missiological Education for the 21st Century."
34. Pocock, "Introduction," 10.
35. Anderson, "Introducing Missiology."
36. Rundle and Steffen, *Great Commission Companies*.
37. Tippett, *Introduction to Missiology*.

the role of language and translation.[38] Two recent studies published in *The Great Commission Research Journal* relied on ecclesiology and theology as well as concepts from the field of qualitative research methodology.[39] Jenkins's essay on "missiology in environmental context" cites numerous sources on environmental stewardship but also employs liberation theology, ecology, and development theories.[40] And Rynkiewich's article on diaspora missiology cites sources on globalization, multiculturalism, hermeneutics, as well as specific ethnographic studies.[41]

In fact, missiological research can be done without direct historical studies, or without delving into anthropological theory. For example, Barram's theoretical essay on biblical values of economic justice, while rooted in the *oikonomia* of Genesis 1–3, does not look at the economics within specific cultural or historical contexts.[42] Additionally, theology may be slim in some missiological research; but the piece may still make a contribution to Christian missions. LaBreche's research on the evaluation of missionary performance relies very little on anthropology, history or theology, but provides important guidelines for missionary educators and administrators.[43] In fact, as I looked over my own missiological research, I noticed that my study of Christianity and animism in Melanesia stood on anthropology, history, and to a lesser extent, theology.[44] However, my study of formal theological education in Vanuatu did not particularly involve historical or theological inquiry—it asked a question from the social sciences: For what reasons do Melanesians avail themselves of theological training?[45]

---

38. Ott, "Power of Biblical Metaphors."

39. Casey, "Identifying and Reaching Ethnic Groups in the City"; Huizing, "In Search of the Healthy Church."

40. Jenkins, "Missiology in Environmental Context."

41. Rynkiewich, "Mission in the 'Present time.'"

42. Barram, "'Occupying' Genesis 1–3."

43. LaBreche, "Missionary Performance Evaluation."

44. Nehrbass, *Christianity and Animism in Melanesia*.

45. Nehrbass, "Formal Theological Education in Vanuatu."

### The Interdisciplinary Approach

An inquiry is interdisciplinary when it combines more than one academic discipline to answer a question.

*Example*: Nurses and anthropologists combined their efforts in an interdisciplinary study to understand how village leaders in India could encourage more handwashing.

What, then, makes the study missiological, if it does not stand simultaneously on theology, social sciences and history? The use of an interdisciplinary approach for making disciples of the *ethne* (Matt 28:16–20; Luke 24:44–48; John 20:21; Acts 1:8) is the common denominator of missiology. That is, it is not the presence of certain academic fields that makes missiology; instead, what makes missiology is a commitment to understanding how best to make Jesus-followers as we cross cultures.

Extreme prioritists (those who believe missionaries should place a higher priority on proclamation of the gospel than on any other activity) may argue that missiology is only useful insofar as more churches are planted. But the command to make disciples of all nations is more richly understood when it is taken in a number of directions. We make disciples of the *ethne* as we educate cross-culturally, as we run businesses in an ethical way cross-culturally, as we care for the sick and provide for other material needs (I elaborate on this argument in ch. 8). In other words, we may be engaged in missiology even when we are not sitting squarely on the three-legged stool of theology, history, and social sciences.

## Limitation 5: Stool Legs Do Not Describe a Meta-Theory

This leads us to a fifth limitation of the three-legged stool. True, just as the legs serve to prop up the stool, each of the disciplines (whether three, four, five or whatever number) serves the single purpose of cross-cultural discipleship. However, the stool metaphor comes up short in explaining how these legs are fundamentally related to each other, or how they synergistically create a new entity. Is there some sort of "unifying field of knowledge" that explains what in the world anthropology has to do with theology, or what education has to do with history? Even a Venn diagram with the blurred boundaries between theology, history, social sciences, etc., fails to represent a unifying field that brings these disciplines together in the first place.

It is God's mission, the *missio Dei*, that really serves as a unifying field around which all our other academic studies are organized. That is, God has been working throughout history and human societies, since the beginning of time, for the central purpose of revealing Himself. In that sense, there is no anthropology for its own sake, or even theology for its own sake. In light of the *missio Dei*, all studies are based on the underlying purpose of understanding who God is and who we are in relation to God.

Additionally, the "one-size-fits-all" characteristic of the stool metaphor fails to depict how missiology is done on a global scale. The questions of missiology are shaped significantly by our own ecclesiastical traditions; so missiology looks different for different "camps." Glasser recognized that there are distinct conciliar, independent, and Catholic missiologies; and these traditions serve as "balancing distinctives" for the discipline.[46]

## Summary of the Three-Legged Stool Metaphor: Does Missiology Have a Leg to Stand On?

Missiology is not a hodgepodge of firmly bounded academic disciplines; nor is it the sum total of knowledge from these various disciplines. The study of Christian missions is something *sui generis*—it is the use of biblical theology, social sciences, education, etc. in order to understand how to make disciples in other cultural contexts. As our knowledge of the world expands and changes, as more voices are added to the choir, missiology changes as well.

Below, I will develop a metaphor of missiology which attempts to rectify the deficiencies of models like three-legged stools, Venn diagrams, and spokes on a wheel. I envision the science of Christian missions more as a river with countless tributaries (theoretical disciplines) that converge at the common goal of making disciples in cross-cultural contexts. As the river moves downstream, it serves multiple communities in endless ways (mission strategies).

But before developing the metaphor of missiology as a river, we need to consider the nature of interdisciplinarity itself, since it is the cross-pollination of ideas that really encapsulates how missiology is done.

46. Glasser, *Missiology*.

## The Nature of Interdisciplinarity

Of course, missiology does not have a monopoly on interdisciplinarity. Collaboration is becoming increasingly popular all over academia, as we recognize that all learning is simply the process of making new connections between several previously un-connected ideas. For instance, social scientists and physicians are working together to solve health problems in the Global South. Mining and oil companies consult anthropologists to understand the communities where they do business. As interdisciplinarity becomes more common, academicians run the risk of collaborating simply for collaboration's sake, or simply because it is trendy. Interdisciplinarity scholar Frodeman asks, interdisciplinary is useful "to what end? Pragmatically put, toward the ends of greater insight and greater success at problem solving."[47] In the case of missiology, the cross-pollination is for the ultimate sake of making disciples of all peoples.

Earlier, I mentioned that one fault of the three-legged metaphor is the tendency to portray the disciplines of missiology as distinct and static. Interdisciplinarity scholars Calhoun and Rhoten explain that this tendency is common within any interdisciplinary field: "The distinctions among the social science disciplines are historically forged and largely arbitrary."[48] The recognition of a blurry overlap between fields marks a paradigm shift in interdisciplinarity. Scholars have moved from collaboration or interaction to integration of their disciplines.[49]

What makes interdisciplinarity different from collaboration is that true interdisciplinary studies often give birth to a new academic discipline. Missiology was the result of what Krohn has called "interdisciplinary fusion"[50]—rather than leaving the boundaries between disciplines firm, a new discipline was born to solve new sorts of problems encountered in the mission field. So interdisciplinarity is not a salad bowl—it requires integrating multiple disciplines to create a new field with distinct research methods, theoretical models, and purposes. And missiologists have argued that their field is not merely a mixture of more

---

47. Frodeman, *Oxford Nandbook on Interdisciplinarity*, xxxii.

48. Calhoun and Rhoten, "Integrating the Social Sciences," 104.

49. Landau et al., "Interdisciplinary Approach and the Concept of Behavioral Sciences."

50. Krohn, "Interdisciplinary Cases and Disciplinary Knowledge", 31.

"legitimate disciplines" like the social sciences, theology, etc.; in the past three decades it has come to be recognized as a field in its own right.[51]

## The Dangers and Difficulties of an Interdisciplinary Approach

While interdisciplinarity is part of being "cutting edge" in academia, it is not a panacea. In fact, it comes at a cost. One danger of such interdisciplinarity is it can give the impression that scholars must be experts in numerous fields in order to make a significant contribution. Staffing schools of mission with diverse specialists can give the impression that to be a mission scholar, one must become an expert on fields ranging from pastoral theology to Islamic studies to international development. Scherer called this tendency "interdisciplinary overload."[52] We must be careful not to send the message that missiologists must be simultaneously economists, theologians, anthropologists, historians, educationists, and demographers. Instead, we must allow scholars to locate themselves within the broad discipline, and to ask what new contributions they can make in the theory and practice of missions.

Also, interdisciplinarity can lead to "disciplinary defaulting" where theorists from certain backgrounds (economics, anthropology, etc.) continue to use terms and theories that are specific to their field, but that do not translate well across disciplines.[53] This leads us to a related danger: rather than fostering cross-pollination, emphasizing separate disciplines can cause further compartmentalization.[54] This is evident in our schools of world mission which are occupied by theologians, historians, anthropologists, linguists, development consultants, and educationists, yet the demanding schedules of academia often impede the interdisciplinary process.

## New Testament Missiology as a Base for a New Metaphor

It is common to talk about the "missionary methods" of the apostle Paul, the founder of Christian missions, but did he actually develop a missiology? Hesselgrave contends that Paul's methods, theology, and

---

51. Scherer, "Missiology as a Discipline and What it Includes"; Tippett, *Missiology*.
52. Scherer, "Missiology as a Discipline and What it Includes," 517.
53. Miller, "Varieties of Interdisciplinary Approaches in the Social Sciences," 1.
54. Adeney, "Telling Stories," 384.

strategies were inextricably linked.[55] While Paul did not have modern anthropology, and was not a historian, he used knowledge from many areas of life to discover how God makes Himself known among the *ethne*. Paul certainly combined the study of salvation history, culture, biblical exegesis, etc., to form a philosophy of missions and missionary strategies. Paul's missiology was defined by a desire to preach Christ to all ethne, and that approach required him to vary his message, style, polity, and methods depending on his target audience.[56]

We see the same sort of flexibility in proclamation, methods, and geographic targeting throughout the New Testament. As Dean Flemming showed, Luke's program for the book of Acts seemed to be the development of a missiology that contextualized the message, the law, and leadership styles for the target audience.[57] For example, Paul adapted his communication style as well as his message for the Jewish agrarians, the Greek philosophers, and the Romans in rural areas.[58] The good news for Corinth was embodied differently than it was in Rome, Thessalonica, or Philippi.[59] In fact, Flemming has shown a flexibility in the missiology of Jesus and Peter, as well as Paul.[60] So while it may be anachronistic to refer to a New Testament missiology, the apostles developed cross-cultural ministry with some of the tools that missiologists use.

For example, Paul's philosophy of missions was dynamic; it expanded and was flexible. The law applied differently to Jews living in Jerusalem than for pagans in the Roman Empire (Acts 15:1–35). As gentiles came to faith, Paul realized that he could have communion with them (Gal 2:11—3:29); and the expansion of the church in his day caused him to work out a theology of the law. Consider how he worked out an approach toward food that had been sacrificed to idols (1 Cor 8:1–13; 10:14–26). It was a theological question, but also an issue of culture, politics, history, and even demographics. Dyrness (after Chester Wood) argued that as Paul understood the geopolitical circumstances of his day, his missiological strategy involved moving the missionary outreach center from Jerusalem

---

55. Hesselgrave, "Paul's Missions Strategy."
56. Schnabel, "Paul the Missionary."
57. Flemming, *Contextualization in the New Testament*.
58. Flemming, *Contextualization in the New Testament*, 70, 74, 85, 130.
59. Flemming, *Contextualization in the New Testament*, 87–88.
60. Flemming, *Contextualization in the New Testament*, 53.

to Rome.[61] Andrew Walls takes note of Paul's interdisciplinarity in solving missiological questions: "Paul ranges over such issues as the ontological status of pagan divinities, the nature of Christian liberty, the Christian duty of loving consideration for other Christians, and the different degrees of Christian maturity."[62]

And Paul's missiology also was directional, as the spirit moved him along. He came to understand that his missionary purpose was to be a light to the gentiles (Acts 13:46–48). The dynamic aspect of Paul's missiology meant that his strategies were unbounded; he could move as the Spirit led; in fact virtually every decision Paul made was based on prayer and the Spirit's guidance.[63] He incorporated a number of influences.

By this point, we have examined the nature of interdisciplinarity, the weaknesses of the old stool metaphor for capturing the essence of missiology, and have tried to gain a sense of a New Testament missiology. Now, we are ready for a new metaphor that may more fully encompass the interdisciplinary nature of the science of Christian missions.

## Missiology Like a River

We understand that the disciplines that inform missiology are expanding, the boundaries between the disciplines are fuzzy, these disciplines converge for a central purpose, and the diffusion of ideas between missiology and the other disciplines is two-way. A river seems to be a metaphor that captures this dynamic and expanding process that is compelled by an unseen force to move onward. While a stool is unchanging, rivers are constantly reinvented. As Heraclitus said, no man ever steps in the same river twice.

A river has endless tributaries; some are large and some have a much smaller influence. At times, some of the disciplines (like communication theory) that influence missiology surge for a time; others (like theology) exert a continual force, while others have a much smaller impact. Theology, though, occupies a unique place in the river. It is both tributary (as a separate discipline) and yet is the *sine qua non* of missiology. That is, if the theological tributary were cut off, the river would cease to be defined as missiology.

61. Dyrness, *Learning about Theology from the Third World*, 189.
62. Walls, "Rise of Global Theologies," 24.
63. Gallagher, "Missionary Methods."

Indeed all of these tributaries expand and change as the cultural currents shift. That is, trends and issues arise which affect how we make disciples across cultures. When the current events included famines, cargo cults, or Marxism, missiology responded. Today, the world's surging currents involve human trafficking, global partnerships, and oral learners; and missiologists are in touch with those global needs and trends. Some streams within missiology rise and then wane; some disappear at the bottom of the river, others have a long "tail life" (discussed more in chapter 11). There are many hidden treasures in a riverbed, and eddies bring up those sediments. Additionally, the river metaphor suggests that ideas that have been latent upstream appear again later on.

How can we find the recursive process in the metaphor of a river? Scholars of missions are often ambassadors of multiple disciplines (earlier I suggested the names of Codrington, Mayers, Lingenfelter, Livermore, Kraft, and others, as such cross-disciplinary ambassadors). They ferry their new missiological knowledge back upstream as they return to anthropology, psychology, theology, etc. to diffuse their ideas throughout those tributaries.

The convergence of major tributaries often is the space that defines the river. While the Nile runs thousands of miles and is fed by endless smaller streams, the convergence in Egypt is symbolic of the river itself. In missiology, the space where these multiple disciplines converge is the purpose of fulfilling the Great Commission. Without that specific convergence, there would be social sciences, history, ethnotheology, etc., but there would be no missiology. Missiology exists when the study of God and the world is employed for the purpose of making disciples across cultures.

And rivers flow directionally. This mixture of theories moves downstream in the form of mission strategies. However, rivers are fluid, and the elements that are mixed up inside of them continue to wield an influence on the river and on future theoretical and strategic contributions. This is the recursive interplay between theory and strategy. What's fascinating is that even the downstream strategies of mission are highly interdisciplinary—with fluid or "fuzzy" boundaries between the theories. Madinger,[64] for instance, has demonstrated that the strategy of orality (evangelism through the spoken, rather than the written word) involves at least seven disciplines: anthropology, linguistics, literacy,

---

64. Madinger, "Coming to Terms with Orality."

social networks, cognition and memory, the arts, and media. And some might say that orality has become a discipline in its own right, with its own technical terms, canonical list of scholars and formative books.

A stool serves best when it does *not* move; but a river moves with purpose. Rivers have a *telos*—a completion. Rivers, like Paul's missiology, are directional—moving toward the goal of making disciples of all peoples. The missionary task is not directed by missiology itself, but by God's work throughout history. Some scholars refer to this theoretical position as Trinitarian missiology.[65] All our efforts in language, culture, and theological studies are carried along by the *missio Dei*; we are participating with God as the Spirit moves.[66] The image of currents carrying along a river reminds us that it is the Spirit of God that provides the forward direction.

But the directionality of a river does not imply narrowness in purpose. A stool's purpose is too narrowly defined for missiology: it is only for sitting. It is the very nature of missiology as an interdisciplinary effort that allows this river to be quite broad, as we make disciples through our various efforts.

## Conclusion

My overall aim here is not simply to substitute one metaphor for another; instead, I am contrasting various metaphors that have been used to describe missiology so that I can paint a vivid picture of what missiology is, and what it isn't—of how missiological research *is* and *isn't* done.

While we may concede that missiology is informed by countless disciplines "upstream," schools of missions have limited resources; therefore the curriculum cannot include an endless stream of courses from philosophers, business professors, sociologists, etc. This is why we end up with a more or less canonical set of courses and faculty from anthropology, history, theology, and education. And even if we concede that the boundaries of missiology are dynamic, expanding, and "fuzzy," schools of missions must design a standardized curriculum. In general, faculty of schools of missions have doctoral degrees in history, theology, or the social sciences, and their courses reflect this. But missiologists use their narrow specializations in broad, interdisciplinary ways. Missiologically-minded

---

65. Zscheile, "Forming and Restoring Community in a Nomadic World," 1, 3.
66. Bosch, *Transforming Mission*, 389–93.

theologians do theological studies in an interdisciplinary way, looking at current economic and social challenges to our theology. Missiological historians do historical studies in an interdisciplinary way, delving into topics like geo-politics and globalization. And our studies in the social sciences span across the disciplines, from education, to the psychology of intercultural adjustment, to economics and community development.

## Move Into Action

Cast your net widely. No questions or data are off-limits when it comes to researching missiological questions. For example, research questions about theological education are also political and economic questions; studies of contextualization are also linguistic and historical studies; an understanding of best practices in community development also requires understanding post-colonial modernities and globalization. Casting your net widely means you will need to develop friendships with thinkers and practitioners who are working in very different missionary fields than you are engaged in. It means you'll be stretched to learn new vocabularies and perspectives.

But casting our nets widely doesn't mean we must be experts on all of these fields. Instead, we must ask ourselves, "What academic disciplines must I look at for solving the problem I'm interested in? And what level of collaboration with other scholars is necessary?" In every case, we are increasingly aware that inderdisciplinarity is fundamental to a holistic missiology.

## Ideas for Further Research

1. Think about other tributaries to missiology. Discover how missiologists have incorporated those fields.
2. Missiology in the West has stood on three legs. Discover the core disciplines that comprise missiology in other parts of the world.

## Review Questions

1. How does the author define missiology?

2. What are the weaknesses of the three-legs stool metaphor?
3. How does the river metaphor improve on the stool metaphor?
4. In what ways is missiology interdisciplinary?
5. How does interdisciplinarity help and hinder the discipline of missiology?

## Reflection Questions

1. What are the strengths and weaknesses of this book's thesis that the foundational question of missiology is how to make disciples across boundaries?
2. What interdisciplinary background(s) do you bring to missiology?

*Chapter 2*

# Connecting Theology to Cross-Cultural Discipleship

THIS CHAPTER EXAMINES MISSIOLOGICAL theology: the way missiologists think theologically in order to inform our best practices of making disciples across cultures. I have deliberately given prominence to theology in this book because, while missiology is immensely interdisciplinary, it is foundationally about a theological question: How can we effectively join in God's desire to make Himself known throughout the world? Yet numerous other theological questions arise through the process of making disciples across cultures: What is the fate of those who have never heard about Jesus? Does God require evangelization of all people groups before the end times? Is the work of the church primarily missions (making disciples across cultures), or is the church's mission broader than that? This chapter gives some tools to navigate theological questions related to missions.

> **Chapter Goals**
>
> *Knowledge goals:*
>
> - Describe the biblical basis for missions without using "prooftexts" or watering down the definition of missions
> - Distinguish between mission and missions
>
> *Action goals:*
>
> - Exegete scripture for answers to tough questions about the way Christianity spreads across cultures

*Heart goals:*

- Commit to joining in God's desire to make Himself known throughout the world.

## Situating Theology in Missiology

We can observe the prominence of theology in missiology at the earliest stages when we note that the first missiologists were situated in schools of theology (and many still are today); rather than in separate schools of missions, or within branches of intercultural studies or anthropology.[1] More than ever, missiologists should give prominence to theology in order to rescue missiology "from drifting (and drowning!) in a sea of social science data and be anchored once gain to its theological foundation."[2]

One reason I use the phrase "missiological theology" in contrast with the more common title "theology of missions" is that the genitive "of missions" can give the impression that missions is a compartmentalized portion of theology, which can be developed by niche theologians the way they would develop a "theology of dance," a "theology of sports," or a "theology in the public square." On the contrary, I share Martin Kähler's conviction that missions is not merely ancillary to "theology proper"; missions is the mother of theology.[3] That is, the missionary task has engendered theological developments over the past two millennia, as the church first expanded throughout the Roman world, and then to the corners of the earth. This cross-cultural contact has continually pressed theologians to answer theological questions.

Missiological theology is not a branch of theology that deals with the occasional biblical imperatives to make disciples. As Wright pointed out, we find throughout the Bible such theological themes as "election, redemption, covenant, worship, ethics and eschatology" which "all await our missiological reflection."[4] From here, Wright argues that it is proper to read the entire Bible with a missional hermeneutic.[5] In fact, Erickson pointed out that even a single missiological question like "the fate of the

---

1. Cerny, "Relationship Between Theology and Missiology," 106.
2. Köstenberger, "Challenge of a Systematized Biblical Theology of Mission," 445.
3. Kähler, *Schriften zur Christologie und Mission*.
4. Wright, *Mission of God*, 65.
5. Wright, *Mission of God*, 61.

lost" is related to all sorts of other issues in systematic theology, such as the nature of God, the nature of humans, general revelation, sin, salvation, Christ, hermeneutics, and the church.[6] We cannot really examine any missiological issue without theologizing.

## Establishing the Biblical Basis for Missiological Theology

Theologians typically use the Scripture in some way to develop their missiology. Two main tactics have been taken, and both have caused some confusion or mission-drift in missiology. On the one hand, some evangelical theologians have developed the "Missions-everywhere-in-the-Bible" approach, which looks for hints of cross-cultural evangelism under every stone in the Old Testament. On the other hand, the conciliar or mainline movement has turned toward a "Mission-of-God" approach, which ostensibly attempts to establish missions in the Old Testament, but eventually widens the term mission (without the "s") to mean everything God wills and does, thus diminishing the aspect of cross-cultural evangelism in missions (with the "s"). After critiquing these two approaches below, I will suggest a third option, which I describe as "systematic missiological theology." This approach maintains the distinctiveness of missions as cross-cultural discipleship (rather than widening the focus to God's mission in general) but admits from the outset that even when missions is not a theme in a particular passage, a missiological hermeneutic can be applied.

### The "Missions Everywhere in the Bible Approach"

In an effort to establish the theological basis for missions, some missiologists have tried to uncover a metanarrative of cross-cultural evangelism throughout the Bible. For example, Cook argued the Old Testament (abbreviated throughout as OT) is about a missionary God who sends a missionary people with a missionary message;[7] Kaiser argued that the New Testament is a continuation of an evangelistic cross-cultural impulse in the OT;[8] and others maintain that "the Bible is from start to

---

6. Erickson, "State of the Question," 32–33.
7. Cook, *An Introduction to the Study of Christian Missions*.
8. Kaiser, *Mission in the Old Testament*.

finish a missionary book."[9] Cerny asserts that the "Bible is a missionary document which developed over centuries as a message and a testimony about the *Missio Dei*. God has been engaged in a mission towards humanity";[10] He establishes that the Bible was written in a missionary situation, dealing with "a problem, a need, a controversy or a threat that the people of God had to deal with in the context of their mission."[11]

Notice that theologians from disciplines other than missiology have also used an "everywhere-in-the-Bible" approach to demonstrate that their own cause is paramount: They argue that their issue is not only *a* theme in Scripture, rather it is *the* overarching theme. After all, finding an overarching theme within the Bible seems like a better way to build a theological case than just finding a prooftext here or there to justify a given position. Stearns, for instance, has argued that social uplift, and especially care of the poor, is a theme that is so predominant in the Bible that nearly half of its verses are related to the topic.[12] This is to imply that if a given issue is a recurring theme in Scripture, it must continue to have relevance today!

However, the notion that "the Bible is a missionary book" is not entirely convincing. Only some of the passages in the narrative histories (Gen 22:18; 26:4), prophets (Isa 42:6; Amos 9:11, 12) and wisdom literature (Ps 67; 116:1) can be considered to have a "missionary message" for their original audience; other passages may have a missionary application if one applies a missionary hermeneutic to the passage, as the authors of the New Testament certainly did in some cases (see, for example, Paul's missionary interpretation of 2 Sam 22:50 in Rom 15:9).

But many passages do not have an overt missionary message. Schnabel[13] has shown that the original reading of Gen 12 does not suggest missions; rather, it answers how God chose Abraham's bloodline and how Israel's descendants ended up in Canaan. Likewise, the books Exodus through Joshua were not originally read as missionary messages—these books primarily recount God's law, and narrate how Israel became a nation of priests. The psalms and wisdom literature "envision a future, divinely-initiated desire by many individuals from many people groups to worship Yahweh, but not because of any necessarily Jewish mission

---

9. Ott et al., *Encountering Theology of Mission*, 3.
10. Cerny, "Relationship Between Theology and Missiology," 107.
11. Cerny, "Relationship Between Theology and Missiology," 107.
12. Stearns, *Hole in our Gospel*.
13. Schnabel, *Early Christian Mission*.

explicitly targeting them, then or later."[14] True, we find ideas in the OT about the God of self-disclosure, who sends his people out, who is jealous for His own glory, and who wants to bless not only Israel, but all nations. And it is also true that these ideas are all building blocks of a theology of missions. But I think many are still not convinced that even Isa 44 and 45, as much as they teach the exclusivity of the God of Israel, were meant to be taken primarily as missionary texts.

Those who would argue that the OT is about missions often end up basing their case on a few hallmark missionary texts that are interspersed throughout the narrative, like Gen 17 and the book of Jonah. Wright pejoratively refers to this as the "text assembly method;"[15] and he demonstrates that such an albeit well-intentioned hermeneutic is actually counterproductive: What was meant to establish missions as a metanarrative in Scripture actually ends up making it seem like an intermittent sub-theme. If missions is truly at the core of God's plan for humanity, then pointing to a few dozen proof texts doesn't do justice to the theme at all.

## The "Mission of God" Approach

In the end, the program of tracing a metanarrative of missions throughout the Bible is only possible if one widens the definition of "missions" significantly. As Schnabel argued, the narrower we define missions, the less we see it in the Old Testament.[16] Two general approaches have widened "missions" to "mission," thus tracing a missional theme through the entire Bible: Some focus broadly on God's general purposes, the *missio Dei*, and some focus a bit more narrowly on the thread of the kingdom of God throughout the Bible.

### *Missio Dei Throughout All of Scripture*

Theologians who focus on *missio Dei* are careful to distinguish between mission and missions, since conflating missions (cross-cultural discipleship) with God's wider purposes is confusing and erroneous.[17]

14. Blomberg, "Mission in the Bible," 64.
15. Wright, *Mission of God*.
16. Schnabel, *Early Christian Mission*.
17. For more on the distinction between Mission and Missions, see Newbigin, "Mission and Missions," 911.

Ever since Georg Vicedom used the term *missio Dei* in *The Mission of God* to refer to God's self-disclosure among the nations,[18] mainline theologians have used the term *missio Dei* to make the point that it is myopic (even narcissistic?) to equate human missionary efforts with the mission of an omnipotent God. God does not need the church to do His mission (again, without the "s"). Indeed, God's plans throughout history have been much broader than just cross-cultural discipleship; and Jesus's vision of the imminent kingdom of God was wider than the Great Commission. Likewise today, not everything the church does is about missions. Wright concludes that the metanarrative of the Bible is not narrowly about missions if "we are thinking of 'missions' and the great and laudable efforts of cross-cultural missionaries."[19] But the Bible is arguably about God's mission,[20] if we define it as God's plan to reveal his holiness and love, first to the line of Abraham and later to the world through Jesus Christ.[21]

In one sense, the *missio Dei* argument is so simple it does not cause any problems for evangelical missiological theology: The entire Bible is certainly about God's mission (without the s) in that it encompasses "everything God plans." However, the *missio Dei* argument is so broad that it is limited in its ability to inform us about missiological theories and strategies, which are more narrowly focused on missions (with the s) as cross-cultural discipleship.

### Tracing the Kingdom of God through scripture

Some missiologists narrow the broader "mission of God" approach a bit by making mission coterminous with the biblical idea of the "Kingdom of God."[22] They argue that we (as the church in general) are not merely in "the missions business"; we are in the kingdom business. While the phrase "kingdom of God" is not found in the Old Testament, van Engen, et al. trace themes of God's imminent and future rule throughout the Bible, hence they find "mission" as a predominant theme in Scripture.

However, such observations about *missio Dei* and the kingdom of God are not particularly missiological claims. They are ecclesiological

---

18. Whitfield, "Triune God; The God of Mission," 19.
19. Wright, *Mission of God*, 531.
20. Wright, *Mission of God*, 29.
21. Wright, *Mission of God*, 369.
22. Van Engen et al., *Announcing the Kingdom*.

claims (which admittedly have missiological implications). That is, if we focus exclusively on mission (without the "s") and end the conversation there, we are engaging in an important theological discussion, but we are not specifically addressing the work of missions (with the "s"). We would be articulating a missional theology without specifying a missiological theology. So while evangelical theology must be informed by the *missio Dei* or the kingdom of God lens, our theology is not complete until we have also addressed a theology of cross-cultural discipleship.

To summarize my point about the biblical basis for missions: God's mission, the kingdom of God, and missions are all important components of our theology; and we must see how these various distinct themes fit together. While theologians may ask a broader question about God's mission (that is, God's overall plan for humanity) throughout the Bible, a missiological theology must focus on what "rational discourse about God"—a typical definition of theology—teaches us about cross-cultural disciple making. Missiological theology asks, *How does our interaction with Scripture shape our understanding of cross-cultural discipleship?*

If missions, then, is a subtheme of a subtheme, and is only intermittently mentioned in the Old Testament, how do missiological theologians use Scripture to inform their missiology? Missiologists do not need to feel anxious by the assertion that missions (that is, cross-cultural discipleship) is not explicitly a theme in the OT (contra the "missions-everywhere-in-the-Bible" approach). Rather than looking for a metanarrative of missions throughout the Bible (which inevitably causes us to resort to the text-assembly method, thus lessening the import of missions), a more credible and fruitful way to think theologically about missions comes to us through the field of systematic theology.

## The Systematic Missiological Theology Approach

Systematic theology is constructed (ideally) by piecing together the best insights from biblical theology. Biblical theology begins with a biblical text and asks questions about what that passage means. These "data" are pieced together to build a systematic theology. For example, a specialist on the Synoptic Gospels will help us see how Jesus Christ is portrayed in Matthew, Mark, and Luke; then Johannine scholars would look at Jesus Christ in John, and Pauline experts would understand who Jesus Christ is in Paul's letters, and so on. A systematic theologian would piece these various scholarly contributions together to answer "Who is Jesus Christ?"

(see Figure 1). At this point, we could even look to the Old Testament to understand what the Scripture as a *system* says about the Messiah from the Psalms, Isaiah, Genesis 1, and so on.

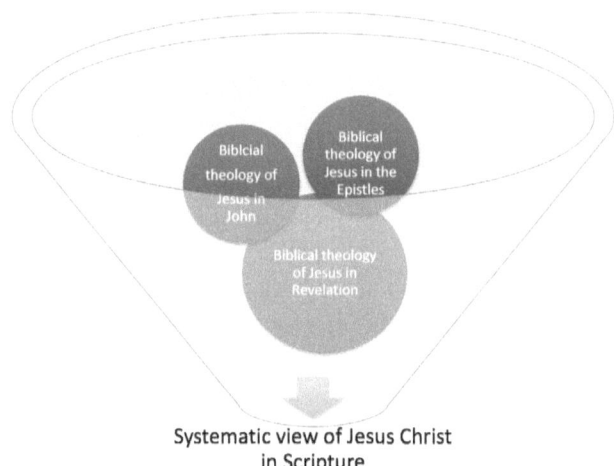

Figure 1: Using biblical theology to build a systematic theology

Yet since the Bible was written over 1,400 years by more than 40 authors in various cultural contexts, it can be extremely complicated to piece together "the biblical view" on any topic. Some might note the multi-vocal stance within Scripture on virtually any doctrine from the role of a deacon or deaconess, to the care of creation, to the nature of the Trinity. God as three persons may be clearly developed in the Gospel of John, or even in the Synoptic Gospels; but we cannot easily say that the Bible, on the whole, is about the doctrine of the Trinity. But if we ask questions about the nature of the Father, Son, and Holy Spirit as we examine Scripture, we can systematically arrive at a theology of the Trinity, even when that wasn't the express purpose of the individual books. Once we have inductively arrived at the doctrine through systematic theology, we can read the Bible with a Trinitarian lens. For example, while there are some passages in Genesis where we see the Trinity at work (like Genesis 1), the Trinitarian interpretation of those passages is only apparent if we have already begun with our notion of a Triune God from the New Testament. We may even say the Old Testament is Trinitarian, but it is systematic theology, not biblical exegesis, which allows us to say this.

I have discussed three ways to establish the biblical basis of missions. Table 1 below summarizes these approaches.

Table 1: Comparison of three approaches to the biblical basis of mission(s)

| "Missions is everywhere" approach | "Mission of God" approach | "Systematic missiological theology" approach |
|---|---|---|
| Finds proof texts of heralding God across cultures | Widens mission(s) beyond cross-cultural discipleship to "everything that God desires and does" | • Maintains a clear definition of missions as heralding God across cultures;<br>• Does not require this theme to be found throughout the books of Scripture;<br>• Forms biblical ideas of missions by studying passages that *are* about missions; and<br>• Can apply a hermeneutic of missions to passages that are admittedly not specifically about missions. |

The third approach—systematic missiological theology—avoids the temptation to water down missions to "everything God does" and also avoids the pitfall of reading missions into every passage of Scripture. Instead, it applies a missiological hermeneutic[23] to scriptural themes, to understand an overall biblical approach toward missions. Typically, systematic theology has tackled six main themes: 1) the nature of God the Father, 2) the nature and work of Jesus Christ, 3), the nature of salvation, 4) the nature of the church, 5) the Holy Spirit, and 6) the nature of the end times. In the remainder of this chapter, I will discuss how missiologists have applied these six major fields of systematic theology to the theoretical and practical aspects of making disciples across cultures.

## Missiological Implications of the Nature and Work of God the Father

Virtually everything we know about God has implications for the work of making disciples across cultures. God is Creator; He owns the universe, and can rightly command His subjects—regardless of culture or background—to obey Him. "God's claim of universal *ownership* is

---

23. This is somewhat (though not entirely) different than Wright's missional hermeneutic, which does not specifically look at the cross-cultural discipleship process, but is wide enough to look at God's plan for humankind in general.

based on the right of creation (e.g., Ps 24:1–2; 89:11–12; 95:3–5)".[24] God is supremely loving and good, so He alone is worthy of the nations' praise (Ps 67). As the creator of a good universe, God blesses and provides good things (Jas 1:17); therefore all people will only find that their hearts find rest and forgiveness in Him. He is unparalleled in power; He is *sui generis*—that means all the other so-called "gods" are in an entirely different category, and are not worthy of our devotion and sacrifice.

The uniqueness of God is such an important missiological theme that much of Christopher Wright's work[25] is devoted to establishing the basis of monotheism in the OT. If God is one, then worship of anything else is idolatry. God is unique—there may be other gods, but since they are mute and powerless, they are not in the same category as YHWH—therefore Moses can say, "There is no other" (Deut 4:35, 39).

## God is Triune

When we come to understand the Triune God as Creator, Redeemer, and Sustainer, we see numerous missiological implications. We see discipleship more holistically than simply calling for "decisions" to follow Christ. We see that the Spirit has been at work in the nations before the missionaries ever arrived. I will discuss some of the missiological implications of God's attributes below.

### God is Creator

As Creator of the universe, God is a King (Ps 47:7) who has established a kingdom and He actively reigns over His creation (Ps 47:8), which He called "good." He takes an active part in relating with humans, who are "very good." In order to establish His kingdom, He commanded humans to have lots of children, to live fruitfully on the earth (Gen 1:28), and to scatter across the globe, using the planet's resources in such a way that people will flourish (Gen 2:15). This first command has been called the creation mandate, or the cultural mandate.[26] This scattering and flourishing has involved everything from building cities and suburbs, to establishing hospitals and schools, to inventing trains, planes, and the

---

24. Wright, *Mission of God*, 80.
25. Wright, *Mission of God*.
26. Nehrbass, *God's Image and Global Cultures*.

internet. Wherever humans use the planet's resources to promote the fruitfulness and multiplication of humanity, they are in obedience to God's plan for His kingdom on earth. Of course, humans have ignored God's plans for the "good creation" and have corrupted His good creation.

This creation mandate has missiological implications. Coming under God's reign is not just about confessing Jesus as Lord, it is about enjoying the fullest blessings of filling the earth and subduing (that is, enjoying or managing) it. Missions, teaching people to obey "all I have commanded" (Matt 28:20) is the act of helping people carry out that creation mandate. Since the church began spreading from the Roman Empire, this extension of the creation mandate has involved spreading literacy across cultures, teaching sanitary health practices and establishing just governments so people can flourish. It also means spreading good business practices that are environmentally conscious.

### *God is Supreme*

"The God who created human beings should be the object of their worship and thanksgiving."[27] But our worship stems out of more than mere obligation. Piper has repeatedly reminded the church that worship is even more significant than thankfulness and giving God His due.[28] Worship is actually God's way of ensuring that we are fulfilled, at peace, content, and whole. A God who is infinitely more lovely, gracious, just and merciful than we are is the only one who can truly satisfy us. It is not that God requires us to worship for His own ego, or even that He requires worship because it is just and fair for us to honor Him. If we are to delight in something that is lovely, we must delight in the Most Lovely. If we are to enjoy something beautiful, we will have most enjoyment in the Most Beautiful. So worship is about delighting in the most Supremely Delightful. Missiologists have understood that the implication is that for people in any time or place to be truly whole and satisfied, they need to worship the Most High. Piper supplies exhaustive support from Scripture that God is ultimately concerned with His own renown, and when God has stepped in throughout history, it was for the express purpose of making His own fame great.[29]

27. Van Engen et al., *Announcing the Kingdom*, 54.
28. Piper, *Let the Nations Be Glad*.
29. Piper, *Let the Nations Be Glad*.

## Profile of a Missiologist: John Piper

*(contemporary)*

Education: ThD University of Munich
Occupation: Professor of biblical studies, pastor, author

John Piper has authored more than 50 books on Scripture and the Christian life, most of which are freely distributed electronically through his ministry "Desiring God."

While Piper did not serve extensively in the missionary field, and did not hold a position in missiology, his theology has profoundly shaped missiological theology in recent decades. Piper's theoretical contribution, which he termed "Christian hedonism" is that the highest pleasure humans can have is to be found in glorifying God. This tenet has strong biblical grounding, and is summarized in the Shorter Westminster Catechism: "What is the chief end of man? To glorify God and enjoy him forever." If this is the chief end of humankind, then the glory of God (and not missions) must also be the chief end of the church. Piper famously stated in his missiological text *Let the Nations be Glad*, "Missions is not the ultimate goal of the church. Worship is. Missions exists because worship doesn't. Worship is ultimate."[1] Christian hedonism has tremendous missiological significance because it is counterintuitive in most settings where the gospel is preached. People typically think Christianity is about following rules to obtain God's blessing, rather than about taking pleasure in the goodness of God. Christian hedonism suggests that "lostness" is not only about eternal punishment, but also about missing out on all the pleasure that comes along with glorifying God.

Some scholars take issue with the notion that the chief end of humankind is to glorify God. Metzger, for instance, argues that such a theory only partially touches on our obligation to obey God.[2] The Trinity's most fundamental quality is the love between the Father, Son, and Holy Spirit; and it is *out* of this love that the Father glorifies the Son. Glory is a result of the greater thing, which is love. So glory is not actually an end in itself; love is. However, even in Metzger's case, the missiological implication is similar to Piper's model: Humanity must be restored to a loving relationship with the Trinity, which will result in praise.

---

[1] Piper, *Let the Nations be Glad*, 17.
[2] Metzger, "Halfway House of Hedonism."

## God is the Sender

God sent Adam and Eve on a commission to be fruitful and multiply. He then sent them out of the garden (Gen 3:23). He sent Abram to a new land (Gen 12:1), and has been sending angels (Ps 91:11; Mark 13:27; Luke 1:26) and prophets (Jer 25:4) to proclaim his message. God asked, "Whom shall I send?" (Isa 6:8). Eventually, He sent His Son. Just like God is a sending God, Jesus is a sender (John 20:21).[30] This theology of sending and self-disclosing is so plain in the OT and NT, that Stephen Holmes suggests that even if the Great Commission passages had never been included in the Gospels and Acts, world evangelization would have been the natural fruit of Christianity.[31] God chose the Son from the foundation of the world (1 Pet 1:20), therefore missions was not "plan B."[32] God is eternally the Father who elects the Son, and who sends Him. Missions (from the Latin *missio* "send") is at the heart of God's eternal character.

The notion of God as sender has transformed how theologians understand missions. The task of the missions is no longer seen as something that originates in, or is even fulfilled by, the church. Rather, it is intrinsic to the *missio Dei*, a work owned and carried out by God.

## God is the Discloser of Himself

God put the stars and moon and sun in the sky to show there is Someone up there (Ps 19). Many cultures in fact do interpret these "signs" to mean there is a creator God. What the psalmist implied was that God is a God who reveals Himself—He is a God of self-disclosure. The Father, Son, and Holy Spirit are eternally communicating to each other, and we are nearest to God when we 1) perceive that communication and 2) declare the knowledge of God to others. Missions is so closely tied to proclamation because God is a God who declares His own nature to humanity.

The primary way God made Himself known was through covenants. He "cut" a covenant with Noah (Gen 9), Abraham (Gen 15), and later with Moses and the People of God (Exod 24:3–8). Jesus made a new covenant (Matt 26:27). God makes promises to His people to bless, redeem, and

---

30. Keener, "Sent Like Jesus."
31. Peters, *Biblical Theology of Missions*.
32. Johnson, "Ecclesiology, Election, and the Life of God."

restore. One of the main ways God redeems is by disclosing Himself to His people.

In the Old Testament, this self-disclosure required the Israelites to tell the nations that God is King, the God of all peoples (Gen 12; Deut 10:1; 1 Kgs 8:41; Ps 22:7; 46:10; 66:4–7; 96:9–10; Isa 2:1–4; 25:6–9, 60; 49:6; Jer 3:17; Ezek 36:22–23; Zech 8:20–23; Mic 4:13).[33]

The continual self-disclosure of God, which involved covenant-making, has clear missiological implications. Our interaction with people who are outside of the covenant should result in disclosing who God is, so they can also become heirs to His promises.

## God's Loving-kindness

One of the most beautiful characteristics of God, *chesed* has no equivalent in the English language, but translators since Miles Coverdell have settled on terms like "loving-kindness" (Hos 2:19). The loaded term carries ideas of grace; but it is also, as we see in the book of Ruth, a dutiful love.[34]

The missiological implication of this untranslatable, dutiful, gracious love is that, as Rick Warren often puts it, "People matter to God." As the apostle put it, "We love because He first loved us" (1 John 4:19 NIV). Missions starts with love for God and humankind.

## God is Judge

God's judgment is based on His character of righteousness and justice. He demands justice for the meek (Deut 10:15–18).[35] When people sin, God appears as judge—from the disobedience of Adam to Cain's anger, to the immorality in Sodom and Gomorrah, to the idolatry of Israel—God cannot stand sin (Prov 6:16–19).

The missiological implication is that since all, through Adam, have sinned (Rom 5:12), the nations are "without excuse" (Rom 1:20) and are in a dire position. They need the redemption of the God who self-discloses and makes covenants.

---

33. Verkuyl, "Biblical Foundation for the Worldwide Mission Mandate."
34. Montgomery, "Hebrew Hesed and Greek Charis."
35. Wright, *Mission of God*, 80.

## Summary of the Missiological Implication of God's Nature and Work

Wright summarizes the missiological implications of the nature of God: God is creator, He owns the nations, governs them, judges them, reveals himself to them, loves them, saves those who turn to him, guides them, and will ultimately bring them peace.[36]

## Missiological Implications of the Nature and Work of Jesus Christ

Systematic theology also focuses on Christology—the study of the nature and work of Jesus Christ. A systematic missiological theology requires us to think about the ways that Jesus Christ's person and ministry inform how we make disciples across cultures. What was Jesus's approach to those who were outside of the covenant that God made to Israel? Did Jesus model cross-cultural ministry? If so, are we to continue His model?

### Jesus's Incarnation

The incarnation is the greatest example of how God reached out to humankind to identify with us and bring us into relationship with Him. Missiologists have long recognized the implications of the incarnation: Cross-cultural workers identify with their host cultures, speak the local languages, eat indigenous foods, and observe the laws of the land. Missionaries attempt to embody the *kenosis* (emptying) in Phil 2:5–11 by taking on the role of servant. They try to act out of humility, as guests or pilgrims.

Of course, the incarnational metaphor of Christian work can only be extended so far; and evangelical missiologists are rightly a bit skeptical about the implications of the term "incarnational ministry." As the World Council of Churches (WCC) began to adopt religious pluralism in the twentieth century, WCC theologians began emphasizing every believer's role in incarnational ministry or "presence evangelism" in order to de-emphasize the unique (and exclusive) role that Jesus Christ played in history. That is, if the gospel can be re-imagined as "the church loving like Jesus did," then the gospel does not have to be rooted in pre-modern

---

36. Wright, *Mission of God*, 104.

miracle stories (which embarrassed twentieth-century mainline theologians) like the virgin birth and resurrection.

Ironically, the biblical passages on the incarnation are actually meant to show the uniqueness of Jesus, not to create a model for disciples to emulate.[37] There is "an ontological gap that forever distances the origins of Jesus's mission from the origins of the disciples' mission."[38] Namely, evangelicals would note, we cannot continue the work of a substitutionary death for the world. It is also questionable whether we are to continue the ministry of the "winnowing fork."[39]

Therefore, while the incarnation does indeed imply a *kenosis*-attitude for all Christians, and suggests that the Word of God must be contextualized, the most profound implication of the incarnation is the urgency for the world to know the unique person of Jesus Christ through the Scriptures, since, as Jesus said, "If you really know me, you will know my Father as well. From now on, you do know him and have seen him" (John 14:7 NIV).

## The Precursor of Jesus's Ministry Model

Biblical scholars are puzzled about the antecedents to Jesus's ministry model. Is Jesus's ministry based on existing rabbinic models? Was Jesus continuing some OT or inter-testamental program of itinerant preaching and healing? If so, does that mean He was masterful at contextualizing his ministry to his time and place? If the OT did not provide such a model for proselytism, where did Jesus capture his model for ministry? Is his ministry model unique? Is it normative for us today?

Some have suggested that wandering rabbis common in the first century. Perhaps religious leaders in the Greco-Roman world such as Cynics or Stoics did some itinerant preaching. Matt 23:15 seems to indicate that Jews were already proselytizing: "Woe to you, teachers of the law and Pharisees, you hypocrites! You travel over land and sea to win a single convert, and when you have succeeded, you make them twice as much a child of hell as you are" (NIV).

On the other hand, Jesus's ministry is clearly unique, yet based on the OT messianic prophecies and apocalyptic literature.

37. Köstenberger, "Challenge of a Systematized Biblical Theology of Mission."

38. Carson, *Gospel According to John*, 566.

39. Deyoung and Gilbert, *What is the Mission of the Church?*; Hesselgrave, *Paradigms in Conflict*.

### The nature of Jesus's ministry

Missiologists are not just interested in the precursors of His ministry, but also in the nature of it. On the one hand, Jesus's stated ministry was not to heal or exorcize, but to preach (Mark 1:38). Yet He did not simply focus on persuading people to believe; His preaching extoled the standards of holy living.[40] Even if preaching was the ostensible focus, the Gospels are clearly organized around a trifecta of preaching, healing, and exorcizing. A truly "representational" missiology, then, would focus on all these aspects of restoring shalom to the people we encounter.

### The Recipients of Jesus's Ministry

Was Jesus's ministry aimed only at the Jews, as He said in Matt 15:24, or was He actually interested in the gentiles as well? And if His ministry was for the Jews, is that normative for our missiology today—or does the Great Commission supersede the Jewish-focused ministry of Jesus?

The Gospels reiterate the OT themes of fulfillment, blessing, and serving as a light to the nations; but they do not portray Jesus and His disciples as missionaries to gentiles. In fact, the consummation or ingathering of the nations were not seen as a contemporary reality for the apostles' time; but rather as eschatological events.[41] Yet Jesus was often aware in His preaching that the Jews would reject Him, whereas the gentiles would accept Him. Jesus's parables of the lost coin, sheep, and son in Luke 15 suggest that God's love extends not only to those who are "found" (Israel) but also to the "lost" (gentiles). And the parable that finally invoked the wrath of Jerusalem was about a vinedresser who transfers ownership of the vineyard to the foreigners (i.e., to the gentiles) because the original chosen people rejected the owner's son (Matt 21:33–46; Mark 12:1–12; Luke 20:9–19).[42]

Some theologians like J. B. Hood[43] have suggested that Matthew deliberately mentioned foreigners in Jesus's genealogy (1:1–17) in order to underscore that salvation through Jesus is for all people. Some of Jesus's ancestors like Tamar and Rahab were Canaanites, Ruth was from Moab, and Bathsheba was probably a Hittite. While the focus of the

---

40. Köstenberger and O'Brien, *Salvation to the Ends of the Earth*, 106.
41 Köstenberger and O'Brien, *Salvation to the Ends of the Earth*, 99.
42 See Hultgren, "Paul's Christology and His Mission to the Gentiles."
43. Hood, *Messiah*.

genealogy was Jesus's descent through Adam, Abraham and King David, the Messiah's family line is diverse in ethnicity and social status (much like any of our own genealogies).

The evangelists also included stories of how Jesus ministered to a Roman centurion (Matt 8:5–13), a Syrophoenician woman (Mark 7:24–30; Matt 15:21–28), a Samaritan woman (John 4), a demoniac from the land of the Gadarenes (Luke 8:26–39), and the thief on the cross (Luke 23:39–43), who was a gentile criminal. What is remarkable about these stories is not just that Jesus had contact with foreigners, or even that He respected and valued them, but that He held some of them up as exemplars of faith, gratitude, repentance, or humility. The multiethnic impulse of Jesus's ministry is one of the most significant theological issues in missiological theology.

As I began this chapter, I argued that we can apply a lens of missiological theology to the Old Testament even where we do not expressly find missions (cross-cultural discipleship) as a theme. The same is true even for Jesus's own ministry. We need not argue that the gospels are *about* Jesus as a missionary to the gentiles. Instead, we can look at Jesus's ministry, to both Jews and gentiles, through a missiological lens. The focus of Jesus's ministry was his own identity as God's chosen one who has the power to forgive sins. He preached that everyone must come under the rule of God. If we specifically look for cross-cultural themes (that is, if we apply a missiological lens) we see that Jesus treated people of all ethnicities with dignity, grace, and mercy. The urgency to come under the rule of God applies to people of all socioeconomic classes, and ethnic backgrounds—regardless of how sinful or holy they perceive themselves to be.

## Missiological Implications of Salvation-History

Within systematic theology, the topic of salvation-history usually focuses on how God worked throughout history to choose the nation of Israel as His own, and then, finally how Christ is the fulfillment of the promises that He made to Abraham. Questions of salvation-history that have a particular missiological significance include: What is the role of Israel in light of the other nations? How can God be concerned for all humanity on the one hand, as our missiology tells us He is, and yet particularly concerned for Israel, as the OT indicates? What is the legitimacy of religions in other cultures? Are other religions beneficiaries of God's revelation—are they at least covered by Christ's universal "yes" to humankind (2 Cor 1:20)? What is the global role of the church in light of salvation-history? Is the church's role today more about interreligious dialog and peacekeeping, or is it about world evangelization, or perhaps about redemption of the *kosmos*? Below, I will examine some missiological theological contributions that have tried to answer these sorts of questions.

## Salvation of Israel and the Nations

Israel, as a chosen nation, poses a problem for a missiological soteriology. If the covenant-making God chose Israel as the locus where He would disclose Himself, how can we claim that He is truly concerned for all peoples? Wright has addressed this question by explaining that it is not a dilemma at all. God's plan for revealing Himself to the world was actually made possible through His covenant with Israel. The mission of God is to bless the nations through a special community that lives righteously. The way God protected, chastised, and forgave this community served as an "education" for the nations. They were to be a "nation of priests." Just like a priest is separate from the rest of the community, Israel was separate from the nations to be God's mediator to the world (Num 6:22–26). As Isa 49:6 said, and Jesus later extended to the believers in Matt 5:14, they were the light of the world.[44]

This specific group called the "people of God" was formed when God made a covenant with Abraham. Finally, a descendent of Israel's greatest leader, King David, became the fulfillment of this "Universalizing particularity."[45] Besides, family lineage was never the key to restoring one's relationship with God; it was always about faith.[46] "Election does not cut Israel off from the nations. It situates that people in relationship with them."[47] Therefore, the election of Israel is not at odds with God's universal mission, it is fundamental to it.[48]

It is important to see that salvation for Israel, and for the early church, was not just about the forgiveness of sins. Salvation meant a state of political peace, prosperity, health, abundant crops, and freedom from

---

44. Wright, *Mission of God*, 43.
45. Wright, *Mission of God*, 256–57, 369.
46. Wright, *Mission of God*, 252.
47. Legrand, *Unity and Plurality*, 14.
48. Köstenberger and O'Brien, *Salvation to the Ends of the Earth*, 41–42, 50.

demons. Grasping that salvation was holistic in the Bible can help us to keep our missiological theology holistic today as well.[49]

But the ultimate salvation was that the "earth will be filled with the knowledge of the glory of the LORD as the waters cover the sea" (Hab 2:14 NIV). Oswalt showed that in the prophets, we see the themes in which Israel's restoration would be a witness to the nations. Israel's defeat of other nations was a witness to the way God blesses those who keep His law. On the other hand, the defeat of Israel by other nations also served to "educate" the nations about God's character. They saw that God judges those who disobey Him. This was a "relatively stable" idea throughout Israel's history from 800 BC to 400 BC.[50] The nations would observe God's sovereignty over Israel in two ways: At times they would become servants of Israel; and at times they would participate in God's blessings.

But Israel would not proselytize the nations. Jerusalem had an eschatological role as the city of righteousness which would become the divine world center—the locus of the ingathering of the gentiles in Isa 2:2–4.[51] "These will I bring to my holy mountain" (Isa 56:6–7, NIV). So the gathering of the nations at the throne of Jesus in Rev 7 is Gen 12's mission accomplished.[52]

True, the Israelites' motivation for interacting with the nations may have been more nationalistic than evangelistic. Yet the diaspora was a sort of centrifugal mission by default, as it resulted in increased contact with gentiles, and the diffusion of the gospel.[53]

## General Revelation and the Origin of the Religions

A missiological soteriology leads us to ask about other religions. Where did these other religions come from? Are they degradations of Yahweh worship? Are they influenced by the Nephilim in Gen 6:4? Are they simply the fruits of creative human nature, misplaced Freudian desires, or are they simply reflective of particular patterns of social organization? Or are they actually the result of territorial spirits?

Some missiologists like to point to passages in the OT where God seemed to be at work *outside* of Israel. Gentiles who either heard from

49. Goheen, *Introducing Christian Mission Today*, 90.
50. Oswalt, "Mission of Israel to the Nations," 94.
51. Oswalt, "Mission of Israel to the Nations," 95.
52. Wright, *Mission of God*, 250–51.
53. Köstenberger and O'Brien, *Salvation to the Ends of the Earth*, 59–67.

God or were used by God include Balaam, Rahab, King Huram of Tyre, Abel, Enoch, Noah, Job, Abimelech, Jethro, Ruth, Naaman and the Queen of Sheeba, and of course, Melchizedek. Richardson's missiological interpretation of these passages led him to coin the "Melchizedek factor."[54] Richardson supplied anecdotes from isolated religious groups throughout the world that seemed to have knowledge of a holy, loving, high God. Richardson did not go so far as to claim that such knowledge was salvific, but he took it as evidence that God has put "eternity in their hearts" (Ecc 3:11 NIV).

Richardson's argument draws on Wilhelm Schmidt's evidence of widespread belief in a unique supreme "sky god" (above the local deities). Schmidt developed a theory of "original monotheism" which argued that as the nations dispersed in Gen 9–11, their ancestral knowledge of YHWH slowly became "degraded" into self-serving ritual and idolatry. This degradation is the origin of the various religions throughout the world today.[55]

Evangelicals do not disagree that God sovereignly uses the nations and their religions for His own purposes to reveal Himself, but they emphasize that such revelation is only efficacious for them to discover "that He alone is God," and does not lead to salvation (see Ezek 8:22–23; 25:5, 11, 16–17; 26:4–6; 29:6, 8, 16; 30:19, 26; 32:15).

The approach one has toward the world's religions seriously impacts his or her missionary strategies. People who see religions as vestiges of Yahweh worship encourage local religious expression. On the other hand, some early church fathers thought the religions were inspired by the devil.[56] This would lead to a proscription of other religions and exclusive emphasis on Christianity.

This core question about missiological soteriology has to do with the fate of those who do not know Christ. A permutation of this question asks, "What is the fate of those who are, by all counts, good people who adhere to their own religion?" These questions have been the crux of missiological theology since the early church days. While the Bible has a lot to say about the other religions, and the fate of those who do not come to faith in YHWH through Jesus Christ, the church has never had consensus on the question of the fate of the billions who have died without hearing the good news. A majority view has consistently

---

54. Richardson, *Eternity in Their Hearts*.
55. Schmidt, *Origin and Growth of Religion*.
56. Sigountons, "Did Early Christians Believe Pagan Religions Could Save?"

prevailed, namely that those who are outside of the faith will suffer eternal punishment. Yet a small number of Christian thinkers have concluded that the notion that a loving God would consign finite humans—whose sin is also finite—to eternal punishment, is logically incoherent, and even abhorrent. Recently, pastor Rob Bell made waves with his popular book *Love Wins*, where he argued that the passages on eternal torture are hyperbole and metaphorical, and do not literally mean people will suffer eternally for their sins.[57]

We get off track when the question is framed (by skeptics) like this: "Would God really send people to hell because they have never heard or had a chance to accept the gospel?" This is a straw man argument, since neither the Bible nor the church fathers taught that failure to *believe* is the infraction that condemns people to hell. The Bible teaches that all people are deserving of hell, and headed there with certainty, because of their own sinfulness (Rom 3:23)—not because of their unbelief. Yet surprisingly, Vatican II reified this straw man argument, by asking about the fate of some who "through no fault of their own" but by simple bad luck of being born in the wrong place, at the wrong time, "without blame on their part, have not yet arrived at an explicit knowledge of God, but strive to live a good life".[58] Vatican II seems to have forgotten that it is not the rejection of the gospel or lack of hearing it that condemns people; it is their sinful state that condemns them (Rom 5:12). But it is hearing the gospel that allows them an opportunity to be saved (Rom 10:9–10).

The debate over the fate of the lost never seems to progress, because it is not really about the fate of the lost. While evangelicals are supremely concerned about the fate of the lost, those with a more modernist hermeneutic see discussions about evangelism and hell as outdated or triumphalist. If a theologian does not believe in supernatural revelation (and therefore, does not believe in divine commands or sin as the breaking of those commands), she obviously is not interested in the question, "how can one be saved?" for there is nothing to be saved *from* in her worldview. Therefore the "fate of the lost" debate is about much deeper issues like the nature of religious truth, the source of religious knowledge, and the underlying problem facing humankind. So a conversation about the fate of the lost is only possible for those who already agree that humanity stands in judgment before God because of sin. It is really just an "in house" question for evangelicals. Nonetheless, three broad theological

---

57. Bell, *Love Wins*.
58. Abbott, *Documents of Vatican II*, 35.

camps—pluralists, inclusivists, and exclusivists—have answered what happens to those who die without explicit belief in Jesus Christ.

## Pluralists

Pluralists like John Hick argue that to think humans are designed for happiness, and yet ultimately destined for hell, is to misunderstand God's love. But keep in mind that for pluralists, the discussion is not really about the nature of God, God's love, or salvation. Again, arising during the modern era, pluralism typically presupposes a materialist (non-supernatural) universe, where miracles are not possible. In this system, if God exists, God does not speak in ways that can be understood in human language, because that would require a miracle. For them, religious beliefs cannot not correspond with truth, because there is no act of divine revelation. Instead, religions are simply human constructs. Therefore, pluralists are left equating religion simply with culture, rather than evaluating them in terms of truthfulness (that is, how they correspond with reality) or salvific-ness (ability to save).

Those who hold to pluralism advocate for a missionary method of interreligious dialog rather than evangelism. If, by dialog, they mean "rational discourse in search of the truth," this would be a noble task. But what they typically mean instead is "sharing our stories" and "mutual enrichment."[59] For example, the project of *Beyond Dialogue* by United Methodist professor John Cobb was to help Christians learn from "truths" of Buddhism.[60]

## Inclusivists

In contrast to universalists, inclusivists believe in the supernatural; so they can accept orthodox Christian doctrines like the atonement of Christ. Yet they find the doctrine of hell to be unimaginably harsh. They conclude there must be some other way for those who do not know Christ to be saved. This position was propagated by the neo-orthodoxy of Karl Barth, based on God's ultimate "yes" to humankind through Jesus (2 Cor 1:20). Inclusivism has been subsequently developed by notable theologians like John Sanders, David Watson, and Clark Pinnock.

---

59. Goheen, *Introducing Christian Mission Today*, 365.
60. Cobb, *Beyond Dialog*.

Surprisingly, since Vatican II, the official Catholic position is one of inclusivism. The *Lumen Gentium*[61] states that salvation is possible outside explicit faith in Christ, and other religions can be a channel of that salvation. Catholic theologian Karl Rahner popularized this inclusivist idea under the moniker "anonymous Christians." Rahner imagined that God-fearing people who do not know of Christ may have "implicit faith" (that is, unconscious faith) which saves them.

Rahner's argument was admired in the mid twentieth century because it seemed to promote peace and tolerance; but the interreligious climate in the twenty-first century alerts us to how offensive the notion of "implicit faith" must be to Muslims, Buddhists, Hindus, and others. Think how misunderstood—even scandalized—you would feel if you discovered that Muslim theologians have decided that, at heart, you are actually an "anonymous Muslim"!

Inclusivism leads to idiosyncratic missiological methods. If all are going to be eternally saved, evangelism is not necessary. In fact, evangelism would just be a triumphalist project of expanding church institutions. Therefore, missionary methods are redefined in humanitarian ways. Many mainline church leaders in the twentieth century went the way of neo-orthodoxy and inclusivism, which is why the WCC missionary methods shifted from "evangelization in this generation" in 1910 to the social gospel and interreligious dialog by the end of the century.

### Exclusivists

Exclusivists hold that people must have explicit faith in Christ to be forgiven for their depravity. They consider special revelation (which we access today in canonical biblical texts) to be the only certain source of religious knowledge. The "noetic effects" of the Fall have rendered general revelation (as God may be known through nature or rational thought) as incomplete, cursed, and subject to decay.[62]

---

61. John Paul II, *Lumen Gentium*, 16.
62. Spencer, "Romans 1."

## Profile of a Missiologist: James Edward Lesslie Newbigin

(1909–1998)

*Education: Queen's College (Cambridge); Westminster College*

*Occupation: Missionary in India; Anglican Bishop; professor of missiology and ecumenism at Selly Oak College (Birmingham, UK)*

Lesslie Newbigin labored for nearly forty years as an evangelist among the Tamil at the Madras Mission in India. There, he worked toward the unity of the congregational, Anglican Methodist, and Presbyterian churches. This "South India miracle" of denominational unity began a lifelong project of his in bringing unity to the church. His position as the General Secretary of the World Council of Churches allowed him to influence ecumenism.

Members at the World Missionary Conference in Edinburgh in 1910 believed that no single church had the resources to accomplish "evangelization in this generation." Therefore, the churches would need to work together. A spirit of ecumenism spread and permeated much of the subsequent conferences and councils that were spawned by Edinburgh, including the International Missionary Council and later, the World Council of Churches. Hesselgrave argued that the "Edinburgh error" was that the participants touted ecumenism without working out theological issues.[1] Billy Graham said "since then the world church has floundered as evangelism was replaced by humanization, the reconciliation of man with man rather than of man with God."[2]

But Newbigin did not sacrifice theology for unity's sake. He called himself a "hopeful exclusivist" and believed Christianity contained truths that are true for all people.[3]

> The relativism which is not willing to speak about truth but only about "what is true for me" is an evasion of the serious business of living. It is the mark of a tragic loss of nerve in our contemporary culture. It is a preliminary symptom of death.[4]

---

[1] Hesselgrave, "Will We Correct the Edinburgh Error?"
[2] Graham, "Why Lausanne?" 25.
[3] Terry et al., *Missiology*, 25.
[4] Newbigin, *Gospel in a Pluralist Society*, 22.

Historically, exclusivism has been the normative Christian understanding of salvation, from Augustine onward. But astute critics may point out that if Augustine found it necessary to debunk pluralism and annihilationism, then both of those interpretations were in fact being argued as far back as the fourth century.

Note that exclusivists do not hold their position because they are cold-hearted or are "holier than thou." Rather, they begin with the presupposition that there is a supernatural world, so supernatural acts like specific revelation are possible. If God *can* communicate, then it is possible that He did indeed reveal Himself through the events recorded in the OT and finally through his Son as recorded in the NT. And His Son said that He is the only way (John 14:6). God's miraculously-revealed word also says that there is no other way by which people can be saved (Acts 4:12). The more certain one becomes the Bible is God's accurate communication to humankind, the more certain she is that Jesus is the only mediator between humans and God (1 Tim 2:5).

Crockett argues that exclusivism was endemic to the first century Palestinian worldview. Paul's language reinforced a social boundary,[63] and Jews would not have conceived of pagans as part of this community. "The exclusive claim is not a footnote to the gospel; it is the gospel itself."[64] In fact, one of the major points in Chris Wright's theology of mission is that the prophets railed on idolatry because it thwarts God's mission:[65] God's mission is to make Himself known, and idolatry obscures Him. This is of missiological significance because the world's religions often contain examples of idolatry: trusting in that which we want, fear, and need. If idolatry is this bad, we cannot settle for missionary method that encourages such idolatry through interfaith dialog.

If explicit faith in Jesus Christ is necessary for salvation, as exclusivists claim (based on Scripture), then many will not be saved. Interestingly, even exclusivists are divided about the ultimate fate of the lost. Historically, the orthodox view (as established in the creeds) is that the lost will suffer eternal punishment in hell. But a minority and recent view is that of annihilationism. Those who hold this view argue that while it is true that people who do not know Christ cannot be saved (so this view fits under exclusionism), the lost will not be condemned

---

63. Crockett, "Will God Save Everyone in the End?" 162.
64. Peters, *Biblical Theology of Missions*, 147.
65. Wright, *Mission of God*.

to hell; instead, they will cease to exist. Seeing Jesus as "the only way" indicates that annihiliationists do have a supernaturalistic cosmology, in contrast to the materialism that is typical of universalism. They allow for the miracle of specific revelation through Jesus and Scripture, so they are open to using Scripture to form their answer about the fate of the lost. To do so, they must argue that Jesus did not really teach hell as eternal punishment. They say his comments about eternal punishment must have been hyperbole. "Many of the passages depicting hell are in the genre of Scripture designated as prophetic, parabaolic, or apocalyptic."[66] The debate centers especially on what "destruction" refers to in Phil 3:19.

## Summary of Major Positions on the Destiny of the Lost

Missiological theologians typically recognize humbly that the Bible is not entirely clear on the fate of those who have never heard; and they find the doctrine of eternal punishment to be somewhat disturbing. Theologians find biblical support for their arguments by "privileging" a certain hermeneutical lens. Rob Bell, Clark Pinnock, John Sanders, and Lesslie Newbigin emphasize God's love, so they see passages about eternal punishment as hyperbole. Exclusivists like John Walvoord and Ronald Nash "privilege" a hermeneutic of justice.

Although I have outlined four major theological answers to the fate of the lost here, it would be erroneous to imply that each of these options has equal representation within Christian hermeneutics. Throughout the church's history, orthodox Christians have been exclusivists, and can find no other way for the lost to be saved; so they concluded that we are compelled to preach Christ until He returns. The debate about the lost is not splitting hairs, and is not a trivial question. If we depart from orthodoxy on this point, we change virtually all other aspects of systematic theology.[67] Table 2 (below) summarizes the various positions on the destiny of the lost, as well as the implications that each position has for missionary outreach.

---

66. Brewer, "Rob Bell and John Wesley on the Fate of the Lost," 128.
67. Van Engen, *Mission on the Way*, 181.

**Table 2: Summary of Theologies of the Lost**

| Position | Description | Verses used as support | Missiological Ramifications |
|---|---|---|---|
| Pluralism | No souls will be lost; all will live on in God's memory or in heaven, because all are made in God's image, and God's self-revelation through nature is salvific | Rom 5:12–21; 14:11; 1 Cor 15:20–28; Isa 52:10; 66:23; Hab 2:14; 3:3; Num 14:21; Ps 97:6; Phil 2:9–11; Isa 45:23; Eph 1:10; Col 1:21–23 (see Brewer, "Rob Bell and John Wesley on the Fate of the Lost," 122). | Missions is about inter-faith dialog; theology is informed by the "truths" in other religions Missionary activities are directed toward social justice |
| Inclusivism | All souls will be saved through the work of Jesus Christ, whether people overtly confessed faith in Him or not. | 2 Cor 1:20 | Proclamation is about ecumenism and emphasizes the benefits of knowing Christ and the church during life on earth |
| Exclusivism | Those who do not explicitly believe in Jesus Christ will suffer eternal punishment | Matt 5:22, 29, 30; 10:28; 18:9; 23:13, 15, 33; Mark 9:43, 45, 47; Luke 12:5; 13:25–29; Rom 6:21; Acts 4:12; Phil 1:28; 3:19; 1 Thess 5:3; 2 Thess 1:8ff; Jas 3:6; 2 Pet 2:4; Rev 14:10; 20:10–15; 23 (see Brewer, "Rob Bell and John Wesley on the Fate of the Lost," 122). | Missionary *activities* are holistic, but may emphasize evangelism and discipleship |
| Annihilationism | Those who did not confess faith in Jesus Christ are condemned but only in the sense that they will cease to exist for eternity | Deut 29:20; Ps 37; Mal 4:1–2; Matt 3:10, 12; 5:30; 10:28, 13:30, 42, 49–50; Luke 16:19–31; Rom 2:8; Gal 6:8; 1 Cor 3:17; Phil 1:28; 3:19; 2 Thess 1:9; Heb 10:39; 2 Pet 2:1, 3; 2:6; 3:6–7; Jude 7, Rev 20:14–15; 23 (see Brewer, "Rob Bell and John Wesley on the Fate of the Lost," 122). | Proclamation is about ecumenism and emphasizes the benefits of knowing Christ and the church in this life. |

## Missiological Implications of the Nature of the Church

Studies of the nature of God, Christology, and soteriology lead us to the next branch of systematic theology: ecclesiology—the study of the nature and role of the church. Missiological ecclesiology asks questions like: Given the nature of God as the owner of all creation, the One who makes covenants to save humankind, what is the role of the church in missions today? Is Paul's model of itinerant preaching and the establishment of house churches normative for the church's role in missions today? When is the right time to baptize new believers? Can enough discipleship be done in one day to lead, in good conscience, to baptism, as with the Ethiopian eunuch in Acts 8?

A great body of missiological ecclesiology focuses on the nature and work of the church in facilitating the expansion of Christianity. In fact, missiology and ecclesiology are so intertwined that Fuller's School of World Mission overlapped significantly with its Church Growth Institute (now the two are the Fuller School of Intercultural Studies).

Church planting models are also informed by missiological ecclesiology. The name apostle, after all, comes from the same root as missionary: those who are sent. For the early church, expansion was central; though fellowship, obedience, and service were also foci. But starting in the book of Acts, multiplication has been a sign of health for the church. If you're not growing, you're dying. If the church ceases to be involved in outreach, it soon ceases to exist. The constant centrifugal force gives the church its life.

But is the church's primary activity in the world to make disciples? Under Christendom (when Roman Catholicism enjoyed political power in Western Europe) the church's mission became less focused on making disciples, and more interested in extending the reach of church institutions into the political and economic lives of subjects in the empire.

Unfortunately, numerous other competing philosophies of missions have distracted the church throughout history. For some, church has become merely a place to teach children morals, a social club, another non-profit for doing relief work, and even a platform for instigating political revolutions. And in the twentieth century, many mainline churches began redefining their role as that of peacemakers—those who bring *shalom* through interreligious dialog.

So missiologists return to ecclesiology in the New Testament—especially in Paul's letters, to inform us of biblical views on the role of the church in missions. Missiological studies of Paul have focused on his turn toward the gentiles[68] and his methods of missions, including the role of finance in his missionary work,[69] his evangelism methods,[70] and his view of the local church in missionary outreach.[71] Much has also been done to understand Paul's "missionary theology" including his reliance on the Holy Spirit,[72] his Christology,[73] his eschatology,[74] and his methods for contextualizing the gospel.[75] Scholars have concluded that the core of Paul's missionary message includes reconciliation,[76] the glory of God,[77] the *missio Dei*,[78] and salvation through Christ.[79]

## Missiological Implications of the Nature and Work of the Holy Spirit

Pneumatology, the branch of systematic theology that seeks to understand the nature and work of the Holy Spirit, has always been closely tied to the study of missions. This is, in large part, because the book of Acts, nicknamed the Acts of the Holy Spirit, shows that the Spirit (and not humans) is on a mission to expand the church to all corners of the world. Missiologist Roland Allen noted the Holy Spirit's central role in the "spontaneous expansion of the church."[80] So "if we are to have a sound pneumatology, we must locate the Spirit first in the context of eschatology and mission."[81]

---

68. Lin, "Jewish Identity Crisis Posed by Paul's Gentile Mission"; Nicklas and Schlögel, "Mission to the Gentiles."

69. Cortez, "Mission-Charity Dilemme"; Lim, "Generosity from Pauline Perspective"; Ogereau, "Paul's Κοινωνία with the Philippians"; Walton, "Paul, Patronage and Pay."

70. Yinger, "Paul and Evangelism."

71. Liubinskas, "Body of Christ in Mission."

72. Berding, "At the Intersection of Mission and Spirtual Formation"; Burke, "Holy Spirit as the Controlling Dynamic."

73. Hultgren, "Paul's Christology and His Mission to the Gentiles."

74. White, "Eschatological Conversion of 'all the Nations' In Matthew 28:19–20."

75. Salisbury, "Paul's First Letter to Timothy."

76. Porter, "Reconciliation as the Heart of Paul's Missionary Theology."

77. Rosner, "Glory of God in Paul's Missionary Theology and Practice."

78. Gaventa, "Mission of God in Paul's Letter to the Romans."

79. Ciampa, "Paul's Theology of the Gospel."

80. Allen, *Spontaneous Expansion of the Church*.

81. Goheen, *Introducing Christian Mission Today*, 100.

## Profile of a Missiologist: Roland Allen

### (1868–1947)

*Education: Oxford; Leeds Clergy Training School*
*Occupation: Missionary to China, Anglican parish priest, lecturer and author*

Roland Allen served in North China with the Society for the Propagation of the Gospel (SPG) until the Boxer Rebellion in 1900. He and his wife returned to China for a short time until he fell ill and they returned again to England, where he served briefly as a parish priest. For the last forty years of his life, Allen did not serve the church in an official capacity; and in fact he became increasingly embittered toward the church's hierarchy. Allen also critiqued the missionary enterprise for getting into ruts where missionaries repeated the same old mistakes.[1]

While we may see Allen's missiology as common sense today, his arguments actually went against the common practices of the Anglican church in his own day. Allen argued that the foreign churches should have Scriptures, hymns, and catechisms in their own language. And like Venn, Anderson, and Nevius, Allen argued that missionaries should raise up local priests and bishops among the most talented leaders in the society. The local church was responsible for evangelizing those around them, and if a community of believers did not have these elements, it was not a church, but still a mission field.[2]

Allen also believed the role of the Holy Spirit was central. He argued[3] that Paul's missionary method, unlike "ours," was to communicate the spirit of the law, under grace, rather than control every aspect of the church.[4]

Some (in Allen's day, as well as today) would critique Allen's methods, since hasty transfer of leadership can result in syncretism and shallow churches. On the other hand, Allen's championing of the preeminence of church planting over any other aspect of ministry would eventually shape Donald McGavran's missiology, as well as many others'.[5]

---

[1] Long and Rowthorn, "Legacy of Roland Allen," 66.
[2] Long and Rowthorn, "Legacy of Roland Allen," 66.
[3] Allen, *Spontaneous Expansion of the Church*.
[4] Long and Rowthorn, "Legacy of Roland Allen," 67.
[5] Long and Rowthorn, "Legacy of Roland Allen," 68.

Not only does the Holy Spirit cause people to repent and believe, thus expanding the church, He compels people to get involved in missions (Acts 2:43–47). When the Holy Spirit causes large waves of renewal, the result is a push for world evangelization.[82] And Lorance has astutely pointed out, on three occasions in the book of Acts the Holy Spirit had the disciples wait before they went further in their missionary work.[83]

Additionally, as the earlier section on salvation-history indicated, the Spirit goes before the evangelist, preparing people's hearts by convicting them of sin and showing them the deficiency of their own idolatry. Paul believed that the preaching of the gospel would be accompanied by a "demonstration of the spirit's power" (Gal 3:3; 1, Thess 1:5; 1 Cor 2:4).[84]

## Missiological Implications of the End Times

In the last two centuries, an area of systematic theology that has received a great deal of focus is eschatology—the study of the end times. For a systematic missiological theology, we need to ask, *What are the missiological implications of Jesus's triumphal return?* Missions is in fact an activity of the end times, as it exists in this "overlapping" of the ages, between the Old Age and the Age to Come—the already-not yet.[85]

What do the end times entail, from a missiological perspective? The wedding banquet stories in Matt 22:8–10; Matt 24:14; and Mark 13:10 are about Jews and gentiles alike being invited into the kingdom of Heaven.[86] So missionary preaching is about salvation from the wrath to come at King Jesus's *parousia*.[87] There will be an ingathering in Mount Zion, like a banquet in Isa 25:6–9. Jesus extended this banquet to heaven, and also used the metaphor of a harvest (Matt 9:37–38). The end times, especially in Jewish tradition, involve not only an ingathering of the faithful, but a purification of the sinner and obedience by the people of God (Ezek 36:24–27).[88]

---

82. Holmes, *Holy Spirit*.
83. Lorance, "Holy Spirit and the Pace of Mission."
84. Burke, "Holy Spirit as the Controlling Dynamic," 143.
85. Goheen, *Introducing Christian Mission Today*, 50.
86. Carriker, "Missiological Hermeneutic and Pauline Apocalyptic Eschatology."
87. Gieschen, "Christ's Coming and the Church's Mission in 1 Thessalonians."
88. Goheen, *Introducing Christian Mission Today*, 54.

Missiological theologians must ask whether global evangelism efforts are a precursor to the *parousia*, as Matt 24:14 can imply. Those who see the rapture as imminent (who are also typically exclusivists) believe there is a tremendous urgency to make disciples of all *ethne* before the Day of the Lord. Pre-millennialists like Robert Saucy and Gordon Lewis are more likely to see not only evangelism, but discipleship of all nations to be both a sign and prerequisite to the return of Christ.[89] On the other hand, the likelihood of making disciples of every ethnic group is such a remote possibility, that to see it as a prerequisite to Christ's return is to view the rapture as not only a long way off, but seemingly impossible.

Amillennialists like Anthony A. Hoekema and Robert Recker, as well as post-millennialists like John Jefferson Davis, take Matt 24:14 to mean that the gospel will continually be preached until judgment day, but they emphasize the sovereignty of God in the end times, rather than the work of the church in hastening Christ's return.[90]

So eschatology is as much a part of the theology of missions as every other branch of systematic theology. Missiological eschatology brings together the issues of salvation history (soteriology) and the work of the church (ecclesiology).

## Conclusion

Systematic missiological theology can extend to a number of areas that we do not have room to include here, such as contextual theology, the missiological implications of theological anthropology, and the missiological implications of angels and demons. At this point it should be obvious that while many passages of God's word are not about missions, a missiological lens can be applied to the entire Scripture to flesh out theories and strategies of making disciples across cultures. Table 3 summarizes the missiological implications of the six theological categories discussed in this chapter.

---

89. Hesselgrave, "Millennium and Missions."
90. Hesselgrave, "Millennium and Missions."

Table 3: Missiological implications of systematic theological categories

| Category from Systematic theology | Missiological topics |
|---|---|
| Missions and the Nature and work of God (missiological theology) | • The implications of the fact that God as creator, unique, supreme, judge, and loving has the right to require all people to worship Him alone<br>• The implications of God as blesser, sender, defender of the weak, covenant-maker and the one who discloses himself |
| Missions and the Nature and work of Jesus Christ (missiological Christology) | • How the church should emulate the model of the incarnation, as a ministry<br>• Jesus's treatment of foreigners a model for missional engagement |
| Missions and the Nature of salvation-history (missiological soteriology) | • How to reconcile God's particular plan for Israel with God's universal plan for the world<br>• The fate of those who have never heard<br>• The evaluation of truth claims in the world's religions<br>• The church's role in interacting with other religions |
| Missions and the Nature and work of the church (missiological ecclesiology) | • The role of the church in the world today<br>• The role of proclamation in relation to other aspects of the kingdom of God<br>• How biblical models of mission (Acts and Pauline missiology) are normative for the church today |
| Missions and the Nature and work of the Holy Spirit (missiological pneumatology) | • How people are led to repentance and belief<br>• The supernatural causes that are behind the expansion of the church |
| Missions and the Nature of the *eschaton* (missiological eschatology) | • The relationship between world evangelization and the *parousia* |

## Move Into Action

Read each passage of Scripture, first, to understand its original intent in its context; don't look for missions in each passage. But consider how the original intent of each passage has implications on some aspect of missions. This chapter has suggested some various action points for using theology to make disciples across cultures:

- Leverage understandings within the host culture related to God, sin, humanity, etc;
- Point out theological errors across cultures;
- Address theological questions that host communities are asking; and
- Encourage disciple makers to recognize the spiritual realm

## Ideas for Further Research

Research in missiological theology can be done using methodologies in the humanities (book study) or the social sciences (gathering empirical research from people). This chapter has argued that humanities-based missiological theology should examine the implications of biblical passages for cross-cultural discipleship. For example:

1. Theologians have developed theodicies (explanations for the existence of evil)—but how do those theodicies inform or challenge the explanations for evil in Hinduism, Buddhism, or animistic societies?
2. How do New Testament passages about order and leadership in the life of the church inform and challenge church life in Christian communities in specific cultural contexts?

Social science research can also inform missiological theology. For example:

1. How do healing practices of Christian communities in specific cultural contexts inform or challenge Western theologies of healing?
2. How do theodicies of Christian communities in specific cultural contexts inform or challenge Western theodicies?

## Review Questions

1. How does systematic missiological theology avoid the problems of the "text assembly method" or the danger of conflating "missions" with "mission?"

2. What is the difference between missions and mission, according to this text?

3. What did Martin Kähler mean by the assertion that mission is not merely ancillary to "theology proper"; rather that "mission is the mother of theology"?[91]

4. How do missiologists use theology to make disciples across cultures?

## Reflection Questions

1. What are the strengths and weaknesses of the pluralist, inclusivist, and exclusivist answers for the fate of those who die without converting to Christianity?

2. What is the biblical basis for missions?

3. Give examples of how you would apply a missiological hermeneutic to texts that are not specifically about missions.

---

91. Kähler, *Schriften zur Christologie und Mission*, 190.

*Chapter 3*

# Connecting the History of Missions to Cross-Cultural Discipleship

I ASKED MY DOCTORAL students in a class on missiological theory and strategy, "Why do missiologists study the history of missions?" "To learn from the past" and "to not repeat the same mistakes" were the common responses. These are two commendable, albeit simplistic purposes for studying any branch of history. But these answers do not help us make that jump from "knowing about the history of missions" to "not repeating the same mistakes." How do missiologists take information about the expansion (and contraction) of Christianity over two millennia and actually make it useful?

Most missiologists agree that history is an essential part of their discipline. This chapter answers, "How do missiologists actually use history?" In order to answer this research question, I have examined more than a hundred articles, theses, and books on the history of missions in order to outline the methodologies and theoretical approaches for doing historical work in missions. And ultimately, I have tried to understand the goals of these historians. Of course, there is not a single answer to this; the methods and goals reflect various theological and theoretical perspectives. Here, I have organized those approaches so that missiologists can learn to read history more purposefully, as well as produce quality historical research of missiological value.

## Chapter Goals

*Knowledge goals:*

- Critique the advantages and disadvantages of viewing the history of missions through "great missionary" biography.
- Describe how the stories of marginalized people can enrich our understanding of the history of missions
- Describe theories about what has caused Christianity to expand and contract over the centuries.

*Action goals:*

- As you write about the history of missions in a specific area, rather than recounting names and dates, highlight best practices for making disciples across cultures

*Heart goals:*

- Psalm 96 implores us to proclaim God's deeds among the nations. Commit to learning how God has worked among the nations, and to retelling those stories in a way that brings Him praise.

## Six Lenses for Interpreting the History of Missions

High quality, original contributions in the social sciences are usually aimed at explaining the world through a deductive-inductive cycle of theory-building;[1] but this purpose is less evident in the field of history. At times, though, historians of missions do help readers make the jump from "what happened" to what should or could happen, why it matters, and what should never be repeated. As Bradley and Muller argued, good history involves moving from description to explanation, with the aim of "assigning causes and construing significance."[2]

Unfortunately, historians' theories can be lost on their readers because such theories are suggested subtly, and with an understandable

---

1. Bendassolli, "Theory Building in Qualitative Research"; Jaccard and Jacoby, *Theory Construction and Model-building Skills.*
2. Bradley and Muller, *Church History*, 52.

degree of tentativeness. And missiologists' historical methods, regardless of how robust and organized, are usually even subtler or not articulated at all. So we end up reading history as simply a list of names and dates, like we did in elementary school. Recently my eighth-grade daughter asked me for help on an assignment in her US history class. As she painstakingly looked up the date that each constitutional amendment was passed, I stopped her and asked if she understood the purpose of the eleventh amendment. Alas, she didn't—partly because her assignment did not include any questions related to the purpose of the amendments. I am surprised that by now better pedagogical methods for history have not thoroughly permeated the middle school curriculum. Rather than memorize the names and dates, why not consider how the amendment was a product of the times? Or what would life be like if it had not been passed? Or what was the controversy regarding the amendment? How did the amendment affect the economy and social life?

These curricular techniques are also possible in the history of missions. Rather than listing the accomplishments of various missionaries, worthwhile histories examine how the actions and beliefs of home churches, missionaries, mission agencies and members of the host culture were indicative of the time. For example, advanced studies on the history of missions would not simply recount where William Carey served, how many wives he had, and how many businesses he set up; instead, they would ask questions like, How was Carey simultaneously emblematic of colonialism, yet also against the grain? What would have happened if Hudson Taylor had not gone to inland China? Why was Mary Slessor a controversial figure in the twentieth century? What do we infer about the plan of God as we study the expansion of the church during the Middle Ages? What would Christianity in Europe be like today if the medieval church had not launched the Crusades?

The history of missions is not always done at that level of theory-building. In fact, since there is no widely accepted missiological historiography, histories of missions vary greatly in approach, methodology and purpose. The *sine qua non* of the histories of missions seems to be the causes and effects of the expansion of the church; but the way these questions are asked can be quite nuanced. Here, I argue that historians of missions have looked at the expansion of Christianity through six major theoretical approaches: 1) by viewing God's guidance of the process; 2) by following the lives of "great missionaries"; 3) by celebrating legacies of mission boards and churches, 4) by highlighting the role of marginalized actors in the missionary effort; 5) by emphasizing specific strategies of missions; and 6) by building missiological theory. Building theory involves several steps, including: Extracting timeless principles and universals, making connections such as social and political influences on the missionary effort, and understanding a phenomenon in its complexity, rather than reducing or essentializing it.

## Locating the History of Mission within Academia

Missiologists use history for the same reason scholars use any field in the humanities: to understand humankind better, which in turn helps us understand ourselves better and know how to respond to our own situations. Further, Christians study the humanities to understand how God and humans have responded in relationship to each other over the millennia.

What gives the history of missions its distinctiveness is the set of questions it explores, like: What caused conversions and numerical growth in the church? What impact did European efforts to missionize the rest of the world have on local cultures? How does the message of Christianity interface with theologies of various cultures? These questions are important to theologians, missiologists, and church historians alike; and scholars from each of these disciplines have studied histories of missions at both the macro and micro level. Therefore no particular branch of Christian thought can claim the history of missions as a subset purely of its own discipline. Church historians may claim it is as a focus within their realm, whereas missiologists may locate it as one of the "legs" of their field. I argue that the history of missions is at the nexus of church history and missiology, as Figure 2 shows below. While Christian scholars from multiple disciplines have a vested interest in these questions, Skreslet pointed out that they are not the only ones examining the history of missions:

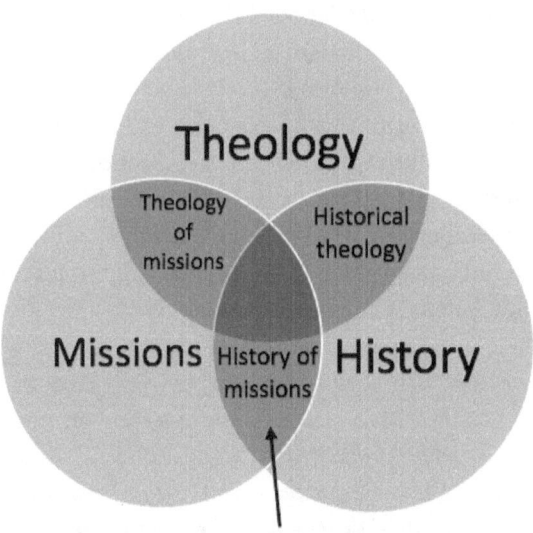

Figure 2: Locating the history of mission within wider Christian disciplines

> Now a growing legion of scholars is being drawn to the study of mission history, among whom we find specialists in politics and economics, Marxists, feminists, historical anthropologists and other kinds of social historians, and Americanists as well as researchers focused on non-Western societies, not to mention religious historians of every stripe who make it their business to study the world's burgeoning collection of faith communities and traditions.[3]

Some questions about the history of missions are more specific to missiologists, such as, What barriers do missionaries face, and how do they overcome those barriers? Or, what can European Christians learn from global hermeneutics?

Most Christian studies of the history of missions have tried to answer a meta-question about *how* Christianity spread from Jerusalem to the ends of the earth, going back to Augustine's argument in *The City of God* that Christianity was more resilient than Hellenic heathenism because of its moral superiority. Harnack famously argued it was the diaspora of Judaism coupled with "Jewish Missionary theology" that paved the way for the spread of Christianity;[4] though this thesis has recently been

3. Skreslet, "Thinking Missiologically About the History of Mission," 59.
4. Harnack, *Die Mission und Ausbreitung des Christentums*.

contested.[5] Latourette[6] and later Meeks[7] theorized that the expansion was possible because early Christian society offered more tangible benefits than the Greco-Roman world did.

On the other hand, historians have had to explain why Christians since the first century experienced persecutions and martyrdom. "Their enemies patently trifled with the truth when they referred to the Christians as 'imbeciles' (Lucian), 'god-forsaken fools' (Celsus), and haters of the human race' (Tacitus) . . . The Christians were generally despised, often hated, by the people among whom they lived. They were accused of being atheists, immoral and unpatriotic."[8]

The spread of Christianity beyond the Near East was also a chief question for Moore.[9] More recently the question of how Christianity became a world religion was taken up by Robert.[10] And Montgomery has specifically applied Diffusion Theory from the social sciences to understand the "lopsided" expansion of Christianity throughout history.[11]

Other histories of missions focus on how the gospel spread in a specific region. Examples include Robinson's study of the Christianization of Europe,[12] or Addison's research on the conversion of Northern Europe during the Middle Ages.[13] The earliest and most prevalent explanation for the spread of Christianity has been the sovereign will of God.

## Following "Providential Guidance" Throughout History

Before the Enlightenment, church history was aimed at showing the continuity and sovereignty of God over time. "History (or at least chronicle) was written not critically, but inspirationally; and in a cosmos perceived as a battleground between God and the Enemy, only one side of the story was worth the telling."[14] Christian historians who focus on

5. Cohen, *Significance of Yavneh and Other Essays in Jewish Hellenism*; Goodman, *Mission and Conversion*.

6. Latourette, *History of Christianity*.

7. Meeks, *First Urban Christians*.

8. Kane, *Concise History of the Christian World Mission*, 30–31.

9. Moore, *Spread of Christianity in the Modern World*.

10. Robert, *Christian Mission*.

11. Montgomery, *LopsidedSspread of Christianity*.

12. Robinson, *How the Gospel Spread Through Europe*.

13. Addison, *Medieval Missionary*.

14. Sharpe, "Reflections on Missionary Historiography," 78.

the history of missions have traced how the Holy Spirit continued the miracle of Pentecost throughout human history, leading inexorably toward world evangelization. By the nineteenth century this inevitable progression of history also contained social evolution and the relentless progress toward "civilization."

This was certainly Philip Schaff's plan in his monumental church history[15]—to "discern the hand of providence and the guiding spirit of Christianity in history."[16] Likewise, Pierson's history of nineteenth century missions argues that the great missionary expansion could only be understood in view of God's superintendence.[17]

Such theological positivism is rarely adhered to these days by historians—even Christian ones; and we cannot presume to even attain a "God's-eye perspective."[18] However, studying history to know God's character is still a superb reason for studying the history of missions. In fact, this is the underlying purpose of Klauber and Manetsch's recent history of evangelical global missions.[19] Nonetheless, a view of Providence is no longer the main theoretical lens for understanding the history of missions. A far more common approach has been the biographical approach.

## Following the Lives of "Great Missionaries"

Scottish historian Thomas Carlyle theorized, "The history of the world is but the biography of great men."[20] Missionary biographies from the Venerable Bede in the eighth century through Carlyle's era commonly approached the research question about the spread of Christianity by focusing on great men (and sometimes great women) of the faith. This approach to history is akin to Bradley and Muller's "great thinker model" within church history.[21]

---

15. Schaff, *Church History*.
16. Bradley and Muller, *Church History*, 20.
17. Pierson, *Modern Mission Century Viewed as aCcycle of Divine Working*.
18. Skreslet, "Thinking Missiologically about the History of Mission," 60.
19. Klauber and Manetsch, *Great Commission*.
20. Carlyle, *On Heros, Hero Worship and the Heroic in History*, 127.
21. Bradley and Muller, *Church History*, 30.

Smith's *Heroes and Martyrs of the Modern Missionary Enterprise* is an example of this biographical approach from the nineteenth century.[22] Examples of "great missionary" histories are still common.[23] For example, Frykenberg recently published a legacy of the *mahatma* "Great Soul" Pandita Ramabai Dongre, who founded the Mukti Mission in India;[24] and Ma published a legacy of the holistic ministry of Mark and Huldah Bultan in Calcutta.[25]

The "great missionary" model can indeed be inspiring. John Piper's history of three Christian leaders, William Tyndale, Adoniram Judson, and John Paton, challenges frontline missionaries to "share in Christ's afflictions," going where it is dangerous to be a witness for Christ.[26] Histories of Lottie Moon,[27] Amy Carmichael,[28] and Gladys Aylward[29] have undoubtedly inspired numerous women—single and married—to work across cultures.

The greatest weakness of missionary biography, from a historiographical perspective, is the tendency to write hagiographies. "Assertions and stories clearly meant to inspire readers are frequently a mixture of truth, exaggeration, and imagination."[30] For example, "Hagiographers are inclined to elevate or denigrate the social and economic status of saints, depending on the writer's basic purpose."[31] Further, missionary biography can have the unfortunate side effect of demotivating the average reader who cannot identify his or her own life with one of these "great" men or women. As Bishop Stephen Neill theorized, from the very beginning, the feature that has allowed Christianity to

---

22. Smith, *Heroes and Martyrs of the Modern Missionary Enterprise*.

23. Davies, *Life and Thought of Henry Gerhard Appenzeller*; Starkes, *God's Commissioned People*; Tucker, *From Jerusalem to Irian Jaya*.

24. Frykenberg, "Legacy of Pandita Ramabai."

25. Ma, "Touching Lives of People Through the Holistic Mission Work."

26. Piper, *Filling up the Afflictions of Christ*.

27. Allen, "Legacy of Lottie Moon"; Allen, "Charlotte (Lottie) Moon 1840–1912"; Flowers, "Contested Legacy of Lottie Moon"; Harper, *Send the Light*; Short, "Lottie Moon"; Sullivan, *Lottie Moon*.

28. Elliot, "Amy Carmichael of India"; Jeyakumar, "Amy Carmichael of Dohnavur 1867–1951"; Jeyaraj, "Amy Carmichael"; Murray, *Amy Carmichael*; Sharpe, "Legacy of Amy Carmichael."

29. Burgess, *Small Woman*.

30. Neely, "Saints Who Sometimes Were," 445.

31. Neely, "Saints Who Sometimes Were," 446.

spread is the countless anonymous lay witnesses—not the unusual great witness.[32]

Also, these biographies can be limited in their capacity for theory-building. The missiological goal for the history of missions, as I mentioned earlier, is not to simply understand a particular person in depth—nor even a period of history, nor to understand the development of a certain doctrine, as historical theologians do. Missionary biography is less useful when it fails to show connections between eras, or fails to look at wider influences (e.g., from culture, politics). However, it is useful when it explores "what made this missionary effective?" Or, "How did this missionary influence future mission work?" Interestingly, though, the more biography takes into account philosophical, cultural, and other historical process, the less it is emblematic of the "great missionary" model of Thomas Carlyle's time. Biographies which include a host of other explanatory factors regarding the causes and results of the expansion of Christianity instead entail a holistic approach to the history of missions.

Interestingly, a permutation of the "great missionary" approach is the "great missiologist" lens, which focuses on the contributions eminent missiologists to the theory and strategy of missions. For example, the *Great Commission Research Journal* often focuses on the legacy of Donald McGavran, including his influence on the church growth movement,[33] and on the theology of conversion,[34] or on the theology of evangelism,[35] and on urban evangelism strategies[36] as well as his own missionary heritage.[37] Historians of missions also examine the legacy of other missiologists like Ralph Winter and Henry Venn.

## Establishing a Canon of Missionary Biography

The biographical approach to missions has tremendous force even today in missiological curriculum. By repeatedly selecting certain "great missionaries" missiologists have developed a canon (albeit loosely defined one) of historical missionaries of which any scholar of mission needs to

32. Neill, *History of Christian Missions*, 24.
33. Van Engen, "Bridges of God."
34. Suarez, "Donald McGavran's Understanding of Conversion."
35. Walters, "Donald McGavran's Theological Foundations for 'Effective Evangelism.'"
36. Walters, "Donald McGavran and the City."
37. McIntosh, "McGavran's Family Heritage."

be aware. We would consider missiological education deficient if the students were unfamiliar with St. Patrick's use of the shamrock to illustrate the Trinity, or with his evangelization of 100,000 (or was it 200,000?) Irish. Likewise, we expect students of missiology to know about Boniface's power encounter among the Frisians as he cut down their sacred oak. And no historical survey of missions would leave out the wide influence of the Jesuits, noting, for example, how Francis Xavier identified with the Japanese upper classes. And what course on history of missions would omit how William Carey set off the modern Protestant missionary movement by arguing that the Great Commission applies to the church today? Additionally, we expect our students to be familiar with the Moravians who sent out thousands of missionaries at a great cost; as well as with John Eliot's Macedonian call to the Algonquin, and Adoniram Judson's experience of a "people movement" among a marginalized ethnic group in Burma. Missiological curriculum certainly includes a study of how Hudson Taylor and Mary Slessor both moved missionary stations from the coast to the inland villages; and we would note that Lottie Moon was so culturally embedded in the girls' school in China that she died of starvation rather than return home.

By this point, it must be clear that the "canon" within the history of missions is neither complete nor uncontested: In a recent informal survey I conducted of professors of missions, participants said the list must also contain such figures as Gladys Aylward, Robert Morrison, C.T. Studd, David Brainerd, Amy Carmichael, E. Stanley Jones, Roberto di Nobili, Matteo Ricci, and David Livingstone. Urbana's list of "21 Missionaries you should know"[38] includes more recent figures like Cameron Townsend, Jim Elliot, Pandita Ramabai, Kenneth Stratchan, and Helen Roseveare. While there is no clearly defined canon of "great missionaries," there are figures who are easily recognized as leaving their mark on the history of missions. Figure 3 (below) shows how this "canon" is created ad hoc as scholars reify the influence of these "great missionaries" by making repeated reference to them.

The presence of such a "canon" of "great missionaries" should raise questions about the outcomes of continuing this sort of history of missions in our curriculum. If the majority of missionary biographies that are available to us are limited in their capacity for theory-building, why

---

38. Voekel, "21 Missionaries You Should Know."

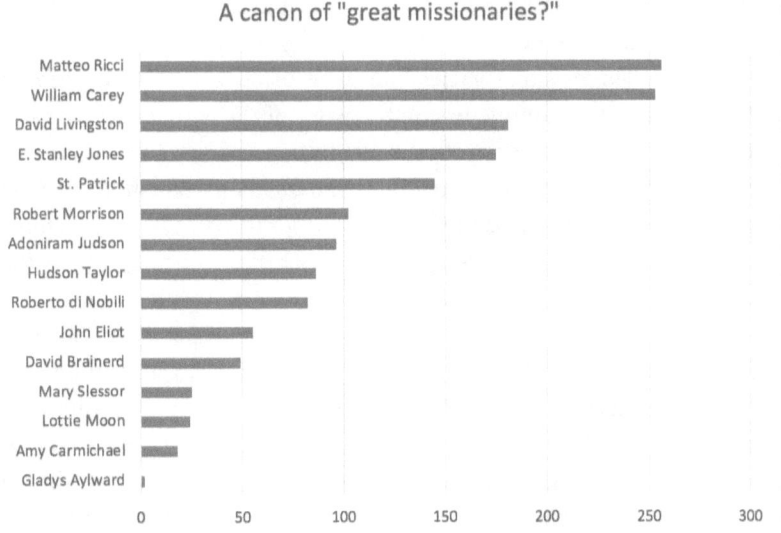

Figure 3: Number of works that reference 15 "great missionaries" in ATLA religious database through 2018

do they occupy the central role in our reading of the history of missions? The field of history has moved beyond the "great man" theory, especially since critical theorists have suggested that this approach endorses the majority voice while silencing cultural minorities (including women). Therefore, by reinforcing this canon, we are not only revealing how behind they times we are, we are also missing out on the *other* valuable ways to do the history of missions (discussed later on in this chapter).

## By Celebrating the Legacy of Mission Agencies, Churches, and Missionary Movements

Sometimes the "great missionary" model is extended to the "mission board legacy." Beckner's history of the French mission to Basutoland is right on the border of a "great missionary" biography and a "mission board legacy" since it traces the work of two missionaries—Eugene Casalis and Thomas Arbouseet—as well as the wider legacy of their mission agency.[39] The study indicates that the success of these missionaries was due to their application of "mission-by-translation" (to use Lamin Sanneh's term) as

---

39. Beckner, "Eugene Casalis and the French Mission to Basutoland."

they became "vernacular agents, inspiring indigenous sentiment and theory laying the groundwork for he founding of a nation."[40]

Wiest called mission legacies "house histories . . . written to preserve early records and to commemorate the work of the early generations."[41] And indeed one of the important contributions of the "legacy model" in the history of missions is making primary data accessible, such as missionary yearbooks and mission board proceedings. An example of an early "house history" would be Reid's history of missions in the Methodist Episcopal Church.[42]

Just as missionary biography is limited in its capacity for theory-building, Wiest notes that these agency-focused histories tend to be restricted in their usefulness. "These writings generally take the form of a chronological or a biographical account and rarely give a critical interpretation or comprehensive coverage of the sources."[43] As Sharpe explained, "Chronicle *becomes* history only when an element of interpretation is added to the chronological record."[44]

But, as with missionary biography, if they are done well, mission legacies can certainly contribute to theory building. For instance, Hood's study of the English Presbyterian Mission in East Guangdong Province demonstrates how the agency's efforts to train local leadership contributed to the self-sufficiency of the church in that region.[45] Similarly, Kovacs showed that the Free Church in Scotland played a central role in shaping civil society and education in Hungary.[46]

## Tracing the Impact of Missionary Conferences on World Mission

Another way historians of missions celebrate legacies is to trace the impact of World Missionary movements and conferences on the expansion of Christianity. What cultural forces, philosophical shifts and personalities led to these "world conferences?" In what ways were the grandiose

40. Beckner, "Eugene Casalis and the French Mission to Basutoland," 75.
41. Wiest, "Maryknoll China History Project," 50.
42. Reid, *Missions and Missionary Society of the Methodist Episcopal Church.*
43. Wiest, "Maryknoll China History Project," 50.
44. Sharpe, "Reflections on Missionary Historiography," 76.
45. Hood, "A History of the English Presbyterian Mission in East Guangdong Province."
46. Kovács, *History of the Free Church of Scotland's Mission.*

plans of these conferences misguided, naïve, or myopic? What was the lasting impact? These missionary conferences serve as a barometer of the missiological thinking of the day. They typically produce statements that are meant to be a consensus of the representatives at the conference.

An early example of a missionary movement is the Haystack Prayer Meeting in 1806, which contributed to the forming of the Student Volunteer Movement (SVM). The World Missionary Conference in Edinburgh 1910 grew out of the SVM and John Mott's leadership.[47] The conference in Edinburgh stood "as an apt symbol for the dawning of a new era — that of Christian mission as a multi-cultural, multidirectional network."[48] The ecumenical spirit from Edinburgh eventually led to the founding of the World Council of Churches (WCC) and many subsequent world conferences on mission. To celebrate the hundredth anniversary of the World Missionary Conference in Edinburgh 1910, the journal *Missiology* devoted considerable space to understanding the conference's legacy.[49] Oborji recently published an African perspective on the impact of Edinburgh 1910 on Christian identity;[50] and Chow published on the effects of the World Missionary Conference on ecumenism and theology in China.[51]

Probably more literature on the history of missions has focused on the impact of the Lausanne International Congress on World Evangelization in 1974 than on any other missionary conference.[52] Some scholars look specifically at how the Lausanne Congress impacted intercultural relations among evangelicals,[53] interpretations of the Great Commission,[54] attitudes toward social action[55] and strategies for urban ministry.[56]

---

47. Nehrbass, "Haystack Revival."
48. Robert, *Christian Mission*, 56.
49. Dawson, "Church and the Edinburgh Missionary Conference"; Thomas, "Springboards for 21st Century Mission."
50. Oborji, "Edinburgh 1910 and Christian Identity Today."
51. Chow, "Protestant Ecumenism and Theology in China Since Edinburgh 1910."
52. Coote, "Lausanne II and World Evangelization"; Engelsviken, "Mission, Evangelism and Evangelization"; Hunt, "History of the Lausanne Movement"; Stanley, "Lausanne 1974"; Stott, "Twenty Years After Lausanne."
53. Chapman, "Evangelical International Relations in the Post-Colonial World."
54. Stanley, "1974—Redefining the Great Commission."
55. Steuernagel, "Social Concern and Evangelization."
56. Bakke, "Urban Evangelization."

Other missionary movements and conferences that are of continued interest to missiologists include Urbana,[57] and Cape Town 2010.[58] A recurrent theme in these world missionary conferences is the space that has been carved out for more marginalized voices in the missionary movement to be heard.

## Highlighting Marginal Voices

As early as 1979, missiologists endeavored to hear the history of missions from the perspective of those who are often less visible in academia such as women, the colonized, the laity.[59] In this approach to the history of missions, stories are presented from non-European perspectives. Ahanotu, for instance, has published a Nigerian view of decolonization—lamenting how the mission agencies lost influence over education as the Nigerian government took control.[60] Koggie, Iveh, and Geysbeek[61] recently told the story of Sudan Interior Mission's (SIM) early twentieth-century efforts in Nigeria by highlighting voices from a Nigerian perspective. And Andrews has recounted how native Americans and black slaves in the Americas shaped Christianity for their contexts and became evangelists.[62]

Indeed, if two thirds of the mission force has been women[63] we should have a great deal of female voices made available in the history of missions. Robert has recounted not only the careers of female missionaries, but has exegeted their theologies and strategies from their journals and letters, showing that the women's missiology engendered a theoretical turn toward holism.[64]

---

57. Beach, "Urbana"; Escobar et al., "Urbana '90;" Howard, "Road to Urbana and Beyond"; Norton, "Urbana."

58. Corwin, "Unpacking Cape Town 2010"; Green, "Report on Cape Town 2010"; Hesselgrave, "Did Cape Town 2010 Correct the 'Edinburgh Error'"; Padilla, "From Lausanne I to Lausanne III."

59. Tasie et al., "History of Mission."

60. Ahanotu, "Nigerian Military and the Issue of State Control of Mission Schools."

61. Koggie et al., "That was the Beginning of Great Things at Miango."

62. Andrews, *Native Apostles*.

63. Tucker, *Guardians of the Great Commission*, 10.

64. Robert, *American Women in Mission*.

## Profile of a Missiologist: Dana L. Robert

*(contemporary)*

*Education: BA (Louisiana State University); MA, MPhil, PhD in Religious Studies (Yale University)*

*Occupation: Professor of World Christianity and History of Mission at Boston University School of Theology*

Dana Robert has authored more than ten books of missiological significance, several of which have earned a place on the list of outstanding books and essential reading in the *International Bulletin of Missionary Research*. She has also authored more than eighty chapters and articles on the history of missions, Pentecostalism, world Christianity, and the role of women in missions. She regularly does fieldwork on Christianity in South Africa and Zimbabwe, and is sought after as a lecturer all over the world.

Robert frames World Christianity as a woman's movement,[1] and has studied the role of friendship[2] and the role of the home[3] in Christian missions. In addition to highlighting the role of women in missions, Robert has researched female missionaries' diaries, letters, and publications to demonstrate how women have contributed to missiological thought. "Without consideration of women's missiological contribution in the history of American, missions, the historical record has been distorted and partial."[4] Robert argues, for example, that women have viewed missions more holistically and relationally than men have. This relational approach of female missiologists has helped bridge the tensions caused by denominational schisms.

Robert's work leads us to ask new questions. What impact will continuing research on women in mission have on the current teaching about mission history and theory? Is there something about women's experience that is essential for both men and women to embrace as an incarnational principle for mission?[5]

---

[1] Robert, "World Christianity as a Woman's Movement."
[2] Robert, "Cross-cultural Friendship in the Creation of Twentieth-Century World Christianity," "Global Friendship as Incarnational Missional Practice."
[3] Robert, "What Happened to the Christian Home?"
[4] Robert, *American Women in Mission*, 417.
[5] Dries, Review of *American Women in Mission*, 215.

Selecting which voices we listen to can shape our priorities, our interests, and our views. For example, by focusing on the factors that attracted people to the Universal Fellowship of Metropolitan Community Churches—especially the teaching that God accepts all people—Wilcox has included a gay and lesbian Christian perspective on the historical narrative of the expansion of Christianity in the USA.[65]

## Challenging the Narrative

Sometimes hearing marginal voices involves challenging the predominant historical narrative. When a historical study focuses on certain events, people, places, by necessity, it must exclude other narratives. "It is the very essence of sound historiography that it be selective."[66] Yet we can change the narrative as we determine the stories that are told, the people who get to come in to focus. For example, the main narrative that has been subverted in the past decades of work on the history of missions has been the simplistic story that "missionaries acted and natives reacted."[67]

On the other hand, publishing on women in missions reinforces the fact that women have had a significant role in the expansion of the church. Similarly, by supplying numerous studies on the expansion of the church in Asia, we become more aware of the breadth, depth, and nuances of Christianity on that continent.

Challenging the narrative can involve getting the timeline right, or demonstrating who the real pioneers were. For example, Adoniram Judson has often been called the first missionary to be sent from the US. However, if we pay attention to the narrative of a freed slave named George Lisle, we learn he went to Kingston, Jamaica to work with African slaves there, and ended up baptizing more than 400 converts.[68] Irvin and Sunquist recount how the first Protestant missionary to Africa was a Ghanaian who was enslaved by the Dutch, renamed Jacobus Elisa Johannes Capitein, was educated in Europe, and returned to Ghana where he translated Christian works in this native Fante language and preached the gospel.[69]

65. Wilcox, "Of Markets and Missions."
66. Bradley and Muller, *Church History*, 48.
67. Skreslet, "Thinking Missiologically about the History of Mission," 60.
68. Kaplan, *Black Presence in the Era of the American Revolution*, 92–94.
69. Irvin and Sunquist, *History of the World Christian Movement*, V2, 323.

Similarly, Kane has challenged the narrative that William Carey inaugurated British missions in 1792. The Society for the Propagation of the Gospel in New England began 150 years before Carey's treatise, and the Society for Promoting Christian Knowledge, also based in the New World, was founded in 1698.[70] Jenkins's *Lost History of Christianity* pokes holes in the dominant (erroneous) narrative that Christianity is a European religion.[71] He tells the thousand-year story of marginalized movements of Christianity in Asia and Northern Africa.

> **World Christianity**
>
> Global Christianity refers to an academic field that examines the practices and beliefs of Christians throughout the world. Some studies in Global Christianity are historical in nature, such as Walls's *History of Christianity in Africa*. Other studies are more focused on how Christian theology has been contextualized wherever it has cross cultural boundaries.

Much of the work in "World Christianity" challenges the narrative that the expansion of the church was effected "from the west to the rest." Kim and Kim's survey of Christian movements on all continents reveals that Christians in the majority world have always been key players in shaping the beliefs, church polity, and worship life of their local congregations.[72] Additionally, Walls's historical survey of global Christianity demonstrates that Christianity has always been multicultural, and the study of Christianity is a cross-cultural (rather than Western-centric) project.[73]

Challenging narratives often involves critique. Nwaka has recently called into question the early evangelization strategies of missionaries in Igboland in the first part of the twentieth century.[74] While historians of missions have typically commended the numeric growth of Christianity, Nwaka maintains that the efforts often led to rivalries and division.

At times challenging the narrative means vindicating those missionaries (or their strategies) that had been previously painted unfairly

---

70. Kane, *Concise History of the Christian World Mission*, 81–82.
71. Jenkins, *Lost History of Christianity*.
72. Kim, *Christianity as a World Religion*.
73. Walls, "Crossing Cultural Frontiers."
74. Nwaka, "Early Missionary Groups and the Context for Igboland."

in a negative light. A recent history of missions in Aneityum (Vanuatu) attempted to vindicate the three Johns (Paton, Inglis, and Geddie) who had been depicted as harsh bullies in previous historical studies.[75] Such a project involves scouring primary sources to challenge the narrative.

Latourette's *Great Century* vindicates missionary efforts in a time when a common narrative depicts Western missionary efforts as paternalistic, concluding:

> Single-handedly and with great courage they attacked the social evils of their time: child marriage, the immolation of widows, temple prostitution, and untouchability in India; footbinding, opium addiction, and the abandoning of babies in China; polygamy, the slave trade and the destruction of twins in Africa. In all parts of the world they opened schools, hospitals, clinics, medical colleges, orphanages, leprosaria. They gave succor and sustenance to the dregs of society cast off by their own communities. At great risk to themselves and their families they fought famines, floods, pestilences, and plagues. They were the first to rescue unwanted babies, educate girls, and liberate women. Above all, they gave to the non-Christian world the most liberating of all messages—the gospel of Christ. They converted savages into saints; and out of this raw material they built the Christian church, which is today the most universal of all institutions. By the end of the century the gospel had literally been taken to the ends of the earth . . . Included in the Christian church, for the very first time, were representatives of "every tribe and tongue and people and nation"[76] (Rev 5:9).

In Latourette's case, challenging the predominant narrative has provided more explanatory scope for the expansion of Christianity than previous studies had done. And the more we challenge narratives and highlight marginal voices, the more that the history of missions can teach us something new, and lead us into fresh directions.

## Underscoring Specific Strategies of Missions

One way to look at the expansion of Christianity is to focus on the role that certain strategies have played in facilitating missions work. Historically, such strategies have included community development

---

75. Barnes, *Aneityum*.
76. Latourette, *Great Century in the Americas, Australasia and Africa*, 469.

and entrepreneurship, deliverance ministries, theological education by extension, Bible translation, oral communication and media missions, and working among ethnic communities in diaspora.

For example, while Arrington's dissertation focuses on the expansion of Christianity among the Lisu of China, her study is more about highlighting the role that vernacular hymnody played in communicating doctrine to oral societies.[77] Elsewhere, Arrington examined how the utilization of ingenious art and architecture in Catholic missions in China helped the church become independent.[78] And several studies have examined the impact of Bible translation on the expansion of Christianity in tribal areas.[79]

## Building Theory

I argue here that the history of missions is most useful to missiologists when the interpretation of the past helps us construct theories about the cross-cultural process of Christianity. Theories are explanations or "central understandings," and are typically constructed by looking at connections in the following way:

- Impact of x on y (Example: impact of technology on expansion of the church);
- Factors that led to x (example: What lead to the Protestant mission era, or to the un-involvement of Protestants in missions? Or What led to the "moratorium on missions"?);
- How historical X led to present situation (example: How did colonialism lead to anti-western sentiment?);
- Evaluation of historical X in light of Y criteria (example: Was Xavier effective in light of his association with the rich?); and,
- Difference between X and Y (What were the differences between Protestant and Catholic missions?)

Below, I will show how historians of missions have used several approaches for building theory including: identifying stages of the

77. Arrington, "Hymns of the Everlasting Hills."
78. Arrington, "Recasting the Image."
79. Fortosis, *Multilingual God*; Sanneh, *Translating the Message*; Smalley, *Translation as Mission*.

expansion of the church, finding "themes" or universals, making connections, and understanding history as a complex interplay of multiple social systems (politics, religion, family life, and so on).

## Understanding Stages and Our Place Within Those Stages

The history of missions, like any other sub-discipline of Christian thought, is the study of *missio Dei*: how God has moved dynamically over time, and how we fit in that bigger picture within our present context. Missionary efforts in the time of apostle Paul, the Roman era, the eastern and western expansion of the church, vary significantly. The Christian church evolves as it expands and contracts—thriving at the edges and wallowing in the heartland.[80]

This oscillating response to Christianity has caused modern historians to divide the history of missions into distinct stages. Gustav Warneck separated Protestant missions into "ages" of mission: Reformation, orthodoxy, pietism, and the present age of mission boards.[81] More notably, Latourette saw the Christian faith moving through five "renaissances" or epochs, representing resurgences and recessions, as it moved from the Roman world to the ends of the earth.[82]

Bosch[83] drew on Kuhn's theory of "paradigm shifts"[84] to describe how the missionary enterprise has changed. As the world situation changes, the church experiences increasing challenges to its worldview and approaches until it reaches a point of crisis. Within Kuhn's theory, these crises lead to a radical shift. Bosch argued Christianity has experienced six of these paradigm shifts: The apostolic paradigm of the book of Acts, the Hellenistic paradigm of the early church fathers; the Catholic (medieval) paradigm; the Protestant Reformation paradigm; the modern Enlightenment era; and an emerging ecumenical paradigm emphasizing social justice and interfaith dialog. This progression of paradigms suggests that no approach toward missions is permanent; the approaches are shaped by inexorable ideological, political, and social forces.

80. Walls, *Missionary Movement in Christian History*.
81. Warneck, *Outline of a History of Protestant Missions*.
82. Latourette, *History of the Expansion of Christianity*.
83. Bosch, *Transforming Mission*.
84. Kuhn, *Structure of Scientific Revolutions*.

Profile of a Missiologist: David Bosch

(1929–1992)

*Education: PhD New Testament, University of Basel*

*Occupation: Missionary among the Xhosa; Professor of Missiology at University of South Africa*

Jonathan Bonk avers that "in the world of mission studies, [Bosch] is surely one of the most significant figures of the twentieth century."[1] Bosch published six books and 160 articles, but is primarily known among English speaking missiologists for *Transforming Mission*. In this "summa missiologica" Bosch applied Thomas Kuhn's theory of paradigm shifts to understand how missions has moved through six paradigms.

Living in South Africa, Bosch seems to have been in a unique position to take an ecumenical stance. His genius lay in his ability to craft a missiology that was, on the one hand, grounded in the Old and New Testaments, yet on the other hand, addressed, with a conciliar tone, contemporary issues like religious plurality and environmental stewardship.

Also, living in Africa during apartheid, Bosch was highly aware of racial injustice. He lobbied for the Dutch Reformed Church to stand against apartheid, and for the church to become an "alternative community" of reconciliation and diversity.[2] Bosch did not live to see the end of apartheid, as he was tragically killed in a car accident in 1992.

---

[1] Bonk, "Christian Mission," 58.
[2] Livingston, "Legacy of David J. Bosch," 30.

---

And Winter constructed three (Protestant) mission eras: The Coastlands Era engendered by William Carey, the Inland Era represented by the pioneer work of Hudson Taylor; and the Unreached Peoples, represented by Cameron Townsend and Donald McGavran.[85] Steffen suggests that we are now in a fourth era: The Facilitator Era.[86] This construction of stages or epochs highlights another use of history: using the past to explain the present.

85. Winter, "Three Mission Eras."
86. Steffen, *Facilitator Era*.

## Profile of a Missiologist: Tom Steffen

*(contemporary)*

Education: DMiss from Biola University
Occupation: Missionary; Professor of Missiology

Tom and Darla Steffen served with New Tribes Mission (now Ethnos 360) from 1969 to 1989. Tom became interested in the study of missions while he was supporting church planting in the Philippines (from 1972 to 1986). He noticed that missionaries were trained to quickly transfer leadership to locals, but in reality, they often lacked a plan for doing so. Steffen studied the successful "phase out" aspect of church planting for his doctoral work at Biola.[1]

While in the Philippines, Steffen was an early adopter of Bible storytelling methods, where Trevor McIlwain was developing Chronological Bible Storying.[2] Orality became a focus for Steffen's publications and involvement in professional missionary organizations.

Whereas prolific missiologists can often follow academic interests that only tangentially serve the church, Steffen's more than one hundred publications (between books, chapters, articles, and reviews) all directly relate to the work of missions. But his career more or less tracked with the popular trends in missiology: the shift away from paternalism in missions,[3] the use of orality and narrative teaching methods,[4] various conceptualizations of shame and honor,[5] and Business as Mission.[6]

Steffen was a key influencer at Biola's School of Intercultural Studies, serving on faculty from 1991 to 2013. But Steffen's sphere of influence was much broader than his university. In addition to his publications, which have been translated into Mandarin, Spanish, Tagalog, and Korean, he has taught adjunct at ten universities, and has served on the board of directors for seven mission agencies from 1997 to present. He has also been hired as a consultant for numerous mission agencies.

I asked Steffen what differences missiology has made for the "boots on the ground" doing missionary work. He told me:

> Missiology helps us look at [missions] through mission history, social sciences, anthropology. Often the missionaries start with mission strategy, and therefore repeat the same mistakes everybody's made back then- because they don't know mission history. But if they can blend those…three together, then the mission strategy has a much greater possibility of being successful.[7]

---

[1] Steffen, *Passing the Baton*.
[2] McIlwain, *Building on Firm Foundations*.
[3] Steffen, *Facilitator Era*.
[4] Steffen, *Reconnecting God's Story to Ministry*, "Orality Comes of Age."
[5] Steffen, "Clothesline Theology for the World."
[6] Steffen, *Business as Usual in the Missions Enterprise*; Rundle and Steffen, *Great Commission Companies*.
[7] Nehrbass, "Profile of a Missiologist."

As they draw on different data or look at different regions of the world, theorists are likely to continue to construct new models to describe additional historical paradigms or stages of the history of missions. Historians also do this sort of theory building on a micro-scale, looking at paradigms of missions within a single mission organization or within a particular missionary strategy. The point in building these theories is not simply to label multiple stages, but to evaluate the effectiveness of each stage within its context.

## Developing Universals From "Themes"

Nineteenth-century church historians wanted to understand objectively history "as it really was." They aimed to apply the scientific method to history so they could deduce laws and timeless principles (or theories).[87] By now, most academicians have all but given up hope for objectivity; and no longer expect human nature to operate throughout history according to "laws" the way physics does. However, we can still use history to theorize about human nature and how people typically respond to missionaries and to the Christian faith.

Rather than studying the history of missions diachronically, this approach utilizes what Bradley and Muller referred to as the "special or synchronic method."[88] We look at a specific issue and see how this has been understood throughout history. This tactic of extracting truths from the study of the history of missions goes back as far as the third-century historian Tertullian who theorized that martyrdom causes the church to spread further.

Current academicians still use history in this way. For instance, Bonk's history of missionaries in Africa and China argues that Christianity spread as missionaries identified with local cultures.[89] Kim's history of Christianity among Koreans living in Myungdongchon village, China, attempts to build on the theory of "people movements" by examining indigenous leadership patterns and the holistic approach of missionary efforts in that region.[90]

---

87. Bradley and Muller, *Church History*, 21; cf. Smith, "Nature and Worth of the Science of Church History."

88. Bradley and Muller, *Church History*, 29.

89. Bonk, *Theory and Practice of Missionary Identification 1860–1920*.

90. Kim, "Myungdongchon."

To consider some other universal principles: Missiologists have tried to look at historical data to determine if Christianity is spread top-down, through influential elites, or if it is primarily a movement at the grassroots. For example, Neill[91] shows how Francis Xavier enjoyed success by reaching the elite of Japan—the "best people yet discovered"; and how Christianity spread rapidly through the Pacific by reaching the kings of Tonga and Tahiti. Irvin and Sunquist's history of the world Christian movement demonstrates that Christianity expanded where colonial powers went: Calvinism spread with the Dutch, who proscribed Catholicism; Catholicism spread with Spanish, French, Italians, and Portuguese, who tried to convince Thomist, Ethiopian, Orthodox, and Coptic Christians to conform to Rome; Lutheranism accompanied Germans in their colonial expansion, and Methodism and the Anglican Church spread in British colonies.[92] Christianity never took hold in Asia, where Asian empires were able to expel missionaries and ban Christianity. Whenever empires lost their influence, religious movements could move in, until a new power arose to endorse one religion and proscribe the rest.

Also, we can easily establish that Christianity spreads in sync with modern medicine and education, as Zvogbo showed from a case study in Zimbabwe.[93] In other cases, especially in Pentecostalism, healings are seen as more important than development, paving the way for the expansion of the church.[94] And Kane summarizes several contributions that history has made to missiological theory: Hasty conversions lead to syncretism or shallowness; lack of training national leadership impedes sustainability of the national church, and the "unholy alliance" of missionaries with colonial powers has often led to bitterness or rejection of the church.[95]

Walls's "indigenizing and pilgrim principles" are examples of universal principles, suggesting these are tendencies that can be seen across time and in various regions.[96] Note that the "indigenizing and pilgrim" principles are credible because they are grounded in historical

---

91. Neill, *History of Christian Missions*.
92. Irvin and Sunquist, *History of the World Christian Movement*.
93. Zvobgo, *History of Christian Missions in Zimbabwe*.
94. Burgess, "South Indian Pentecostal Movement in the Twentieth Century."
95. Kane, *Concise History of the Christian World Mission*, 71.
96. Walls, *Missionary Movement in Christian History*.

data—so we see that history is an essential part of building missiological theory.

The contributors to *Christianity Reborn: The Global Expansion of Evangelicalism in the Twentieth Century* have argued that evangelicalism spread because of two universal human tendencies: indigenization and globalization.[97] On the one hand, as evangelical churches became de-westernized, they became more palatable to Africans, South Americans, and Asians. On the other hand, the homogenization of global culture in the twentieth century facilitated the spread of evangelicalism. In fact, Robert has argued that the unique role of missionaries throughout the centuries has been acting as bridges between the local and global.[98]

## Making Connections and "Filling in the Gaps"

Theory-building also involves making connections between eras, events, ideas, and social pressures. This process involves moving far beyond "transcribing stories of heroic missionary action" by "taking into account large-scale social patterns of which the missionaries themselves may have been only vaguely aware. It means asking about the ways in which factors like geography, economics, organizational theory, and politics not only influenced missionary choices but also perhaps shaped evangelistic outcomes."[99]

An example of this sort of connection which is widely accepted among church historians is the impact that Emperor Constantine's legalization of Christianity (through the Edict of Milan in AD 313) had on the Western fusion of political and religious power. To take another example in wide use: Scholars have connected the *Pax Romana* (especially the safety of traveling on Roman roads between districts) with the quick spread of Christianity in the first few centuries.[100] And much more recently, Robert has established how capitalism and the Enlightenment idea of free choice spurred the birth of missionary sending agencies. Such a scenario enabled commoners to hear the call from God to go overseas, and senders could "invest" in the mission work for heavenly returns.[101]

97. Lewis, *Christianity Reborn.*
98. Robert, *Christian Mission*, 176.
99. Skreslet, "Thinking Missiologically About the History of Mission," 59.
100. Ramsay, "Imperial Peace."
101. Robert, *Christian Mission*, 46–47.

The more interdisciplinary missiology becomes, the more it connects the history of missions to politics, gender, identity, technology, healthcare, economic development, etc. For example, Hastings showed the historical connection between Bible translation and nation building.[102] Wiltgen's study of Gold Coast Missions looks at how the slave trade, tropical diseases, war, national politics impeded the growth of Catholic Missions.[103] Watkins[104] studied how literacy has led to church growth. And Morrison's study of seventeenth Jesuit missions among the Montagnais Indians is an excellent example of connecting communication theory and worldview to missionary efforts.[105]

## Revealing the Complexity

Theory-building is not about simplifying; it is about understanding issues in their complexity. Within the history of missions, theory building involves understanding the cross-cultural process of Christianity from multiple angles. For example, Friesen's survey of nineteenth-century missions demonstrated that missionaries were not monolithic in their approach to indigenous religions.[106] Instead, their responses ranged along a continuum from radical displacement to moral reconstruction, to fulfillment, to affiliation.

Discovering a variety of paradigms and approaches opens up new possibilities for us; it gets our creative juices going and makes the "different" seem a bit more familiar to us. Being critical of previous "paradigms" is a sly way of being critical of ourselves, as we often repeat those errors (e.g., paternalism, the mission station).

## Conclusion

Studies of the history of missions can be carried out in many different ways; I have only been able to give examples here of six major theoretical lenses missiologists employ to understand the expansion of Christianity. The theoretical approach will depend on the purpose of the study. But

102. Hastings, *Construction of Nationhood*.
103. Wiltgen, *Gold Coast Mission History*.
104. Watkins, *Literacy, Bible Reading, and Church Growth through the Ages*.
105. Morrison, "Discourse and the Accommodation of Values."
106. Friesen, *Missionary Responses to Tribal Religions at Edinburgh*.

I argue that quality histories of missions make clear which theoretical lens is being employed. First of all, what research question does the study attempt to answer, and how is it tied to the overarching question within missiology regarding the expansion of Christianity?

Biographies can inspire; mission agency legacies can help preserve primary data; tracing the Hand of God in the expansion of the church can establish theological convictions; thematic historical studies can help us evaluate certain missiological strategies. In any case, to make the leap from "what happened" to "what we should learn from history," the history of missions will involve constructing theories with practical applications. A missiological historiography that is focused on constructing theory involves recognizing multiple perspectives and giving voice to the marginalized. To be credible (and useful), histories must examine issues in their complexity, which includes recognizing the contested or controversial issues that arise.

Lastly, the history of missions is most useful when it seamlessly interacts with the other disciplines on which missiology stands, such as theology and the social sciences. In fact, further work on missiological historiography should delve deeper into how historians have made those connections.

## Ideas for Further Research

This chapter has suggested that further missiological historical research would be most useful if it generates theory. There is a need for further research like the following:

1. Revisit the expansion of Christianity in a specific cultural setting, but tell the story from "below" (from the position of the marginalized, or those who are not typically recognized).

2. Revisit the expansion of Christianity in a specific cultural setting, but focus on the missionary strategies that were used.

3. Find alternate explanations for the barriers that hindered the expansion of Christianity in a specific cultural setting.

## Move Into Action

As you read and write about the history of missions, keep your focus on questions about making disciples across cultural boundaries, such as:

1. What models and trends historically facilitated making disciples in other cultures?

2. How have historical barriers and geo-politics impacted the way Christianity spreads various contexts?

## Review Questions

1. What does this book suggest is the foundational question of missiological historiography?

2. How do missiological historians build "best practices" based on the history of missions?

## Reflection Questions

1. Which of the six approaches toward the history of missions (discussed above) do you find most useful? Which approach do you find least useful?

2. What place does "Providential guidance" have in your understanding of the history of missions?

*Chapter 4*

# Connecting Anthropology to Cross-Cultural Discipleship

EVER SINCE EDWARD TYLOR published *Anthropology*,[1] missiology has had a love-hate relationship with anthropology.[2] On the one hand, missionaries provided valuable field notes to nineteenth-century "armchair anthropologists" like Edward Tylor and James Frazer. Whiteman recounted the contributions of numerous early missionaries such as Robert Codrington, Charles E. Fox, John Batchelor, Maurice Leenhardt, Henri Alexandere Junod, and William and Charlotte Wiser, who recorded the folklore, ritual, social organization, magic and religious practices in their missionary fields.[3] Additionally, academic-minded missionaries and anthropologists share similar goals of strengthening the self-determinacy of vulnerable minority people groups; and both often possess a genuine desire to describe—or even explain—the worldviews, values, and rituals of the peoples they encounter.

---

1. Tylor, *Anthropology*.
2. Hiebert, "Missions and Anthropology."
3. Whiteman, "Anthropology and Mission."

## Chapter Goals

*Knowledge goals:*

- Explain how biblical Christianity critiques and coheres with anthropological theories about human nature and cultures.
- Explain how missiology has borrowed from theories of culture to make the gospel relevant in various cultural contexts.
- Explain how the study of culture helps missionaries deal with the stress of crossing cultures.

*Action goals:*

- Work with Christian leaders in other cultures to understand how the obedience to Jesus would impact their economic systems, kinship systems, leadership styles, and worldviews.

*Heart goals:*

- Commit to being a lifelong learner of your own culture and of other cultures.

On the other hand, anthropologists often deem the missionary aim of cross-cultural discipleship to be ethnocentric and imperialistic. Meanwhile, missiologists typically believe that cultural relativism, which is foundational within much of anthropological theory, undermines the absolutist claims found in Scripture. Further, since the nineteenth century, thinkers within the sciences have looked down on Christianity as irrational, wondering *How could missiologists possibly contribute to such an esteemed science as anthropology?* Fundamentalists sometimes responded to this unwanted criticism by turning away from science and toward anti-intellectualism. Evangelical and conciliar missiologists stayed somewhere in the tension between the social sciences and Christian missions. These "push and pull factors" have contributed to an identity crisis of missiologists: To what degree is it an anthropological discipline? How can we redeem anthropology for the purpose of cross-cultural discipleship?

Despite the troubled relationship between these fields, the cross-pollination between missiology and anthropology has led to a number of fruitful discoveries that have advanced both fields. Below I will describe the rocky relationship between anthropology and missiology, and then I will trace some major contributions of anthropology to the study of missions, and will survey how missiologists have employed these theories to further the practice of cross-cultural discipleship. I conclude that anthropology—the study of humans in their cultural environment—is an essential component for engaging in cross-cultural discipleship. Becoming a follower of Christ requires bringing all aspects of life—everything in culture—under the lordship of Christ. And anthropological inquiry serves as an excellent avenue for achieving a holistic view of the ways Christ can be lord of our cultural spheres (e.g., the distribution of power, the use natural resources, organization into family units, or the assignment of role and status).

## Critiques Anthropologists Have of Missiology

Why would the study of humans in their cultural contexts be problematic for missiologists? Cannot missionaries also be anthropologists? Indeed, "Good missionaries have always been good anthropologists".[4] As Hiebert maintained "no one would be consider adequately trained for cross-cultural missions now without some understanding of cultural anthropology."[5]

Yet some see missiological anthropology as an oxymoron. As Tertullian posed, "What hath Athens to do with Jerusalem? What concord is there between the academy and the church?"[6] Working through this ambivalent relationship can help us be sensitive to areas where missiology has unnecessarily adopted anthropological themes that are at odds with Christianity, and where missiology has gone too far in distancing itself from perfectly useful theories within anthropology.

Missionary anthropologist Alexandre Junod explained that anthropologists have two main criticisms of missionaries: their common lack of understanding of the indigenous cultures where they work, and their lack of understanding about the degree to which Christianity

---

4. Nida, *Customs and Cultures*, xi.

5. Hiebert, *Anthropological Reflections on Missiological Issues*, 9.

6. Tertullian, *Praescr.* ch. 7.

will likely change those local cultures.⁷ As Stipe et al. explained, many anthropologists have negative attitudes toward missionaries because "primitive cultures are characterized by an organic unity,"⁸ and any major change to social structures or worldview (such as Christianity) would bring disastrous disruption to that steady state. Also, Stipe et al. concluded that many anthropologists are critical of missionaries for holding "religious beliefs [that] are essentially meaningless."⁹ This criticism is based on the fact that many scientists are materialists (that is, they do not believe in the supernatural), and cannot accept any religion except their own rigid belief in materialism.

But the relationship between missiology and anthropology has been more complex (and in fact more positive) than Junod and Stipe et al.'s descriptions above. Below, I will work through criticisms anthropologists have levied against missiology and will show how missiologists and Christian anthropologists have responded to these criticisms.

### "Christianity Must Be Just Like Any Other 'Primitive' Religion"

Early anthropologists had a vision of an ideal civilized society, and argued that any practices in European society which were contrary to their ideal civilization were actually due to the persistence of savage or barbaric practices from our cultural-evolutionary past. As staunch rationalists, nineteenth-century founders of anthropology such as Edward Tylor and James Frazer were especially convinced that belief in the supernatural was erroneous, and would eventually disappear from civilization. For example, Larsen has shown how Edward Tylor, who was raised as a Quaker, evaluated cultural data through his own Quaker lens in such a way as to expose "paganisms that have survived into the present, but which need to be purged."¹⁰ Tylor told stories of "savage cultures" in order to "make familiar religious practices that his [Christian] readers had always accepted as understandable come to appear strange and savage."¹¹ For instance, Tylor repeatedly argued that "the Catholic attitude to

---

7. Junod, "Anthropology and Missionary Education," 214.
8. Stipe et al. "Anthropologists Versus Missionaries," 66.
9. Stipe et al. "Anthropologists Versus Missionaries," 166.
10. Larsen, *Slain God*, 36.
11. Larsen, *Slain God*, 48.

saints on high is no different from ancestor worship—or polytheism—or idolatry."[12]

Likewise, while British anthropologist James Frazer was ostensibly supplying cultural data from around the world to generate anthropological theory, his more subtle agenda was to "expose the savage beneath the sacred" in any religion, including Christianity.[13] For example, Frazer suggested that the story of Jesus's death and resurrection was originally an annual ritual reenacting the death and rebirth of a god. Anthropologists have insisted such pagan roots also engendered the Passover, the Eucharist, and the priestly system. They have also attempted to trace Judeo-Christian stories such as the flood to neighboring mythical traditions, so that divine inspiration of these narratives could be subverted.[14] The reasoning seemed to be if a biblical story is based on a "savage" myth, then the biblical story is savage too, rather than divinely inspired. If early anthropologists could prove that Christianity was really a carryover from primitive culture, then surely civilization would eventually relinquish such unnecessary vestiges.

This model of cultural progression from savage to civilized was based on social Darwinism. "'The Englishman,' of course, was the very model of modern, civilized *homo sapiens*."[15] Tylor and Morgan believed that humanity must evolve along these subsequent stages, "Age of Magic" and "age of religion" and on to the age of rationalism, just like civilizations move from the stone age to the bronze age and so on.[16] Since the nineteenth century, this idea of unilineal evolution has been entirely abandoned not because scholars "reject evolution *per se*, but because the unilineal scheme simply does not fit the data."[17] Cross-cultural workers have discovered as many as 15,000 distinct ethnolinguistic people groups each with distinct cultures, which cannot fit into a neat evolutionary scheme. Even Darwinians now disagree with Tylor and Morgan's stages, reminding us that evolution does not necessarily lead to progress.[18]

---

12. Larsen, *Slain God*, 18.
13. Larsen, *Slain God*, 61.
14. Larsen, *Slain God*, 63.
15. Larsen, *Slain God*, 21.
16. Larsen, *Slain God*, 41.
17. Nehrbass, *God's Image and Global Cultures*, 96.
18. Larsen, *Slain God*, 31.

Interestingly, by the mid-twentieth century, anthropologists turned this notion that modern civilization has vestiges of barbarism (such as religion) on its head: It became fashionable to describe pre-modern societies in ways that were suspiciously similar to the anthropologists' own ideals of a utopian society. They then reasoned that obstacles to obtaining this utopia in modern society are caused by the degradation from our early roots in superior "primitive societies." For example Margaret Mead imagined that Samoan teen girls enjoyed the sort of sexual freedom and empowerment that was idealized by the sexual revolution in the US, whereas prudish ideas from Christianity had removed such "freedoms" from the Western world.[19]

## "Science is Rational; Christianity is Irrational"

Related to the claim that Christianity is as "savage" as "primitive religions" was the claim that Christianity was at odds with the rationalism necessary for producing scientific knowledge. Evans-Pritchard explained "It would therefore be useless for me to pretend that social anthropology is not predominantly rationalist in outlook . . . Anthropology has always been . . . considered, not unjustly, as anti-religious in tone, and even in aim.'"[20] Such rationalists created a false dichotomy "by exaggerating both the extent to which Europeans are rational and the extent to which primitive people," and Christians, are irrational.[21]

While it is true that the earliest anthropologists were so committed to rationalism that they could not accept religious belief, many important anthropologists who came after Tylor and Frazer rejected rationalism, and made room for the supernatural in their cosmologies. Anthropologist (and Roman Catholic) Mary Douglas concluded that hyper rationalism does not advance science; it is simply one pole on the pendulum swing within academia from super-religious to anti-religious. She contended one could find secularists among the savages[22] just as one can find religiously faithful scientists. And in fact, she argued that the pendulum had already swung back: Rationalism was waning for the most part, although "you will meet the occasional old-fashioned

---

19. Mead, *Coming of Age in Samoa*.
20. Quoted in Larsen, *Slain God*, 95.
21. Larsen, *Slain God*, 89.
22. Larsen, *Slain God*, 141.

anthropologist who takes all religion for mumbo-jumbo."[23] Whiteman agrees that "at the beginning of the twentieth century, anthropology as a discipline was becoming established and recovering from its obsession with evolutionary" or secular-rationalist thought.[24] In fact, Larsen has shown that for some seminal anthropologists such as Sir Edward Evans-Pritchard, Victor Turner, and Mary Douglas, not only was materialism not to be accepted *a priori*, but Christianity (or Catholicism, for all three of these) was also a viable belief system—even for world-renowned anthropologists.[25]

## "No Serious Anthropologist is a Christian"

Yet somehow the impression that anthropologists cannot be Christians has persisted. Goldschmidt told the American Anthropological Association (AAA) "Missionaries are in many ways our opposites; they believe in original sin."[26] Evans-Pritchard wrote to Alfred Kroeber in 1965 to confirm that "no American anthropologist adhered to any religious faith."[27] Elsewhere Evans-Pritchard explained that "religious belief was to these anthropologists absurd, and it is so to most anthropologists of yesterday and today."[28]

Yet Larsen's study of the journey to faith of Evans-Prichard, Douglas, and Turner concludes that anthropology has not been persistently inimical to Christianity. In fact, the field has experienced a "progression away from rationalistic errors and towards veritable faith."[29] Anthropology has been the site of "deconversions and conversions, gain and loss, doubt and faith."[30] This progression has followed the wider scholarly movement away from the positivism of modernity to the pluralism (or epistemological uncertainty) of postmodernism.

Today, many missiologists belong to anthropological societies like the American Anthropology Association (AAA) and publish in

23. Larsen, *Slain God*, 167.
24. Whiteman, "Anthropology and Mission," 400.
25. Larsen, *Slain God*.
26. in Priest, "Missionary Positions," 33.
27. Larsen, *Slain God*, 96.
28. Larsen, *Slain God*, 96.
29. Larsen, *Slain God*, 223.
30. Larsen, *Slain God*, 224.

anthropological journals, thus challenging the notion that one cannot be a missiologists and anthropologist.

## "The Agenda of Christianity is at Odds with Anthropology"

When I was studying for my undergraduate degree at the University of California, I told people I would eventually be a missionary. Some chided me, "You mean you'll go in and change the culture?!" Those with a vague familiarity with the social sciences imagined that cultures could remain untouched by outside influence, and would continue in some sort of idyllic homeostasis. Change would mean disruption, which must be harmful; and besides, conversion to a Western version of Christianity would epitomize imperialism.

But Hiebert[31] and Whiteman[32] have demonstrated that from the inception, anthropologists have not been in agreement over the extent to which practitioners should be change agents. The Ethnological Society was founded in 1843 by ideologues who wanted to salvage as much of an idyllic "primitive" way of life as possible before it was replaced with European languages and ideas. Such anthropologists saw missionaries as meddlers or worse, perpetrators of ethnocide. "Missionaries appear[ed] to be undermining the very cultures which most social scientists would like to find left in a 'virtually uncontaminated' state."[33]

On the other end of the spectrum, some maintained that anthropologists had a duty to be change agents. They observed "indigenous peoples . . . were being mistreated in colonial encounters. This religiously motivated concern, in turn, led on to a scholarly interest in 'savages.'"[34] Abolitionists formed the Aboriginal Protection Society (in 1838) and later the Anthropological Society (in 1863) to serve their applied anthropological agenda of "civilizing" aborigines so that they could have the political voice and education levels necessary for protecting their lands and society.

By the 1930s, applied anthropology moved away from notions of "civilizing" natives, and focused more on social issues that indigenous communities face. Missiological thinking was also influenced by this new

31. Hiebert, "Missions and Anthropology."
32. Whiteman, "Anthropology and Mission."
33. Trompf, "Missiology and Anthropology," 148.
34. Larsen, *Slain God*, 16.

empowering posture toward culture. The rise of cultural anthropology facilitated this shift in missiological attitudes.[35]

Nonetheless, the accusation of missionary-induced ethnocide persists. A classic example is Lauriston Sharp's[36] argument that introduction of steel axes (by none other than missionaries, of course) would eventually cause the demise of the Yir Yoront, an aboriginal Australian group. Sharp argued that stone axes were part of a totemic system that held up social life; so taking away the stone axe would involve "hacking at the supports of an entire cultural system."[37]

Note that Sharp[38] was writing in a period of positivism in academia which expected the human mind (and societies) to go through stages of development. Functionalism was a widespread theory at the time—every cultural feature must fulfill a certain biological or social need, or else it would have been weeded out by natural selection, and would have disappeared. So functionalists believed all cultural features must exist for some (often hidden or long forgotten) reason. If missionaries took the cultural feature away, the whole system would be in peril, just like taking away any system in a living organism can be fatal.

Sharp's[39] thesis was intriguing, partly for its simplicity, and especially since it made missionaries culpable for culture loss. A Google search of "steel axes" returns Sharp's original study along with thousands of sources that have referenced it. By now, the functionalism of Sharp's theory has been largely abandoned; but anthropology textbooks continue to republish Sharp's story of these stone axes that propped up an entire society. Sharp's analysis (whether accurate or not) demonstrates the interrelatedness of cultural spheres. Even the business world latched on to the Sharp's narrative of "unintended consequences" to warn about the potential dangers of technological change.

Some thirty years after Sharp's theory (that a simple introduction by missionaries can bring down a culture) had become accepted as "fact," John Taylor followed up on the aboriginal groups in the Edward River region where Sharp had worked.[40] Taylor found that while language

35. Nishioka, "Worldview Methodology in Mission Theology."
36. Sharp, "Steel Axes for Stone-Age Australians."
37. Sharp, "Steel Axes for Stone-Age Australians," 21.
38. Sharp, "Steel Axes for Stone-Age Australians," 21.
39. Sharp, "Steel Axes for Stone-Age Australians," 21.
40. Taylor, "Goods and Gods."

use had mostly shifted to English, many indigenous beliefs, rituals, and social systems persisted, despite the disappearance of the stone axe. Taylor suggested that the real cultural changes among the Yir Yoront were connected to the more stationary lifestyle of a mission station, than simply the adoption of steel axes. Living near a mission station (for church and school services) means shifting toward agriculture, and burying corpses rather than leaving them to decompose in taboo areas. Taylor painted a more complex and believable picture of culture change than Sharp had done.

But unlike Sharp's scintillating narrative,[41] Taylor's work isn't repeated in textbooks. Popular culture prefers the idea that a simple "mistake" like handing out steel axes can have drastic consequences, especially if done by missionaries. Like the Coca-Cola bottle in the film *The Gods Must be Crazy*[42] Sharp's steel axes are really metonyms for the harm salvage anthropologists believed would come to societies through cultural changes like modernism or Christianity.

However today, anthropology recognizes that cultures are constantly changing; and responsible practitioners (anthropologists, but not necessarily missionaries) should even get involved in advocating for culture change at times. Perhaps the antipathy toward missionaries that persists in anthropology is not based on a commitment to keeping cultures static; rather it has to do with competition for access to the precious human resources that serve as "data" for field workers. Salamone[43] reported that in a survey of 202 anthropologists in the AAA, 68 percent opposed missionary endeavors; but the highest percentage were young "romantic" males who had not yet established themselves in their academic careers, and who saw missionaries as threats to limited resources (the people they study). "The greater the power a missionary has in determining the anthropologist's success, the greater the hostility between them."[44]

Just as anthropologists' postures toward culture and culture change have varied greatly, so have those of missiologists. Whiteman suggests we have seen this change in a shift from colonial-style "missionary anthropology" to postcolonial "missiological anthropology."[45] Some

41. Sharp, "Steel Axes for Stone Age Australians."
42. Uys, *Gods Must be Crazy*.
43. Salamone, "Missionaries and Anthropologists," 58–60.
44. Salamone, "Missionaries and Anthropologists," 66.
45. Whiteman, "Anthropology and Mission," 405.

missionaries have had an antithetical approach toward culture learning, and have been more imperialistic. Others, especially Edwin Smith, Eugene Nida, Louis Luzbetak, Charles Kraft, and Sherwood Lingenfelter adopted a posture toward culture that was in step with anthropological thinking, which has advanced missiology.

## Anthropological Concepts that Shaped Missiology

Evangelical missiologists' ultimate purpose for studying culture is to make disciples across cultures, as Jesus Christ commanded. We have discovered that anthropology can offer tremendous assistance toward reaching that aim. Eugene Nida, who made anthropology accessible to missiology, explained:

> No one must imagine . . . that cultural anthropology is the answer to the problems of Christian missions, but it can aid very materially in the process by which the missionary endeavors to communicate to others the significance of the new way of life made possible through the vicarious death of the Son of God.[46]

Anthropology allows cross-cultural workers to make sense of their new environment. Cultural analysis helps missionaries to interpret the unfamiliar rituals, social structures, and symbols around them. It helps them discover underlying fears, motivations, and values of the people they are discipling. Missionaries move across cultures to be agents of change, and their chances of instigating change—whether in education, community development, or worldview—depends heavily on their ability to interpret and navigate the Other's culture.

Understanding the Other can also help missionaries cope with the stress of living in other cultures. We are more accepting of practices and beliefs that seem strange to us if we can see that they make sense in their own context. So a measure of cultural pluralism and knowledge of cultural values can help missionaries deal with culture shock.

The reasons for incorporating anthropology into missiology are multiple, but can be summarized in the following figure:

---

46. Nida, *Customs and Cultures*, 23.

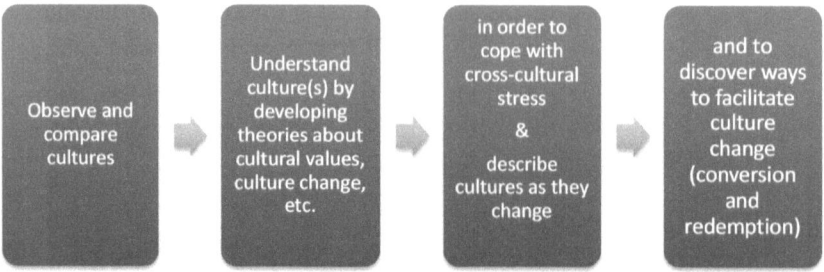

Figure 4: Why missiologists use the study of culture

As early as 1910, delegates at the World Missionary Conference at Edinburgh recognized the need for missiologists to engage in culture-learning and analysis:

> It is, therefore, clear that the missionary needs to know far more than the mere manners and customs of the race to which he is sent; he ought to be versed in the genius of the people, that which has made them the people they are; and to sympathise so truly with the good which they have evolved, that he may be able to aid the national leaders reverently to build up a Christian civilisation after their own kind, not after the European kind.[47]

Missiologist Charles Kraft expounded on a number of ways anthropology is useful for missiologists.[48] Anthropology has given us the concepts of culture and worldview, which enable us to distinguish between surface behaviors (for example, birthday parties) and underlying structures (e.g., how a birthday party, as a rite of passage, strengthens social ties, hierarchy, reciprocation of gifts, etc). Additionally, anthropology has taught us to think of humans as belonging to entire systems. When we are proclaiming the gospel, for example, we are not just asking individuals to provide intellectual assent to an idea, we are addressing interrelated economic, political, social, and religious structures. The methodology of anthropology (a framework of cultural pluralism, plus ethnographic methods like participant observation, interviews, etc.) has reduced an element of cultural imperialism and ethnocentrism for many trained missionaries, and has allowed culture-crossers to gain an emic perspective.

---

47. "World Missionary Conference, 1910," 170.
48. Kraft, *Anthropology for Christian Witness*, 4–13.

In this section, I will describe four specific ways that anthropology has shaped missiology, including the concepts of culture, cultural systems, culture change, and cultural pluralism.

### How the Concept of Culture Shapes Missiology

The concept of culture is "anthropology's most significant contribution to missiology."[49] Before modern anthropology, Westerners used the term culture to refer to that which is civilized, refined, and well-bred. Culture, then, was singular—and epitomized by Western European society. Those who did not eat with forks or attend the opera or organize into democratic government were thought to have "no culture." Anthropology subverted that notion and taught us that culture is plural—there are many cultures, with various ideas about what comprised the "good," refined, or well-bred. Culture—everything humans think, do, and believe as members of a society—is learned rather than innate. People in other societies behave in ways that are "common sense" for them. That is, their politics, economics, pastimes, rituals, and religion are all ways they make sense of the world around them. As Geertz maintained, culture is the sum of the "meanings embodied in symbols" by which societies "communicate, perpetuate, and develop their knowledge about and their attitudes toward life."[50] The notion that the world's ethnolinguistic groups each comprise a unique culture has compelled students of culture to try to gain in an insider perspective.

### How Seeing Cultures as Systems Shapes Missiology

Anthropology has also taught us to look at cultures as integrated systems, rather than as beliefs and behaviors that are adopted piecemeal. We learned that "cultures are not a heap of lifeless items but rather integrated wholes."[51] Anthropology enables us to move from just describing what we see to understanding how the parts of the system are integrated. It also allows us to look below the forms of culture for underlying functions. So

---

49. Luzbetak, *Church and Cultures*, 133.
50. Geertz, *Interpretation of Cultures*, 89.
51. Luzbetak, "Applied Missionary Anthropology," 166.

discipleship becomes this job of "untangling cultural knots."⁵² Luzbetak uses the example of pigs in Melanesia:

> To an American, a pig is nothing more than a potential sausage or canned source of income for certain individuals. To the New Guinea native the pig is incomparably more, for the animal is intermeshed with practically every aspect of native life. In fact, native life would be impossible without the pig. The pig, for instance, is regarded as the most important ritual animal, without which religion would be impossible. The pig is the chief source of security, for the pig must be sacrificed to placate pork-hungry ancestors and deceased relatives on whom the wellbeing of the clan members depends. In time of serious illness no cure is possible except by means of pig-sacrifices. No child is born into the world successfully and no tribal battle is won except through pig-sacrifices. Without pig sacrifices there is no security possible. The pig has also a very important economic and social role to play. Pigs, for instance, are exchanged for the precious pearl shell and form the most important part of the family wealth. Although pork is eaten on a feast-or-famine basis, it is the main and usually the only source of animal protein in the native diet. An exchange of pork seals friendships between individuals, families, lineages, and larger social groups. In fact, a friend is referred to literally as "my fellow pork-eater." Distribution of pork climaxes all major festivities, such as birth ceremonies, engagements, weddings, and food exchange between friendly groups. Without pigs it would be impossible for a boy to be initiated into the tribe and thus become a full-fledged member of his social group with all rights and privileges annexed to such membership. The number and quality of pigs gives the owner prestige. A pigless adult would, in fact, be a kind of Stone Age "tramp" or "hobo." A woman's value as wife depends largely on her skill in caring for pigs, and one of the major tests which a young woman must go through during her trial marriage is that of pig raising. It is impossible to acquire a wife except with pigs as an essential, if not main part of the bride-wealth.⁵³

When early missionaries encountered new cultures, they attempted to bar "heathen practices" like puberty rituals or garden magic, without recognizing the reverberations this ban would have on economy, social ties, status, etc.

52. Luzbetak, "Applied Missionary Anthropology," 171.
53. Luzbetak, "Applied Missionary Anthropology," 168–69.

The task of the missiological anthropologist is to understand how these cultural systems are interrelated, to identify the most salient cultural features and symbols by determining which ones are connected robustly to economics, social structure, worldview, etc. If parts of culture are related, then discipleship in one area will have ripple effects in other areas. For example, Junod's essay on Bantu marriage traced the consequences of removing the bride price. "We have to admit that we have acted somewhat too hurriedly here, in destroying or ignoring, forgetting that killing or ignoring a custom does not kill the need which created the custom, a need which is not always bad."[54]

Further, missiological anthropology can help us understand how these salient cultural features impact the process of conversion, discipleship and church growth, leadership and other areas of Christian life.

> With the emergence of the functional/structural schools of anthropology . . . cultures were presented as organic wholes in which the various parts were interdependent and all contributed to the whole. This development in anthropology caught the attention of many missionaries who then pursued studies in anthropology and applied these insights to missionary principles and practice. For example . . . concepts of leadership, patterns of organization and support, methods of communicating the gospel, and the process of making religious decisions would be drawn from and identified with the local culture (e.g., William Smalley 1958). Stress was placed on the unique configuration of each culture. Missionaries in evangelism and church growth were challenged to adapt to these differences.[55]

### How the Comparative Method Shapes Missiology

The concept of culture has also given us the comparative method in anthropology, which reveals differences across cultures. The point of the comparative method is not as much to isolate dependent variables in order to "prove" why cultures have different features. Instead, the comparative method can show the wide variety of experiences within an ethnic group or a national group. For example, sometimes we compare urban and rural experiences, or Christian and non-Christian experiences, or rich and poor.

---

54. Junod, "Anthropology and Missionary Education," 221.
55. Barney, "Challenge of Anthropology to Current Missiology," 173.

Some applications of the comparative method within missiology include Rice's comparison of Ilocano and Kalahan decision-making processes in the Philippines.[56] Both groups are more collectivist, down to the decision to convert to Christianity; but the Kalahan are much more formal in the process of group decision-making. To take another example, Smalley looked at three ethnic groups in Northern Laos, the majority Lao as well as two minority groups Khmu, and Meo. "In spite of the fact that in many cases the same individual missionaries work among the three groups . . . the differences in the response of the three groups to the Christian message are striking."[57] Smalley explains that the Meo have responded to western contact with the industriousness that leads to revitalization, whereas the Khmu have experienced more demoralization due to modernization. The comparative method shows the extent to which "one size does not fit all."

### How Cultural Pluralism Shapes Missiology

The concept of culture allowed us to see that much of what people think, do, and make is culturally-patterned. Ideas about who is eligible for marriage, or who God is, or how to prepare a meal, are not universal; they are the result of innovations and the diffusion of cultural sharing throughout history. People do what makes sense to them, in their context. This observation gave us a sense of cultural relativism. We learned that

> ideas about morality, "politeness," "respect" etc., are relative to a specific culture . . . Virtually all of the acceptable practices, beliefs and actions shared by members of a society are relative to a specific context. We would not expect people from far away continents to have the values we have, or enjoy the same foods we enjoy or believe the same things about God that we do, any more than we would expect them to speak the same language we speak.[58]

In fact, as early as Gustav Warneck, missiologists understood that culture itself could be seen as "neutral."[59] Note that "neutral" is a sort of euphemism for "relative."

---

56. Rice, "Evangelism and Decision-making Processes."
57. Smalley, "Gospel and the Cultures of Laos," 47.
58. Nehrbass, *God's Image and Global Cultures*, 108.
59. Barney, "Challenge of Anthropology to Current Missiology," 172.

## Missiologist Profile: Gustav Warneck

### (1834–1910)

*Education: Theology, Halle University; PhD University of Jenna*

*Occupation: Pastor, professor of missions*

Gustav Warneck is known as the founder of German missiology, though his chronic lung disease prevented him from serving in cross-cultural missions. He was a pastor, and championed missions in his preaching. He became the first chair of "missionary science" in Germany, at Halle University (now Martin Luther Universität). He achieved wide recognition, publishing more than thirty books "and ten times that many articles" on missions and also founded a German language missiology journal.[1]

Warneck championed missions from the pulpit. "Convinced that the pastor is the key person to promote . . . mission spirit and recruitment in his own congregation, Warneck labored tirelessly on mission sermons and lessons for the preacher's use."[2]

Like Henry Venn, Warneck's mission plan involved three stages that move from individual conversion to the establishment of local churches: 1) gathering of individual believers; 2) forming them into congregations; and 3) joining of local congregations into a communion.

Warneck's *missionslehre*—theology of mission—argues that the gospel is supracultural; that is, it is relevant to all peoples because it transcends cultural norms. For Warneck, cultural patterns may be neutral, so the missionary's job is not to Westernize, but to learn culture and make the gospel relevant in that context.

Warneck's taxonomy of missiology involved three sub-disciplines: 1) history of the expansion of the church (which he termed world-history); 2) practical theology (providing an apologetic for missional activity) and 3) theology (especially the theology of conversion, which he termed kingdom-history).

Warneck was also ahead of the times as he advocated a worldwide missionary council with regular conferences for the sake of unifying the church in efforts to fulfill the great commission.[3]

---

[1] Kasdorf, "Legacy of Gustav Warneck," 105.
[2] Kasdorf, "Legacy of Gustav Warneck," 104.
[3] Neill, *History of Christian Missions*, 402.

Interestingly, the tremendous degree of cultural variations is just the data that philosophical relativists needed to justify the notion of philosophical relativism: If cultures have different views of good and bad, clean and unclean, who is to say that any one of those cultural systems is more correct than any other? Contemporary anthropology *presupposes* cultural relativism, in part to intentionally mitigate the problems of ethnocentrism. As Bennett's highest stage of "ethnorelativity" concludes, "there is no absolute standard of rightness [or] 'goodness' that can be applied to cultural behavior. Cultural difference is neither good or bad; it is just different."[60]

While missiologists quickly saw the value of understanding cultural pluralism, they have had to reconcile this value with the philosophical relativism that runs deep in academia.

> Whole sections of Africa showed no evidence of a belief in the Fall (and therefore a need for redemption) in their cultures, yet lived decently and humanely. Quite diverse patterns of sexual mores did not seem to bring with them the wages of sin, as one would have expected from a Christian ethical perspective. Indeed, anthropology's cataloguing of the sheer diversity of forms of human life called into question whether one could generalize about much of anything. If that were the case, then Christianity faced the prospect of having to forego its claim to be the universal religion.[61]

Missiologists typically do not interpret cultural pluralism to mean that there is no objective standard. In fact, Mary Douglas found that "relativism was a good servant, but a bad master."[62] Cultural variety just serves to reveal how vastly creative humans can be in developing their own political, social, and religious systems. Yet as fallen creatures, we corrupt each of these cultural systems, no matter what society we belong to.

## How Models of Culture Change Impact Missiology

Anthropologists discovered that cultures are not static; they are the composite of innovations and the hybridization of innovations that are brought in from neighboring societies. Tippett noted that societies' responses to rapid changes like colonialism or modernization can

---

60. Bennett, "Towards Ethnorelativism," 26.
61. Schreiter, "Anthropology and Faith," 286.
62. Larsen, *Slain God*, 143.

involve submersion, demoralization, conversion, or revitalization.[63] Revitalization was a concept Tippett gleaned from Wallace's[64] study of the stress that marginalized societies experience when they undergo rapid cultural change, often resulting in nativistic movements or cargo cults. Strom's study of the Mizoram showed how Christianity helped a minority ethnic group in India cope with the loss of self-determinacy under colonialism.[65]

Recently, missiologists have been studying how cultures are changing due to globalization. Grenham looked at how the Sakalava people of Madagascar turn to their folk religious system to cope with the pressures of globalization.[66] And Adogame's study of Pentecostalism and modernization in Africa makes the fascinating point that globalization is now facilitating the reversal of influence—now African Pentecostalism is exported across the world.[67] The expectation that cultures are constantly changing helps missiologists develop dynamic understandings of people groups, rather than static generalizations.

## How Ethnographic Methods Impact Missiology

Anthropology has taught missiologists to be students of culture. Those who do not put the effort into learning their host cultures seem to assume that humans are simply blank slates that can receive a new religious system, believe it in its entirety, and put it into action. Most missionary trainers realize that cross-cultural workers must be students of their host culture; but cultural intelligence was not always standard.

Throughout the past century, anthropology has given the ethnographic methods to study cultures. Ethnography can be either quantitative or qualitative. Quantitative methods include measuring cultural data that can be counted, often to isolate dependent variables. For example, does income affect how many wives an African man will have? Or what is the relationship between education level and likelihood of conversion?

The qualitative paradigm attempts to gain an insider perspective. Qualitative ethnographic study is an iterative process of observation, interview, analysis, and generation of new data through interviews as well

63. Tippett, *Introduction to Missiology*, 189.
64. Wallace, "Movements Revitalization."
65. Strom, "Christianity and Culture Change Among the Mizoram."
66. Grenham, "Reconstructing Christian Culture."
67. Adogame, *Who is Afraid of the Holy Ghost?*

as the examination of archival data. For example, what are Indo-American attitudes about education?[68] Or to take another example, Flinn's study of Catholicism on the island of Pollap used software called ANTHROPAC to do a "pile sort," which enabled her to elicit 20 participants' views of women's work.[69]

Malinowski set the example that cultural analysis requires extended experience in the field "to grasp the native's point of view . . . to realize his vision of the world."[70] Extensive fieldwork allows missiological anthropologists to separate the ideal culture as described by informants from the actual experience the fieldworker observes.

Various branches within anthropology have added to our toolbox for doing ethnographic study. Social anthropology, for example, gave us tools like genograms and kinship terminology to understand kinship systems. Levi-Strauss taught us to analyze myth for underlying dyadic cognitive structures (like sacred/profane, shame/honor).[71] Geertz taught us that ethnographic descriptions must be thick—a feat that is only possible through extended period of immersion in the society. Applied anthropology has taught us to explore indigenous attitudes and structures that may serve as obstacles to such an agenda.[72] For instance, Colby interviewed Huistan and Zinacantan Amerindians in Mexico to understand motivations for having their girls read (e.g., so they can earn money, assimilate to Latino culture, become smart) as well as their cultural obstacles to literacy (e.g., they should be doing household chores, Indians shouldn't try to be like Latinos).[73] Anthropology has taught us that cultures are complex, so culture learning is hard work. Proper anthropological training gives missionaries a number of theories and labels to help them understand their new cultural context.

## How Anthropology Helps Missiologists Address Discipleship Holistically

By this point, it must be clear that understanding a host culture well enough to engage in holistic discipleship requires a wide array of study.

68. Colby, "Indian Attitudes."
69. Flinn, *Mary, the Devil, and Ttaro*.
70. Malinowski, *Argonauts of the Western Pacific*, 25.
71. Levi-Strauss, *Structural Anthropology*.
72. Geertz, *Interpretation of Cultures*.
73. Colby, "Indian Attitudes."

It requires addressing these integrated cultural systems. Figure 5 below shows how this systematic and holistic study of cultural study would look:

Figure 5: Discipling the cultures we cross

Cross-cultural discipleship involves addressing these integrated systems within culture, from cultural identity, to ritual, to myth and symbol, and so on. Below, I will survey how missiological anthropologists have studied various cultural systems to advance the theory and practice of missions.

## *How the Study of Identity Shapes Missiology*

Related to the concept of culture is the concept of identity. Our cultures help us make meaning of our identity as children, parents, siblings, employees, bosses, and establish our religious identity, ethnic identity, and so on. Our identities are formed at the intersections of race, gender, religious identity.

The study of identity is newer within anthropology, and missiologists have only recently begun to uncover identity formation in their host cultures. For instance, Selka studied what it means to be an afro-Brazilian evangelical in a context of Roman Catholicism.[74] And Barton examined efforts to construct a more unifying national identity in post-civil war Rwanda. He argued "God's mission seeks not to eliminate identities per se, but to eliminate the enmity between them, thus calling people to accept and welcome the 'other as other' in the name of Christ. Therefore, in the current climate in Rwanda, and despite impressive indicators of social and economic progress, the call of mission may increasingly require a subversive posture."[75]

Missiological anthropology involves working through the meanings of these identities so that disciples can find their new identity in Christ while redeeming (rather than surrendering) their cultural identities.

*How the study of social organization shapes missiology*

Bringing social life under God's rule is also part of discipleship. One of the early concerns for missionaries was how to reconcile discipleship with non-western views of courtship, marriage, polygamy, and bride price. I will expand on each below.

### How the study of marriage and sexuality shapes missiology

Early missiological anthropologists asked, *Could a polygamist be a follower of Christ? If he must divorce all but one wife in order to be admitted into the church, wouldn't that also be a sin?* Trobisch's interview with an African man using the pseudonym Omodo reveals how inadequately missionaries had understood marriage and social organization in Africa. Omodo believed in Jesus and supported the church financially, but could not be a church member.[76] Meanwhile, Omodo's first wife, who had in fact bullied Omodo into taking a second wife in order to raise the prestige of the home and ease some of the burden of domestic duties, was allowed to join the church, because she technically was not guilty of polygamy.

Missionaries also asked, *Are animistic couples considered truly wedded in God's sight?* If traditional societies do not recognize a couple as legitimately married until they bear children, is it the case that the couple

---

74. Selka, *Religion and the Politics of Ethnic Identity in Bahia*.
75. Barton, "Confusion and Communion," 229.
76. Trobisch, "Congregational Responsibility for the Christian Individual."

is fornicating up to the point in time where the tribe recognizes them as married? And what should be the Christian response to bride price? Or how does Christianity respond to cultures where marriages are arranged more for the agenda of the men who arrange these marriages than for the welfare of the couple and their children?

Anthropological theory has brought to light how much of our social relationships are about duty, obligation, reciprocity, and role. The maintenance of virginity until marriage, for instance, is often not as much about personal purity as it is about keeping the value of the thing-to-be-traded (the bride) for the dowry that will be exchanged. Reyburn pointed out the way that social organization, gender, modernization and economics are all integrated in ways that cause problems for the discipleship among the Kaka in Cameroun:

> Wives produce children and gardens, girl children produce dowry and provide personal service and are valuable for increasing garden income . . . Wives have a great desire to own, and if they do not find that they receive an equitable proportion of the cash income from their labor, they are anxious to seek other means of securing money. This they may do by encouraging and helping the husband to secure other wives. This gives each wife an opportunity to free herself from the close control of her husband, to sell her garden produce in a market town, to find employment, and to have financially rewarding extramarital sex relations . . . What is needed rather is a reorientation of both men and women concerning money and wealth.[77]

These questions about how social structures must be reorganized under the rule of God do not have easy answers.

## How the Study of Exchange and Patron-Client Social Structures Shape Missiology

Social systems also help us work out how we will share economic resources. Hiebert developed a three-fold taxonomy for these types of social structures: small-scale oral societies, peasant, and industrial.[78] Each of these has its own particular patterns for engaging in exchange, and for delineating status and role.

---

77. Reyburn, "Polygamy," 266.
78. Hiebert, *Transforming Worldviews*.

## Profile of a Missiologist: Paul Hiebert

### (1932–2007)

*Education: PhD Anthropology, University of Minnesota*
*Occupation: Professor of missiology*

Paul Hiebert was "arguably the world's leading missiological anthropologist."[1] He published over 180 articles and 13 books on missiology and anthropology, covering such topics as spiritual warfare, church planting, globalization, and short-term missions. Much of Hiebert's examples came from India, where he grew up and served as a missionary for six years.

Hiebert's greatest theoretical contribution was the incorporation of numerous tributaries into missiology, including anthropology, philosophy, and even mathematics. Drawing from Hegel's thesis-antithesis-synthesis model, Hiebert gave missiologists the model of critical contextualization.[2] He modified the fuzzy set theory from mathematics for missiology, noting that religious views are not binary: devotion to Christ is not as clear-cut as evangelical discourse would imply. Hiebert adapted the model of organic and mechanistic metaphors from organizational psychology to demonstrate how cosmologies within cultures tend toward personal deities (ghosts, demigods, God) or impersonal forces (karma, manna, fate).[3] He brought philosophy into missiology by introducing us to critical realism. His model of "the flaw of the excluded middle" was likely influenced by the "law of the excluded middle" in logic.[4] And he adapted Leslie White's threefold taxonomy of culture (the affective, evaluative and cognitive domains) to create a model for culture change.[5] He also adapted anthropologist Marvin Harris's threefold taxonomy of social organization to help explain worldview differences between tribal, peasant and industrial societies.[6]

---

[1] Priest, "Paul G. Hiebert."
[2] Hiebert, *Anthropological Insights for Missionaries.*
[3] Hiebert et al., *Understanding Folk Religion.*
[4] Hiebert, "Flaw of the Excluded Middle."
[5] Hiebert, *Anthropological Insights for Missionaries*, 31.
[6] Hiebert, *Transforming Worldviews.*

The tribal system tends to rely on exchange. Mauss theorized that in most societies, there is no such thing as a free gift.[79] "Gifts" are exchanged

79. Mauss, *Gift.*

to create asymmetrical relationships, where people with certain roles are indebted to reciprocate down the line. Such a view of gift giving and exchange profoundly affects the way people understand themselves in relationship to others and God. Irwin suggested that this sort of gift-indebtedness, which he termed a "liability complex," affects Chimbu attitudes of the atonement. "When a clan feels it has paid enough for Christ's grace by attending church services and communion, it returns to its former way of life again."[80]

Peasant societies are often arranged around a patron-client system, which has received much attention in missiological anthropology.[81] Missionaries negotiate their own role in these contexts as potential patrons. This is complicated in light of the current discourse on post-colonialism.

## How the Study of Gender, Status, and Role shapes Missiology

Societies also organize themselves around status and role. These roles can relate to gender, kin relation, leadership position, etc. Roles typically appear in pairs. We are never fathers, leaders, or parishioners in a vacuum—we "occasion" these roles in relation to others: father-son, boss-followers, parishioner-priest. Hiebert helped missionaries think through the role of the missionary in their new cultural context.[82] The change in role is more significant for the missionary than even their drastic change in location. Numerous studies have looked at how Christian missions is impacted by cultural ideals of leadership,[83] gender,[84] and the intersection of gender and leadership.[85]

---

80. Irwin, "Liability Complex Among the Chimbu Peoples of New Guinea," 219.

81. Chinchen, "Patron-Client Relationship Concept"; Dierck, "Teams that Work"; Fox, "Money as Water."

82. Hiebert, "Critical Contextualization."

83. Forman, "South Pacific Style in the Christian Ministry"; Loewen, "Leadership in the Choco Church."

84. Eriksen, *Gender, Christianity and Change in Vanuatu*.

85. Adeney, "Esther Across Cultures"; Hibbert, "Considering a Gendered Approach to Church Planting in Muslim-Background Contexts."

## How the Study of Rituals Shapes Missiology

Anthropologists helped us understand that rituals are not merely pastimes. They serve functions within a society, either to maintain order, or restore order in times of crisis. Some rituals serve as rites of passage, where they ensure the spiritual safety of those who are undergoing a life change such as birth, puberty, marriage, or death. These transitions in life are seen as "liminal" phases[86] where the spirit world is more active, so special rites such as the killing of chickens, extra washings for purification, or the blowing of conch shells and beating of drums, are used to ward off evil. People also follow special taboos during these spiritually-charged times in life, such as abstaining from sexual intercourse, shaving, or handling sharp objects.

Social anthropology poses that rituals are structurally maintained because they are a way for stabilizing social relationships. For example, a wedding is about the groom and bride, but also the extended families, and making sure everyone is still in relationship.[87]

From the earliest efforts at cross-cultural discipleship, missionaries have grappled with the extent to which "pagan" rituals should be encouraged. A number of pagan rituals were disconcerting for cross-cultural Christian workers in early colonial contact, including the strangling or immolation of widows (e.g., *sati* in India), and even cannibalism. One of the persistent rituals that still plagues the Christian church in Africa is female genital mutilation (FGM). Schafroth studied FGM in African societies and concluded "FGM is a violation of the God—given female body and should be eradicated in the Christian Church by forming associations, using appropriate education and alternative initiations rites"[88] by removing the secrecy surrounding the puberty rite, and by capitalizing on the notion that women are equally made in God's image.[89] A quantitative study revealed that puberty rituals in Sri Lanka are a polarizing issue.[90] Many of the Christians prefer to replace these controversial rituals with a functional substitute.

---

86. Van Gennep, *Rites of Passage.*
87. Hiebert et al., *Understanding Folk Religion,* 288.
88. Schafroth, "Female Genital Mutilation in Africa," 527.
89. Schafroth, "Female Genital Mutilation in Africa," 539.
90. Kim, "Comparative Missiological Study of Sinhalese Buddhist."

## How the Study of Worldview Shapes Missiology

While the term worldview was originally developed within German philosophy,[91] anthropology did much to bring the concept of worldview into missiology. One of the most significant missiological contributions regarding worldview is Hiebert's model of the "Flaw of the excluded middle."[92] Hiebert showed that worldview largely determines how a society will syncretize or accommodate Christianity. He argued that the "high religion" of many Christian missionaries focuses on ultimate questions like salvation from sin, while ignoring day-to-day issues for adherents to "folk religions." The cosmology of these folk religions contains countless spiritual beings like ghosts, demons, as well as impersonal forces like karma or the evil eye. It is these middle-level spiritual realities that seem to explain this-worldly problems like drought and sickness, as well as successes such as a plentiful harvest or the birth of a child. When Christianity fails to address this middle realm, its relevance to the lives of many people is severely limited.

A number of missiological studies have focused on this clash of worldviews. In Mexico, Pitarch explored the worldview of Tzeltal Christians, especially regarding their soul.[93] Their belief that each human possesses four to thirteen souls presented challenges for Christian doctrines of the free will or the eternal destiny of the soul. Hiebert also used the worldview concept to show how within the Hindu context, the universe is highly hierarchal, yet with a great deal of fluidity between the supernatural and natural, or between spirit and matter.[94] Only Brahman is reality; everything else is illusion, from high gods, to lesser gods, to priests, then rulers, merchants, down to outcastes, to high and low animals, and finally to plants and the inanimate world. This can seriously skew Hindu background believers' concepts of God and human responsibility.

### WORLDVIEW SHAPES IDEAS OF POWER, HEALING, SORCERY

Worldviews are the underpinning of many religious activities within a culture. Religion is not just the interaction with spiritual beings and

---

91. Kant, *Critique of Judgment*.
92. Hiebert, "Flaw of the Excluded Middle."
93. Pitarch, *Jaguar and the Priest*.
94. Hiebert, "Missions and the Understanding of Culture," 54–55.

forces (discussed above) but the generation of fortune (such as harvests or healing) as well as the avoidance of misfortune such as avoiding sickness, drought, or other curses. The anthropology of religion has given missiologists a number of tools for analyzing spiritual practices such as witchcraft, sorcery, clairvoyance, magic, etc. Hiebert's framework of organic and mechanical analogies organizes spiritual power into a two-dimensional model: Some cultures tend to harness power through mechanical forces that are other-worldly (like fate or karma), or this-worldly (like charms, amulets, the evil eye).[95] Other cultures tend to harvest spiritual power through personal forces that are other-worldly (God, angels, demons) or this-worldly (powerful shamans).

Worldview shapes views of sickness and healing. Joshi discovered that traditional healing in Nagaland (India) has been combined with Christian views of healing. "It was generally held among the Kruna that conversion to Christianity would make such power for healing ineffective. In the beginning [converts to Christianity] had also thought that their power to heal would be lost upon conversion, but this did not happen."[96]

Worldview also helps explain misfortune; and traditional communities often blame sickness and disasters on human agency, such as moral failings, sorcery, or witchcraft. A number of missiological studies focus on the social impact of witchcraft accusations. Harr's study within an African society suggests that alleviating poverty may reduce the frequency and intensity of such accusations.[97] The strategy may include involving the church and police in peacemaking efforts. Zocca's volume focuses on witchcraft and sorcery accusations in Papua New Guinea. Such accusations give women who are known to be witches a measure of prestige or agency, while also placing them at risk of violence. These accusations also provide an explanation for misfortune. Also, the fear of retribution by a sorcerer can be an important deterrent to bad behavior.[98] But how can cross-cultural workers reconcile this worldview with following Christ? Perhaps social life would be more secure if Christians from animistic backgrounds would learn to attribute misfortune to "nature spirits, ancestral ghosts, evil spirits, Satan or even God" rather than attack suspected witches or sorcerers in their villages.[99]

---

95. Hiebert, *Anthropological Reflections on Missiological Issues*, 194.
96. Joshi, *Matter of Belief*, 144.
97. Harr, *Imagining Evil*.
98. Zocca, *Sanguma in Paradise*, 337.
99. Zocca, *Sanguma in Paradise*, 298.

## Worldview Shapes Ideas of Sin and Salvation

A prime worldview concern for evangelists is the notion of sin and salvation—what is humankind's problem and how do we find escape from sin and suffering? The cross-cultural process has taught us that societies have wildly different ways to describe the primary problem that humans face, as well as the way they achieve salvation.[100]

## Worldview in Poetry, Mythology, and Proverbs

Since worldview is invisible, it cannot be studied as readily as material culture or ritual. Anthropologists turn to poetry, proverbs, and mythology to discover an underlying worldview. Missiologists mine such cultural data (poetry, proverbs, myth) to understand how worldview impacts a society's reception of the gospel. For example, Woodhouse explores images of the divine in Iranian poetry to understand why Iranians in diaspora are relatively more accepting of Christianity than Muslims from other backgrounds.[101] Woodhouse suggests that images of Jesus as healer, sage, and moral exemplar serve as an entry point for the gospel. Moon studied 629 proverbs among the Builsa in Ghana to help the local Christian church critically examine 13 core values related to God, marriage, and morality.[102] And Aasland's study of Kazakh proverbs indicated college students in Kazakhstan were shifting from collectivism to individualism.[103]

The study of myth is a bit more controversial for missiologists. Some are hesitant to learn, let alone publish, the myths of host cultures, for fear of encouraging the repetition (and belief) in such "pagan" ideas. Other missiological anthropologists see great value in encouraging people in their host culture to tell these stories. Loewen tells the story of a Bible translator, working among Amerindians, who never bothered to ask about the local cosmology.[104] The missionary's failure to explore folklore kept him in the dark about indigenous ideas of sickness, views of the origin and destiny of humankind, explanations of illness, health, and

---

100. Scotchmer, "Symbols of Salvation"; Strelan, *Search for Salvation*; Wilson, "Search for Salvation."

101. Woodhouse, "You are Jesus."

102. Moon, *African Proverbs Reveal Christianity in Culture.*

103. Aasland, "Narrativization of Kazakh Proverbs."

104. Loewen, "Myth and Mission."

healing, natural phenomena such as the horizon, drought, the moon's phases, not to mention the value of myth in properly structuring a story.

When missionaries speak about God, and other important worldview constructs like creation and Satan or demons, they must be aware of how these concepts are already present in the indigenous mythological corpus. For example, McCollum and Ifamut tell how the Seram in Indonesia have myths of creation, exodus, and wandering, but their myths do not contain a God who directs history and works for His glory.[105]

Missiologists must also understand how host cultures reinterpret Scripture within their own mythology. Some Vietnamese, for instance, incorporated Noah into their own flood story, and determined that the curse of Ham must refer to their neighboring ethnolinguistic groups.[106] The missionaries concluded that by "correcting" the mythology, missiologists could help with the peacemaking effort while "introducing the gospel via terms already understood and valued by the people."[107]

Myth can teach missionaries about the host cultures' view of time. Varughese's study of the concept of time and historicity in Hindu mythology raises a number of issues for proclamation of the gospel.[108] Since Hindu mythology is cyclical, it tends to underplay the uniqueness of events in history (like the incarnation). Also, the tendency to mythologize history often causes people from Hindu backgrounds to see Jesus Christ as mythological rather than historical.

## How the Study of Material Culture Shapes Missiology

Missiologists have also spent a great deal of time exploring how aspects of material culture—arts, music, handicrafts, technology, foods, architecture—shape local expressions of Christianity. For example, Meyers's study of twelve churches in Mozambique revealed that indigenous Christians sing very few songs that are locally composed—they hybridize global worship traditions by adapting western hymns and praise choruses to a tempo or rhythm that is more localized. She concludes, "A non-contextualized missionary legacy, globalization, and

---

105. McCollum and Ifamut, "Liana-Seti Origin Myths."
106. Gregerson, "Rengao Myths," 352.
107. Gregerson, "Rengao Myths," 300.
108. Varughese, "Sense of History and Apologetics in a Hindu Context."

urban youth culture have significantly impacted preferred worship styles in Beira churches."[109] To take another example, Hamilton's volume on "the art of rice" demonstrates how growing rice is a spiritual activity in Asia.[110]

## Conclusion

Anthropology enriches missiological theory and practice in multiple ways. It helps mitigate ethnocentrism among cross-cultural workers; and helps us make sense of the "common sense" in our host cultures. It helps us look beneath these outward cultural forms like ritual and symbol for underlying meanings in worldview and cultural values. Anthropological methods give us the tools to see how social, political, religious, and technological systems are interrelated. The theories of ritual, kinship, and exchange have helped missiologists understand the social organization in their host cultures. Missiologists have used the comparative method to understand the breadth of human experiences.

Yet often anthropological theories are not accepted wholesale by missiologists. Instead, they are modified to better explain the data they observe, and to better inform missiological practice. For example, insofar as anthropology relies on materialism and denies the supernatural, it cannot achieve a full understanding of humans in their cultural context. Humans bear God's image and live in a universe that is both material and spiritual; so a holistic view of culture must include such spiritual themes. For example, when rationalist anthropologists reduce religious ideas to some an underlying social or psychological purpose, they only see in part. As Sir Edward Evans-Pritchard argued, the "conception of God cannot be reduced to, or explained by, the social order."[111] Anthropologists have repeatedly gotten it wrong when they found meanings in religion that the practitioners themselves did not see. Mary Douglas agreed that "religions can be described but not further explained; reductionism leads to shallow and false conclusions and must be avoided."[112] Victor Tuner as well felt that ritual needn't be reduced to underlying social structures. It has value in and of itself.[113]

109. Meyers, "Contextualization is Complicated," 264.
110. Hamilton, *Art of Rice*.
111. Quoted in Larsen, *Slain God*, 111.
112. Larsen, *Slain God*, 68.
113. Larsen, *Slain God*, 184.

Below, Table 4 summarizes some anthropological contributions to missiology, as well as the weaknesses in these theories. And I have summarized how missiologists have provided some corrections to these theories.

Table 4: Missiological applications of prominent anthropological theories

| Anthropological contribution *proponents* | *Description* | *Weaknesses* | *Missiological applications or corrections* |
|---|---|---|---|
| **Particularism; Cultural Pluralism** *Franz Boas* | "Culture" is plural—there is no single civilization or modernity | Relies on philosophical relativism—that there is no objective standard for right and wrong | Cultural pluralism encourages missionaries to see cultures from an emic and etic perspective, but does not require missiologists to be philosophical relativists |
| **Semiotics: culture as a web of meanings** *Clifford Geertz; Ferdinand de Saussure; Charles Peirce* | Cultures use changing and contested symbols to point to underlying meanings | Assumes relativism | Eugene Nida argued for dynamic equivalence: cultural forms can vary, you must know what the underlying form means to a particular person or group |
| **Integrated systems approach** *Leslie White* | Cultures are integrated systems | Can de-emphasize the degree to which systems are in competition with each other | Realized discipleship will have social, political, and economic consequence (cf Hiebert's systems model; Kwast's onion model.) |
| **Functionalism** *Bronislaw Malinowski* | Cultural "forms" (ritual, symbol) have underlying functions to meet biological needs | Reduces humans to animals; Does not take into account numerous features of culture which don't seem to serve a basic human need; Presents culture as static and homogenous; Reifies basic functional explanations of culture while denigrating emic explanations | Caused missionaries to value cultural features: rather than view other behaviors and beliefs as "childish" or "primitive." This view caused missionaries to see how such elements actually made sense within the cultural logic (cf. Alan Tippett's functional substitutes). |
| **Social functionalism** *Emile Durkheim* | Cultural "forms" (ritual, symbol) have underlying functions to maintain social structure (hierarchy, leadership status) | Does not take into account numerous features of culture which don't seem to preserve social structures; Presents culture as static and homogenous; Reifies social functional explanations of culture while denigrating emic explanations; | Encouraged missionaries to work within existing social world, such as kin relations, leadership structures, and gender roles; Helped missionaries understand their role in reciprocal relationships |
| **Taxonomy of Economic production** *Elmer Service* | Divides societies into categories based on the type of market activity | Makes sweeping generalizations | Paul Hiebert recognizes that worldviews in tribal, peasant, and industrial societies will vary |

Here, I have only been able to describe a handful of ways that the study of humans in their cultural contexts serves as a tributary to missiological theory. Much more research could be done on the ways culture change may explain the process of conversion—or how the process of conversion enlightens the theory of culture change. Or, how gender and race issues impact the process of cross-cultural disciple-making. Culture is expansive, covering societies' ideas (worldview), actions (ritual), social organization (gender, status, role, leadership), as well as their technologies and arts. Few missiologists would be familiar enough with each of these avenues of anthropological exploration to make use of them all in their fields where they work. Instead, missiologists tend to follow up on the leads that help solve the problems they encounter in the field.

## Move Into Action

The exciting thing about missiological anthropology is that many of the world's ethnolinguistic groups have barely been studied. Use the tools of anthropology to understand how the world's various rituals, worldviews, kinship systems, and economic systems shape, and should be shaped by, the gospel.

## Ideas for Further Research

The field is wide open for many more ethnographies, narrative studies, and comparative studies, such as:

1. Do qualitative studies on attitudes in a particular culture regarding church life and outreach—how do the findings challenge previous anthropological works on that particular cultural group? How can those findings enrich the global church's idea of church life and outreach?

2. Collect conversion narratives from a particular culture—what do these narratives teach us about the emic understandings of kinship, role, gender, worldview, etc.?

## Review Questions

1. Describe the love-hate relationship between anthropologists and missiologists.

2. Describe how anthropology helps cross-cultural workers carry out holistic discipleship.

3. How do missiologists use anthropology to make disciples across cultures?

## Reflection Questions

1. How have studies of missiological anthropology added to theoretical knowledge about the nature of humankind?

2. How have studies of missiological anthropology helped cross-cultural workers deal with the stress of crossing cultures?

*Chapter 5*

# Connecting Intercultural Studies to Cross-Cultural Discipleship

> Chapter Goals
>
> *Knowledge goals:*
>
> - Describe basic features of communication that differ across cultures.
> - Discuss how the theories of cultural value orientations can improve your building of trust and rapport across cultures.
>
> *Action goals:*
>
> - Collect empirical data (speech or actions) in another culture and use intercultural theory to explain the communication patterns in that culture.
>
> *Heart goals:*
>
> - Search your heart for instances of ethnocentrism.

BECAUSE MISSIONS IS THE task of making disciples across cultures, missiologists have been highly interested in theories related to the process of crossing cultures, or intercultural studies (ICS). Below, I will discuss three main lines of inquiry that are central to the field of intercultural studies, and show how these foci shape the study of missions.

### Crossing Cultural Boundaries

primarily refers to working with people who self-avow as members of an ethno-linguistic group that is different than one's own ethno-linguistic group. However, other ways to cross cultural boundaries may include crossing a national border, working with members of another religion, generation, or socio-economic status.

## Intercultural Communication

Even though the discipline of intercultural studies has a missiological focus at many Christian universities, at secular universities the term "intercultural studies" is usually understood to mean more narrowly "intercultural communication." The study of intercultural communication may belong more broadly to the academic department of communication(s), rather than to anthropology. In these settings, students may have courses on rhetoric, mass media, and negotiation theory. Students may even analyze commercials or court transcripts in other languages to understand how speakers from different cultures use persuasion or resolve conflict. Below I will discuss the tools of intercultural communication studies, and show how missiologists have used these tools for the study of missions.

### Intercultural Studies:

is the academic field that examines the experiences of people who cross cultural boundaries

### Cross-cultural:

There is no widely accepted distinction between cross-cultural and intercultural. The two may be synonymous. But to avoid confusion, it is best to pick one term and use it consistently.

### Multicultural:

Containing more than one culture.

### Multiculturalism:

A commitment to representing a diversity of cultures.

## Communication Patterns Across Cultures

As American businesses began setting up shop overseas, the cultural faux pas committed began adding up. Pringles tried to sell smoky bacon flavored chips with the tag line "Ramadan Mubarak." Pepsi ran an ad in China that was supposed to say "it gives you life"; but the translation came out more like "it brings your ancestors back from the dead." Not to be outdone by miscommunicating in China, the name Coca-Cola sounds in Mandarin like "bite the wax tadpole." And a legend has it (albeit one that is well-debunked) that Chevy tried to sell a car in Mexico with the name "nova" which means in Spanish "doesn't go"—supposedly drastically affecting the sales.

Big business blunders in multinational marketing, many documented by Ricks,[1] teach us the importance of understanding the Other culture's communication patterns if we plan to accomplish anything in that setting. All cross-cultural activity—whether marketing, managing, developing, or discipling—involves communication; therefore, the study of crossing cultures must include a study of communication patterns.

After WWII, the US government realized its Foreign Service Officers (FSOs) needed to understand enigmatic (and even hidden) cultural differences in places like Japan, Germany, and Russia. They set up the Foreign Service Institute (FSI) to offer training for its FSOs. The themes of cross-cultural training were adopted by other multinational organizations, such as the Peace Corps, multinational corporations, and missionary organizations, so their personnel could avoid committing cultural blunders. Much of the early training focused on understanding differences in verbal and non-verbal communication patterns. In terms of verbal communication patterns, interculturalists looked at the way different cultures use direct or indirect speech, questions, metaphors, humor and satire, verbal dueling, euphemisms, slang, and even silence:

- When is it appropriate to tell a joke in a speech?
- Can you answer with a direct "no" in this culture, or do you have to hint at it?
- Can a manager give a direct command, or make suggestions like "we should all do it this way"?
- How do you interrupt in another culture? How do you show you are done with the conversation?

---

1. Ricks, *Big Business Blunders*.

As far as non-verbal communication goes, culture-crossers were taught to think about proxemics (how other cultures use personal space), haptics (the significance attached to touching), olfactions (the significance attached to smell), oculesics (how other cultures use eye contact), and kinesics (how other cultures use gestures).[2]

- How much personal space is necessary in this culture?
- What signal am I sending if I wear jewelry, or shorts, or long hair?
- What does the "thumbs up" mean in this culture?
- What's the proper way to accept a gift in this culture?

Such features of verbal and non-verbal communication are the core of most intercultural communication curricula. For example, Moreau et al. introduce students of missiology to how culture affects verbal and non-verbal communication patterns as well as differences in time orientation, gender roles, and notions of the "in-group."[3]

Charles Kraft and David Hesselgrave were pioneers who applied the field of intercultural communication to cross-cultural discipleship. Kraft argued that missionary communication must be "receptor-oriented," so missionaries must understand communication patterns in their mission fields.[4] Hesselgrave introduced missiologists to intercultural communication themes such as verbal and non-verbal codes, and high context speech. He noted that when we apply ICS to missiology, we are really dealing with *three* communication patterns and three cultural value systems: the biblical culture,[5] the missionary's culture, and the "respondent's" culture.[6] And because missiologists have always placed the Bible above "culture," they have typically understood that Christianity must, at times, *confront* both the missionary's culture and the so-called target culture.[7]

Note that much of early cross-cultural training (CCT) was fairly simplistic: Memorize this list of ten or twenty rules (which you may find

2. Ricks, *Big Business Blunders*, 15.
3. Moreau et al., *Effective Intercultural Communication*.
4. Kraft, *Communication Theory for Christian Witness*, 80.
5. I problematize the concept of a "biblical culture" in Nehrbass, *God's Image and Global Cultures*, 38–40.
6. Hesselgrave, *Communicating Christ Cross-culturally*, 73.
7. Mayers, *Christianity Confronts Culture*; Livermore, *Cultural Intelligence*; Hiebert, "Critical Contextualization."

in a travel guide to that country) and you should be okay. The problem is, it's impossible to give culture-crossers all the knowledge they'll need to "know before they go." It is much better to give them the tools to exegete the meanings of verbal and non-verbal communication patterns on their own.

Additionally, such generalized "rules" for going into another culture were also highly reductive. As a professor of intercultural studies, whenever I told my class, "Steak is important in Argentina," an Argentinian student would inevitably take issue with me. Or if I said, "It's important to greet every person individually in Honduras, rather than giving a generic 'hello' to the group," a Honduran in the class would respond, "I've never heard of such a rule." Therefore, interculturalists are learning that it is essential, when making generalizations about other cultures, to ensure that communication "rules" emerge from actual cultural data. Instead of saying "Japanese always use 'we' in persuasive speech," actually analyze commercials in Japan, and report how persuasive speech was used *in those commercials*. Instead of saying "Nobody shows up on time in Saudi Arabia," actually observe various types of meetings there, and report on who showed up when.

## Facework and Identity Management

Early interculturalists theorized that intercultural communication involved Speaker A, from culture A, encoding his message with verbal and non-verbal communication. He would send this communication to Speaker B from culture B, who would decode the language, gestures, body language, gaze, metaphors, etc., according to Speaker B's cultural background.[8] More recently, interculturalists have come to realize that communication is even more complicated than that. First of all, we probably never achieve true parity when we communicate in our own cultural contexts, let alone across cultures. Think of how you are even misunderstood by your own family members at times! When people communicate, they fall on a continuum from near total misunderstanding, to partial parity, to nearly complete agreement on what is being communicated.

Additionally, when two people communicate across cultures, they may possess prejudices about the other culture; they are often in an

---

8. Hesselgrave, *Communicating Christ Cross-culturally*, 29.

asymmetrical power relationship with the other speaker; and they may have contrasting purposes for their communication acts. Think of how the terrorist attack on 9/11 impacted communication between Anglos and people from Muslim majority countries. Communicators always encode and decode messages through their filter of values, intentions, and beliefs.[9] Therefore miscommunication across cultures can happen not just when we misunderstand someone's verbal and non-verbal cues, but also when we fail to understand their intentions and prejudices.

Interculturalists have discovered that much of communication is about managing identity. We project verbal and nonverbal cues to "occasion"[10] our identities: We project ourselves as suburban professionals, or Californian surfers, or evangelical Christian leaders, and so on. Ting-Toomey theorized that communication is achieved when "both communicators successfully meet all these mutual identity needs, expectations, attunements and cravings."[11] Sometimes we miscommunicate across cultures when we are unaware of how identity is "indexed" or "occasioned" for our interlocutors from other cultures.

Some missiologists have become interested in how communication relates to identity management. Charles Kraft's essays in the late 1960s and early 1970s focused on how missionaries should break the mold of the typical colonist.[12] He developed a Christian ethic that breaks the chains of ethnocentrism, and applied the incarnation to communication theory.

I recently studied how identifying as American impacts missionary work. The participants in my study explained that sometimes people (from the USA or from other cultures) use anti-American sentiment to demonstrate that they are enlightened and sophisticated. Anti-American sentiment can also use nationalistic discourse to reinforce an "in-group"—an important part of identity management. The 19 participants in my study also noted that when they are identified as American (or when Canadians are mis-identified as US Americans) they must either challenge or leverage the stereotypes they encounter.[13]

---

9. Gudykunst, "Anxiety/uncertainty Management (AUM) Theory of Effective Communication," 289.

10. Hua, *Exploring Intercultural Communication*, 294.

11. Ting-Toomey, "Identity Negotiation Theory," 222.

12. Kraft, *Culture, Communication and Christianity*, 172–233.

13. Nehrbass, "Controversial Image of the US American in Missions."

Much of this identity management has to do with upgrading "face." Face is our "negotiated public image, mutually granted each other by participants in a communicative event."[14] What makes this so complicated is that cultures have different patterns for upgrading face and for "threatening" another's "face." Sometimes we miscommunicate across cultures when we fail to understand how face is upgraded or threatened in the cultures of our interlocutors.

## Cultural Values in Communication

A main focus of intercultural communication studies is the ways that communicators from different cultures hold different values. Even if the two are speaking a mutually-understood language, they may derive different meanings, because of their cultural backgrounds. These different values can cause "noise"[15] that impedes successful communication. Much of the missionary training in the twentieth century had to do with "peeling back the layers" of culture to get at underlying values and beliefs.[16]

Kluckhohn and Strodtbeck,[17] and Hall[18] developed a vocabulary to describe these clashing values, such as cultural differences in power distance, time orientation, or uncertainty avoidance. Hofstede surveyed 100,000 IBM employees in more than 70 nations to map how these values vary from country to country.[19] The World Values Survey (WVS) collected data from 80 countries to understand how culture affects attitudes about democracy, education, religion, and capitalism.[20] It was a massive study, examining over 400 values in the domains of ecology, emotions, health, leisure, morality.[21] How does culture impact our motivation for work? Our attitudes about getting paid? Our attitudes about work holidays? And so on.

Many other cultural value orientations have caught the attention of interculturalists. Benedict's study of Japanese society honed intercultural

---

14. Hua, *Exploring Intercultural Communication*, 65.
15. Steffen, "Minimizing Crosscultural Evangelism Noise."
16. Kwast, "Understanding Culture."
17. Kluckhohn and Strodtbeck, *Variations in Value Orientations*.
18. Hall, *Silent Language*; *Beyond Culture*; *Hidden Dimension*.
19. Hofstede, *Culture's Consequences*.
20. Inglehart, *Human Values and Social Change*.
21. Inglehart et al., *Human Values and Beliefs*.

theories of shame and honor,[22] which have had much currency in missiology recently.[23] Mary Douglas described the dyadic values of the sacred and the profane—a theme that has received less attention in missiology. Lingenfelter and Mayers' small book *Ministering Cross-culturally* was the seminal text that introduced missiologists to cultural value orientations. Their "model of basic values" covered six dyadic values that were placed in opposition to each other: time versus event orientation, holistic versus dichotomistic thinking, crisis versus non-crisis orientation; task versus person orientation; status versus achievement focus; and concealment versus exposure of vulnerability.[24] Elmer's *Cross-cultural connections*[25] includes a similar list of value orientations, but adds low versus high "worship expression," and guilt versus shame.

Elsewhere, I have outlined more recent critiques on the project of reducing cultural values to simplistic dyads:[26] Cultural differences rarely obey international boundaries; nations contain wide culture variations. And all cultures tend to display a mixture of event *and* time orientation, or dichotomistic *and* holistic thinking, and so on.

### Applying Cultural Value Theory: Grid/Group

One of the value orientations that has had the most currency in missiology is that of "grid and group." Social anthropologist Mary Douglas used a two-dimensional model to show the wide diversity among the world's cultures regarding the above two-value dimensions. She plotted the individualism/collectivism value on one axis, and distribution of power (hierarchy/egalitarianism) on the other axis. Douglas labeled these "two independent variables affecting the structuring of personal relations" as "grid" (for the power distribution value) and "group" (for the self-construal value).[27]

Douglas's original use of the grid/group model was more esoteric and theoretical than it was practical. She wanted to demonstrate that religion

---

22. Benedict, *Chrysanthemum and the Sword*.

23. Muller, *Honor and Shame*; Georges, "From Shame to Honor;" Wu, "How Christ Saves God's Face."

24. Lingenfelter and Mayers, *Ministering Cross-culturally*.

25. Elmer, *Cross-cultural Connections*.

26. Nehrbass, *God's Image and Global Cultures*, 174–211.

27. Douglas, *Natural Symbols*, 57.

is socially-constructed—the product of a group's social structure.[28] She theorized that a highly stratified caste system like India would project highly stratified structures onto their legends about the pantheon; and highly individualistic and egalitarian cultures would lack formal religious structures. "Individuals in different social settings, Douglas argues, are biased towards different cosmologies. People do not believe what makes no sense to them, and what makes sense to them depends on their social environment."[29]

Yet missiologists discovered that Douglas's grid/group theory can help explain (and resolve) conflict that arises over leadership styles when more than two cultures are attempting to steer a church or mission organization.[30] Sherwood Lingenfelter also used the model to understand how the differences of social structure between the missionary's home culture and host culture can lead to conflict over the use of possessions and wealth.[31] Judith Lingenfelter even used the grid/group theory to explain different ecclesiastical understandings of the social gospel.[32]

Students of the Lingenfelters, as well as other missiologists, applied the grid/group model to their own research, including its usefulness for church leadership,[33] for business as mission,[34] for changing social structures in German on the life of the church,[35] for understanding the relationship between social structure and cosmology in the Vineyard Christian Fellowship,[36] and for understanding the way that individualism in the mid-Western USA shaped an intellectual, rather than ecstatic, religious experience for fundamentalists.[37] Note that since the latest missiological publication on grid group theory was in 2007, this particular model that may be reaching the end of its "tail life" (see ch. 11).

28. Douglas, *Natural Symbols*, 57.

29. Spickard, "Guide to Mary Douglas's Three Versions of Grid/Group Theory," 153.

30. Lingenfelter, "DNA of the Church."

31. Lingenfelter, "Possessions, Wealth, and the Cultural Identities of Persons."

32. Lingenfelter, "Why Do We Argue Over How to Help the Poor?"

33. Pattison, "Shame and the Unwanted Self"; Weaver, "Toward a Cross-cultural Theory of Leadership Emergence."

34. Russell et al., "Suits or Sandals."

35. Koeshall, "Toward a Theory of Dynamic Asymmetry and Redeemed Power.'"

36. Loewen, "Faith Vineyard Christian Fellowship."

37. Davis, "From Effervescence to Knowledge."

## Profile of Missiologists: Sherwood and Judith Lingenfelter

*(contemporary)*

*Sherwood's Education: BA, Wheaton College; PhD (anthropology) University of Pittsburgh*

*Judith's Education: BA Wheaton College; MLS State University of New York; PhD University of Pittsburgh*

*Sherwood's Occupation: Missionary to the Yap (Micronesia); Professor of intercultural studies and provost at Biola University and Fuller Theological Seminary*

*Judith's occupation: Missionary to the Yap (Micronesia); Professor of intercultural studies at Biola University*

Sherwood and Judith Lingenfelter are both career missionary-scholars who shaped the field of missiology by publishing on cross-cultural leadership, sustainability of community development projects, culture change, wealth in missions, church planting, contextual theology, homosexuality and gender identity, third culture kids, multicultural education, and ethnographic research methods.

One of the Lingenfelters' most significant contributions was the development and missiological application of the grid/group model, among other value orientations, in *Ministering Cross-culturally*. The Lingenfelters' reference of these value orientations as "social games" brought a bit of cultural relativism to evangelical missionaries.[1] Rather than insisting that all cultures must look like our own, we should play the hierarchy game in a hierarchal culture; and play the egalitarian game in an egalitarian culture.

---

[1] Lingenfelter and Mayers, *Ministering Cross-culturally*.

# Cross-cultural Leadership, Negotiation and Conflict Resolution

Contrary to Maxwell's contention that his 21 rules for leadership are irrefutable in all cultures,[38] many interculturalists have found that virtually all aspects of leadership and followership are impacted by cultural norms

---

38. Maxwell, *21 Irrefutable Laws of Leadership*, xx.

(as the Grid/Group Theory above would indicate). Culture guides how a leader is chosen, what the leader's duties are, how a leader is found to be legitimate, how a leader is deposed, the length of a leader's term, and how a leader's successor is chosen.

Certainly cultural value orientations like the grid/group above affect leadership norms. Cultures that lean toward uncertainty avoidance and collectivism do not reward leaders for being innovative—leaders and followers in these cultures are legitimate insofar as they reinforce the status quo. Lingenfelter,[39] Elmer,[40] and Livermore[41] have helped Christian leaders understand how cultural value orientations and culturally-determined communication patterns impact the way we lead across cultures. Much of this scholarship on Christian cross-cultural leadership also underscores the importance of creating rapport across cultures, and of modeling aspects of the Incarnation.

Missiologists have gathered culture-specific data on how leadership and followership vary across cultures. For example, Rupp studied the ways that millennial missionaries to China have different leadership models than the house church pastors.[42] Umer interviewed church leaders and laypeople in Ethiopia to understand models of leadership and followership there.[43] Others have studied how models of leadership differ among first—and second-generation immigrants.[44]

## Intercultural Adjustment

As Christians began crossing cultures to make disciples, missiologists were concerned that high rates of attrition (sometimes defined as failure to return to the field after a certain length of time overseas) could be attributed to difficulties in adjusting to the host culture.[45] Therefore,

39. Lingenfelter, *Leading Cross-culturally*.
40. Elmer, *Cross-cultural Servanthood*.
41. Livermore, *Leading with Cultural Intelligence*.
42. Rupp, *Sherpas and Shepherds*.
43. Umer, "Relational Theory of the Leadership-Followership Process."
44. Cho, "Understanding Leadership"; Hong, "Church Splits in Korean-American Churches"; Winney, "Impact of Strategic Planning Training."
45. It turns out that failure to get along with colleagues, health problems, and family problems all rank higher as contributing factors to missionary attrition than difficulties of adjusting to another culture do.

missiology has utilized studies on the acculturative process to help missionaries adjust better.

Little research has been done to understand factors that impact how missionaries adjust to other cultures. However, numerous studies have been done to understand factors in general that impact acculturation, including the impact of study abroad programs,[46] and the acculturative experiences of international students.[47]

## Acculturation

is the process of adjusting to another culture. Acculturation takes on several forms, including *assimilation* (losing one's heritage culture to fit in with the new culture), *separation* (finding co-ethnics to socialize with, and not assimilating to the new culture), and *integration* (retaining one's culture of heritage, but participating in the new culture).

## Enculturation

is the process of teaching cultural patterns to others.

Missiologists have picked up on these studies on acculturation to improve missionary work. Below I will discuss how interculturalists have contributed to understandings of culture shock and how they have defined and measured the competencies necessary for crossing cultures.

## Culture Shock Prevention

Crossing cultures can be disorienting. People in the host culture don't behave the way you would expect. You have lost your "props" that help you make sense of life. You find that you no longer know how to tell a joke, or buy groceries, let alone how to talk about things that matter. Kalvero Oberg described this disorienting phase as "culture shock."[48] But "shock" is probably not the best way to describe the experience. A better term is "change induced stress." Often the stress is manifested with complaining:

46. Granados, "Academic and Spiritual Impact of a Semester Abroad Program."
47. Chamberlain, "Factors Impacting Openness To Christianity."
48. Oberg, "Cultural Shock."

- "The food is terrible";
- "People never show up on time";
- "The people are so lazy"; or,
- "You have to bribe the police here."

In the mid-twentieth century, it was imagined that cultural adjustment must look like a U-curve. You start out in a "honeymoon phase" with the exciting new culture; then you are disoriented, disillusioned, and frustrated—you are practically a kindergartener as you learn all over again how to send a package at the post office, how to hail a taxi, and how to order at a restaurant. But as you become familiar in your new environment, you climb back up the U-curve as you reach a new homeostasis.

The U-curve theory (UCT) took on a number of adaptations. Gullahorn and Gullahorn modified this "u" model to look more like a "w."[49] The expatriate still experiences a "honeymoon phase," disillusionment, and adaptation. But eventually, he will receive a home assignment. He initially has anxiety about this, and his anxiety turns to a genuine depression as he experiences nostalgia for "the way things were in my heritage culture" as well as disappointment about the new life he is establishing. According to the "w" theory, a healthy individual will eventually work through this "reverse culture shock" and the line graph will ascend to normalcy.

Still other theorists developed other models to explain the psychological adjustment to a new culture. Young Yun Kim theorized adjustment was more like an upward spiral,[50] and so on. Interculturalists recognize that we adjust on different levels at different rates. And the *emotional* adjustment may very well follow something like a u-curve, whereas one's interpersonal skills or technical skills in a host culture may sharply increase without a dip. Ward has noted that sojourners experience acculturation on at least two levels: psychological and socio-cultural.[51] Indeed, our adjustment to the physical surroundings, to the workplace, and to interpersonal relationships will likely follow different trajectories.

While all these curves and spirals caught the imagination of missionary trainers, unfortunately, these models are usually not based on

49. Gullahorn and Gullahorn, "Extension of the U-Curve Hypothesis."
50. Kim, *Becoming Intercultural*.
51. Ward and Kennedy, "Psychological and Socio-Cultural Adjustment During Cross-Cultural Transitions."

empirical research. Kealey's study of 277 expatriates showed that while 50 percent of the sample experienced stress during adjustment, only about 10 percent of cross-cultural workers actually experience the typical "u" curve.[52] Therefore, the "u" curve is not really typical at all, calling into question the generalizability of the model.[53]

Even if no single model can capture what cultural adjustment is like, the experience does involve a level of adaptation. Storti[54] noted that culture-crossers really experience two different kinds of "flexing" as they adjust to another culture. On the one hand, when we move across cultures, we must change the behaviors we are doing which irritate people in the host culture. (We shouldn't order beef in parts of India where cows are sacred. American women may need to wear dresses in parts of the world where shorts are immodest). On the other hand, when we cross cultures, we also need to be flexible about behaviors and beliefs of people in our host culture that irritate us. (When I tried to drive anywhere in the South Pacific, ten to twenty people would jump in the back of my pickup. I was at first irritated; but then I had to remember, "I am the guest. Their behavior seems reasonable to them. I am the weird one for being irritated." I needed to be flexible).

Lingenfelter and Mayers caught on to the idea of flexing, and explained to the missionary world that cultural adjustment is not a zero-sum game: learning to be flexible with time orientation doesn't make the American missionary less American. Learning to respect authority in Japan does not make the Brazilian missionary any less Brazilian. In fact, letting these cultures change us can enrich us. Lingenfelter and Mayers referred to this give-and-take of cultural adjustment as becoming "150% persons."[55] The authors imagined that you relinquish, say, 25 percent of your heritage culture as your cross-cultural interactions challenge your assumptions. Perhaps you become less individualistic, or less consumeristic. And as you encounter other cultures, you add to your repertoire of vocabulary, perspectives, and experiences, taking on, say, 75 percent of the new culture. Thus resulting in a 150 percent person.

52. Kealey, "Study of Cross-cultural Effectiveness."
53. Jackson, *Introducing Language and Intercultural Communication*, 209.
54. Storti, *Art of Crossing Cultures*.
55. Lingenfelter and Mayers, *Ministering Cross-culturally*, 117–124.

INTERCULTURAL STUDIES & CROSS-CULTURAL DISCIPLESHIP 147

Note that the 150 percent person, like Reed's "bicultural approach,"[56] was formed in a time when missions involved crossing *one* culture. Yet in the twenty-first century, we've discovered that almost nobody works in exclusive bi-cultural settings. We are all regularly dealing with people from diverse cultural backgrounds. To be culturally intelligent doesn't mean giving up parts of your home culture and "becoming like" the Other. Instead, cultural intelligence is our ability to behave appropriately in any cultural context, and to communicate effectively with people from any cultural background. Below, I will discuss how intercultural studies and missiologists have tried to define and measure the competencies for crossing cultures.

## Competencies for Crossing Cultures

How would we define or measure cross-cultural effectiveness? Cross-cultural effectiveness could be defined as "achieving one's goals when crossing cultures." Such goals may include selling a certain number of products, logging a certain number of "decisions for Christ," completing a term in the field, or self-reporting high satisfaction in a cross-cultural context.

Yet what skills are necessary for being effective? Imagine a group of college students goes on a short-term mission trip to Mexico. One, a missionary kid (MK) who grew up in South America, knows Spanish and is familiar with South American cultures. She should do well on the mission trip. However, when the team arrives at their host church in Mexico, she keeps her ear buds in and hesitates getting off the church van to join in the activities. She has cultural knowledge, but lacks motivation. On the other hand, one enthusiastic teen on the mission team lacks Spanish skills, but wants to build rapport; so she goes around hugging everyone in sight. She has motivation but little cultural or linguistic knowledge. Other members of the team may know it's inappropriate to wear shorts in church, but refuse to leave their comfort zone, and wear the shorts anyway. They have knowledge, but do not change their behavior.[57]

---

56. Reed, *Preparing Missionaries for Intercultural Communication*.
57. This scenario is modified from Livermore, *Serving Jesus with Eyes Wide Open*, 113–15.

To move seamlessly across cultures, one must possess the knowledge, strategy, behavior, and motivation to cross other cultures.[58]

Numerous other interculturalists have developed models that describe cross-cultural competence.[59] Most of these models recognize that competence includes a combination of knowledge, skills, and abilities.[60] For example, drawing from Vygotsky's Social Learning Theory, Chen's intercultural communication competence model involves the cognitive, affective, and behavioral domains.[61] While the vocabularies differ slightly among theorists, the competencies tend to include flexibility, tolerance, humility, empathy, autonomy, and the ability to work in teams.[62] Intercutluralists then go on to develop instruments that measure each of these traits, such as Bennett's *Ethnocentric Stages of Development*,[63] the Multicultural Personality Questionnaire,[64] or the Intercultural Adjustment Potential Scale.[65] And the Cultural Intelligence (CQ) instrument measures a subject's self-perception in these four areas, to predict a subject's effectiveness in working across cultures. Some empirical studies have correlated high CQ scores with quantifiable outcomes like low levels of culture shock.[66]

Yet as much as MNCs and mission agencies would like to know objectively whether their candidates possess flexibility, tolerance, etc., there is no reliable way to measure these traits. All the intercultural competence instruments rely on self-reporting—rather than measuring whether a subject is tolerant, they really just measure the extent to which a subject believes himself to be tolerant. This inherent weakness in the instrument calls into question whether these instruments can actually predict cross-cultural effectiveness.

---

58. Livermore, *Cultural Intelligence*.

59. Many of the models in this section are well summarized in LaClare, *Wearing Different Hats*.

60. Cross et al., *Towards a Culturally Competent System of Care*, iv-v; Lonborg and Bowen, "Counselors, Communities, and Spirituality"; Pope et al., "Multicultural Competence in Student Affairs."

61. Chen, "Relationships of the Dimensions of Intercultural Communication Competence."

62. Ruben, "Guidelines for Cross-Cultural Communication Effectiveness."

63. Bennett, "Towards a Developmental Model of Intercultural Sensitivity."

64. Van der Zee and Van Oudenhoven, "Multicultural Personality Questionnaire."

65. Matsumoto et al., "Development and Validation."

66. Ang and Van Dyne, *Handbook of Cultural Intelligence*.

## Conclusion

This chapter provides an overview of how missiologists use intercultural studies in their models and theories of cross-cultural discipleship. I reviewed three main themes in intercultural studies: intercultural communication, intercultural adjustment, and intercultural leadership. These lenses each have their own, longer histories in academia; but each has been more recently incorporated by missiologists in order to facilitate the task of making disciples across cultures. Being highly interdisciplinary, ICS has taken on many other inquiries, including post-colonial criticism and racial identity studies. And missiologists are applying these lines of inquiry to their studies of missions as well. In fact, most of the theories discussed in chapters 9 and 10 are influenced by ICS.

## Move into Action

How often do you hear cultural stereotyping that unfairly portrays another culture as backward, exotic, unchanging, or simplistic? Use the tools discussed above to promote understanding across cultures, for the sake of building rapport.

## Ideas for Further Research

In previous decades, research in intercultural studies focused on comparing value orientations between cultures. More up to date missiological-oriented ICS research could include the following types of studies:

1. Collect actual speech about religious topics between people in specific cultural settings, and demonstrate the degree to which intercultural communication theory explains or fails to explain those features.
2. Perform qualitative studies on how people in specific culture groups avow their cultural identity, and how they diverge from or contest attestations about their cultural identities.
3. Research how people actually experience culture shock and deal with it, rather than relying on older models that were not developed through empirical research.
4. Decide how you would measure cross-cultural effectiveness.

## Review Questions:

1. Give examples of how miscommunication happens when people from different cultures interact.
2. How does ICS differ from anthropology?

## Reflection Questions:

1. Are there principles of leadership which are true in all cultures?
2. Describe a way you have significantly changed, due to your experiences of crossing cultures.

*Chapter 6*

# Connecting Development Theories to Cross-Cultural Discipleship[1]

## Julie Martinez and Kenneth Nehrbass

EVANGELICAL THINKERS LIKE BRYANT Myers, Ron Sider, and Richard Stearns revolutionized missiology by showing how cross-cultural discipleship is tied to issues of poverty and injustice: While discipleship is about equipping people to carry out the first commandment (Gen 1:28, be fruitful and multiply, fill the earth and enjoy/subdue it) and to obey the most important commandments (to love God and others), people in every culture have broken relationships with God, their government, their land, their peers, and themselves. These broken relationships impede them from flourishing and multiplying. Discipleship can often be instrumental in restoring these relationships, and can empower people to flourish in their relationships with God, social groups, their nation and their land.

This chapter describes how evangelical missiologists have connected theories of development with their models for development-as-missions. First, we need to address a troublesome chapter in the history of missiology: missiologists were deeply divided in the twentieth century over the role of development.

---

1. Portions of this chapter are modified from Martinez, "Transformational Development Outcomes in Cambodia."

## Chapter Goals

*Knowledge goals:*

- Describe the holistic nature of discipleship.

*Action goals:*

- Discover ways you can be engaged in advocacy on behalf of a marginalized group.
- Learn the needs of a marginalized group, and see how you can help them restore the broken relationships that cause that marginalization.

*Heart goals:*

- Commit to obeying the first commandment (Gen 1:28), the greatest commandments, and the Great Commission (Matt 28:19–20).

## The Great Schism Over Development-As-Missions

Even though Jesus clearly linked discipleship with justice and social action (Luke 4:19–22), twentieth-century missiology was plagued over the question of whether social action is an equal or subservient partner to the proclamation of the gospel. Between the 1930s and 1980s, many mainline churches changed their missions-focus from proclamation to social actions: Working with orphans, civil rights, digging wells, protecting the environment, and later, issues like economic development and sex trafficking became more prominent whereas proclamation faded to the background. What led to this shift? Did the world all of a sudden have more physical suffering than ever? Was the world so well evangelized that proclamation was no longer a major push for missionaries?

There are actually several reasons for the mid-century shift from evangelism to social uplift. Some are genuine issues or problems that should inform our missiology (e.g., decolonization and abject poverty). Such issues should lead us to do cross-cultural work that is holistic and addresses physical needs. Other influences (e.g., secularism and communism) have served as distractions to missions. Eight reasons for the shift are listed below. Note how the controversial nature of some of these reasons has fomented the controversy over the role of social action as a missionary strategy:

1) Secularization. As western society began to separate issues of faith from "real life," even church-goers, clergy, and mission leaders in the mainline churches thought less and less about the supernatural, heaven, sin, and forgiveness. Church, and the work of the church, was only valuable insofar as it had a secular value such as promoting peace, education, or development.[2]

2) Communism. The experiment of Marxist-style socialism had a tremendous influence in South America in the 1960s and 1970s. This ideology influenced Latin American theologians and missionaries. "Outreach" was re-imagined as a program of ushering in the revolution (which became coterminous with the "Kingdom of God"). The work of missions became about equality, or really, about upending the established political and economic systems.[3]

3) Civil rights abuses. The world saw tremendous suffering and abuse of humans in the twentieth century, and Christians grappled with their role in perpetuating or alleviating these problems.

4) The stigma of fundamentalism. If fundamentalists were seen as culturally-clueless evangelists who only wanted to make converts, mainline missionaries wanted to distance themselves from this image by emphasizing a different missionary approach.

5) A reaction to the church growth movement. Donald McGavran and David Hesselgrave emphasized that missions is not just about proclamation, but persuasion: The church must be growing or missionaries are not doing their job. The multiplication model made sense to evangelical missionaries, but was controversial to mainline missionaries. The distaste for such an emphasis on numerical growth and persuasion led mainline missiologists to focus more on other areas of mission.

---

2. Rauschenbusch, *Theology for the Social Gospel.*
3. Novak, *Will It Liberate?*

6) Anti-establishment rebellion of the 1960s. Many theologians of the 1980s and 1990s grew up during the hippie movements of the 1960s and 1970s. Jesus was envisioned as a wandering magician whose main purpose was to upset the established conservative religious and political system of the day.[4] This anti-establishment, free-thinking attitude permeated missiology in mainline seminaries. Religion was only good insofar as it promoted peace; and evangelism was seen as divisive.

7) Decolonization. As nations gained their independence from Europe between the 1950s and the 1990s, the image of the European missionary who comes to teach or transform was increasingly challenged—both in the west and in the global south. The mainline church either called for a moratorium on missionaries from the West,[5] or for a re-imagining of the role of Westerners: No longer would western missionaries preach and teach, they would learn and serve.

8) Social problems. The famines, wars, earthquakes, tsunamis that have such devastating impacts on the global south captured the hearts of many missionaries.

As some mainline churches sidelined proclamation in favor of social action, evangelicals and fundamentalists became wary of portraying their work as humanitarian, lest they be confused with theologies that moved away from orthodoxy. Evangelicals arguably stayed highly involved in issues of justice, education, medicine, relief; but missionaries were sensitive to the fact that their supporting constituencies might pull their funding if they suspected the missionaries were "distracted" by social effort, at the expense of evangelism and discipleship.

## Evangelical Answers to the "Social Gospel" Schism

Much of the twentieth-century debate between social gospel and prioritism (an emphasis on proclamation) is really a strawman argument: Christians have, in practice, not particularly separated word from deed. Even staunch priorititsts, when working in dire conditions due to war and poverty, often meet the needs of those around them. Remember

4. Crossan, *Historical Jesus*.
5. Castro, "Moratorium."

Latuorette's comments (in ch. 3) about foot binding, etc. Protestants often see education as essential for discipleship, thus lifting people out of poverty. Escobar and Driver argued that Protestantism has historically had numerous other modernizing effects, as reform governments voice a "preference for the Protestant presence." Often Protestants are framers of democratic constitutions.[6] Woodberry has masterfully shown that Christian missionaries brought healthcare, democracy, market activities, and education.[7]

Sociologist Rodney Stark put it this way:

> To cities filled with the homeless and impoverished, Christianity offered charity as well as hope. To cities filled with newcomers and strangers, Christianity offered an immediate basis for attachments. To cities filled with orphans and widows, Christianity provided a new and expanded sense of family. To cities torn by violent strife, Christianity offered a new basis for social solidarity. And to cities faced with epidemics, fires and earthquakes, Christianity offered effective nursing services.[8]

Consider the following ways that missionaries were involved in empowering the marginalized:[9]

- Nevius introduced orchards in Shantung (now Shandong) China;
- Basel missionaries introduced coffee in Ghana;
- James McKean Eliminated smallpox, malaria, and leprosy in Thailand;
- Missionaries helped abolish "blackbirding" in the Pacific;
- Missionaries abolished forced labor in Congo;
- William Carey "waged war" against *sati* (widow emollition) in India; and,
- Moravian missionaries brought about the abolition of the slave trade in the Virgin Islands and Surinam.

However, evangelicals were divided throughout the twentieth century over the place that social action had in missions work. Some

---

6. Escobar and Driver, *Christian Mission and Social Justice*, 22–40.
7. Woodberry, "Missionary Roots of Liberal Democracy."
8. Stark, *Rise of Christianity*, 161.
9. Dennis, *Christian Missions and Social Progress*.

believed social action would be a necessary consequence of evangelism: As societies came under the rule of God, governments would treat people justly, people would get educations, and economies would thrive. Others believed social activity would be a suitable "bridge to evangelism." The Lausanne Committee for World Evangelism eventually settled on a third option, called holistic mission: "Social activity not only follows evangelism as its consequence and aim, and precedes it as its bridge, but also accompanies it as its *partner*."[10]

In 1983 the World Evangelical Fellowship Consultation on the Church in Response to Human Need in Wheaton, IL arrived at a similar conclusion: "the mission of the church includes both proclamation of the Gospel and its demonstration."[11] "Only by spreading the Gospel can the most basic need of human beings be met: to have fellowship with God."[12]

This approach came to be known as integral mission. Rene Padilla explained,

> Integral mission or holistic transformation is the proclamation and demonstration of the gospel. It is not simply that evangelism and social involvement are to be done alongside each other. Rather, in integral mission our proclamation has social consequences as we call people to love and repentance in all areas of life. And our social involvement has evangelistic consequences as we bear witness to the transforming grace of Jesus Christ.[13]

Social action, as a missionary method, is as old as Christianity. It is rooted in the cultural mandate and in Jesus's inaugural address in Luke 4:18–19 (as he read from Isa 61):

> The Spirit of the Lord is on me,
>   because he has anointed me
>   to proclaim good news to the poor.
> He has sent me to proclaim freedom for the prisoners
>   and recovery of sight for the blind,
>   to set the oppressed free,
>   to proclaim the year of the Lord's favor. (NIV)

---

10. Stott, "Evangelism and Social Responsibility," sec. 4 c, *emphasis in original*.
11. Samuel and Sugden, *Church in Response to Human Need*, sec 26.
12. Samuel and Sugden, *Church in Response to Human Need*, "Introduction."
13. Micah Network, "Micah Network Declaration on Integral Mission," 1.

Being a follower of Jesus involves caring for the widow, the orphan, the poor, and advocating for those who are treated unjustly (Prov 31:9, Isa 58:1–3, 5–10). The Old Testament has a robust theology of flourishing; God's plan for meeting the world's needs was that the Israelites would live as part of God's covenant community. This kingdom community included the godly characteristics of kindness/faithfulness (*hesed*), and compassion (Exod 22:21–22; Ps 82:3–4; Jer 22:3). Sider avers "All strands of biblical literature display major concern for the poor, hungry, and oppressed, even though diverse strands emerged in very different historical settings over the course of two millennia of history."[14] A great deal of the biblical message focuses on issues of flourishing, such as: justice, treatment of the poor, care for the widow, sojourner, and the orphan. In fact, as Stearns pointed out, if we took away all these passages on justice, compassion and poverty, we would have a major "hole in our gospel."[15]

Social action is not limited to the four works Christ expressly mentioned in his inaugural address (good news to the poor, freedom for the captive, sight for the blind, and release of the oppressed). Such empowerment involves (but is not limited to) anything that keeps people from flourishing, including the current pressing global needs:

- Hunger;
- Unsanitary conditions and unsafe water;
- Disease: AIDS, polio, TB, typhoid, etc.;
- Homelessness;
- Refugees;
- Orphans, left behind children;
- Social unrest due to income inequality;
- Addictions;
- Trafficking, sex crimes, and slavery;
- Education inequality and illiteracy;
- Racism and ethnic conflict;
- Tyrants and rebels;
- Environmental destruction; and
- Women and children at risk of abortion

---

14. Sider, *Rich Christians in an Age of Hunger*, x.
15. Stearns, *Hole in Our Gospel.*

When Mary discovered she was pregnant with the Son of God, she sang a *magnificat* that predicted a God-directed society which would upend these social injustices (Luke 1:52–53). The hungry would be fed, and prideful rulers would be dethroned. The Messiah's reign brings in a more just kingdom where people flourish. For missionaries throughout history, especially in the industrial age, community development (education, entrepreneurship, training in sanitation, etc.) have been the route for helping people flourish.

And in fact, today, many evangelicals take it as a given that cross-cultural discipleship must entail restoring these relationships between God, self, land, others and government. Missionaries are increasingly entering the field to engage in social uplift. Evangelism and discipleship was the primary activity for 65 percent of missionaries in 1998, whereas 15 percent said their primary activity was relief and development. In 2016, the number of those primary engaged in evangelism and discipleship moved down to 44 percent, whereas those whose primary activity was relief and development moved up to 23 percent.[16]

## Theories that Inform Community Development

Much of development discourse focuses on concepts of improvement. What needs improving and how it is improved depends on who is having the conversation. Some would say that "there can be no fixed and final definition of development, only suggestions of what development should imply in particular contexts."[17] Yet development theory is closely intertwined with economic theories. As scholars argued competing theories about how economies grow, conflicting strategies for aiding the development of poorer communities were also developed.

### Development as the Westerner's Burden

The end of World War II is a significant marker for development theory and practice.[18] Many theorists define the launching point of modern

---

16. Newell, *North American Mission Handbook*, 58.
17. Hettne, *Development Theory and the Three Worlds*, 15.
18. Knutsson, "Intellectual History of Development"; Pieterse, "After Post-Development"; Thorbecke, "Evolution of the Development Doctrine and the Role of Foreign Aid."

development theory and the modern era of development with Truman's declaration in 1949: "The old imperialism—exploitation for foreign profit—has no place in our plans. What we envisage is a program of development based on the concepts of democratic, fair dealings."[19]

The end of the war marked a ramping up of modernization and an intensified belief that modernity could save the world.[20] The war also accelerated the decolonization process due to the crises facing impoverished states of the European nations and their inability to maintain their empires. Two world powers stepped into the power vacuum created by decolonization: the United States and the Soviet Union. Due to the political and economic positional polarity of both superpowers, competition for dominance led to the notion that a lack of development in surrounding nations is a threat to national security at home.[21] The modern conception of US development theory was birthed out of fear—the fear of the rampant spread of communism and the need to contain it.[22] US efforts in community development were imagined to contain the threat of communism.

## Modernization and Development

The Big Push Theory characterized development in the 1950s. This theory included large-scale investment in many different sectors and the planned industrialization of underdevelopment countries. Industrialization was seen as "the engine of growth."[23] The influx of foreign aid was to intended to trigger international and domestic economic growth and thwart the spread of communism. Development was seen as being equal to economic growth[24] and the GNP was the all-encompassing measurement of this growth.[25] Mainstream development in this era was based on modernization and Keynesian economics where the GNP played a starring role.

19. Truman, "Inaugural Address."
20. Pieterse, "After Post-Development."
21. Knutsson, "Intellectual History of Development."
22. Rist, *History of Development*.
23. Thorbecke, "Evolution of the Development Doctrine and the Role of Foreign Aid," 5.
24. Thorbecke, "Evolution of the Development Doctrine and the Role of Foreign Aid"; Hettne, *Development Theory and the Three Worlds*.
25. Knutsson, "Intellectual History of Development."

Many western economists in the 1960s were highly optimistic about world-scale modernization and development. This decade is known as the "heyday of modernization."[26] Walt Rostow, an advisor to both President Kennedy and President Johnson, later articulated and coalesced modernization theory in his seminal book, *The Stages of Economic Growth: A non-Communist Manifesto*.[27] Rostow mapped out the blueprint for a country's modernization process by detailing a five-stage economic progression that each nation would pass through on the way to modernization. The process starts with a traditional (exchange-based) economy and ultimately ends with industrialization and mass consumption. "The success of Rostow's book was thus due not to its originality but, on the contrary, to its roots in a tradition that assured for it a certain legitimacy."[28] Rostow's influential Stages of Growth model also shaped and informed US foreign aid for two decades; linking foreign policy with development theory.[29]

The sixties did mark a significant change in development with the creation of aid agencies. USAID was founded in 1961, and the United Nations established the United Nations Development Program (UNDP) in 1965. Additionally, many humanitarian relief organizations (secular and Christian) began to include development activities as a standard service. These included organizations such as World Vision, Oxfam, Catholic Relief Services, Tear Fund, and others.

## Alternative Development

Although the 1960s introduced changes to the theory and practice of development through the creation of aid organizations, it was in the 1970s that clear lines began to be drawn with a new participatory and people-centered approach.[30] The Gross National Product (GNP) as the sole measurement of development began to be questioned. Suspicions increased regarding the effectiveness of the trickle-down theory, which was the backbone behind the macro-level policies of Walter Rostow[31] and

26. Knutsson, "Intellectual History of Development," 12.
27. Rostow, *Stages of Economic Growth*.
28. Rist, *History of Development*, 103.
29. Reid-Henry, *Political Origins of Inequality*.
30. Pieterse, "After Post-Development."
31. Rostow, *Stages of Economic Growth*.

Milton Friedman.[32] Many remained poor despite their nation's growing GNP. The new primary objective of aid was not the increase of the GNP, rather, the goal was to increase the standard of living for the poor.[33]

Increasingly, grassroots movements were replacing top-down approaches to development. Development was shifting to a basic needs approach. Many governments became decentralized, thus granting people greater voice when it came to making decisions about the services they required. Using the basic needs approach, development policies were being directed at the poorest of the poor. As Yusuf and Stigletz note,

> It is now clear that trickle-down, which can take many years to reach the lower income levels, must be supplemented by policies of inclusion that lessen sharp disparities in incomes and assets, enhance human capital accumulation and employment opportunities, and help provide safety nets for the more vulnerable elements of a society.[34]

Development continued to be redefined in the eighties and nineties; and modernization theory lost sway as postmodernism impacted all areas of thought. Many academics no longer believed that modernization was the route for improving the life of the poor. Even mainstream development no longer focused exclusively on economic growth.[35] During this time, development practitioners placed a greater emphasis on the culture and values of poor and indigenous societies,[36] and human development became the bottom line objective.[37] Thus the United Nations introduced the Human Development Index (HDI) as an alternative to the GNP for measuring progress or development.

## Transformational Development Theory

Transformational Development (TD) is rooted in the tenets of the Christian faith, specifically targeting the redeeming power of the gospel to achieve positive social, economic, and Christian spiritual change. TD

---

32. Friedman, *Capitalism and Freedom*.

33. Thorbecke, "Evolution of the Development Doctrine and the Role of Foreign Aid."

34. Yusuf and Stigletz, "Development Issues," 232.

35. Pieterse, "After Post-Development."

36. Sen, "Well-Being, Agency and Freedom."

37. Ranis, "Human Development and Economic Growth."

seeks to transform those conditions which obstruct the poor and prevent them from improving their well-being.[38] Faith in the redeeming and transformative power of God is an essential feature of transformational development theory.

The term transformational development was born out of the Wheaton Statement of 1983 entitled "Transformation—the Church in Response to Human Need."[39] The Wheaton Statement refined this definition of transformation as "the change from a condition of human existence contrary to God's purposes to one in which people can enjoy fullness of life in harmony with God." The term transformation was chosen to ensure that Transformational Development agencies do not simply practice development like secular agencies and then tack on a prayer meeting at the end to maintain their Christianity. It was produced as a result of wrestling with the tension between social action and evangelism.[40] The term transformation was used to forge an integral relationship between both evangelism and social responsibility.[41]

The unique contribution of Christians to development is the creation of a new community "where all relationships are being redeemed."[42] Development has "salvific intent"[43] as it seeks a positive change materially, socially, and spiritually in the life of the poor. Spiritual transformation is key. "In this way, TD seeks faith acquisition as the seed for development, from which material and social transformation can be pursued."[44] TD begins with a vision for the future that is implemented in the now.[45]

### Recovering Identity—Spiritual Transformation

At the heart of transformational development is the desire to help others uncover their true identity. Part of discovering this identity is finding the answers to fundamental questions. The biggest and most important

---

38. Woolnough, "Christian NGOs in Relief and Development."
39. Sugden, "Transformational Development."
40. Sugden, "Transformational Development."
41. Vinay and Sugden, *Missions as Transformation*.
42. Sider in Bragg, "Beyond Development to Transformation," 165.
43. Sugden, *Gospel, Culture and Transformation*, 40.
44. Gorlorwulu and Rahschulte, "Organizational and Leadership Implications for Transformational Development," 200.
45. Sugden, "Transformational Development."

question is "Who am I?" Two other questions are key in transformational development. They are "Where am I going?" and "What am I worth?" All three issues comprise aspects of identity. Scripture answers these questions by revealing the true identity of every human being—we are known by God, being loved by God, and being made in the image of God.

When addressing issues of identity with the poor, it is important to grasp the impact that poverty has had upon the identity of the world's poorest people.[46] Jakumar Christian has written about "marred identity" as the most fundamental and debilitating impact on the poor.[47] The psychological impact of poverty cannot be underestimated. This marred identity can be likened to miasma. Miasma is like slime that seeps "into people's fundamental sense of their value, threatening their global sense of self."[48] "For most practitioners, addressing this embedded sense of powerlessness is one of the most difficult challenges when working with the poor and oppressed."[49]

Prilleltensky speaks of "human interactions being 'marred' by disrespect, exclusion, humiliation and erasure of identity."[50] Poverty brings a diminishing sense of self and identity and chronic shame. At every turn and in every way the poor's feelings of inferiority, lack of agency, sense of powerlessness, lack of voice, and oppression is reinforced and perpetuated by the existing cultural systems, political and power systems, community relationships, and the poor's current physical reality. As Myers put it, "marred identity is the perceived inability to act because individuals have come to believe that they have neither the right nor the social space to do so."[51] Marred identity produces hopelessness and deep shame.

Shame is not just an individual matter, but it is highly social. Poverty can create a marred identity that can also lead to chronic shame, which is an "unwanted, polluting condition for groups."[52] Chronic shame is produced by rejection, marginalization, objectification, or boundary

---

46. Christian, *God of the Empty-handed*; Myers, "Progressive Pentecostalism, Development, and Christian Development NGOs."

47. Christian, *God of the Empty-handed*.

48. Pattison, "Shame and the Unwanted Self," 17.

49. Myers, "Progressive Pentecostalism, Development, and Christian Development NGOs," 117.

50. Prilleltensky, "Poverty and Power," 6.

51. Myers, *Walking with the Poor*, 127.

52. Pattison, "Shame and the Unwanted Self," 13.

invasion that causes the person to feel inferior, worthless, abandoned, isolated, defiled, depleted, and in pain.

Transformational change within an individual possessing a marred identity and chronic shame is a painstakingly slow process. There are no Superman miracles. Transformation requires the gradual "surrendering and rebuilding of identity."[53] Identity reconstruction can only be achieved by and through the power and love of the Holy Spirit. Hope is a powerful ingredient in the remaking of an individual.

### Material Transformation and an Understanding of Poverty

The rhetoric of development and poverty has over the past few decades come to be redefined and relabeled. Robert Chambers introduced the concept of *poverty as entanglement* where the poor are entangled in a poverty trap of material poverty, physical weakness, powerlessness, isolation, and vulnerability.[54] Chambers defined development as a move from ill-being to well-being.[55] John Friedman proposed that poverty is derived from a lack of access to social power in which the household is under the influence of power from four different domains: state power, political power, economic power, and social power.[56] Pieterse countered with the idea that "poverty is not simply a deficit."[57] He and others believe that the western view of poverty is pauperizing.

Myers agreed that poverty reduction is certainly a component of material transformation, and he used the term *physical sustainability* to describe material transformation of the poor.[58] Physical sustainability is the ability to create wealth. Yet Myers noted that many other levels of transformation are necessary.

Amartya Sen also broadened the concept of development to include various levels of freedom. Sen describes underdevelopment and development with the terms "unfreedom" and "freedom." Anything that is an impediment to freedom is an unfreedom. Underdevelopment is seen broadly in the form of unfreedom and development is considered as a process of "removing unfreedoms and extending the substantive

53. Pattison, "Shame and the Unwanted Self," 19.
54. Chambers, *Rural Development*.
55. Chambers, "Poverty and Livelihoods."
56. Friedman, *Empowerment*.
57. Pieterse, "After Post-Development," 177.
58. Myers, *Walking with the Poor*.

freedoms of different types that people have reason to value."⁵⁹ Sen's thinking about poverty can be summarized as follows: Poverty is a lack of choices, and a lack of choices equals less freedom.

Succinctly put, the discourse on development and poverty is no longer just about economics but is more holistic. It involves the well-being of the whole person. But TD is not just about empowering individuals to recover their sense of identity and generate wealth, it is about transforming society as well.

## Social Transformation

If the cause of poverty is broken relationships (relationship to God and others), then the "transformational process must begin and end with different kinds of relationships."⁶⁰ The recognized contributions of broken systems are the roadblocks they create for bringing substantive change and transformation. Vinay and Sugden defined TD as enabling

> God's vision of society to be actualized in all relationships, social, economic, spiritual, political so that God's will may be reflected in human society and his love experienced by all communities, especially the poor.⁶¹

In many nations, systems are established and maintained to protect power and to keep the poor impoverished. TD seeks to bring reconciliation to relationships—between the powerful and the powerless; between rich and the poor. A biblical example of this principle is found in the exodus. This event displays God's concern for the powerless and showcases his ongoing engagement with the powerful.⁶² God desires the powerful to spend their power on behalf of the powerless.

## Postcolonial Responses to Development

Postcolonial thought has also weighed in on development theories by critically interpreting the effects of colonization. Critics argue that the colonial era produced uneven relationships between Western empires and their colonies. Today, even as many of those nations have

---

59. Sen, *Development as Freedom*, 86.
60. Myers, *Walking with the Poor*, 185.
61. Vinay and Sugden, *Missions as Transformation*, cover page.
62. Crouch, *Culture Making*.

gained independence, the asymmetrical relationships are perpetuated in globalization through the peddling of Western ideology, culture, knowledge, and business practices.[63] The vast differences between the global north and the global south are apparent. The realities of this power distance sensitize missiologists to the issues facing the global south, as they look at how development is related to access to resources (including knowledge and money), a balance of power, and a quest for agency and self-determination. For example, Western stakeholders and Western funds usually drive the development model, indicating that there is "a decidedly postcolonial grammar"[64] embedded in the community development discourse. It is recognized increasingly that development is about power—its operations, its geographies, and its highly uneven distribution and strategies for achieving it. The analysis of power is therefore central to contemporary development studies.[65]

Deep within the development dialogue and debate there is an "unconscious" ethnocentrism.[66] Postcolonial theory also seeks to address the spacial incongruities that exist in development with such terms as the third world. "Post colonialism, therefore, attempts to re-write the hegemonic accounting of time (history) and the spatial distribution of knowledge (power) that constructs the Third World."[67] Postcolonial theory also recognizes that nomenclature is tied to power. Words create worlds. It also must be acknowledged that in modernization theory, knowledge is controlled and produced by the West.[68] Post-colonialism seeks to give the marginalized a voice by seeking to increase agency among the poor and oppressed.

Postcolonial Community Development theories incorporate Said's theory of Orientalism[69] to understand how the Oriental v. Occidental dyad affects today's development discourse: How do unacknowledged biases and prejudices affect development projects?

---

63. Zhang, "Global-Local Dialectic in Postcolonial Approaches in Communication Studies," 91.

64. Krishnaswamy, "Postcolonial and Globalization Studies," 3.

65. McEwan, "Postcolonialism, Feminism and Development"; Crush, *Power of Development*; Radcliffe, "Popular and State Discourses of Power."

66. McEwan, "Postcolonialism, Feminism and Development."

67. McEwan, "Postcolonialism, Feminism and Development," 95.

68. McEwan, "Postcolonialism, Feminism and Development."

69. Said, *Orientalism*.

## Profile of a Missiologist: René Padilla

*(contemporary)*

*Education: BA and MA from Wheaton College; PhD (New Testament) from University of Manchester, UK*

*Occupation: Parachurch administrator, author (theologian), professor*

Born into a poor Christian family in Quito, Ecuador; René Padilla was raised in an environment that was anti-evangelical, and educated in a system that was Marxist with atheistic leanings. After attending Wheaton College, he returned to South America to work for the International Fellowship of Evangelical Students; but he noticed that his excellent Bible training had not prepared him "for the sort of theological reflection that was urgently needed in a revolutionary situation!"[1]

At this point, Latin American theologians like Gustavo Gutierrez were introducing a new hermeneutic: Socialists in Latin America wanted a revolution, and they found legitimization in the book of Exodus for expelling the capitalist bourgeoisie. Conversion came to mean solidarity with the poor; the kingdom of God was equated with a socialist movement. Missions was conflated with revolution. "The building of a just society . . . to participate in the process of liberation is already, in a certain sense, a salvific work."[2]

In the West, mainline churches were also redefining missions in terms of ecumenism and social justice. Evangelicals pushed back by avoiding any discourse that appeared to be tied to the social gospel. They continued to engage in justice and improving the lives of the poor, but they spoke of the priority of evangelism. So both liberal and evangelical movements created a "false dichotomy between evangelism and social justice."[3]

Padilla, along with Orlando Costas, and Samuel Escobar helped form a response to Liberation Theology which was not only relevant for Latin America, but for the global evangelical missionary movement. This response became known as "integral mission," a conceptualization of missions that attends to the needs of the mind, body, and soul. This refreshing missiology impelled the Lausanne Congress to define "Christian Social Responsibility."[4] Padilla devoted his career to the holistic gospel, becoming the international president of Tearfund, president of the Micah Network, and General Secretary of the Kairos Foundation.

While Padilla brought social justice into mainstream evangelical missiology, his approach toward justice, poverty, and equality from 1974 to the present has reflected the Marxist underpinning of development theory.[5] Padilla is against multinational corporations and seems to view capitalism as responsible for the poverty in the global south. "The main (though by no means the only) reason for the material poverty that prevents millions and millions of people from covering their basic needs is the spiritual poverty of a small minority of Mammon worshippers in the transnational class generated by corporate capitalism."[6] Because modernization theory is still a dominant model in international development, Padilla's missiology is more relevant when he speaks about holism than when he gets into areas of economics.

---

[1] Padilla, "My Theological Pilgrimage," 97.
[2] Gutierrez, *Theology of Liberation*, 72.
[3] George, "Constructing Latin American Missiology," 32.
[4] Atallah, "Tribute to René Padilla and Samuel Escobar."
[5] George, "John R. W. Stott and C. René Padilla Critiqued," 38.
[6] Padilla, "Globalization of Greed," 43.

## Evaluating Development Strategies

Are there community development efforts that work and ones that don't? While many community development organizations perform assessments on their projects, empirical research on CD is hard to find, hard to read, and hard to interpret. Development organizations especially do not make it easy to find assessments on projects that failed, even though this information can be very helpful to theorists and practitioners. Below we will discuss two ways in which CD has been evaluated with empirical evidence: studies on the efficacy of community involvement, and studies that measure the improvement of peoples' lives.

### The Efficacy of Community Participation

The level of oversight in development projects ranges from paternalistic, to guided, to non-directed. It is unlikely that any modality or sodality which supports missions through empowerment would describe itself as paternalistic; nonetheless, an organization run by expatriates which determines the needs in a community, the manner for addressing those needs, and the metrics for success, would be paternalistic. For example, certain large churches hire indigenous church leaders and require them to send reports based on the sponsoring church's metrics. This model would be fall somewhere between "guided" and "paternalistic."

In recent decades, many involved in missions-as-community-development have become sensitive to paternalistic models, because in addition to being unsustainable (when the sponsor withdraws, the money dries up), they demean the receiver by taking away agency and perpetuating a victim status, or at least a receiver status. To combat this, Myers,[70] Corbett et al.,[71] and Lupton[72] offer guided models for missions-as-empowerment, such as Asset Based Community Development (ABCD) or Participatory Learning and Action (PLA). The participatory models encourage marginalized communities to identify the problems they face, understand the resources they have to address those issues, and select pathways for addressing those problems.

---

70. Myers, *Walking with the Poor*.
71. Corbett et al., *When Helping Hurts*.
72. Lupton, *Toxic Charity*.

Some researchers have carried out empirical research to assess the effectiveness of participatory models. One study showed that PLA and lecture methods have about equivalent effectiveness, and could be used in combination.[73] PLA is especially effective when addressing issues that require self-reflection[74] or when the goal is to connect "ideas, assets and people."[75] Therefore, PLA may be most useful when the goal (and not just the process) is to have communities value their resources and relationships. For example, one short-term project aimed at encouraging young people to maintain their residence in a rural Wisconsin town showed that over four years people felt more positive about their hometown because of the ABCD process.[76] In fact, ABCD and PLA seem to be most effective when the goals of the project are better reached through community accountability, such as quitting smoking[77] or paying back micro loans.

Participatory strategies may have a much wider utility. Some public health studies show that PLA projects aimed at neo-natal health in LDCs decreased infant mortality;[78] therefore this type of community involvement has been judged to be a cost-effective way of decreasing illness connected to poor sanitation.[79]

Others believe that even a moderate amount of oversight such as PLA or ABCD is paternalistic. These practitioners want sponsors to just send money, without interfering in the process by providing planning and oversight. Examples include the charity Give Directly, which provides internal and external empirical research that suggests sending money to Africa without strings attached leads to outcomes of better health, education, and empowerment of women.[80] It may be fair to place Operation Christmas Child or Toys for Tots in this category, since these

---

73. Kamath and Udavakiran, "Effectiveness of Participatory Learning Activity."

74. Stuttaford and Coe, "The 'Learning' Component of Participatory Learning."

75. Yeneabat and Butterfield, "We Can't Eat a Road."

76. Andresen, "Evaluating an Asset-Based Effort to Attract and Retain Young People."

77. McGeechan et al., "A Coproduction Community Based Approach to Reducing Smoking Prevalence."

78. Seward et al., "Effects of Women's Groups Practising Participatory Learning and Action."

79. Sinha et al., "Economic Evaluation of Participatory Learning and Action."

80. Haushofer and Shapiro, *Short-term Impact of Unconditional Cash Transfers to the Poor*.

models for empowerment involve the redistribution of wealth in the form of children's toys and clothing, without a great deal of oversight, sustainability, or conditions for receiving the gifts.

### Measuring the Improvement of People's Lives

When we travel to some of the world's poorest communities, we have seen community health buildings that have been converted to personal living quarters; we discovered water pumps that no longer functioned. I remember when a church that led a short-term mission to Mexico placed a plumbed toilet in one community to increase sanitary conditions; but after the STM left, the community removed the toilet and converted the room to a pastor's office. One of my students' churches donated an air conditioner to a church in Algeria, but the church couldn't afford the electric bill. These concerns about lack of sustainability are widespread. For example, at any given time, one third of handpump wells in sub-Saharan Africa are nonfunctional.[81]

Do the anecdotes above suggest that these projects were a waste of time and money? How should we assess the effectiveness of CD projects? The number of lives saved? The sustainability of the project after the CD project is implemented? The number of people baptized as a result?

Occasionally researchers carry out empirical studies to evaluate a project. For example, Pocol and McDonough did a mixed methods survey of 30 women who had previously been involved in a beekeeping project in Romania that was aimed at raising the standard of living in that area. The participants said their beekeeping was small-scale, but did bring extra income.[82]

Wydick, Glewwe, and Lane studied child sponsorships with Compassion International in six countries:

> Child sponsorship resulted in 1.03–1.46 additional years of completed schooling for sponsored children over a baseline of 10.24 years for unsponsored children. Impacts on primary schooling range from 4.0 to 7.7 percentage points over an untreated baseline of 88.7 percent. Impacts on secondary school completion are greater and highly significant, ranging from 11.6 to 16.5 percentage points over a baseline of 44.9 percent;

---

81. RWSN, *Sustainable Rural Water Supplies*.
82. Pocol and McDonough, "Women, Apiculture and Development."

accounting for marginally significant spillover effects pushes the figure somewhat higher, to 13.7–18.5 percentage points. Tertiary education point estimates of impact are smaller, from 2.1 to 3.6 percentage points, but these are realized over a small baseline of 4.3 percent.[83]

Based on the research that development economists have amassed on CD efforts, Wydick[84] compiled a list of the most effective CD projects in terms of "bang for your buck." Bringing clean water to villages was considered the most impactful project (per dollar spent) because at an average cost of $10 per person, infant mortality could be reduced from 35 to 50 percent. Other projects high on the list included deworming, mosquito nets, child sponsorships, and wood burning stoves.

Community development workers must continue to research the efficacy of their methods and to measure their outcomes. They may fear that publishing their results would bring criticism; but high quality research on the impact of community development models will ultimately save lives and improve economies, as we learn what works, and what doesn't.

## Conclusion

Development as a missionary strategy is based on the biblical command to be fruitful and multiply. Over the centuries, missionaries have been involved in numerous strategies for helping people in their cross-cultural settings to flourish. These strategies incorporate spiritual, political, entrepreneurial, educational, and sanitary practices. But in a postcolonial setting, missiologists are not agreed on the role of western money, western power, and even the role of economics in directing development.

## Move Into Action

Evangelicals have a robust foundation for getting involved in holistic development efforts. But are these efforts working? We theologize a lot about the causes of under-development, but are we making a difference? This chapter has raised the need for more empirical research on the effectiveness of CD projects.

83. Wydick et al., "Does International Child Sponsorship Work?" 396–97.
84. Wydick, "Cost-Effective Compassion."

### Ideas for Further Research

Researchers could do the following sorts of studies:

1. Interview project managers about why projects failed.

2. Perform longitudinal studies on the impact of business-as-mission projects that help poor communities start their own companies.

### Review Questions

1. How does economic development relate to discipleship?

2. How is "holistic missions" different than simply giving a "hand-out?"

### Reflection Questions

1. What are the dangers and advantages of sending money to constituents in least developed nations?

2. How do you respond to the holism-prioritism debate?

*Chapter 7*

# Connecting Education to Cross-Cultural Discipleship

REBECA BURNETT AND LEANNE DZUBINSKI

IN THE EARLY DAYS of the modern missionary movement, which most scholars agree started in 1792 with William Carey's establishment of The Particular Baptist Society for the Propagation of the Gospel Among the Heathen, missionaries' primary emphasis was sharing the gospel of Jesus Christ with those who had never heard. Early missionaries went to exotic-sounding places like India, China, Hawaii, and Burma, among others. Most of them were married, and many of the women were just as committed to spreading the gospel as their husbands were. However, the doors for direct ministry were sometimes not open to women, due to mission policy or host culture practices. Some served in settings where women were strictly secluded; others worked in places where the physical needs were so great that they felt compelled to address both spiritual and physical needs simultaneously. For these and other reasons, many "missionary wives" soon found themselves involved in education as one way to gain the trust and hearts of the people they came to serve.[1] Indeed, Tucker and Liefeld explain: "It was in the sphere of education perhaps more than any other that women in the Third World were influenced by women's missionary work."[2] Some held literacy classes for adult women,

1. Seton, *Western Daughters in Eastern Lands*.
2. Tucker and Liefeld, *Daughters of the Church*, 330.

others established schools for girls. Especially in settings where preaching and direct evangelism were problematic for women, education provided a way to establish relationships, gain trust, and share the gospel.

**Chapter Goals**

*Knowledge goals:*

- Discuss how missionaries have used formal, non-formal, and informal education to make disciples across cultures.
- Explain how culture affects the way missionaries contextualize education, support students, and mentor students across cultural boundaries

*Action goals:*

- Create a means for determining the effectiveness of education in making disciples across cultures.

*Heart goals:*

- Appreciate the impact of education as ministry for making disciples across cultures.

Of course some women also preached, and some men also used education as a missionary strategy. Still, to some degree, the use of education as a missionary strategy could be considered a distinctly female approach to missions for certain contexts. Women missionaries established schools for girls and colleges for women in many countries; they also brought professional education such as medical training and theological education to women. Male missionaries were more likely to establish theological colleges and seminaries to educate national church and ministry leaders than they were to focus on primary and secondary education.

The use of education in mission has continued to the present day, encompassing the spectrum from formal theological education in colleges and seminaries, to organization- and church-based training for missionaries and Christian workers of all types. However, intercultural education as a missiological discipline is not often discussed in books on missiology. Therefore, the purpose of this chapter is to show how missiologists connect educational theories with the task of making disciples across cultures.

One straightforward way to categorize studies related to intercultural education is by types of educational approach. Educational literature often classifies education as occurring in three main formats. First is formal education, which is typically associated with the granting of a degree or diploma by a recognized educational institution. Next is non-formal education, which would include the type of education often done through churches, mission agencies, and other institutions that need a trained workforce but are not themselves primarily educational institutions. Finally, informal education (sometimes called incidental learning), is the type of learning people do in ordinary life. Learning the best route home at high-traffic times of day, or learning which vendor in the market typically has the best prices for certain items would be considered informal or incidental learning.

For clarity in understanding how missiologists and scholars use intercultural education, we frame this chapter in terms of formal and non-formal educational approaches. In our review of the studies of formal education, we divide the discussion into considerations of effectiveness, contextualization, outcomes, and preparation (preparing students through short-term cross-cultural experiences). In our review of non-formal education, we divide the discussion into missionary training, i.e., training people to take the gospel across cultural boundaries, national ministry training, i.e., training people to spread the gospel within their own cultural groups, and a discussion of orality in education.

## Formal Education as Mission Strategy

Formal education as part of a missionary strategy has been used to good effect over the last 200-plus years. From primary schools to theological institutions, education as a way of winning people to Christ and developing them as disciples has proven highly successful. A review of studies of formal education done by missiologists in the last 25 years shows a focus on four main areas. First is evaluating the effectiveness of Christian education, particularly for the sake of spiritual development. Second, a major theme in educational missiology is the contextualization of education (i.e., ensuring that education carried out in different settings around the globe is, indeed, appropriate for those settings). Third, educational missiologists are interested in the academic outcomes of higher education, Christian and secular, on graduates, particularly in carrying out subsequent ministry post-graduation. Fourth, educational missiologists want to understand the impact of formal missiological training and programs such as study abroad which provide cross-cultural experiences for students. We discuss each of these four missiological themes of formal education below.

## Effective Formal Education is Holistic

Primary and secondary education as a missionary strategy started as early as 1834, with the founding of the Female Education Society (FES), which was first known as the Society for Promoting Female Education in the East.[3] The goal of the FES was to recruit and send godly female educators to India and China. There they were to establish schools and recruit and train local women as Christian teachers who would teach and evangelize; the work of the FES continued for a span of 75 years. Like all other work of missionaries, education as a missionary strategy has received sustained criticism for being an arm of colonialism and westernization, for creating power imbalances in countries by providing access to education to only a limited number of people, for importing the denominational bickering from western nations, etc.[4] And partly for those reasons, the FES itself eventually closed. But education as a mission strategy did not cease; it has continued right up to today.

Missiological studies on the effectiveness of formal education primarily focus on the way in which education is holistic—addressing cognitive, social, affective, and spiritual needs. These studies examine the ability of an educational program to achieve specific goals, such as fostering spiritual development along with academic development of students. For example, one missiologist discovered that preschool teachers in Korea used their own spiritual experiences as a basis for nurturing young children. Developing the teachers themselves in the faith was crucial for their ability to help the children grow in faith. A second crucial factor in that study was a contextualized Korean spirituality rather than

---

3. Seton, *Western Daughters in Eastern Lands*.
4. Holmes, *Educational Policy and the Mission Schools*.

## Profile of a Missiologist: Isabella Thoburn
### (1840–1901)

*Education: Wheeling Female Seminary; The Art School of Cincinnati*
*Occupation: Founder, Isabella Thoburn College, Lucknow, India*[1]

Isabella Thoburn was a pioneer missionary educator in India in the late 1800s. A native of Ohio, she became a school teacher by age 18 and also worked as a nurse during the Civil War (1861–1865). In 1869, the Woman's Foreign Missionary Society of the Methodist Episcopal Church (WFMS) raised funds to send Thoburn to India. She was the first single woman sent out by the WFMS.[2]

In India, Thoburn confronted racism, classism, and sexism in establishing her girls' school. Some missionaries opposed educating Indian people for any purpose beyond reading the Bible; some upper-caste Indians opposed educating lower-caste people or mixing castes in an educational setting; both missionaries and Indian people opposed the education of girls. She launched her school in a house called "Ruby Garden" with just seven girls and a guard posted at the entrance for protection.[3] Within a short amount of time the school grew to include a high school, and then a college.

At every stage, Thoburn invested in the lives of her students. She offered education and literacy, along with prayer and spiritual training. And she maintained her standards, as Montgomery explains: "The girls' school and college was firm in its stand that there be no caste lines, no race lines."[4] Thoburn summed up her views on education in an address to the Ecumenical Missionary Conference in 1900, held at Carnegie Hall:

> The power of educated womanhood in the world is simply the power of skilled service. We are not in the world to be ministered unto, but to minister. The world is full of need, and every opportunity to help is a duty. Preparation for these duties is education, whatever form it may take or whatever service may result.[5]

Shortly after Thoburn returned to India, she passed away from cholera. Montgomery characterizes Thoburn's thirty years of service to girls and women in India with these words: "Rarely has there been a more beautiful life of service than that which Isabella Thoburn poured out in [her] Ruby Garden of girls."[6]

---

[1] https://www.itcollege.ac.in/.
[2] Montgomery, *Western Women in Eastern Lands*, 168.
[3] Montgomery, *Western Women in Eastern Lands*, 169.
[4] Montgomery, *Western Women in Eastern Lands*, 173.
[5] Quoted in Montgomery, *Western Women in Eastern Lands*, 174.
[6] Montgomery, *Western Women in Eastern Lands*, 171.

a Western-based approach to discipleship. This study highlights both the importance of paying attention to the spiritual development of children from a very young age and the importance of education that is local and contextualized, reflecting the needs and values of the society itself.[5] Another educational missiologist studied junior high and high school teachers in Kenya, and discovered that teachers were able to foster holistic development of their students by attending to spiritual, emotional, and intellectual development of students.[6]

While some missiologists are accustomed to studying one specific culture in depth, in today's globalizing world, an increasing number of students study in multicultural settings. This may include multicultural classrooms in the USA or formal education in other regions. For example, one study took globalization into account by examining the educational and spiritual needs of cross-cultural children who grow up in multiple cultural environments.[7] Multicultural children have unique developmental needs as they process their experiences and learn to live as global Christian citizens. Similarly, another study examined the well-being of Korean missionary kids (MKs) who were studying in American universities, in order to support them while far from both their parents and home country.[8] These studies highlight the importance of education as part of holistic academic and spiritual development for students worldwide.

Missiologists also want to understand the effectiveness of higher education as part of Christian mission. Not surprisingly, such studies are frequently able to point out strengths of such education, and can also suggest areas for improvement. For example, T. D. Ng's study of community-building experiences for seminary students in Manila reinforced what educators have long-known: Smaller classes promote better interactions between students and teachers, leading to more effective education.[9]

Formal education is not always accessible, however, especially in majority-world countries. In such cases, building a case for the effectiveness of education can also include questions of access and

5. Jang, "Global Missions Perspective."
6. Im, "Desired African Teacher."
7. Lee, "Teaching and Learning Around the Cycle."
8. Lee, "Factors Affecting the Well-being of Korean Missionary Kids."
9. Ng, "Study on Community at a Theological Institution in Manila Using Victor Turner's Theory."

affordability. Woodmansee found that making an affordable Master of Education program available through a Baptist mission society in Haiti was strategic in developing effective teachers for local schools.[10]

Another question that educational missiologists sometimes ask is how Christian programs compare with secular ones in terms of effectiveness. In a study of Christian English-language instruction in Korea, M. Lee found that students from two schools did have a competitive economic advantage due to English skills and a better preparation for a globalizing world, but that they also became somewhat "Americanized" through the process.[11] These mixed findings draw attention to another major issue of great interest in the themes of educational missiology: the contextualization of education.

## Contextualization of Education

Many early western missionary educators saw themselves clearly and definitely as bringing western culture and values to their students. Letters from early missionaries—men and women—often described what they considered to be appalling living conditions, lack of education and literacy, and the desperate needs of women, girls, boys, and sometimes men who they met in their new homes. Missionaries, and missionary women in particular, intentionally brought their Western learning, including literacy, math, homemaking skills, and so forth, at least initially as part of their evangelistic outreach.[12] An important component of their two-pronged educational and evangelistic strategy was the introduction of "Bible women"—local women who attended classes with missionary women to learn the fundamentals of literacy and the gospel, and then were sent out by the mission as itinerant evangelists. Bible women were a major factor in the spread of the gospel in Japan, China, and India, among others. Missionaries also trained local women to be teachers themselves, leading to an expansion of local schools and an increase in access to education for children in many societies.

However, the concept of contextualization did not become important until many decades later, as mission theory shifted to be less Euro-centric and colonial, and more indigenous. (See chapter 9 for a more thorough

10. Woodmansee, "Haitian Educational Leaders' Perceptions."
11. Lee, "Benefits and Challenges in Globalization in Christian Higher Education.".
12. Hardage, *Mary Slessor—Everybody's Mother*.

discussion of contextualization.) Today's educational missiologist is often highly interested in the question of contextualization: To what degree is a given school or seminary providing education that is contextually appropriate and useful for the spread of the gospel in the local setting? Such studies often examine educational institutions that were started by westerners, or perhaps by locals who received their own training in the West and have potentially imported western ways into a non-western setting.

This question of the contextualization of education is perhaps one of the most-asked and most-studied by educational missiologists today. Lingenfelter and Lingenfelter proposed a four-part model for understanding teachers and learners based on cultural variations in values.[13] They recommended educators understand the role of the hidden curriculum, the responsibilities of a Christian teacher, the differences between western and local approaches to knowledge, and the interaction with local cultural values. Their study continues to inform educational missiologists working to contextualize their practice.

Given that many of the earliest evangelistic educational efforts took place in Asia, numerous studies examine schools and institutions in that area of the world: Korea, East Asia, Malaysia, and India have all come under study. But studies on the contextualization of education are not limited to that geographical region. Institutions in Europe and the US have also come under scrutiny.

In many instances, educational institutions that were originally run by western missionaries have successfully transitioned to well-contextualized models. For example, Grant described an Indian theological institution, founded 47 years prior by American missionaries, which was appropriately preparing students for ministry in India.[14] Grant's work showed that, overall, the school was properly Indian in its approach and educational philosophy. While maintaining its Indian-ness, she argued, Christian values were actually transforming traditional Indian practices for the better. For example, rather than following traditional Indian values of caste, the school had implemented egalitarianism based on the priesthood of all believers.

Formal theological institutions in other parts of the world have also become contextualized. Bar's study of a Christian college in Melanesia

---

13. Lingenfelter and Lingenfelter, *Teaching Cross-culturally*.
14. Grant, "Theological Education in India."

found that the college largely reflected Melanesian values, though there were still areas for further contextualization, like hiring more national faculty.[15] Manna likewise examined a youth ministry degree program in Ukraine that had been started by Americans and had become largely localized. Based on that context, Manna proposed a model for contextualizing theological education that could be of use to other, nationally-run institutions that were originally founded by westerners.[16] These studies are encouraging because they show the flexibility and adaptability of educators in varied contexts.

Other studies have examined the degree of contextualization within the curriculum,[17] instructors' pedagogies,[18] and the process of mentoring[19] on student preparation in specific locations. Studies such as these help educational missiologists to critically interrogate the convergence of Western, local, and scriptural values such that the gospel can be preached effectively by seminary graduates.

## Formal Education as Preparation for Mission

A third area of missiological interest related to formal education is its use as training or preparation for making disciples across cultures. Numerous educational missiologists have sought to understand the relationship between formal educational preparation through programs like study abroad or short term mission trips as part of the formal curriculum and missionary training embedded in the formal educational process. (Note that in a later section on non-formal education we discuss the myriad of types of missionary preparation that exist among agencies and training schools; however in this section we focus only on training done through formal educational institutions).

15. Bar, "Development of a Contextualized Indigenous Education System."
16. Manna, "Indigenous Contextualization Model."
17. Houger, W. "Recipient Driven Curriculum for Asian Assemblies of God Bible Schools"; Lee, "Holistic Curriculum Development."
18. Houger, "Instructors' Pedagogies as the Frame of Influence for East Asian Assemblies of God Bible Schools."
19. Kim, "Study of the Relationship Between Academic Mentoring"; Olsen, "Czech Social Relations"; Sumule, "Impact of Informal Mentoring."

## Experiential Learning in Formal Education

Missiologists have discovered that formal preparation for missionary work is strongest when it involves experiential learning. Some Christian colleges and universities have formal programs of internships or short-term mission trips built into the degree requirements. Understanding the impact and outcomes of such programs is of interest to educational missiologists. For example, La George listened to the experiences of students who had received formal educational preparation for mission and then went on a short-term mission project. Her survey of over 1,000 students and graduates of a formal training program, 380 of whom actually participated in a short-term mission (STM) trip, demonstrated that short-term mission trips continued to positively impact students' and graduates' attitudes toward God and towards their own involvement with global missions.[20] The students reflected that as a result of these trips, their lives were changed, that their eyes were opened to the many needs of those around the globe and that the gospel came alive to them in different and powerful ways. LaGeorge's study also contained several key implications: First, the application process for the program was changed to require students to formulate beforehand a description of their motivations for embarking on a mission project and how the trip would help them in their vocational goals. Second, the need for fostering additional partnerships between the university and host missionaries was highlighted. Third, classroom content should include additional language and cultural training. And finally, La George's study stressed the need for some type of reflection once the students returned (see chapter 10 for more discussion on the outcomes of STM).

Study abroad programs also have a profound impact on undergraduate students. Granados interviewed students who enrolled in a semester-long study abroad in Israel, and found that study abroad had a positive impact for students both academically and spiritually.[21] Women in particular reported positive academic outcomes from their study abroad programs. Dinani's year-long study on the development of intercultural competence among African-American students who studied abroad showed that not only did study abroad increase students' intercultural competence, but they also reported a faith development

---

20. La George, "Short-term Missions at the Master's College."
21. Granados, "Academic and Spiritual Impact of a Semester Abroad Program."

process.²² The role of faith became even more important for some of her students as a result of being immersed in a new culture. This finding suggests that students' faith can develop through secular as well as faith-based programs. Additionally, Dinani's focus on African-American students, who are an underrepresented population in study abroad, offered important knowledge about the development of intercultural competence and faith among this group.

## Outcomes of Educational Programs

Educational missiology also investigates the outcomes of educational programs. Educators want to understand the impact of their work so they can continually improve their practice; institutions benefit from having a clear understanding of the outcomes of their degree programs; and students, reasonably, want to know that the time, effort, and money they invest in their studies will have useful results. A number of factors affect the outcomes of education, such as the ability to adjust the curriculum, the use of ongoing training, and the ability to address "hidden curriculum."

Campbell's work blended the theory of multiple intelligences with experiential learning theory.²³ She started by training American teachers, who then traveled overseas and taught the theories and their classroom use to missionary and national educators. These educators then taught the theories to nationals in various locations throughout Asia. At each stage, Campbell examined both the usefulness and the contextual adjustment of the theories as they progressed through the various levels of reproduction and adjustment. Even though she tried this strategy in several different Asian countries, her results were consistent: The use of these two theories was received very positively by the national educators and by the students they taught. While there was some hesitation by the nationals in having to learn and eventually adopt these new theories, they talked about "owning" the material and style of teaching to a greater extent than before these theories were introduced. As a result, teachers contextualized the theories and adapted them to best fit the needs of their students.

Effective education for Christian workers requires ongoing education, much like other professions require continuing education credits to maintain certification or licensure. Mathew's study of

22. Dinani, "Impact of Ethnic Identity Stage Development."
23. Campbell, "Experiential Learning Approach to Faculty Training."

secular university education for Pentecostal ministers in India reminds educational missiologists that education is not a one-time event; rather, encouraging lifelong learning is important for those involved in Christian ministry.[24]

Yet the outcomes of formal education in missionary work are not always positive. S. Y. Kim[25] discovered that while Dominican Republic pastors in New York had a favorable attitude towards education, in practice they believed it was not only unnecessary but actually irrelevant to their chosen work. In this case, the educational outcomes could be described as far from satisfactory, and educational missiologists—who typically believe in the value of education—should keep the barriers to such education in mind as they implement contextually appropriate changes so that theological education would be more likely to be embraced.

An important aspect of education that has been identified but is often overlooked is known as the "hidden curriculum." The hidden curriculum consists of underlying values and beliefs which are not explicitly stated but are nevertheless embedded in the educational process. These values can impact the access and benefit of education for marginalized groups. Both racist and sexist ideologies have been highlighted as underlying value systems frequently found in educational materials and programs. Mbuva used this concept to compare two Christian higher education institutions, one in California and one in Kenya, examining the explicit, implicit, and hidden curricula in each.[26] Through this comparison, he was able to show how the social context shaped all aspects of the curriculum. Such knowledge enables Christian educators to be intentional and careful about all aspects of the curriculum that they provide to students. Likewise, missiologists have focused on groups of students at higher risk of non-completion. For example, Vara investigated what helped Hispanic students to succeed in a predominately white, Christian environment.[27] Student success fell into five domains: academic, social, interpersonal, spiritual, and institutional. Students had positive experiences with faith, support networks, and participation in activities that valued Hispanic culture, which in turn promoted student success. These underlying values may even affect the way first-generation college students who

24. Mathew, "Study of the Effects of a University Education."
25. Kim, "Theological Education Among Dominican Republic Pastors."
26. Mbuva, "A Comparative Study of Two Religious Training Schools."
27. Vara, "Academic Success Among Hispanic Students."

study at predominately white Christian institutions choose their majors.[28] In order for college administrators to better serve their at-risk student groups and increase their likelihood of success, many colleges and universities are creating curricular and co-curricular programs that come alongside at-risk students with the intent to narrow the gap which many of these students face. By identifying the "hidden curriculum" and making appropriate, empowering changes, these at-risk students stand a much better chance of success.

## Summary of Formal Education as a Missionary Strategy

Over the last three decades, educational missiologists have been interested in understanding formal education's impact on spiritual formation, strategies to contextualize education, education's outcomes, and the way education prepares students for vocational and professional service. The missiological studies discussed in this section suggest that formal education can be effective in making disciples when it is holistic, contextualized, experiential, and inclusive.

## Non-Formal Education as Missionary Strategy

The importance of the intersection of missions and non-formal education cannot be understated. It is often within the confines of everyday life where missionaries are most effectively using education to evangelize and support the growth of new Christian disciples. In this section, we look at the ways non-formal education is helping send agencies, missionaries, and nationals in the transmission of the gospel across cultural boundaries in a variety of settings. In many cases, the success of non-formal education draws on adult learning theory: missionaries need to see how their training is relevant, and it must draw on their own life experiences.

### How Sending Agencies use Non-Formal Education

The importance of non-formal education begins even before missionaries arrive on the field. A search of some of the largest mission agencies reveals that many of them have created and developed their own non-formal missionary training curriculum. This curriculum looks different from

---

28. Burnett, "It's a Major Decision."

agency to agency; but at the core is the desire to train the missionaries they send with basic skills to succeed cross-culturally in various settings throughout the world.

Some agencies have chosen to assess and redesign their existing training curriculum. One agency, New Tribes Mission (NTM—now called Ethnos 360) identified the importance of evaluating their training materials based on shifts within missions. They evaluated how well their existing curriculum was preparing their missionaries as they were entering the mission field, specifically in the Global South region. Strauss described and analyzed the design and delivery of intentional and integral missionary training of NTM.[29] He recognized how the shift of Christianity to the Global South provided unique opportunities for ministry partnerships with the North. Therefore, a reevaluation of missionary training is one important area of collaboration between North and South, especially when local church leaders have specific, unique needs that can only be met through specific skills. Strauss offered tested and verified strategies and methodologies for designing and delivering missionary training. As a result of these recommendations, NTM completely redesigned their training curriculum to include relational and experiential learning rather than traditional classroom approaches. To this day they use and continuously revise the updated curriculum.

Other educational missiologists have looked at how missionaries are adapting in cross-cultural settings. Austring studied the relationship between cultural adaption and adult learning for Assemblies of God missionaries in Latin America.[30] Specifically, he looked at the effectiveness of the training that took place before these missionaries arrived in the countries they were serving and how the impact of training (based on adult learning theory) increased or faded over time. Through interviews and surveys, he found that missionaries found the training useful but there was little follow-up by the sending agency once they arrived on the field. New missionaries also faced less-than-supportive interactions with veteran missionaries on the field, who had unfavorable views of the adult-learning-based training. Yet the new missionaries found the training essential and compatible with doctrine on the empowerment of the Holy Spirit.

---

29. Strauss, "Design and Delivery of Intentional and Integral Missionary Training."
30. Austring, "Analysis of the Role of Adult Learning Theory."

## How Missionaries Use Non-Formal Education

Non-formal education within missions does not only pertain to the training of missionaries who intend to minister in settings outside their home country; it also includes the way missionaries use education in their day-to-day life.

For example, women missionaries are taking advantage of non-formal education to develop leaders in Tamil Nadu, India. Lowell used interviews, life histories, and archival sources to gather rich data that showed that women missionaries were planting the seeds of leadership formation into the lives of their young students.[31] Over time, these seeds grew and formed leadership skills in these young students who matured and secured leadership positions at the national and district levels. The study revealed the dedication that these women missionaries had, and highlighted their persistence in their development of young leaders through non-formal education.

Women missionaries often use non-formal education to adapt their leadership styles as they learn to navigate a largely male-based structure. Even when they have shown their effectiveness, female missionaries often face even greater challenges than male missionaries. For example, women missionaries in predominately patriarchal evangelical mission organizations have had consciously and sometimes, subconsciously, learned to accept and follow the gender roles that were prescribed within their sending agencies and local settings.[32] Some of these women learned how to use gender roles to their advantage and development of their leadership. But sadly, deeply entrenched, unequal structures favoring men often stymied how successful these women could be in leadership. The non-formal lessons they encountered affected how and to what extent they could minister and lead.

Non-formal education within missions can be seen throughout urban settings around the globe. One educational missiologist explored contextualized leadership development in urban Cambodia.[33] Church leaders saw a need for training and leadership development for young men and women in their congregations. They created their training for emerging leaders based on the knowledge of Cambodian Christians. This particular model was developed after interviews with church leaders

---

31. Lowell, "Educational Contributions."
32. Dzubinski, "Playing by the Rules."
33. Suh, "Exploring a Contextualized Leadership Development Model."

from two of the largest Christian churches in Cambodia. They took into account the historical and cultural knowledge possessed by these young leaders, and they formed a model based on the needs that the nationals identified. The result was a training model based on spiritual formation that provided a strong foundation and support system for these emerging leaders.

Non-formal education is also helping urban missionaries within the United States, and it plays a role in imparting cultural adaptability to missionary candidates wishing to serve in highly diverse, multi-cultural cities. Ruder studied a group of urban mission candidates in response to their sending agency's realization of the need for cultural adaptability training as a core component of their training curriculum.[34] The agency developed a survey to measure cross-cultural adaptability and administered it to their urban missionary candidates. The study found evidence of notable increases in cross-cultural adaptability after the training took place. This allowed the sending agency to not only evaluate the effectiveness of their training, but also allowed them to make a case for continuing such training.

## How Church Leaders Use Non-Formal Education

Educational missiology considers how church leaders across the globe use non-formal education. Non-formal education has been used over time and observed in great detail. It takes on many forms and permeates day-to-day life. This form of education is not used exclusively by sending agencies and missionaries. Nationals in the countries where missionaries are serving use it extensively. They may intuitively understand, better than outsiders, the settings within which such education will take place.

In many instances, nationals are best equipped to know the challenges and pitfalls they may face in a non-formal educational setting. Yang researched how a highly homogenous society like Korea would face the challenge of globalization.[35] He focused specifically on how Korean Christians could use globalization to develop leaders within their churches. He observed six classes of Koreans engaged in leadership training within a family ministry. The curriculum was based on Experiential Learning (EL) where all members of the family could interact. EL's focus on the relationship between teacher and student

34. Ruder, "Competencies and the Changing World of Work."
35. Yang, "Experiential Approach to Korean Family Ministry Leaders' Training."

proved to be a positive style of teaching because of the Korean ideal of respect between teacher and student. The study confirmed the need for a strong trust relationship between the teacher and student. In fact, this relationship is key for training leaders in Asia.

## The Use of Orality in Education

The impact of orality on adult learning also blurs the boundaries between education and evangelism (Note that orality as a missionary strategy is further described in chapter 10). Missionaries learn to teach using narrative teaching methods through formal education, taking classes, and learning orality as an academic sub-discipline. Once in their target setting, however, they use non-formal means to transmit their learning. Primarily an evangelistic approach, their work can nevertheless be considered an educational strategy. The goal is to teach the Bible through oral rather than written means. By means of songs, memorization, story-telling, drama, and other non-written communication forms, orality-minded evangelists seek to communicate the gospel among low-literate people.

For example, in her study in rural Java, Marantika researched *macapat*, a Javanese poetic song genre. Her longitudinal study took place in four rural communities in two provinces.[36] These communities were small-scale farming areas. Most of the population were day laborers or engrossed in farm work, and most did not pursue advanced education. The nationals' mode of learning was not reading, but oral, and specifically musical orality. Marantika found that using *macapat* as an entry point for teaching the Bible was highly effective. This method of musical poetry and teaching had been used for centuries to teach moral and religious values. The Christian nationals and missionaries translated the Gospel of Matthew into *macapat* for the churches in four communities. The result was an innovative, culturally appropriate, and effective tool that these nationals could use to spread the gospel.

In another example, in a small, rural community in southwestern Ethiopia, formal educational methods were used in a non-formal setting to study 50 sermons that were delivered by pastors and how these sermons were a telling glimpse into values and best ways to present the gospel. Through recordings, transcriptions, and analyzation of these 50 sermons, Anderson learned that the character of the preacher

---

36. Marantika, "Use of a Culturally Sensitive Song Form, Macapat."

was key to the reception of the gospel message.[37] Homiletics aside, the preacher's reputation and style was more important than the actual message content. The result was the formation of a theory of how to teach preachers to deliver their message and live a spirit-filled lifestyle that was contextualized to this area of Ethiopia.

Another study of orality, set in Cambodia, looked at how adults with limited formal education (ALFE) benefited from non-formal education. In this particular study, Thigpen sought to understand how ALFE learned most effectively.[38] She observed that ALFE in Cambodia were largely oral learners. The ALFEs observed were adults ranging in age from 18 to 83 years and had six or fewer years of formal schooling. These adult learners preferred to learn in connected ways (learning from trusted individuals and in a spiritual setting) and through relationships (where they did not feel a sense of shame in not being able to read). Thigpen observed that the most successful way to teach the gospel was to repackage biblical ideas into stories, parables, metaphors, and dramas. It was also essential to take the element of shame away from the gospel message and teach in a positive, redemptive style.

Finally, Parsons looked at a highly marginalized group which is often the recipient of Christian evangelism but less often recipients of Christian education.[39] He found an oral, narrative-style gospel presentation to be effective among homeless men living in a shelter. Oral strategies may be particularly well-suited in situations where shame from challenges such as homelessness or low literacy are present.

Oral education strategies bring us full circle to the "Bible women" of a century ago. Attaining a high level of education or literacy has never been a prerequisite for understanding the gospel; the current orality movement, like the Bible women movement, recognizes and capitalizes on the different ways people can hear and transmit the gospel message.

---

37. Anderson, "Implicit Rhetorical Theory of Preachers in Wolaitta Ethiopia with Implications for Homiletics Instruction in Theological Education."

38. Thigpen, "Connected Learning."

39. Parsons, "The Impact of a Contextualized Narrative Curriculum on Gospel Understanding."

### Summary of Non-Formal Education as a Missionary Strategy

Non-formal education is used in all stages of mission work by cross-cultural missionaries and nationals alike. This training is often on-the-job, and allows adult learners to incorporate their own life experience. Missionaries learn best when they can connect theories to their own goals in the missionary field.

While formal education obviously has its place in missions, non-formal education has some advantages within a cross-cultural setting. Not confined by regulations and accreditation, non-formal education can be adapted to fit settings that are unique and challenging. It also provides access to individuals beyond those who have been formally educated. And it empowers people with little formal education to speak into the education of themselves and the next generation.

## Conclusion

In the early 1900s, Anne Grenfell accompanied her husband, a medical doctor, to Newfoundland and Labrador. Their assignment was to bring medical care and the gospel. Anne quickly found herself running an orphan asylum and a school, which provided ample opportunities to both educate and share the gospel.[40] Missionaries like her, both men and women, have paid close attention to those whom society deems less valuable. Women, ethnic and racial minority groups, non-literate people, orphans, and homeless people have all been recipients of the gospel through educational approaches.

Educational missiologists have taken seriously the mandate to bring a transformative, holistic gospel message—one that addresses both the spiritual and practical needs of people. Ultimately, a combination of both formal and non-formal education is ideal as missionaries endeavor to spread the gospel, the good news of Christ across the world.

The following table shows the types of questions that are tackled by educational missiologists:

---

40. Grenfell and Spalding, *Le petit nord*.

**Table 6: How missiologists use education to make disciples across cultures**

| Mode of education | Topic Missiologists study |
|---|---|
| Formal education | **Effectiveness**: To what degree is the curriculum holistic? How does it impact spiritual growth? How does affordability affect accessibility? How does language choice impact instruction? How do multicultural classrooms affect education? How does the size of the classroom affect education? |
| | **Contextual education**: What are differences in approaches to knowledge? What are indigenous pedagogies? How can formal educational institutions be indigenized? How does curriculum reflect indigenous, biblical, or western values? |
| | **Preparation for cross-cultural work**: How do short term missions or study abroad prepare students' involvement in missions? How does exposure to other cultures increase students' faith? |
| | **Outcomes**: What barriers are there to education? How does education impact the lives of marginalized people? |
| Informal education | **Training missionaries**: How can relational and experiential learning prepare people for working overseas? How do missionaries, as adult learners, need to have their training tailored to the needs of adults? How do women learn leadership skills "on the job" in a male-dominated career? How do missionaries working in urban settings adapt to their context? |
| | **Training church leaders**: How can experiential learning be adapted to highly hierarchal contexts? |
| | **Narrative pedagogy**: How is the gospel message transmitted through song, dance, dramas, and symbols? |

## Action Point

Cross-cultural competency is the key to effective cross-cultural education. Non-formal and formal educational methods must be contextualized to the local values, expectations, and pedagogies.

## Ideas for Further Research

Many studies have been done on the effectiveness of various educational strategies, including the implementation of those strategies in cross-cultural settings. More research is needed on the effectiveness of education as a cross-cultural discipleship strategy. The following sorts of studies could be done:

1. Interview pastors in missionary-led training programs to see how their ministry practices changed based on their experiences with theological education.
2. Contextualization is tricky. Interview local believers (men and women) to understand the impact of cultural values on education, then develop recommendations that allow the gospel message to reach all members of a society.

## Review Questions

1. How does spiritual formation relate to formal and non-formal education, as a missionary strategy?
2. How does contextualization relate to formal and non-formal education, as a missionary strategy?

## Reflection Questions

1. What opportunities do missionaries face as they use education to make disciples across cultures?
2. What challenges do missionaries face as they use education to make disciples across cultures?

## *Part II*

# The Distributaries Of Missiology

THE THESIS OF THIS book is that the various tributaries of missiology all converge for the purpose of making disciples across cultures. Granted, the fields of psychology, history, theology, education, anthropology, etc., can converge for a multitude of reasons, not just to help us understand how to make disciples across cultures. For example, such tributaries may be combined to form a historical theology, or a theological anthropology. But any reason for interdisciplinarity other than cross cultural discipleship does not produce missiology. Something—some central purpose—must be at the center of these converging disciplines to make missiology unique. The *sine qua non* of missiology, I argue throughout this book, is the Great Commission.

Part 1 of this book covered various ways that missiological fields are put to use for the purpose of cross-cultural discipleship. A summary of how the disciplines covered can facilitate cross-cultural discipleship is included in the following table:

Table 7: Connecting Missiological theory to Missionary practice

| Missiological Theology | • Leverages understandings within the host culture related to God, sin, humanity, etc; <br> • Points out theological errors across cultures; <br> • Helps address theological questions that host communities are asking; and <br> • Encourages disciple makers to recognize the spiritual realm. |
|---|---|
| Missiological History | • Helps uncover models and trends that historically facilitated making disciples in other cultures; <br> • Identifies historical barriers and geo-politics related to sharing to the gospel in certain contexts. |
| Missiological Anthropology | • Helps identify how rituals and symbols can be redeemed to glorify God without promoting idolatry; <br> • Helps the disciple maker understand how to transmit the gospel through social networks in the host cultures. |
| Intercultural Studies | • Helps missionaries deal with culture shock; <br> • Helps culture-crossers work seamlessly across cultures by communicating and behaving according to the host culture's values; <br> • Encourages missionaries to be reflective about paternalism in light of postcolonialism. |
| Missiological Education | • Helps training and leadership practices to fit the host culture's context. |
| Transformational Development | • Provides a theological impetus for addressing physical needs; <br> • Integrates the best of economic theory to ensure development is sustainable. |

However, as I mentioned in chapter 1, missiologists are not simply foragers who take the best of other disciplines; they actively research to generate their own explanatory and categorizing theories about how humans respond to the gospel. And scholar-practitioners within missiology also generate models of "best practices." The second part of this book covers seminal models and theories that are idiosyncratic to missiology. First, though, I must begin by (finally) defining what evangelical missiologists mean by "cross-cultural disciple making," since that is a key part of my definition of missions, and missiology.

*Chapter 8*

# Defining Cross-Cultural Discipleship

WHILE THE TERMS "CROSS-CULTURAL discipleship" and "intercultural discipleship" have appeared in missiology,¹ shockingly little effort has been put into studying how the numerous missionary strategies fit under a single rubric of cross-cultural discipleship, even though discipleship is the essence of the missionary task. Practical theologians have put much effort into developing discipleship models; but typically make little effort to understand the extent to which their models are transferrable to other cultural contexts. Likewise, some scholars have focused on the process of crossing cultures (see chapters 4 and 5, on missiological anthropology and intercultural studies) but these models seldom touch on how to cross cultures for the express purpose of making disciples. In fact, in a survey of twenty Christian universities, only one (Providence) offers a missions or ICS class called cross-cultural discipleship. The phrase barely turns up in internet searches or in scholarly databases.²

---

1. Davis, *Making Disciples Across Cultures*; Hibbert and Hibbert, *Walking Together on the Jesus Road*; Moon, *Intercultural Discipleship*; Yount and Barnett, *Called to Reach*.

2. A search for the terms "cross cultural" or "intercultural" with the term "discipleship" yielded no journal articles in ATLA in 2018; and only 17 dissertations in the Proquest Dissertation series. None of these dissertations is actually on the topic of cross-cultural discipleship.

## Chapter Goals

*Knowledge goals:*

- Critique definitions of discipleship, missions, and missionary.
- Explain how discipleship relates to areas of life like healthcare, economics, and social life.

*Action goals:*

- Teach others to obey all Jesus has commanded.

*Heart goals:*

- Know which sphere(s) of life in which you are most likely to help others learn how to obey "all that Jesus commanded."

Why the lack of works that focus on cross-cultural discipleship, if it is the essence of missions? Understandably, most missiologists focus instead on specific aspects of the missionary task, such as cross-cultural leadership, or church planting, or cross-cultural evangelism. And some focus on discipleship in certain communities, such as Little's work on Muslim communities,[3] and Beattie's edited volume on sharing the faith in Asia.[4] But these regional studies of discipleship do not attempt to lay down the implications for cross-cultural discipleship in general.

Often missiological work focuses on specific missionary methods such as community development, Bible translation, vernacular media, healthcare, etc.; but missiologists are not always clear how these strategies relate to the foundational missiological purpose of furthering cross-cultural discipleship. In fact, while all of these methods are typically seen (by academics, cross-cultural workers, and their supporting churches) as missionary in nature, they are not typically placed all under the rubric of cross-cultural discipleship.

---

3. Little, *Effective Discipline in Muslim Communities*.
4. Beattie, *Ministry Across Cultures*.

To make the connection between the multiple missionary methods and the central task of making disciples, we must work through the sticky task of defining discipleship.

## What Is Discipleship?

### Defining Discipleship

Discipleship is the process of teaching people to obey all that Jesus commanded. Some have focused more on the teachings, and some focus more on the actions; but both aspects are essential.

Jesus used various motifs to describe what He meant by "disciple." He told some simply, "Follow me" (Matt. 4:19). The authors of the gospels never spell out criteria for who among the crowd following Jesus was a disciple and who wasn't. It's safe to say that there was no specific criteria for membership; disciples were those who came to Jesus for teaching (the core of the word "disciple" is one who adheres to the teachings of another). Davis suggests that perhaps the reason that practical theologians cannot agree on a definition of disciple is that it is, after all, a fuzzy (rather than bounded) set.[5] Discipleship is not a program, or a twelve-step process. It is a lifelong process of transformation, and it is personalized—so it is a bit fuzzier to define.

Another motif for discipleship is based on Jesus's teaching of the kingdom of God. Those who are under the rule of God, in whom the kingdom is growing (Luke 17:21), are disciples.

Two main activities have characterized missiological understandings of making disciples: proclamation and obedience. Below I'll explore both briefly.

### Discipleship as Proclamation

Church growth missiologists understood discipleship as primarily about proclamation. Wagner argued the process of discipling involved helping

---

5. Davis, *Making Disciples Across Cultures*, 29–32.

unbelievers to make a commitment to Christ.[6] Wagner deliberately distinguished this activity from a separate stage, perfection, which involves teaching people to obey Jesus.[7] Yet this narrow definition of discipleship is no longer in wide use. Scholar-practitioners now recognize that discipleship is more than bringing people to conversion.

## Discipleship as Bringing Into Obedience

In the Great Commission, Jesus seems to define disciple as those who "obey everything I have commanded" (Matt 28:20 NIV). Yet "followers of Jesus" can be difficult to identify. What, *in toto*, is classified as "everything that Jesus commanded"? Jesus may have been referring to a broader set of commands, including the Sermon on the Mount, His warnings to the Pharisees and other religious leaders, and His parables. In fact, it is probably fair to say that the commands in the rest of Scripture (the epistles, Torah, wisdom literature, etc.), being the Word of God, are also under the rubric of "everything I have commanded."

The rather exhaustive possibilities of what it means to obey "everything God commands" suggests that making disciples is about exegeting the "whole counsel of God" (Acts 20:27 ESV) across all cultures. Perhaps, rather than search for an exhaustive list of every command that must be taught (and followed) to be Jesus's disciple, we can turn to Jesus's summary:

> "Teacher, which is the greatest commandment in the Law?"
> Jesus replied: "'Love the Lord your God with all your heart and with all your soul and with all your mind.' This is the first and greatest commandment. And the second is like it: 'Love your neighbor as yourself.' All the Law and the Prophets hang on these two commandments." (Matt 22:36–40 NIV)

The all-inclusive taxonomy of loving with all our heart, soul, and mind suggests that following "all the law" requires thinking like God does, valuing the things that God does, and treating others like God does. Discipleship is about getting the priorities right, the doctrines right, and about living holy lives.

---

6. Wagner, "What Is 'Making Disciples'?"
7. Rainer, *Book of Church Growth*.

Note that missiologists do not agree on the exact role of obedience in becoming a disciple. Some practical missiologists argue that obedience is the only mark of a disciple,[8] and believe that traditionally, the church has over-emphasized knowledge of orthodox doctrines as a prerequisite for becoming a disciple. But other missiologists emphasize that discipleship must also encompass orthodox beliefs.[9]

To reiterate, if missions is defined as cross-cultural discipleship, it involves far more than persuading people to convert. This is why the slogan for Tokyo's 2010 commemoration of Edinburgh 1910 changed the theme from "evangelism of the world" to "Making disciples of every people."[10] Discipleship is a lifelong process of helping people to love God with their intellect, volition, and behavior. Following Jesus involves re-examining religious ideas about salvation, grace, and works (Eph 2:8–9). But following Jesus also means reordering our business dealings to flow out of humility, love, and service. It involves, for example, changing our attitudes toward leadership (Matt 20:25), how we handle money (Jas 5:1–6), our view of the poor (Jas 2:1–7), and how we talk to others (Eph 4:29). Even by Edinburgh 1910 missiologists recognized that missions involves a wide range of activities including "evangelism, translation, education, medicine, literature, industrial training."[11] Cross-cultural discipleship involves enabling bodies of believers to bring all areas of life under the reign of God, including their politics, educational systems, business practices, pastimes, etc. (see Figure 6).

---

8. Smith, *T4T*.
9. Terry, "Missiology of Excluded Middles," 348.
10. Yeh, *Polycentric Missiology*, 66.
11. Yeh, *Polycentric Missiology*, 14.

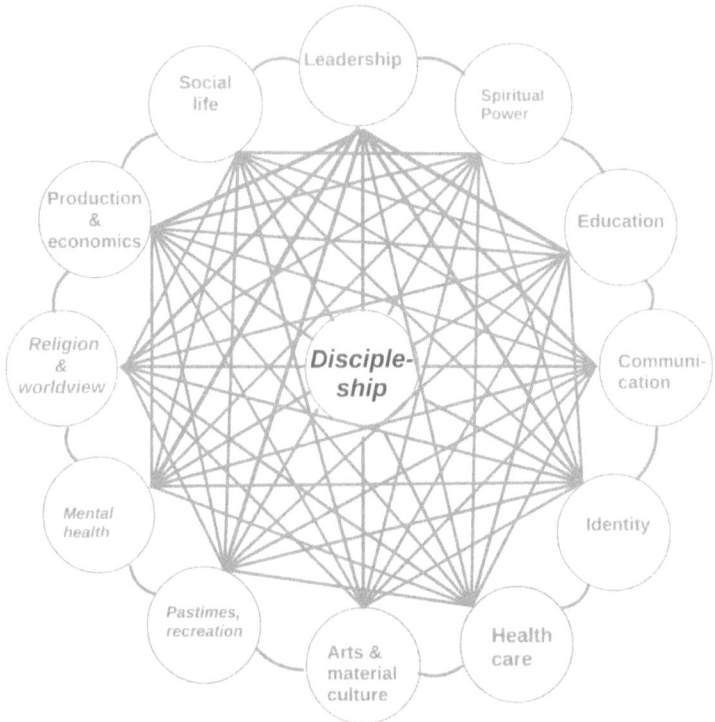

Figure 6: Bringing all aspects of life under the reign of God[12]

## What Is Cross-cultural Discipleship?

Cross-cultural discipleship is any activity that helps people across cultures to bring these spheres of their lives under the lordship of Christ. Below, I'll explore the people who make disciples across cultures, as well as the strategies they use.

12. Adapted from Nehrbass, *God's Image and Global Cultures*, 147 used by permission.

*Who Is Engaged in Cross-cultural Discipleship?*

> **Defining Missionary**
>
> A missionary is someone who is sent by a Christian community primarily for the purpose of making disciples across cultures.

At this point I must address the uncomfortable issue that if missions is cross-cultural discipleship, then some very important work that we do as the church is *not* missions, either because it does not cross cultural boundaries, or doesn't result in disciple-making. Drawing a boundary inevitably means excluding some work from the definition of missions (though such work may be missional and strategic for the church). Consider the following true examples among the students in a graduate degree program in missions:

- Sharon, from the USA, teaches English in Thailand. She was not sent by her church, is not under a mission agency, and receives a salary from her university. While she is working cross-culturally, she does not see herself as a missionary because her presence in Thailand is not particularly about making disciples.
- Miguel, from the Philippines, is studying theology and missions in the USA, but plans to plant churches among his own ethnic group in the Philippines. He considers himself a church planter, but not a missionary.
- Carmen, from the USA, is financially supported by members of her own church to do the bookkeeping for a mission organization in West Africa. She does not particularly "teach them to obey all Jesus has commanded," but her mission organization does have an overall plan to make disciples. Carmen sees herself as a missionary because of her important role in an organization that is doing cross-cultural discipleship.

Of course, the term missionary gets many Christian workers in trouble in parts of the world, and they have learned not to use the term at all—even if they know (and their host country knows) that they are missionaries! Maybe the labels aren't important: who cares if you recognize me as a missionary or not? But on the other hand, if the missionaries are one of the main subjects of focus for missiologists, they'd better be pretty precise about who these missionaries are (and aren't)—while allowing for some "fuzziness."

## Move into Action

If a cross-cultural worker digs wells but has no overall plan for "teaching them to obey all Jesus commanded," then while she is obeying the first commandment to manage the earth for the flourishing of humankind, her work is not part of the narrower aspect of the church's mission to make disciples across cultures. And in all fairness, I must add, if an organization plants churches and hands out tracts, but is not actually "teaching them to obey all Jesus has commanded," then it, too, is not actually making disciples.

Of course, in our day-to-day experience, the set of activities which are involved in making disciples is fuzzy. Healthcare can be done in a way that teaches people to obey Jesus, or it can be done without touching on issues of discipleship. A Christian could work cross-culturally in such a way that she makes disciples in her secular workplace, or she could hide her light under a bushel. By defining missions somewhat narrowly as cross-cultural discipleship, I am not as much excluding certain *activities* as I am focusing on the setting (does it cross cultural boundaries) and strategy (does it make disciples) that drives those activities.

## Ideas for Further Research

1. Do a qualitative study to give voice to a Christian community's understanding of "discipleship."

2. Study biblical scholars' understandings (over time) regarding what Jesus meant by "obey all I have commanded."

## Review Questions

1. What is meant by "discipleship"?

2. What is meant by "missions"?

## Reflection Questions

1. How do you feel about the criteria this book uses to distinguish between missions and other ministries or other cross-cultural work?

2. How do you personally settle the tension between evangelism-as-proclamation and discipleship that encompasses all areas of life?

*Chapter 9*

# Seminal Theories of Cross-Cultural Discipleship

IN ORDER FOR ANY academic field to be seen as a discipline in its own right, scholars within the field must have developed their own theoretical contributions (and even idiosyncratic methodologies for arriving at those theories). Note that two of the theories below are self-named "principles": The Homogeneous Unit Principle and the Pilgrim Principle. While it is not tidy to use two different monikers such as "principle' and "theory," the word "principle" is widely tied to those two particular theories. In the end, the nearly interchangeable use of "principle" and "theory" needn't concern us too much, since "principle," like "theory," can be used to refer to an explanation of the way things are.

## The Indigenizing and Pilgrim Principle

Christianity has always existed in a tension between indigenous and counter-cultural expressions of the faith. Church historian Andrew Walls's categorizing theory (briefly introduced in chapter 3) referred to these poles as the indigenizing principle and the pilgrim principle.[1]

---

1. Walls, *Missionary Movement in Christian History*.

> Chapter Goals
>
> *Knowledge goals:*
>
> - Discuss how theories that were developed in missiology impact the way we make disciples across cultures.
>
> *Action goals:*
>
> - Rather than simply accepting seminal theories that shaped missiology, critique those theories; and conduct rigorous research to generate new understandings (theories) of how the gospel spreads across cultures.
>
> *Heart goals:*
>
> - Commit to generating new knowledge (theories based on actual data) that will help others understand better how Christianity spreads across cultures. This chapter covers nine seminal theories that were developed by missiologists.

> The former refers to that aspect of the gospel which accepts every believer as they are, irrespective of cultural background and geographical location. The latter refers to that aspect of the gospel which is nowhere completely at home, the part that challenges believers to constantly reassess their cultural norms and to become ever more Christ-like in their thoughts and actions.[2]

Walls's main thesis was that because of the indigenizing nature of Christianity, the faith has been lived out in a plurality of expressions as it has become indigenized in such diverse cultures.[3] "The gospel of Jesus Christ can be expressed in any language and become 'at home' in any culture; followers of Jesus do not need to abandon their cultural or ethnic identity when converting to Christ." And yet, conversion "involves the dialectical tension between what we are becoming—the new humanity in Christ—and the familiar patterns that have shaped us."[4]

---

2. Muller, "'Indigenizing' and 'Pilgrim' Principles of Andrew F. Walls Reassessed," 313.

3. Walls, *Missionary Movement in Christian History*.

4. McDermott and Netland, *Trinitarian Theology of Religions*, 165.

Walls's pilgrim principle highlights situations where contextualization is undesirable.[5] Sometimes disciples of Jesus simply won't feel at home in their own culture. In that case, they have more in common with other Christians throughout the globe than they do with those of their own ethnic culture.

> Just as the indigenizing principle, itself rooted in the Gospel, associates Christians with the *particulars* of their culture and group, the pilgrim principle, in tension with the indigenizing and equally [sic] of the Gospel, by associating them with things and people outside the culture and group, is in some respects a *universalizing* factor.[6]

The pilgrim principle serves to curb contextualization. Sometimes Christianity will not feel "contextualized"; it will be counter-cultural.

## The C1–C6 Spectrum

The C1–C6 scale is a categorizing theory which measures the degree to which a believing community fits within the wider society. Note that the "c" stands for Christ-centered communities, not contextualization. This model, developed by John Travis is meant to be descriptive of six types of ecclesial communities in the Muslim world, and is not meant to denote one type as better than any other.[7] The scale moves from a transplanted church (C1) to progressively more cultural relevance, to C5 and C6, which are so culturally embedded they may be syncretistic:

- C1: Global denominational churches using foreign language;
- C2: Global denominational churches using the local vernacular;
- C3: Indigenous church using vernacular;
- C4: Indigenous churches using vernacular and "biblically permissible" cultural (Islamic) forms;
- C5: Christ-centered communities of "Messianic Muslims"; and,
- C6: Small groups of secret believers who are incorporated into wider Muslim communities.

---

5. Walls, *Missionary Movement in Christian History*.
6. Walls, *Missionary Movement in Christian History*, 8.
7. Travis, "C1–C6 Spectrum after Fifteen Years."

The main controversy of the C1–C6 scale has been whether C5 constitutes true converts from Islam, or only people who are still on their journey toward Christianity. Do converts need to be gathered into church communities to be considered followers of Christ? As Travis and Travis put it 17 years after they first developed the C1–C6 scale,

> From a Biblical perspective, can a person be truly saved and continue to be a Muslim? Doesn't a follower of Christ need to identify himself as a Christian and officially join the Christian faith? Can a Muslim follower of Christ retain all Muslim practices, in particular praying in the mosque toward Mecca and continuing to repeat the Muslim creed?[8]

Proponents of C5 contextualization are enthusiastic about "Messianic Muslims" "who reject or modify unbiblical Islamic teachings, yet they still see their lives woven together by the social fabric of Islam."[9] These movements have become known as Insider Movements, and the C1–C6 scale is an important part of the discourse in the Insider Movement debate.

A weakness of the C1–C6 scale is that it attempts to measure two factors which are only sometimes related. Its rubric often conflates the degree of religious freedom with the extent to which a church is contextualized in a Muslim context. For example, C6 believers are often under such a threat of persecution that they cannot risk attending public worship services or carrying Bibles. And it is likely that only societies with wide religious tolerance would engender C1 churches (where Christian worship is done openly in a foreign language). But the degree of religious tolerance in a society does not always determine the extent to which a church is contextualized. A church can be moderately contextualized (C4 or 5) to a Muslim community even when the society enjoys wide religious freedom, as it does in the USA. So the C1–C6 scale is most useful when it is clear about the feature it is measuring. It should focus on the varying responses of contextualization in Muslim contexts rather than correlate contextualization with persecution. And the scale will be more useful as it is modified and updated for changing cultural contexts.

The C1–C6 spectrum caught the imagination of missiologists. Williams has cleverly shown how the scale could be used to describe different approaches toward worship in the USA.[10] C1 would be "high

---

8. Travis, "C1–C6 Spectrum after Fifteen Years," 13.
9. Travis, "C1–C6 Spectrum after Fifteen Years," 53.
10. Williams, "Revisiting the C1–C6 Spectrum in Muslim Contextualization."

church" denominations which have pews, sixteenth-century hymns, and the organ. The priest wears vestments and carries incense. On the other end of the spectrum, C6, individuals identify as believers, but listen to "crossover" bands like U2, and don't meet in church buildings at all. In the middle of the scale we find seeker sensitive churches which use overtly Christian lyrics but have worship bands and clothing styles that reflect contemporary popular culture. Allison engaged in a similar project regarding the church's relevance to postmodernism, modifying the C1–C6 scale to the CM1–CM6 scale.[11] CM1 would represent Christian language that is so entrenched in propositional truths that postmodern communities found little crossover with the church. Moving to the middle of the spectrum, churches would maintain creedal Christianity but would meet the felt needs of postmoderns (by providing a sense of community, for example). CM6 would represent closet Christians existing in a post-Christian culture.

The spectrum easily connects to other missiological concepts. For example, Williams[12] connects the C1–C6 scale with Hiebert's model of critical contextualization.[13] The C1 level represents Hiebert's "denial of the old" which causes Christianity to seem foreign. The C5 and C6 level reflect Hiebert's uncritical contextualization, which leads to syncretism. And the middle levels embody Hiebert's critical contextualization.

The C1–C6 spectrum raises questions about which type of contextualization is desirable. Should churches look different than their surrounding cultural context? Is it possible to have "Churchless Christianity?"[14] What about cases where Muslim Background Believers (MBBs) find non-contextualization to be desirable? For example, some MBBs in Indonesia reject the hijab so that they can signal that they have converted. Or some worshiping communities in the South Pacific prefer the music style of Hillsong over their indigenous forms of dance and music, which are perceived to be the content of "darkness" (heathenism).

## People Proups, Unreached People Groups and Affinity Blocs

The theory which categorizes human societies into people groups "and the subsequent emphasis on unreached peoples (as opposed to unreached

   11. Allison, "Evaluation of Emerging Churches on the Basis of the Contextualization Spectrum."
   12. Williams, "Revisiting the C1–C6 spectrum in Muslim Contextualization."
   13. Hiebert, "Critical Contextualization."
   14. Hoefer, *Churchless Christianity*.

'fields') has been globally seismic in the transformation of missions."[15] It is hard to imagine the missionary enterprise without "people groups"; but the theory is actually a fairly recent development in missiology.

Before the Lausanne Congress on World Evangelization in 1974, missiologists typically strategized about church planting at the national level. They spoke of reaching Nigerians, or Chinese, or Aboriginal Australians. By the mid-1970s, missiologists began to understand the deep significance of ethnic identity, in additional to national identity. Stafford[16] says this revelation came to Ralph Winter through his exposure at Fuller Theological Seminary to Donald McGavran's "homogenous unit" principle (discussed later in this chapter). If people are most likely to worship and learn about God from those who are most similar to them, then missions will have its greatest impact when it is tailored for people who share a cultural background. Missiologists began to take note that, for example, Javanese Muslims have a very different culture than animists in West Timor or West Papua, even though all three groups live in the nation of Indonesia.

These "homogenous units" of shared ethnicity, language, material culture, ritual, and religious background were eventually termed "people groups." The 1982 Lausanne Committee Chicago meeting defined a people group as the "largest unit where gospel can spread without running into cultural or social barriers." It would seem that the most basic way to distinguish people groups would be along language barriers. However, language barriers are fuzzy; what one person sees as a dialect another sees as a different language indeed. And missiologists have noted that languages cross ethnic boundaries, social statuses, and even religious boundaries. Beginning with the world's 7,000 distinct languages,[17] the Joshua project took into account features such as religion, and ethnicity,[18] to arrive at a list of over 16,000 people groups.

Once people groups were identified, strategists began to catalog these groups in terms of evangelistic response and need, for the purposes of prayer.[19] And mission organizations began to direct mission resources to the fields (i.e., people groups) that were 1) seen as "ripe" (receptive), or 2) to those where no work has been done. If it were not for the concept

15. Piper, "John Piper's Personal Tribute to the Late Ralph Winter," para. 6.
16. Stafford, "Ralph Winter."
17. Lewis et al., *Ethnologue*.
18. "Global Statistics."
19. Johnstone and Mandryk, *Operation World*.

of people groups, mission mobilizers would not have come to emphasize *unreached* people groups in the 1990s.

## Profile of a Missiologist: Ralph Winter

### (1924-2009)

*Education: BS Engineering, Cal Tech; MA Columbia University; MDiv from Princeton University; PhD in anthropology and linguistics from Cornell University*

*Occupation: Missionary; Mission Agency executive; professor of missiology*

Ralph and Roberta Winter served with the Presbyterian church among the Mam of Guatemala from 1956 to 1966. There, Winter developed a model of theological education by extension (TEE), where local pastors can receive theological training by distance education, rather than leaving their support system and churches in order to receive education at an expensive theological institute.

After returning to the USA, Winter began teaching missiology at Fuller Theological Seminary. The president of Fuller at the time, David Hubbard, told Winter "for missiology to gain academic respect, missiologists needed a professional society that sponsored regular meetings, published a scholarly journal and promoted publication of monographs in the field of missions studies."[1] So along with his colleague Gerald Anderson, Winter was instrumental in founding the American Society of Missiology (ASM) in 1972. He later founded the US Center for World Mission (Now called Frontier Ventures), a missionary think tank that houses the Perspectives on the World Christian Movement, the *International Journal of Frontier Missiology*, William Carey International University, William Carey Publishing, and the popular magazine *Mission Frontiers*. Winter personally published over 200 articles and books on missiological issues through these channels.

One of Winter's most significant contributions was the development of the notion of "people groups." Winter also developed the taxonomy of two structures for God's redemptive mission: sodalities (parachurch organizations) and modalities (denominational mission boards), as well as the E1, E2, and E3 scale for cultural similarity, where E1 encompasses similar cultural environments, and E3 evangelism would involve significant cultural differences.

---

[1] Shenk, "Dr. Ralph Winter and the American Society of Missiology," 92.

The concept of people groups has now been amended to include seventeen major "affinity blocs," including the Arab world, East Asians, Eurasians, Jews, Malay, North Americans, Pacific Islanders, etc. As affinity blocs are highly reductive and do not take into account these major differences in ethnicity, language, or religion, the concept may appear to be a regression from "people groups." However, affinity blocs are also a missiological application of the homogenous unit principle: Mission strategies within the Arab world will be conceived differently than they will among North Americans or East Asians.

The concept of people groups, combined with the twentieth-century push for "evangelization in this generation" led to the discourse of unreached people groups. Once these unreached people groups could be identified, mobilizers of missions suggested adopting people groups, especially in a geographic region missiologists called the 10/40 window, which is discussed below.

## The 10/40 window

As the twentieth century was closing, missiologists developed a reductive theory that "97% of the persons who inhabit the least evangelized countries" live in a space between Turkey and China, in the latitudes 10 to 40 degrees north.[20] This geographic area became known as the 10/40 Window. Luis Bush, an evangelist from Argentina, recounts how he developed the theoretical concept:

> At the July 1989 Lausanne II Conference in Manila, I stated in my plenary session that most of the unreached people groups "live in a belt that extends from West Africa across Asia, between ten degrees north to forty degrees north of the equator. This includes the Muslim block, the Hindu block, and the Buddhist block . . . we must refocus our efforts in evangelization."[21]

The 10/40 Window became a prescriptive model that mobilized many efforts for church planting in the 1990s and 2000s, as mission organizations began focusing their church planting strategies, personnel, and media on populations in this region. Churches began praying for the people groups in the 10/40 Window.[22] The goal of these efforts was the

20. Bush, "Getting to the Core of the Core."
21. Bush, "A Brief Historical Overview of the AD2000 and Beyond Movement and Joshua Project," 1.
22. Daugherty, "Praying for the Lost in the 10/40 Window"; Wagner et al., *Praying*

establishment of a self-supporting, self-multiplying, and self-governing church among every unreached people group.

The impetus to "finish the task" can be tied to eschatology. Hastening the evangelization of every ethnolinguistic people group, called "closure theology" by some, became a sort of "dubious attempt to trigger the second coming of Christ by fulfilling the conditions of Matthew 24:14."[23] The problem is, in reality, humans cannot be divided into bounded, distinct, and static ethnic groups. The lines between ethnolinguistic groups are fuzzy and dynamic.[24] If the lines between *ethne* are contested and changing, it would be impossible to delineate a time (in the future) when people of all *ethne* have an established church. Some say the rhetoric of finishing the task is also dangerous as it conflates the Great Commission with the task of planting self-supporting churches.

The 10/40 Window has drawn other criticisms. The concept is neater as a theory than human geography is in reality; so it suffers from imprecision:

> Indonesia, the largest Muslim country in the world, does not fall within the parameters of the 10/40 window (see also Coote 2000). Later attempts to redraw the Window but keep the language still left people struggling with such anomalies as the fact that Kazakistan [sic] and Malaysia fall outside the boundaries, and yet the Philippines are inside. In fact, the northern two-thirds of the Philippines falls inside, while the southern third is outside, just the opposite of what the Window proposes.[25]

The imprecision of the 10/40 Window raises issues about other missiological attempts to generalize large population groups. For example, we are aware that the countries in the southern hemisphere are significantly poorer than those in the northern; so using the term "global south" to refer to people living in poverty can be highly misleading. In fact, however, the majority of people who live on less than a dollar a day actually live north of the 10/40 Window, in Bangladesh, Burkina Faso, Laos, Liberia, Cambodia, China, Haiti, India, Mali, Niger, Turkmenistan, Uzbekistan, and Papua New Guinea. Terms like the "majority world," "third world," and "two-thirds" world may be attempts to correct the

---

*through the 100 Gateway Cities of the 10/40 Window.*

23. Coote, "AD 2000" and the "10/40 Window," 160.
24. Nehrbass, *God's Image and Global Cultures*, 70–72.
25. Rynkiewich, "Corporate Metaphors and Strategic Thinking," 219.

imprecision of the North-South dyad; but these terms are also ambiguous and contested. Additionally, scholars in intercultural studies often use the East-West dyad to refer to cultural differences (in terms of hospitality or honor, for instance); yet such generalizations are imprecise, contested, reductive, and subject to "identity freezing."[26]

But the 10/40 Window can be useful even without a tie to faulty eschatology, outdated ideas about ethnicity, and geographic imprecision. The tremendous value is that it causes mobilizers of missions to think about issues like *priority*. Is India or China more deserving of missionary efforts than Germany or Canada (which have both become quite secular)? Does focusing on the resistant peoples of Asia diminish or compete with our efforts in Africa, the Pacific, South America, or other pockets of the world where it is not currently in vogue to send missionaries?

## The Homogenous Unit Principle (HUP)

"Probably the most controversial idea of the Church Growth Movement was the elaboration of the Homogeneous Unit Principle (HUP)."[27] The HUP is a reductive theory about human nature, which states "People like to become Christians without crossing racial, linguistic or class barriers" therefore "conversion should occur with the minimum of social dislocation."[28] That is, church planting efforts should focus on "homogenous units" which McGavran defines as "simply a section of society in which all the members have some characteristic in common."[29] McGavran avers "the great obstacles to conversion are social, not theological."[30] People will not give a church a fair hearing if they stick out in the congregation like a sore thumb. Birds of a feather flock together.

The HUP is a product of the discourse of contextualization and the notion of people groups: The gospel must be presented to people in ways that are culturally familiar to them, including indigenous language, worship style, architecture, and so on. The HUP suggests that church growth efforts will be most effective if they are directed at homogenous units (which *can* be taken to mean ethnolinguistic people groups).

26. Nehrbass, *God's Image and Global Cultures*, 100–101.
27. Pickett, "Caste-Sensitive Church Planting," 178.
28. McGavran, *Understanding Church Growth*, x.
29. McGavran, *Understanding Church Growth*, 85.
30. McGavran, *Understanding Church Growth*, 156.

It is significant that the HUP was conceived by missiologists who worked in India, since India is one of the most socially stratified nations. Caste identity can significantly limit South Asian's interactions with others who are of higher or lower standing. Therefore, it would seem, church ministry would be easiest among people of the same caste. The HUP suggests that church planting efforts should focus on these homogenous units, like the Dalits or the Brahmins.

The HUP is so controversial because it seems to subvert the value of diversity, the cross-pollination of theological thought, and the unity of the body of Christ. This emphasis on distinct worshiping communities may seem to contrast Gal 2:28, "there is neither Jew nor Gentile, neither slave nor free, nor is there male and female, for you are all one in Christ Jesus" (NIV). Yet, Wagner argued, "Gentiles do not have to become Jews, females do not have to become males . . . in order to enter into and share the blessings of God's Kingdom."[31] The HUP was meant to reify cultural difference, not to cause cultural divisions. As Steffen mentioned, "McGavran believed the homogeneous unit was a necessary starting point. He also believed it was not the end point. Homogenous churches could and should eventually become more heterogeneous."[32]

In an effort to win numbers, is McGavran's HUP sacrificing a depth of theology and Christian community that could be gained through a heterogeneous (multicultural) church?[33] Is it better to see HUP churches as a temporary means for bringing people into the church until they grow in their faith and become more open to worshiping with others?[34]

> The witness of separate congregations in the same geographical area on the basis of language and culture may have to be accepted as a necessary, but provisional, measure for the sake of the fulfillment of Christ's mission.[35]

---

31. Wagner, "How Ethical is the Homogeneous Unit Principle," 18.
32. Steffen, *Facilitator Era*, 28.
33. Plueddemann, "Needed."
34. Plueddemann, "Needed," 12.
35. Newbigin, "What is 'A Local Church Truly United'?" 124.

## Profile of a Missiologist: Charles Peter Wagner

*(1930–2016)*

*Education: PhD (Social Ethics) from University of Southern California*

*Occupation: Missionary in Bolivia; professor of church growth at Fuller Theological Seminary's School of World Missions*

C. Peter Wagner authored over 70 books on church growth, spiritual warfare, healing and prayer. He impacted missiology by connecting church growth to church leadership by applying Donald McGavran's model of church growth to the American pulpit. Churches do naturally grow when church members bear children—a phenomenon Wagner referred to as biological growth. But healthy churches also will necessarily experience "conversion growth." As with McGavran's model, the *telos* of missionary outreach was not simply evangelism but church growth.

Yet numbers were not the only metric of success. Wagner's model can be described as follows: Cells of believers + congregation + celebration = church. He coined the term "body evangelism" to describe the three "p's" of evangelism: presence, proclamation, and persuasion for people to join a church body.

As with his colleague Charles Kraft, Wagner's thought moved from missiology to spiritual warfare later on in his career. Ministry must include power encounters—a notion influenced by Wimber and Springer's *Power Evangelism*.[1] Wagner noted that in the twentieth century the Holy Spirit was first manifested widely among Pentecostals at the Azusa Street revival, and later among mainline and Catholic churches during the charismatic renewals in the 1960s.[2] Wagner and other thinkers at Fuller School of World Mission may have sensed the need for evangelicals to grab hold of this Holy Spirit fervor without becoming outright Pentecostals.[3] Wagner termed this movement of Holy Spirit within evangelicalism the "Third Wave."

As a strong personality who touched on sensitive issues, Wagner was a controversial figure. The notion that missionary success can be measured by numerical growth has been controversial since McGavran and Wagner began forming these ideas. Elizondo and Castuera contended with Wagner, suggesting that Providence is more of a contributing factor than missionary intentionality.[4] Wagner's affiliation with the New Apostolic Reformation (NAR) movement was also controversial.

---

[1] Wimber and Springer, *Power Evangelism*.
[2] Stetzer, "C. Peter Wagner (1930–2016)."
[3] Bialecki, "Third Wave and the Third World."
[4] Elizondo and Castuera, "Responses to the Article by C. Peter Wagner."

As with other concepts in this chapter (such as "redemptive analogies"), the homogeneous unit principle is more useful as a descriptive theory than as a prescriptive model. It is undeniable that people form together in groups of shared values, language, and beliefs. This is basic to cultural and social anthropology. HUP discourse is about recognizing how groups designate the ingroup and the outgroup. The question is, how will Christians, no matter which ingroup, respond to their outgroups? "Homogeneity may be good or bad, depending on *how it is used*. My suggestion is that, in keeping with the aims of Christian growth, we should take a position that attempts to reinforce the strengths of homogeneity but to overcome the difficulties."[36] If the HUP is more descriptive than prescriptive, missiologists can challenge the tendency for churches to be so homogenous. We must be mindful of the ethnocentrism that seems to be inherent in any socially constructed group. How can we be relevant to a bounded "ingroup" yet also challenge that group to widen its boundaries?

And in fact, the expansion of Christianity has shown that the HUP is not a necessary (let alone desirable) factor of church growth. "The [early] church not only grew, but *it grew across cultural barriers*." The New Testament "provides plenty of examples of how the barriers had been abolished in the new humanity."[37] Further, in an era of globalization, there are no more homogenous units. Even isolated tribes have members who move to capital cities and intermarry with other groups.[38] And in fact, societies have never existed in homogenous groups; rather, classes and ethnically distinct groups have been interdependent in wider social networks.[39] Hyatt describes a growing trend of multiculturalism as a church growth strategy in this era of globalization.[40]

In summary, while the HUP has gained great attention in the missiological community, causing us to think about unity and cultural diversity in the church, the model may be more academic than real, and may not have impacted the way we actually do missions.[41] In reality, issues of heterogeneity and homogeneity are much more complex than the HUP supposed.

---

36. Kraft, "Anthropological Apologetic for the Homogeneous Unit Principle in Missiology," 125.
37. Padilla, "Unity of the Church and the Homogeneous Unit Principle," 29.
38. Nehrbass, *God's Image and Global Cultures*, 71.
39. McClintock, "Sociological Critique of the Homogeneous Unit Principle."
40. Hyatt, "From Homogeneous to a Heterogeneous Unit Principle."
41. Gration, "Homogeneous Unit Principle."

## Profile of a Missiologist: Donald McGavran

### (1897–1990)

*Education: BA (Butler University); BD (Yale); MA (College of Missions, Indianapolis); PhD in education (Columbia University)*

*Occupation: Missionary to India; Dean of Fuller Theological Seminary's School of World Missions*

Donald McGavran was a third-generation missionary to India. "The young McGavran was put in charge of 80 missionaries, five hospitals, many high schools and primary schools, evangelistic work and a leprosy home."[1]

McGavran is considered the father of the church growth movement because he devoted his academic career to understanding why churches grow. He "developed a field research method for studying growing (and non-growing) churches, employing historical analysis, observations, and interviews to collect data for analysis and case studies."[2]

Concerned by discourse about a "moratorium on mission" from the mainline church, and the redefinition of mission as "everything the church does outside its four walls" (including the social gospel), McGavran became convinced of the need for a return to missiological curriculum.[3] He established missiology at Fuller in an era when missions was disappearing from the curriculum of mainline seminaries.[4]

McGavran noticed that while conversion is an individualistic phenomenon in European cultures, it has consequences for a person's wider social network in many traditional societies. Therefore conversion is often a collective decision. At times, conversions are decided *en masse*—a phenomenon that McGavran called a "people movement." The missiologist's task would be to facilitate such a movement.

McGavran articulated two controversial concepts in *Understanding Church Growth*. First, he coined the Homogenous Unit Principle: "People like to become Christians without crossing racial, linguistic, or class barriers."[5] McGavran also argued for a "harvest theology" (based on Matt 10:11–14) that focused on a people group's receptivity to the gospel. If receptivity ebbs and flows, missionaries should strategically focus their efforts on the areas where they will harvest the most fruit. This strategy is markedly different than the 10/40 window model and discourse of Unreached People groups that permeated missiology at the end of the twentieth century.

---

[1] Pickett, "Caste-sensitive Church Planting," 178.
[2] Hunter, "Legacy of Donald A. McGavran," 158.
[3] McGavran, "My Pilgrimage in Mission."
[4] Hunter, "Legacy of Donald A. McGavran," 159.
[5] McGavran, *Understanding Church Growth*, 160.

## The Modality/Sodality Model

Is world missions the job of the local church, or of professional mission agencies? Winter's categorizing theory of modalities and sodalities argues that the task belongs to congregations as well as professional guilds.[42] Local churches play an important role in identifying missionaries in their midst, sending them out, and planting denominational or "daughter" churches. And such missionary outreach has, in return, a healthy impact on the local church. As Newbigin put it, "An unchurchly mission is as much a monstrosity as an unmissionary church."[43] In the book of Acts, churches were already sending out missionaries who planted other churches.[44] Winter called these congregations "modalities."[45]

Yet many tasks related to world missions require a guild of skilled workers who are professionally accountable to an organization related to their specialty. Winter called such mission agencies sodalities, from the Latin word *sodalis* or "companion."[46] Medieval examples of sodalities were the monasteries. They were guilds of "professional" clergy who promoted social welfare and the study of Scripture. Today, these sodalities are parachurch organizations that specialize in Bible translation, media production, economic development, legal advocacy, orphan care, teaching English, etc. It is highly unrealistic for even mega churches to identify enough experts in their midst who could be sent out to do Bible translations of high quality; the task is more suited to organizations that focus strictly on Bible translation. This can be true of community development agencies as well. Of course, this raises the question of whether local churches are even equipped to send out church planters in foreign countries—is the task really "transferable" from one's home soil to a foreign setting? Does this task also require a specially trained guild?

Since sodalities are not connected to a denominational body, they often emphasize aspects of individual discipleship without a great deal of enthusiasm for church multiplication. On the other hand, denominations often become myopic in their need to multiply, without emphasis on the whole person, or on deep training before baptism.

---

42. Winter, "Two Structures of God's Redemptive Mission."
43. Newbigin, *Household of God*, 201.
44. Ott and Wilson, *Global Church Planting*.
45. Winter, "Two Structures of God's Redemptive Mission."
46. Winter, "Two Structures of God's Redemptive Mission."

Smither has argued that Winter's sodality/modality model can give the inaccurate impression that during the medieval period, missionary efforts were not normative for local congregations, only for sodalities such as monastic missionary orders.[47] Quite to the contrary, Smither argues that it was normal for church leaders (such as Boniface, Patrick, Basil, and Augustine of Canterbury) to mobilize local congregations for cross-cultural outreach. Missionaries were essentially sent by both the local church and the universal church.

Of course, the world has changed drastically since the times of Boniface and Basil. While the church may still be the primary impetus for world missions, the reality is that much missionary work is done nowadays through sodalities. The overwhelming majority of those who serve in cross-cultural evangelism are affiliated with a sodality, because mission agencies lend credibility to a missionary's work, plus they offer a level of support and accountability that seldom comes from local churches. However, very few missionaries are actually commissioned by sodalities. In fact, the local congregations they have contact with are the ones funding their work, praying for success, and visiting them on the field. In this sense, Smither's thesis is undeniable: Even in light of the proliferation of sodalities, in the end, it is the church (that is, the universal church) which actually sends out the majority of those who make disciples across cultures.[48]

## The Emic/Etic Distinction

Do anthropologists seek to describe culture "from a native point of view," or from a more objective, theoretical or global point of view? Is it even possible to get a native—let alone objective—point of view? This debate about how to do anthropological analysis is often referred to as the emic/etic distinction. Kenneth Pike, the eminent linguist in the Summer Institute of Linguistics, is often (correctly) credited as the originator of the emic/etic distinction[49]—a categorizing theory which became a significant, albeit controversial, model for missiological anthropology. Pike later reminisced:

---

47. Smither, "When the Church was the Mission Organization."
48. Smither, "When the Church was the Mission Organization."
49. Pike, *Language in Relation to a Unified Theory.*

> I do not know where my material will fit in history 100 years from now. My best guess would be to look at the footnotes of the last ten years. The only concept of mine which is mentioned often is *emics/etics*. Perhaps this idea will survive because it insists on the relationship of the observer to the data, as against an abstract science in which the observer is somehow eliminated in principle even when this would be impossible in fact.[50]

Few authors explain how Pike arrived at the terms emic and etic. The terms come from the field of linguistics. Linguists are interested in two types of speech sounds in any given language: the phonetics and the phonemics. Phonetics covers all possible sounds that can be found in that language. But not all these sounds actually carry meaning to the hearers. Sometimes, for instance, speakers of American English pronounce the letter "t" with a small puff of air afterwards, as in the word "take." But sometimes that small puff of air connected to t (and k and p, in American English) disappears, as in the word "stop." The puff of air, called aspiration, is not meaningful in American English. But it is a meaningful distinction in some other languages like Korean. In contrast to phonetics, which examines all sounds of a language, phonemics only examines those sounds which are recognized by native speakers as important or meaningful. Phonetics, then, is the outsider's perspective of a language, gained through scientific study; and phonemics is the insider's perspective on the language, gained through immersion from birth.

Pike believed that "verbal and nonverbal activity is a unified whole."[51] Therefore, he borrowed the suffixes emic and etic from linguistics to describe a similar phenomenon in cultural description. The etic view is the outsider's, based on theory that has been constructed at a more global level. The emic view is the insider's, and may or may not wholly agree with the etic view.

Anthropologist Marvin Harris found emics and etics to be a useful distinction when discussing the phenomenon of the sacred cow in India.[52] The emic understanding is that cows are not eaten because they are inherently sacred. The etic view takes into account other reasons for not eating beef, such as the agricultural benefits of keeping cattle alive for pulling ploughs and producing dung for fertilizer and cooking fuel.

---

50. Pike, in Kaye, "Interview with Kenneth Pike," para. 44.
51. Pike, *Language in Relation to a Unified Theory*, 2.
52. Harris, "Cultural Ecology of India's Sacred Cattle."

The emic/etic distinction raises a number of questions. Is the cultural insider to be taken at his word when he describes the meaning of his own culture? He is, after all, the expert informant on his own culture. And is it paternalistic for social scientists to insist that emic explanations (about why Hindus don't eat cows, for example) are not the "real" or "scientific" explanations? "For Pike, emic and etic standpoints are not incompatible; rather, they represent two pictures of a stereoscopic view."[53] Pike was an idealist (like many evangelicals in the twentieth century). For idealists, underlying ideas are at the center of what drives culture. So Pike's goal was to get the "native point of view." Marvin Harris, a cultural materialist, disagreed with Pike, insisting that culture is not always driven by an underlying worldview. This debate over emics-etics became the subject of a special session at the American Anthropological Association in 1988.[54]

The emic/etic distinction also raises questions about perspectivalism. Is the etic observer any more objective than the emic one? Or are they both subjective? And if the goal is to "grasp the native's point of view, his relation to life, to realize his vision of his world,"[55] then the question arises, "Which native?"[56] If all views are subjective and contested, then there really is no etic/emic bifurcation—there are simply multiple perspectives. The most obvious difficulty with the emic/etic distinction is that sometimes outsiders become so familiar with a culture, they can "speak" it like a native; and likewise, sometimes insiders become so adept at anthropological theory and cross-cultural studies, they can analyze their own culture as an outsider would.

In summary, missiologists have found the emic/etic model useful for culture learning and analysis[57] and for understanding cross-cultural hermeneutics.[58] But the bifurcation is fuzzy, rather than discrete.

## The Flaw of the Excluded Middle

Missionaries from the west tend to focus much of their energy on explaining how to get saved, which involves working through theories of the atonement with their target audience. And they tend to help with

53. Mostowlansky and Rota, "Matter of Perspective?" 323.
54. Headland et al., *Emics and Etics*.
55. Malinowski, *Argonauts of the Western Pacific*, 25.
56. McGee and Warms, *Anthropological Theory*, 342.
57. Steinbronn, "Missiological Bridge-Building Based Upon an Emic and Etic."
58. Craffert, "Is the Emic-Etic Distinction a Useful Tool."

the material needs for the here-and-now, by bringing medical care, technology, literacy, etc. And people from other religious backgrounds may even embrace both the technology and the missionaries' ideas about salvation from the punishment of sin. But what happens when a hurricane is looming, or when there is a drought, or when an elder in the village falls ill? Why do people in the fields where missionaries work so often turn to shamans, divination, rituals, and magic, for the pressing needs of daily life? Hiebert noted this phenomenon in India. South Asian Christians understood the ultimate, big idea teachings of Christianity, but had a hard time seeing how it was relevant to daily life.[59] Missionaries were in error to emphasize the eternal benefits of Christianity while omitting Jesus's relevance in cases of witchcraft, sorcery, or other misfortunes. Hiebert called this explanatory (or reductive) theory the "flaw of the excluded middle."

Protestant interest in spiritual warfare and charismatic expressions of faith are essentially responses to the flaw of the excluded middle. Pentecostals address this "Excluded Middle" by calling on the name of Jesus to combat the power of territorial spirits, fate, shamans, etc. Out of Pentecostalism was born the prosperity gospel, which also made Christianity relevant for practitioners' daily experience by promising a spiritual solution for securing health, wealth, happiness. Mainline Protestants typically conceptualize Christianity in terms of securing eternal life, and the charismatic renewal in mainline churches made Christianity relevant to this present world. By the 1980s, evangelicals also began to be interested in issues of spiritual warfare and charisma. Wagner referred to this rise of interest as the "Third Wave" of the Holy Spirit. The Third Wave filled in this "excluded middle" for evangelicals.

## Redemptive Analogies

Richardson's concept of "redemptive analogies" was based on his experience with the Sawi in Indonesia.[60] The Sawi, who held treachery to be a high ideal, concluded that Judas was the hero of the New Testament. Being in a constant state of war with neighboring tribes, the warfare would reach a hiatus whenever the tribe would offer a "peace child" to live among the rival tribe. As long as the child survived among its enemies, the villages were at peace. Richardson explained to the Sawi that God

---

59. Hiebert, "Flaw of the Excluded Middle."
60. Richardson, *Peace Child*.

sent us his Peace Child, and even though we killed Him, God still wants peace with us. The story of Jesus as a Peace Child served as a "redemptive analogy" among the Sawi, by making the gospel relevant to their cultural logic.

Richardson suggested a reductive explanatory theory: "God has imbedded in the rituals, ceremonies, history, and memory of primitive cultures concepts that portray key elements of the gospel."[61] People who were not privy to God's special revelation, like Melchizedek in Gen 14, seem to have an amount of general revelation that prepares their hearts for God. Richardson referred to the preparatory knowledge of God as the Melchizedek factor. And yet, the Sodom factor corrupts this knowledge of God.

Are Richardson's concepts of redemptive analogies and the Melchizedek factor prescriptive or descriptive?[62] If they are descriptive theories, they serve to inspire us about God's far-reaching grace as He has come before the missionary in societies from the Karen of Burma to the Incas to Indonesia, and has revealed himself (to some extent). However, the models are more problematic if they are taken to be prescriptive for missions in general. The implication is that these redemptive analogies lie dormant until a herald of the gospel can bring in the missing pieces. If churches could just discover these redemptive analogies, revival would ensue.[63] This notion excited mission mobilizers. In fact, after years of seeing few conversions, a supporter told me, "That's because you did not find the redemptive analogy. Once you do that, people will convert." Moreau reports that a missionary among the Momina of West Papua lamented that a colleague "had overlooked numerous potentially helpful but less significant bridges in searching for a single key [redemptive analogy]."[64]

Demarest and Harpel suggest that what Richardson has described are not redemptive analogies, but rather non-redemptive analogies, since such cultural logics, without the special revelation of Christ, only point to the inability of culture to bring people redemption.[65] This is not just an issue of semantics; evangelical theologians have critiqued Richardson for teetering near inclusivism, by apparently accepting general revelation as redemptive (see chapter 2).

61. Richardson, *Eternity in their Hearts*.
62. Richardson, *Eternity in their Hearts*.
63. Hrangkhuma, "How Redemptive Analogies Can Help Churches Grow."
64. Moreau, *Contextualization*, 148.
65. Demarest and Harpel, "Don Richardson's 'Redemptive Analogies.'"

## Profile of a Missiologist: Don Richardson

*(contemporary)*

Education: Prairie Bible Institute; Summer Institute of Linguistics
Occupation: Missionary to the Sawi in West Papua, Missionary spokesman, author

Don Richardson never taught full time at a university, and his publications would be considered popular rather than academic. Yet his theories of redemptive analogies, the Melchizedek factor, and original monotheism captured the imagination of missionaries and mobilizers of missionaries.

Richardson provided data from around the world that suggested that God has planted the notion of a Supreme Being deep within the human psyche.[1] This is a simplified version of Wilhelm Schmidt's massive "culture-history."[2] Like other "diffusionary anthropologists," Schmidt believed that cultural elements (bows and arrows, ideas about exogamy or endogamy, religion, etc.) must have been diffused from a proto-civilization. For Schmidt and Richardson, this uber civilization was directly inherited from Noah's descendants, so it must have had a vestige of belief in one high God. The original culture, then, was monotheistic, but subsequent diffusion and cultural innovations led to increased interest in ritual and "middle level" religious activity, to the near extinction of belief in the high God. Yet spanning from the Karen of Burma to the ancient Incas, to Sub Saharan African religions, tribal peoples seem to have a name for the High God who seems to have forgotten them. Perhaps if missionaries would just reintroduce these peoples to their long lost belief in God, they would experience a collective conversion. Richardson's stories of mass conversions in these tribes caught the imaginations of missionaries and churches, especially through his involvement in the US Center for World Mission's missionary course called Perspectives on the World Christian Movement.

It is worth pointing out that Scripture does not attest to original monotheism; in fact, it often emphasizes the lostness of other religions. Further, the overwhelming data from around the world do not support Richardson's claim to a near universal knowledge of a high God. Nor is this actually a problem for missions, for, as Adeney suggested, people do not need to find coherence with their own religious background to convert.[3] They may come to Christ as they recognize their sinfulness, felt needs, or dissatisfaction with their religion.

Aside from the critiques of his Melchizedek factor and model of redemptive analogies, Richardson shaped mission mobilization by championing the cause of frontier missions, Bible translation, as well as the importance of learning local cultures.

---

[1] Richardson, *Eternity in their Hearts.*
[2] Schmidt, *Origin and Growth of Religion.*
[3] Adeney, "Review of Eternity in their Hearts."

## Conclusion

Missiology is most credible and useful when it produces theories that are explanatory. The theories above explain phenomena such as: people come to Christ in homogenous groups, cultures differ in construals of the individual-collective dimension, missions is done through the church and parachurch organizations. Many other theories have been developed; in fact, most dissertations related to missions should generate an explanatory theory and perhaps a prescriptive model. As these models and theories are developed over time, the discipline of missiology comes of age, and even fragments as academics become polarized about the validity of some of these theories.

## Ideas for Further Research

Many missiological models have been tested "in the lab" of academia, but have not been extensively researched in the field. Some examples include:

1. Interview Muslim background believers to understand how their integration of gospel and culture challenges and informs the C1–C6 spectrum.

2. Gather data on the preaching of the gospel in specific cultural setting to see how it informs and challenges the notion of redemptive analogies.

3. Perform quantitative studies on conversion experiences to understand how cultural contextualization is correlated with likelihood of conversion.

## Review Questions

1. What is the difference between a theory and a model, in this book?

2. How are missiological theories and models in missiology generated?

## Reflection Question

1. What missiological theories are most useful to your work? (Note, this may include models that are not discussed in this chapter.)

*Chapter 10*

# Seminal Models for Cross-Cultural Discipleship

OVER THE CENTURIES, THE church has experimented with countless methods for making disciples across cultures. Some "teach them to obey all Jesus commanded" through overtly ministerial activities such as planting churches, teaching in international seminaries, exorcising demons, and preaching to crowds at college campuses. But missionaries are engaged in numerous other activities such as leadership development, medical ministry, relief and aid, orphanages, broadcasting, education. In 2016, 23 percent of missionaries said their primary activity was development and relief, 18 percent said education, and 14 percent said mission support.[1] Each of these activities aims at bringing spheres of life under the lordship of Christ as they explore biblical teachings. For instance, community development and business as mission seek to transform the economic lives of disciples as they fulfill the first commandment to flourish through productive work; theological education by extension (TEE) and leadership training help church leaders be more Christ-like; healthcare as mission seeks to provide biblical views of sickness causation and healing.

---

1. Newell, *North American Mission Handbook*, 58.

## Chapter Goals

*Knowledge goals:*

- Discuss how various missionary methods (below) are connected to discipleship

*Action goals:*

- Critically examine the advantages and drawbacks of using various missionary methods for disciple-making.

*Heart goals:*

- Commit to using your skills and vocational background to engage in the missionary models that are most suited to you.

Yet all of these strategies for missions are also interrelated. For example, health care missions has an aspect of sociality, education, and economic development. Figure 7 below shows how various missionary strategies are integrated, yet fit together in the bigger picture of making disciples across cultures.

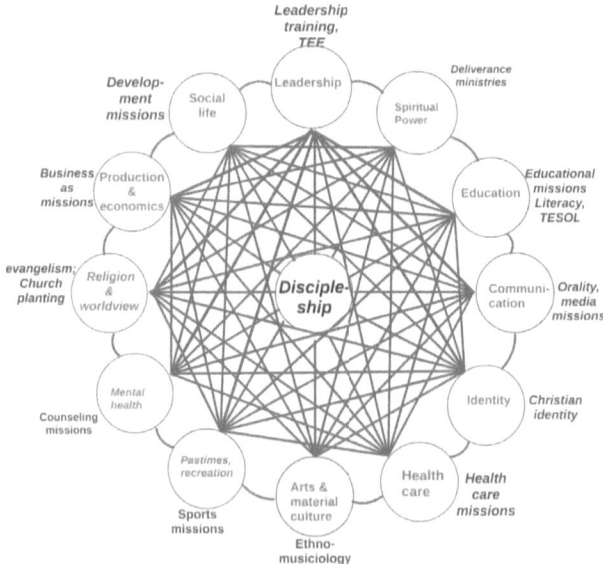

**Figure 7: Missionary methods as means for making disciples across cultures**

This is not to imply that each missionary strategy has a one-to-one correlation with a specific sphere of culture. Leadership training may impact many aspects of life such as politics, business, and church life. And the diagram above is not exhaustive. Missionaries have developed numerous methods for discipling people across cultures to bring the spheres of their lives under the lordship of Christ.

Note that while we may think of fancy methods such as ethnomusicology or business as mission as "cutting edge," none of these methods are actually new. The apostle Paul contextualized the gospel for his audiences 2000 years ago; Christianity has long spread through the Bible story telling methods used by the International Orality Network; the church has traditionally done community development wherever it spread the gospel. Paul didn't even invent the missionary strategy of tentmaking; people have always had to find work when they move to a new setting. And Bibles have been translated since the Jewish scribes translated the Old Testament into Greek in the third century BC (the translation is known as the Septuagint).

## The Three-Selves Model

The missiological model that has had the greatest impact is arguably the "three-selves" or independent church model:[2] Missionaries should aim to plant churches that are self-governing, self-supporting, and self-propagating. Henry Venn and Rufus Anderson were early promoters of these "three selves," but the desire to establish churches and an indigenous missionary force can be traced back at least to the time of William Carey.[3] Anderson's model for indigeneity focused on native leadership, whereas Venn was more concerned about avoiding dependency.[4] Venn wrote,

> Regarding the ultimate object of mission . . . to be the settlement of a native Church, under native pastors, upon a self-supporting system . . . as it has been happily expressed, "the euthanasia of a mission" takes place when a missionary, surrounded by well-trained native congregations, under native pastors, is able to resign all pastoral work into their hands.[5]

---

2. Shenk, "Origins and Evolution of the Three-Selfs in Relation to China," 28.
3. Shenk, "Origins and Evolution of the Three-Selfs in Relation to China," 28–29.
4. Shenk, "Origins and Evolution of the Three-Selfs in Relation to China," 29.
5. Hawks and Perry, *Journal of the General Conventions Church*, 6:345.

Venn urged other members of the Church Missionary Society (CMS) to establish indigenous churches in their field, and the "three-selves" model spread throughout Africa as well, as mission societies established divinity schools to train up native pastors who would lead their own self-multiplying churches.[6]

## Three Self Model

### Why it works:

The Three-self model has recognized the dignity of local leaders and the value of host cultures.

### What it might miss:

God never intended us to be self-sufficient. The church should always be learning from, participating with, and giving to, Christians across cultures. The Three-self model tends to under-emphasize interdependence.

John Nevius developed a similar plan for indigenous churches in China, arguing that the "old plan" of paying native evangelists caused dependency on the missionaries. "Nevius paid a visit to Korea in 1890 and his plan was later credited with having played an important part in the growth of the church there."[7] Could the rapid church growth in South Korea be attributed to the early use of the indigenous method?

The three-selves model has been widely adapted. Bosch, for example, suggests the model must include a fourth self: self-theologizing.[8] And Tippett suggested that a self-sustaining church has six, not three, marks: self-image, self-functioning, self-determining, self-supporting, self-propagating and self-giving.[9]

Even though the three-selves model is one of the oldest missiological models, it is just as relevant today, as people are still unraveling colonialism, and as nationalism remains strong. But the push for indigenous churches is also coming under scrutiny in an era of globalization. Isn't it more

---

6. Nkonge, "Church Missionary Society's Burden."
7. Shenk, "Origins and Evolution of the Three-Selfs in Relation to China," 30.
8. Bosch, *Transforming Mission*.
9. Tippett, "Indigenous Principles in Mission Today."

realistic for churches to be interdependent, rather than independent? Is self-determination really the litmus test of a healthy church?

### Profile of a Missiologist: Henry Venn

### (1796–1873)

*Education:* Queens' College, Cambridge (BA; MA; BD)

*Occupation:* Anglican Priest

Even as the modern Protestant missionary movement was gathering steam, Henry Venn was already arranging the euthanasia of missions.[1] It's not that Venn was opposed to cross-cultural evangelism; rather, he was concerned about the paternalistic effects of the mission station.[2] The ultimate goal, Venn argued in one of his many instructions to missionaries, was not just individual conversions, but the establishment of indigenous churches:

> The object set before us is not only to induce a few individuals of every nation to flock into the Christian Church, but that all nations should gradually adopt the Christian religion as their national profession of faith, and thus fill the universal church by the accession of national churches.[3]

Venn argued national churches must be self-governing, self-propagating, and self-supporting. An example his commitment to this three-self model, Venn established eight bishoprics overseas[4] including that of freed slave Samuel Crowther, who became the first ordained bishop in Africa beyond colonial limits.

Venn was adamant that missions is not about westernizing or "civilizing the natives";[5] rather the host culture is of fundamental importance, so missionaries must learn the vernaculars and translate scriptures and educational curriculum into those languages. Venn petitioned the British government to establish vernacular education in India, and to build economic infrastructure in West Africa.

---

[1] Shenk, "Henry Venn's Legacy," 18.
[2] Terry et al., *Missiology*, 439.
[3] Shenk, "Henry Venn's Instructions to Missionaries," 470.
[4] Anderson, *Biographical Dictionary of Christian Missions.*
[5] Terry et al., *Missiology*, 209.

## Models of Contextualization

Should people have to give up their culture to become Christians? When missionaries gain a convert, does the host culture lose a citizen? Missiologists want to avoid transplanting their own cultural version of Christianity, on the one hand, or fostering a syncretized religion on the other hand. So they seek to make Christianity orthodox yet relevant to their host cultures.

### Contextualization of Christianity

is the process of making the faith fit the cultural patterns (language, leadership style, rituals, etc.) of the host culture. Contextualization is the core activity of cross-cultural discipleship.

But the indigenization of Christianity is not a forced or artificial process; it is organic. Local communities "automatically" shape Christianity to fit within their preexisting cultural frameworks, often resulting in a hybridized or idiosyncratic version of the Christian church. For example, societies adjust the architecture, language, leadership norms, musical style, preaching style and even the message brought to them by missionaries. Shoki Coe[10] referred to this process of indigenizing Christianity as contextualization.

> Coe described contextualization as a continual interplay between the transcendent text of Scripture and the ever changing context in which it must be interpreted. He recognized that effective incarnational ministry depends on a continual willingness to face Scripture's summons to transformation in the midst of changing social, political, and economic circumstances.[11]

Contextualization is of interest to scholars in multiple fields, since it delves into issues of biblical studies (how did the authors of Scripture shape God's messages to fit their cultural contexts?), theology (what aspects of Christianity are supra-cultural?), anthropology (how do communities hybridize a global religion?), and intercultural communication (how do we proclaim the gospel in a way that makes sense to the Other?). Below I will discuss biblical and missiological models of contextualization.

---

10. Coe, "Contextualizing Theology."
11. Wheeler, "Legacy of Shoki Coe," 78.

## Profile of a Missiologist: John Mbiti

*(contemporary)*

*Education: BA Makerere College (Uganda); ThB (Barrington College); PhD (Theology) University of Cambridge.*

*Occupation: Anglican Parish priest; professor of New Testament at University of Bern (Switzerland); professor at the Ecumenical Institute of the World Council of Churches (Geneva)*

John Mbiti, from the Akamba tribe in Kenya, attempted to find common ground between Christianity and African Traditional Religion (ATR). He "published over 400 items including books, articles, essays, poems, and book reviews in the fields of Christianity, theology, biblical studies, ecumenics, literature and African religion."[1]

As a professor of New Testament and religion in East Africa, Mbiti helped ministerial students see how Christianity could be relevant in their own contexts. He tells the (perhaps autobiographical) story of an East African who went to Europe for nine years to receive advanced theological training. When he returned to his village, a woman fell to the ground, screeching and foaming at the mouth. The only thing this educated pastor could think to do was to take the lady to the hospital; but the villagers protested, "It's 50 miles away" and, "She is possessed. Hospitals will not cure her."[2] So the minister began to wonder whether his excellent theological training is in fact impotent in the country of his birth.

The missiological significance of Mbiti's work has to do with how the Gospel is communicated and lived out in animistic contexts. Mbiti was "one of the first to attempt to systematize and analyze, from an insider's perspective, the African understanding of the world in which we live and how that understanding affects the Africans' view of Christianity."[3]

The difficulty of this project of contextualization is that Christianity, missions history, and local religions can be very difficult to reconcile. To address this tension, Mbiti offered a sort of updated Wesleyan quadrilateral, arguing that theology for Africa must take into account four studies: scripture, the history of Christian thought, the traditional African worldview, and the "theology of the living church."[4]

---

[1] van Wyk, "Mbiti, John Samuel."
[2] Wilson, "John S. Mbiti."
[3] Moreau, "Critique of John Mbiti's Understanding," 36.
[4] Kinney, "Theology of John Mbiti," 66.

## Biblical Models of Contextualization

Is contextualization biblical? The Old and New Testaments both legitimize, to some extent, the surrounding cultural context by citing concepts from surrounding religions and holy books. Terry et al. point out that the New Testament uses of king, messiah, and *logos* are all appropriations of Ancient Near Eastern cultural ideas.[12] Num 21:14 quotes the "book of the wars of the Lord"; Josh 10 and 2 Sam 1 both quote the book of Jashur, Jude quotes the Assumption of Moses; Paul quotes the Cilician poet Aratus in Acts 17:16–34 and quotes Meander in 1 Cor 15:33.[13] Without making a claim about whether these extra biblical passages are truly revealed by God, we can observe that prophets and evangelists made use of the cultural ideals held by their audiences. Missiologists turn to such examples when they form their own models of contextualization.

The "Jerusalem Council" in Acts 15 is the quintessential passage on contextualization. How could gentiles make Christianity "their own" without offending their Jewish brothers and sisters in Christ? The early church decided that Christianity allowed tremendous leeway for cultural features.

Flemming argued that the evangelists in the New Testament contextualized their message for their audiences.[14] The entire book of Romans made the gospel relevant to a Jewish audience, with its focus on the destiny of Israel, and with no mention of the Lord's Supper or the Second Coming. Flemming demonstrated how Paul contextualized his sermons for three different audiences: the Jewish leaders in Acts 13, the unsophisticated gentile in Acts 14, and the educated philosopher in Acts 17.

Contextualization is a sticky issue, because sometimes cultural norms need to bend or be broken in order to conform to Scripture. Remember that the cross of Christ is meant to be a stumbling block—it cannot be "shaped" to fit each culture's sensibilities. And yet, Flemming observes, even the message of the cross was contextualized for different audiences. In Colossians, the cross represents victory; in Philippians, it represents humility; and in 1 Corinthians it represents foolishness and wisdom.[15]

---

12. Terry et al., *Missiology*, 319.
13. Tennent, *Theology in the Context of World Christianity*, 54.
14. Flemming, *Contextualization in the New Testament*.
15. Flemming, *Contextualization in the New Testament*.

The discussion of contextualization in Scripture raises issues about the degree to which cultural-religious knowledge should be legitimated. The degree to which missionaries are willing to "fit the gospel" into local cultural knowledge is largely determined by their view of indigenous religions. Missionaries who see religions as products of the devil will advocate a "replacement model," whereas those who see religions as some form of general revelation will advocate a "fulfillment model" of contextualization.

## *Theological Questions Raised by Contextualization*

In addition to contextualizing tangible aspects of culture (church architecture) and social aspects (like leadership structures) local churches also shape theology through their own cultural norms. These so-called ethno theologies can be both enlightening and problematic to theologians. Of course, all theology is ethno-theology, since all theologians operate through their own cultural lens. Contextual theologies are essentially applied hermeneutics. They are interpretations of the scriptural message, filtered through a certain cultural context.

Such filtering has been going on since Moses wrote the Pentateuch, but contextual theology boomed in a post-colonial context as societies were experimenting with Marxism. Ethno-theologians asked: In what way does the gospel liberate humans? Is it a social, religious, and political liberation?[16] Similarly, theologians asked how the gospel can be good news for African American communities.[17] More recently, contextual theologians have asked: In what way is the atonement not only about removing guilt, but bearing and removing shame?[18] How does Christianity relate to the Native American emphasis on spirituality?[19] How can we make the gospel relevant to Melanesian societies where the ultimate value is retribution or reciprocity, rather than grace?[20] In what way is the gospel good news to the immigrant?[21]

16. Gutierrez, *Theology of Liberation*.

17. Bradley, *Liberating Black Theology*; Cone, *Cross and the Lynching Tree*; Fields, *Introducing Black Theology*; Jones, *Is God a White Racist*?

18. Wu, "How Christ Saves God's Face . . . and Ours."

19. Jenkins, *Dream Catchers*; Kidwell, *Native American Theology*; Twiss, *Rescuing the Gospel from the Cowboys*.

20. Ahrens, "On Grace and Reciprocity"; Nehrbass, *Christianity and Animism in Melanesia*.

21. Davidson and Garcia, "Welcoming the Stranger."

Actually, the phrase ethno-theology is misleading, since ethnic groups do not maintain a consensus about their interpretation of Christian theology. Just because a theology has the word "African" or "Thai" in the title doesn't mean that it is representative of people in that ethno-linguistic grouping. For example, many evangelical theologians in Latin America were not in agreement with many tenets of liberation theology,[22] and responded by forming *mision integral* (integrated missions). This theology, while contextual to Latin America, had a strong impact on global evangelicalism, as it encouraged holistic thinking about Christianity.[23]

The ethno-theologies in any culture arise in response to several factors, including missions history, denominational influences, views of Scripture, plus the traditional culture and traditional religion (see Figure 8 below).

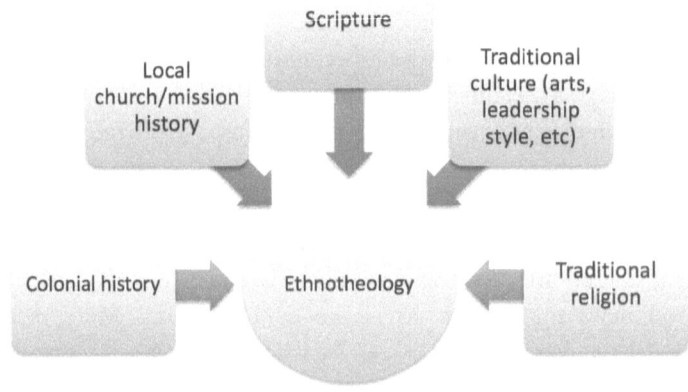

Figure 8: Factors influencing an ethno-theology

### Determining the Kernel

We know that the gospel is not like a plant to be transplanted, but more like a seed to be sown so it will grow on its own in soils all over the world. But how do we know what that "seed" is? Ancient Judaism didn't have this difficulty of separating the "essentials" from the "translatables,"

---

22. Escobar et al., "Latin America Critique of Latin American Theology."
23. Padilla, "Integral Mission and its Historical Development."

because Judaism sought to maintain a cultural, geographic, and linguistic homogeneity wherever it was practiced (though it, too, was influenced by the sitz im leben). Islam also tries to remain homogenous by translating Arabic and its *umma*. But Christianity tries to be limitless in cultural translatability. What parts of Christianity are essentials in each culture?

The answer to that question is not black and white. The answers fall on a continuum. On the left side of the spectrum, Karl Barth argued that only Jesus Christ was the "word" and no human language could encapsulate that word. On the right end of the spectrum, Carl F. Henry and John MacArthur argue that the "plain meaning of the text" is not blurred by culture, and can be directly expressed and understood in any context. Most missiologists fall in the middle of this continuum—there are some "plain meanings" that are transcultural, whereas other aspects of the Christian faith are shaped by the cultural context. But how do we know what falls in each of these two categories?

The church has typically answered this question through cross-cultural councils where they worked out creeds, like the Apostle's Creed or the Nicene Creed. Going back in Christian history, the affirmation that "Jesus is Lord" was a simple, non-negotiable tenet across cultures. We could look at the sermons in the book of Acts to see what Paul considered to be the "kernel" of the Christian faith. More recently, the Lausanne Covenant and Chicago declaration solidified a global consensus on the essentials of the Christian faith.

Why should the global church collaborate to work out the "kernel" of the gospel? Why not just stick to the wisdom of the early church fathers or to Western theologians? The reason working out this kernel must be a global project is that we are all myopic, and cannot see the full implications of the gospel. Westerners long focused on the judicial aspect of the atonement, and paid less attention to the power that Christ gives over the demonic. Pacific Island Christians often focus on the healing and wellness that Christ brings, but may pay less attention to the truth claims in Scripture. We need to hear each other's voices to get the big picture.

But I don't mean to imply that we're in the situation of the blind men who are all touching different parts of the elephant. God has not left us blind, groping in the dark. He is an effective communicator who has revealed Himself in Scripture (Isa 46:10) Instead, we are all like people standing around the elephant with sight; but for too long, we have been comfortable just looking at the part of the elephant that's in front of us.

We need to get up and walk around the elephant. Discussing biblical theology at the global level allows us to do that.

This leads to another issue of contextualization: how do Christians determine which aspects of their culture are sinful, and should be relinquished, and which are neutral, and which are in fact positive? When it comes to outright sins, it's pretty easy: if the Bible forbids it, don't do it.

But a lot of culture isn't that simple. Let's take an example: Suppose an animistic community holds a large yam harvest celebration. Some Christians say "This is a pagan event. The first yams are offered to dead ancestors. It's idolatry." But other Christians say, "No, we now, in our hearts, are thinking about God when we do our yam celebration. It's simply a thanksgiving service." And other Christians say "No, it's not a spiritual event at all. It's a large party, with no spiritual significance." While others say, "It is impossible to make an offering to dead ancestors, they have no power. They are gone. So even if people think of this as a pagan event, it has no efficacy." How can the church proceed? This was exactly the situation in Rom 14:14–23. Paul was saying the event (meat sacrificed to idols, or yam celebrations, or whatever), in and of itself, has no spiritual meaning except that which you attach to it. For the one who thinks it's a pagan event, he better not do it, because then he'd be choosing to do something he believes is a sin. For the one who sees it as a party, let him do it as a party. For the one who thinks it can be redeemed as an event that honors God, let them do that! In many cases, then, indigenous churches are not monolithic in their approach to contextualization.

### Missiological Models of Contextualization

While contextualization theories delve into theological issues (like determining the non-negotiable or supra-cultural aspects of the gospel), usually studies of contextualization have focused on how theories of intercultural communication can help missionaries proclaim the gospel in culturally relevant ways. For example, De Nui and Lim focus on how to communicate the gospel to those from Buddhist backgrounds.[24]

Missionaries have not agreed on the extent to which Christianity must be "translated." Is it proper to find a dynamic equivalent for communion elements or baptism? How are Paul's commands about women's conduct in 1 Cor 7 and 11 to be translated for modern

---

24. De Nui and Lim, *Communicating Christ in the Buddhist World*.

European audiences? Numerous factors impact theorists' positions on contextualization, including their view of Scripture, the value they place on culture, and their view of culture change. Those with a high view of culture, and a low view of Scripture, may be quite willing to swap cultural "forms" with biblical ones, whereas those with a high view of Scripture are usually hesitant to deviate from the forms found in Scripture.

## Denial Model

A small number of theologians are suspicious of the discourse of contextualization,[25] imagining that they had identified a supra-cultural version of Christianity in the New Testament, and all cultures could, and in fact must, conform to that version. They worry that the discourse of contextualization is influenced by postmodernism's tenet that truth cannot be known. For this camp, the gospel contains propositional truths which simply need to be taught across cultures. John MacArthur's "Final Word on Contextualization" avers:

> Each of the churches [Paul] founded had its own unique personality and set of problems, but Paul's teaching, his strategy, and above all his message remained the same throughout his ministry. His means of ministry was always preaching—the straightforward proclamation of biblical truth. By contrast, the "contextualization" of the gospel today has infected the church with the spirit of the age. It has opened the church's doors wide for worldliness, shallowness, and in some cases a crass, party atmosphere. The world now sets the agenda for the church.[26]

Such theologians are concerned that scholars of contextual theology are making too much of a deal about cultural differences. I refer to this model as the "denial model" since such theologians deny that all interpretations of the gospel are cultural.

This criticism of contextualization comes from the wounds of the modernist-evangelical debates of the twentieth century. When the group called the Theological Education Fund began talking about "appropriate Christianity," the *telos* was a Christianity that was appropriate when measured according to the standards of the local culture, not when

---

25. Henry, "Cultural Relativizing of Revelation," MacArthur, "Contextualization and the Corruption of the Church," Geisler, "Response to Paul G. Hiebert."
26. MacArthur, "Contextualization and the Corruption of the Church."

measured according to the standards of Scripture. So some evangelicals became suspicious of "contextualization" because it seemed like a disguise for cultural accommodation. Geisler, for instance, argued "contextualization is *not* the most crucial problem of communicating the gospel to another culture. Rather it is the problem of communicating a theistic gospel to those holding a nontheistic philosophical worldview."[27]

Note that most evangelicals eventually adopted a conservative vision of contextualization, called Dynamic Equivalence.

## Dynamic Equivalence

### The Theory of Dynamic Equivalence

is one of the most significant innovations in missiology. It is a reductive theory of human nature that argues that cultural innovations such as language, ritual, and art are "signs" which vary from culture to culture, but which point to underlying meanings that are grasped in any culture.

### The Model of Dynamic Equivalence

prescribes that missionaries and Bible translators should express the underlying meaning of Christianity according to the varying cultural forms (such as language or ritual).

Many evangelicals balance their esteem of cultural backgrounds, on the one hand, with a value of Scripture on the other. They have typically held to a model which Moreau referred to as the translation model.[28] This model assumes that God has supernaturally revealed a supra-cultural "kernel" of the gospel which takes on different forms.[29] Anyone who translates a discourse assumes that the speaker's words are variable, almost random, symbols which represent a more stable underlying message. The meaning can be repackaged in any number of other forms (languages). Translators refer to this theory of translation as "dynamic equivalence." For example, Koyama's *Water Buffalo Theology* puts the orthodox messages of Christianity into Buddhist forms. Jesus

---

27. Giesler, "Response to Paul G. Hiebert," 139.
28. Moreau, *Contextualization*.
29. Schreiter, *Constructing Local Theologies*, 8.

is the *arhat,* and salvation is *Nirvana.*[30] Luzbetak referred to this model as "accommodation," which he defined as "the respectful, prudent, scientifically and theologically sound adjustment of the Church to the native culture in attitude, outward behavior, and practical apostolic approach."[31] Note that the term "accommodation" has taken on a stigma of "syncretism" so Luzbetak may not have used that term today to describe contextualization.

Dynamic equivalence theories are shaped by Charles Pierce's work on semiotics. Pierce theorized that cultural activities like ritual and art are "signs" which point to underlying meanings. These signs are specific to particular cultures; but the underlying things signified exist at a deeper ontological level; that is, they are transcendent and supra-cultural.[32] For example, in first-century Palestine, a rabbi typically sat down to speak; in modern Western society, the preacher usually stands. These are varying cultural "forms" which signify an underlying meaning of authority. To take another example, South Asians often cremate corpses, Arabs usually bury them or put them in caves, some Pacific Islanders toss them over the side of a canoe, and some Mongolians leave them to be eaten by animals. These are varying "forms" of an underlying meaning about proper respect of the body of a loved one.

## The Anthropological Model

The approach Moreau described as the "anthropological model" of contextualization would be seen as syncretism by many evangelicals.[33] Modernist scholars, those who encourage this more radical form of contextualization, are typically less interested in transmitting supra-cultural "kernels" in Scripture. Instead, they emphasize the way in which God, the creator of all, has been revealing Himself in a general sense within all cultures. Such scholars see missionary efforts as imperialistic and even disruptive to local cultures. Instead they want to emphasize the value of indigenous culture. After all, Christianity is not a western religion. In an era when the center of gravity of Christianity is shifting from Europe to Africa, missiologists recognize that they should give voice to majority

30. Koyama, *Water Buffalo Theology,* 59.
31. Luzbetak, *Church and Cultures,* 341.
32. Hiebert, *Gospel in Human Contexts,* 27.
33. Moreau, *Contextualization.*

world theologies. These contextual christologies ask local communities "Who do you say that I am" rather than "who did the missionaries say I am?"[34] Such theologies are more diverse than global evangelicalism. For example, Prior encouraged church leaders in Vanuatu to find images of God in cultural images like the annual yam ceremony, the dolphin and the octopus.[35] Some African theologians have attempted to connect the worship of Jesus with indigenous ideas of healers and ancestors[36] and even to incorporate ancestor veneration into the life of the church.[37]

## Summary of Contextualization Models

### Contextualization

*Why it works:*

Makes sure Christianity "hits home" in the host culture.

*What it might miss:*

Since no host culture is homogeneous, there is no "one way" to contextualize the gospel for any culture. Christians in any culture will disagree on how much cultural continuity and discontinuity is appropriate.

All models of contextualization operate in the tension between continuity with the cultural background and cultural discontinuity for the sake of obedience to Christ. Evangelical missiologists tend toward "translation" or "dynamic equivalence" models which emphasize the authority of Scripture but also recognize the value of culture.

Evangelical missiologists have devoted so much time to contextualization because they believe that a culturally relevant gospel is the only one that will be seen as good news in a given culture. As Hiebert argued,[38] contextualization is the only way to ensure that the local church

---

34. Tennent, *Theology in the Context of World Christianity*, 109.
35. Prior, *Gospel and Culture in Vanuatu*, 4.
36. Stinton, *Jesus of Africa*.
37. Jebadu, "Ancestral Veneration."
38. Hiebert, "Flaw of the Excluded Middle."

will not practice what Bulatao first referred to as "split-level Christianity" where they pray on Sunday and see the shaman on Monday.[39]

Contextualization is an essential part of missiological discourse in this era of World Christianity. It is "utterly scandalous that students of western theology know more about the theology of heretics long dead than they do about the living theology of hundreds of millions living in Africa today."[40] Traditional sending countries can learn a great deal from contextual theologies. The atonement, for example, is not just a judicial metaphor, but has ramifications for restoring honor and reincorporating people into God's family. Additionally, majority world theologies add to our understanding of spiritual power and spiritual warfare; often these societies have less cultural distance from the cultures in the Bible than western societies do.[41]

Yet in an era of globalization, the discourse of contextualization is changing, and may in fact be waning in importance. Global evangelicalism (from Billy Graham, to Hillsong, to Willow Creek and Saddleback) is a homogenizing force. Communities are torn between identifying with, on the one hand, a sense (imagined or real) of global evangelicalism, and on the other hand, their own religio-cultural identities. Additionally, in multicultural urban centers, churches are too heterogeneous to contextualize the gospel for a specific ethnic group.

## Multiplication Models

"Mission that does not include evangelism is missing the core."[42] Hearing and believing the good news of Jesus Christ is certainly an early step in becoming a disciple. Some have noted that persuading someone to believe requires pre-evangelism, since many cultural backgrounds do not share Judeo-Christian concepts of God, grace, and sin; and many people do not know the thread of redemption from Adam, Noah, Abraham, and on to Christ.

Views of the role of discipleship in missiology tend to be polarizing. On the one hand, some argue for what Terry has called "indiscriminate sowing"—proclaiming the gospel to the 3 A's (anyone, anywhere,

---

39. Bulatao, *Split-level Christianity*.
40. Mbiti, "Theological Impotence and the Universality of the Church," 16–17.
41. Tennent, *Theology in the Context of World Christianity*, 14, 93.
42. Moreau et al., *Introducing World Missions*, 83.

anytime) and proclaiming it just once, and moving on. Such advocates believe that the promise that "my word be that goeth forth out of my mouth: it shall not return unto me void" (Isa 55:11 KJV) exonerates the evangelist from his or her lack of cultural knowledge. So these "rapid-proclamation" advocates tend to have a one-size-fits-all model. On the other end of the continuum, missiologists have argued for lifestyle or relational evangelism, and believe that the gospel must be tailored to communities. In reality, though, practitioners are not forced to choose one or the other, and may balance the both (see Figure 10).

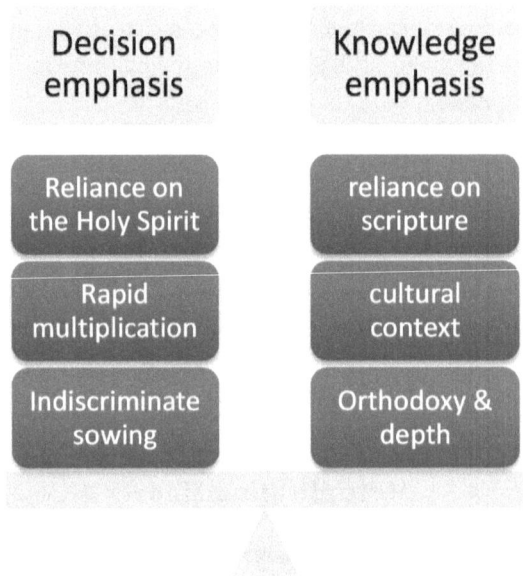

Figure 10: Balancing proclamation and discipleship models

Billy Graham's stadium evangelism was more on the left-hand side of the balance. Many other organizations such as Cru (formerly Campus Crusade for Christ) and Youth With a Mission (YWAM) generate crowds and preach to the masses, on whom, remember, Jesus had compassion (Matt 9:36). On the other side of the balance, Coleman's *Masterplan of Evangelism* emphasized focusing on "a few good men and women" rather than on the masses.[43] Coleman argued that just as Jesus chose the twelve, evangelism was primarily about developing long term relationships.

43. Coleman, *Masterplan of Evangelism*.

Crowds are fickle, and many quickly turn away from Christ—instead, focus on those who show true potential for growth without neglecting the masses. Models which emphasize rapid multiplication run the risk of being simplistic or reductive, and of implementing a one-size-fits-all approach.

## Multiplying Through Narrative Methods

"If we are serious about reaching the unreached peoples of the world, we cannot afford to rely on a strategy that half the world does not use or understand!" Herbert Klem made this argument to missionaries, encouraging them to "take a hard second look" at their dependence on literacy.[44]

In 1981, Trevor McIlwain, a missionary in the Philippines, presented an oral Bible story method for sharing the gospel with animists who had no background in Judeo-Christian thought.[45] He contended that since the Bible is one overarching story, and since the Bible lays out God's plan more or less chronologically, disciple-makers should teach the Bible as one story chronologically.[46] Before people from tribal backgrounds could confess Jesus as Lord, they would need to understand the "chiasm of history" from creation, to sin, to the nation of Israel, Jesus's work, the church, judgment, and the new Creation. Oral methods, chronological Bible teaching (CBT), chronological Bible storying (CBS) or just "storying," have become a popular and effective approach in many missions agencies that work among animistic,[47] Muslim, and Hindu regions. Specialists in narrative methods train indigenous evangelists to tell key stories, and send them out to form small groups who first study the stories and then become trained to go out and form more story groups, and so on.

Oral methods gained a theoretical foundation in the 1980s as missionaries picked up on the work of Walter Ong,[48] who theorized that oral cultures think differently than literate cultures do. He argued that people from oral societies (who made up the majority of the world's population at that time), prefer to communicate with concrete narrative

---

44. Klem, "Dependence on Literacy Strategy."
45. McIlwain, *Building on Firm Foundations*.
46. Steffen, "Orality Comes of Age."
47. Terry, "Chronological Bible Storying to Tribal and Nomadic Peoples."
48. Ong, *Orality and Literacy*.

rather than with abstract concepts. Oral cultures emphasize emotions whereas literate cultures emphasize logic.

While the orality movement has enjoyed tremendous success in the past twenty years, some missiologists would note limitations and even ideological fallacies in the movement. For example, is it paternalistic to say that because people are illiterate, they cannot, or should not, be engaging in literacy? In a globalizing age, isn't literacy a tool where marginalized oral communities are exercising self-determination, and whereby they improve their standards of living?

Additionally, many would argue that the ability to follow complicated abstract propositional arguments is aided by literacy; and such reasoning capacities are necessary for achieving a full understanding of Scripture.[49] Is it debilitating for oral communities (especially when such communities aspire to literacy) to encourage them to seal themselves off from traditions of abstract propositional thinking? Remember that Jesus spoke in plain propositions to his disciples so they could understand his point plainly; but He spoke in parables to the crowds and religious leaders in order to confuse them (Matt 13:10–13).

Is it ethnocentric for western scholars to even assume that pre-literate communities are less inclined to reason with abstract logic? And is it naïve to think that orality is necessarily linked to a capacity for fidelity in storytelling? Note that the orality movement presupposes the "oral-formulaic theory" that pre-literate folks are able to memorize large chunks of narrative and repeat those stories verbatim, ensuring fidelity of the story over generations.[50] If Ong had studied anthropology, rather than English, and if he had spent extensive time living in oral cultures, instead of relying on other historians' works, he may have discovered what many anthropologists have argued: Oral story-telling often contains a "nugget" of the narrative that is preserved as the story is transmitted; but each storyteller also composes elements of the story on the spot. Therefore oral stories often eventually contain numerous contending versions. This presence of "competing" versions of a narrative is not typically a problem for pre-literate people, who tend to be more comfortable with ambiguity than people from literate societies are. But the evolving nature of oral narrative is problematic for evangelicals who focus on the fidelity of the stories.

49. Piper, "Missions, Orality and the Bible."
50. Armstrong, "Efficency of Storying."

## Oral Methods: Bible Storytelling

*Why it works:*

Orality helps get the gospel out to the unreached quickly, in ways they most easily grasp.

*What it might miss:*

Many concepts in Christianity are complex; and globally, evangelical Christians rely on both oral storytelling as well as careful study of Scripture.

To summarize the benefits of the orality movement: 1) communicators are sensitive to the pedagogical and communication styles of their audiences; and 2) the work of evangelism and discipleship is accelerated, as it has been divorced from the prerequisite of literacy. And to summarize the criticism of the orality movement: Literacy has provided two tremendous benefits over illiteracy: 1) literacy ensures fidelity of the story (a concern many people have with the storying movement); and 2) literacy encourages critical thinking and precision in a way that orality cannot.

## Multiplying through Church Planting

From its beginning, the church growth movement has recognized that new converts must be formed into church communities, so they can be discipled. Church planting is tied to leadership development, since multiplying churches require an indigenous force to proclaim the gospel in the cultural context, and to lead the church. So the church planting endeavor has typically involved what Shank called the "four fields": evangelism, discipleship, church planting, and leadership development.[51]

### The Types of Church Planting

Church planters are not agreed on the way that churches should be planted. Should a church split when it becomes large, and create "daughter

---

51. Shank, *Four Fields of Kingdom Growth*.

churches"? Or should new spinoffs be considered simply satellite campuses of a single church entity? Is the location of a "big church" totally unhelpful, and church planters should focus instead on small groups of believers who meet in houses, abut occasionally gather in loosely connected larger meetings? Should denominations and megachurches in the US send out their best emissaries to plant denominational "sister churches" abroad? Or is church planting the job of sodalities like Ethnos 360 and Frontiers?

The answer to all these questions seems to be "yes." It depends on the setting. For example, the multi-site (satellite) and mother-daughter church plants seem to work well in urban and suburban areas, but may not be a viable model in many village and tribal settings. And an emphasis on multiethnic church planting may be unattainable in mono-cultural settings.

### The Role of the Missionary Church Planter

Missiologists are also not agreed on the role of the missionary church planter. Is the missionary a vision caster who facilitates a church planting effort, and passes the baton as soon as possible? Or do missionaries need to invest themselves long term? Virtually no missiologist thinks that the colonial model of paternalism should be perpetuated. In fact, even during the height of colonialism, missiologists (ever since Henry Venn, John Nevius, and Rufus Anderson) emphasized that church planting should be an indigenous effort. In 1900, bishop A. R. Tucker of Uganda was suggesting the parameters of partnership models that are considered "cutting edge" today.[52] However, despite a legacy of missiologists who touted interdependence, the history of church planting seems to have been largely paternalistic, and we are only now moving into the "facilitator era."[53]

One major reason that frontier missionaries emphasize indigenous church planting movements is that Christians from Asia and the Middle East seem to have more success planting churches in their own regions, whereas people from European descent have less success. Daniels and Arlund's qualitative study on "near culture" workers found a number of reasons for this position of advantage: Christians from Asia and the

---

52. Neill, *History of Christian Missions*, 221.
53. Steffen, *Facilitator Era*.

Middle East are familiar with persecution, they do not have as many cultural barriers to cross in order to behave appropriately among their target audiences, and they place a greater emphasis on relational values rather than ministry tasks.[54] Also, these workers do not embody the stigma of colonialism. Church planting movements embody the grassroots effort of church multiplication.

## *Church Planting Movements*

Right now, in about 200 regions of the world, new churches are growing at rates of 25 percent to 50 percent annually. In a certain Islamic region of West Africa in 2000, there were fewer than 85 churches, and today there are more than 450. In a certain Asian Hindu and Buddhist setting, the number of churches grew from 21 to 205 in five years.[55] What leads to such explosive growth? Can we learn from those "church planting movements" (CPMs) and find best practices to help encourage the same sort of growth in more resistant areas?

CPM is both a descriptive theory and a prescriptive model. On the one hand, like McGavran's idea of "people movements," CPM describes the "rapid multiplication of indigenous churches planting churches that sweeps through a people group or population segment."[56] On the other hand, the model is prescriptive in that it encourages converts to Christianity from the very beginning to become trained to go out and plant new churches. They cannot be satisfied simply with proclaiming the gospel to the Any3 (any time, to any people, in any place), but must aim for the establishment of new churches.

Garrison recognized that CPMs include five stages: entry, gospel, discipleship, church formation, and leadership development.[57] Other missiologists have parsed out church planting into similar phases, sometimes including a phase-out.[58] These models recognize that church planting cannot begin with evangelism; it requires a preparatory phase of building relationships, language and culture learning, and challenging worldview assumptions. And church planting does not end with the

54. Daniels and Arlund, "Fruitful Near-culture Church Planters."
55. Slack, "Just How Many Church Planting Movements Are There?" 13.
56. Garrison, *Church Planting Movements*, 21.
57. Garrison, *Church Planting Movements*.
58. Steffen, *Passing the Baton*.

establishment of a church; it is a never-ending process of developing leaders who will go out and repeat the five steps of church planting.

The success of CPMs depends on training indigenous laity to go out and plant churches. Steve Smith developed Training for Trainers (T4T) as a prescriptive model for getting the local church on board right away with church planting. T4T emphasizes four "fields": evangelism, discipleship, church planting, and leadership development.[59]

*One Size Doesn't Fit All*

While critics of models like CPM and T4T typically do not dispute that indigenous church planting movements are essential and exciting, they do have some concerns. First of all, it can be difficult to determine what constitutes a church. Does a short-lived small gathering of not-yet-baptized people who may or may not be able to articulate the gospel, with no institutional structure, count as a church? Second, reports of CPMs may be highly exaggerated.[60]

But more significantly, like much church growth literature of the twentieth century, the emphasis not only on growth, but on rapid growth, invites a criticism about depth. Can church leaders from barely-reached people groups really be trained rapidly to evangelize?

Last, the more prescriptive a model is, the more it appears to be one-size-fits-all. Coker's critique of T4T warns us to beware of "assembly-line evangelism."[61] And beware of our tendency to turn our enthusiasm for a model into a zeal that excludes any other model. Just like there is no one model of church planting that fits all settings, there is no clear model for the role of the missionary that fits all settings. In fairly unreached contexts, where education is also low, an emphasis on "get in, and get out" may be naïve or premature. It would be desirable to train preachers and evangelists in a matter of weeks or months, but not all contexts can receive theological training at the same rate or depth. In some cases, missionaries may need to be present for an extensive period to lay a "firm foundation."

---

59. Smith, *T4T*.
60. Garrison, "10 Church Planting Movement FAQs."
61. Coker, "Review Essay."

## Multiplication

*Why it works:*

Multiplication models help us keep the focus of Jesus's final command: make disciples. And making disciples means we train followers of Jesus, among other things, how to make more disciples!

*What it might miss:*

At times the emphasis on rapid growth can lead to shallow growth, or a temptation to inflate numbers. Christian thinkers do not agree on how rapidly people can convert and learn enough about the Christian life to become disciple makers.

## Multiplying through Diaspora Ministries

Globally, about 244 million people live outside of their country of birth.[62] Babel scattered the nations, and ironically, this new wave of scattering is bringing them back together. In the past, those who felt a call to work with Nepalese or Somalis typically moved overseas. Now South Korean Christians are discovering they can reach Nepalese right in South Korea; Minnesotan Christians can reach Somalis in their own cities.

### Diaspora Missions

involves making disciples among people from ethnolinguistic groups who live outside of their land of heritage.

### Diaspora Missiology

was defined by Wan as "a missiological framework for understanding and participating in God's redemptive mission among people living outside their place of origin."[1]

---

[1] Wan, *Diaspora Missiology and Beyond*, 215.

62. Nacpil, "Church in the Twenty-first Century Diaspora," 69.

This new missionary method is often called diaspora missions. Wan pointed out that there are several types of diaspora missions,[63] including missions *to* the diaspora (e.g., ethnic Kenyan churches reach out to Chinese immigrants in Kenya) and missions *through* the diaspora (e.g., Chinese Christians in Kenya reach out to secular Chinese there) and missions *beyond* the diaspora (Chinese Christians in Kenya reach out to non-believing East Africans in Kenya).[64]

Below I will discuss three types of diaspora missions: international student ministry, so-called "reverse missions" and refugee ministry.

### *International College Ministry*

International students make up a large portion of the global diaspora. In 2016, 4.8 million students studied abroad,[65] temporarily removing themselves from their religious (or highly secular) context at home. The liminal period causes them enough anxiety that they seek out new networks of friends, and are open to new experiences and worldviews. For this reason, many international student ministries, such as Cru's "Bridges" program, locate on college campuses to make friends with international students and tell them about Jesus.

Multiple studies have shown that a major factor that contributes to international students' openness to Christianity is their exposure to Christian friends.[66] Students who converted also said answers to prayer and dreams were factors that brought them to faith; and to a lesser extent, they appreciated receiving a systematic defense of the Christian worldview.[67]

### *Reverse Missions*

While the USA is still the country that sends the most missionaries, Brazil is number two; and "nearly half of the world's top missionary-sending

---

63. Wan, "Diaspora Missiology and Beyond."
64. Gong and Nehrbass, "Reaching Out to Diaspora Chinese in East Africa."
65. Migration Data Portal, "International Students."
66. Ramanayake, *Evangelizing International Students in the United States*; Rawson, *Evangelizing East Asian Students*; Wang and Yang, "More than Evangelical and Ethnic."
67. Chamberlain, Factors Impacting Openness To Christianity Among Graduate Students."

countries are now located in the global South."⁶⁸ As Christianity declines in Western nations, and grows in the global South, the missionary force is increasingly comprised of Christians from the countries that used to be considered mission fields; and these majority world missionaries are often working in the countries that used to be the typical sending countries. To put it another way, the flow of the missionary force has more or less always reflected global immigration flows, which have reversed in the past century.⁶⁹ Under colonialism, missionaries moved from European nations along with those who left for economic reasons: Portuguese migrants settled in Brazil, French settled in Tahiti, British settled in Kenya, and so on. In the twenty-first century, net migration flows involve Brazilians moving to Portugal, Tahitians to France, and Kenyans to the UK. These economic migrants bring their fervor for Christianity along with them, and make disciples in their new contexts.

This missionary method, described as reverse missions, involves several strategies. Consider these two examples: An evangelical denomination in Nigeria sends church planters to work among Nigerians who live in Europe. And a Brazilian woman joins an international Christian media missionary organization based in the USA. The first example is a diaspora missionary method we might call "ethnic diaspora missions." The second is an example of the internationalization of the missionary force. Both examples show that the missionary force is now from everywhere to everywhere. But the moniker "reverse mission" would seem to imply something a bit different than both of these examples: Christians from the global South reaching secular folks of European descent. While this may be happening, it does not seem to be the typical way that ethnic minority churches do their outreach.⁷⁰

*Refugee Ministries*

Over 65 million people have been forcibly displaced outside their home country. Not just in western nations; in fact, the UN reports that 84

---

68. Steffan, "Surprising Countries Most Missionaries Are Sent From and Go To."

69. Hanciles, "Migration and Mission."

70. Adogame, "Mapping Globalization with the Lens of Religion," 210; Asaju, "Colonial Politicization of Religion," 285.

percent of global refugees have located in developing nations, especially Turkey, Pakistan, Lebanon, Iran, and Uganda.[71]

Often, Christians point to biblical examples of refugee crises as the foundation for engaging in such cross-cultural outreach: the Israelites lived as refugee-slaves in Egypt; the Torah had multiple commands for Israelites to love the foreigner among them (Exod 23:9; Lev 19:33–34; Deut 10:18–19); and in order to flee Herod's genocide, Joseph and Mary took Jesus as refugees to Egypt. The differences between those biblical examples and the modern-day refugee crises (or opportunities)[72] are significant.[73] But the biblical command to love our neighbor is applicable to all time periods, political situations, and ethnic groups.

Like international students, refugees are aware that they have many needs, such as learning the language of their host culture, getting a driver's license, attaining housing and furniture, finding medical help, and furthering the education for themselves and their children. Various organizations connect refugees and Christians who are eager to help meet these needs, and to develop cross-cultural friendships.

## Discipling Across Cultures through Cultural Production

Disciples learn to glorify God within their own cultural context as they learn to use their own music, books, poems, paintings, dance, movies, games, and all other cultural products in ways that bring honor to Him. Below I discuss some ways that cross-cultural workers have tried to make disciples through cultural products, including: the arts, Bible translations, and broadcast media.

### The Arts as a Missionary Strategy

In many pre-literate communities, arts are a way of communicating doctrine. Christians around the globe have used music and visual arts to communicate theology. The Lisu, a minority group in China, loved to sing, so early missionaries translated a hymnbook that became a central part of Christianity for the Lisu. "The Lisu hymns serve as a theological mediator for Lisu Christians, bridging the gap between the text-intensive

---

71. Edmund, "84% of Refugees Living in Developing Countries."
72. Kaemingk, *Christian Hospitality and Muslim Immigration in an Age of Fear.*
73. McDowell et al., "Bible and Immigration."

religion that is Christianity and the oral world of Lisu culture."[74] While it has been common for Christian communities to adopt western art forms in church, communities have also adapted their own cultural forms to the Christian message. Members of the Ivorian Senufo church in the Ivory Coast, for example, have composed indigenous songs in their "mother music" (analogous to their "mother tongue"). These songs are efficacious for attracting people to the church, providing comfort, and teaching theological doctrines.[75]

Arts are also a way of expressing our emotions and shaping our identity. One of the primary activities (in fact, the highest priority) of a church, and of any disciple of Jesus, is worship. Worship involves sounds, artifacts, scents, and actions. From earliest times, humans have made images to aid in their worship of God; they have constructed elaborate altars and sanctuaries; they have worshiped to the smell of incense or the scent of the fat of their sacrificial lamb; they have recited liturgies and poems; they have sung along with the harp and lyre; and they have danced to the beat of drums. All of these art forms are cultural productions, which can be used to glorify the creation, or the creator, or which can be used to glorify the self or an idol. Generally, ethnodoxologists agree that "there is no such thing as Christian art or pagan art or morally causal art, even though there are Christian or pagan contexts in which it can be made."[76]

Since we bear the image of God, we are highly creative and cannot help but sing, sculpt, compose, play, and build. Yet, since we are fallen, we use our cultural products to exploit, denigrate, or exclude. Cross-cultural discipleship involves helping new believers to redeem their cultural productions. Hall recommended that every church planting team would include someone who can contextualize worship music.[77] Indigenous and biblical forms of music will avoid the pitfalls of 1) blindly adopting foreign forms of music which are not relevant to the community; or 2) blindly retaining indigenous forms of musical and dance expression that convey demonic or sinful messages within that context.

---

74. Arrington, "Christian Hymns as Theological Mediator," 140.
75. King, *Pathways in Christian Music Communication*.
76. Best, "God's Creation and Human Creativity," 16.
77. Hall, "10 Reasons Why Every Church-planting Team Needs a Worship Leader."

## Bible Translations as Missions

In the past 50 years, the pace of Bible translation has been accelerating rapidly. Yet there is a long way to go: Just under 500 translations of Scripture had been completed between the first and eighteenth century; yet in the past 200 years, over 2,000 additional translations have been completed. Still, more than 2,500 of the world's 7,000 languages do not have a single verse of Scripture.

An indigenous church can survive without Scripture in its language, as the Irish church did from the time of St. Patrick until the translation was done in 1602, or as the Thomas Christians in India did until the Bible was translated into Malayalam in 1811.[78] But access to the word of God is an extremely important part of becoming a disciple of Jesus.

Don Richardson's *Peace Child*[79] and Neil Anderson's *In Search of the Source*[80] inspired many Westerners to get involved directly in Bible translation, and encouraged countless others to support the effort. Bible translation, "the most complex intellectual activity in which any person can engage"[81] is a strategy of discipleship through cultural production. The Bible translation process sets in motion a lifelong habit of thinking about the meaning of God's word and working out ways to communicate that meaning to others. The task of translation requires critical thinking, exegeting God's word, using commentaries, engaging in community-wide discussions on the meaning of the text, and searching for just the right word in the vernacular that captures the idea in Scripture. And this process is often contagious: Once Bible translation consultants work with communities to translate a New Testament, the local leadership often captures the vision, and begins producing Bible study materials, primers, and Old Testament translations in their language.

Sanneh theorized that the an ingenious aspect of Christianity is that it is infinitely translatable, unlike Islam, which is so tied to Arabic and Mecca.[82] In contrast, Christianity is fundamentally about God making himself known to every person in every context. As Walls put it, "Incarnation is translation. When God in Christ became man, Divinity was translated into humanity, as though humanity were a receptor

78. Smalley, *Translation as Mission*, 21–22.
79. Richardson, *Peace Child*.
80. Anderson, *In Search of the Source*.
81. Fortosis, *Multilingual God*, 1.
82. Sanneh, *Translating the Message*.

language. Here was a clear statement of what would otherwise be veiled in obscurity or uncertainty, the statement 'This is what God is like.'"[83]

### Profile of a Missiologist: Lamin Ousman Sanneh

### (1942–2019)

*Education: MA (University of Birmingham, England) PhD (Islamic Studies) University of London*

*Occupation: Professor of History of Religion (Harvard) and then professor of World Christianity and History at Yale Divinity School*

Lamin Sanneh, originally from Gambia, converted from Islam to Catholicism. His academic career has focused on Islam and Christianity. He has authored over two hundred scholarly articles and of more than a dozen books on Islam and African expressions of Christianity. Additionally, he "is an editor-at-large for *The Christian Century* and a contributing editor for the *International Bulletin of Missionary Research*."[1]

The first edition of Sanneh's book *Translating the Message* enjoyed wide popularity among missiologists because it argued that Islam destroyed culture whereas Christianity preserves culture (often protesting colonialism) by encouraging contextual expressions of faith and vernacular Bible translations.[2]

Sanneh's argument was that missions is a twofold process of diffusion and translation (or vernacularization). Note how this is similar to Walls's indigenizing and pilgrim principle. Sanneh argues that once the message has been translated, it becomes the property of the community that received it. Hence, the answer to his question *Whose religion is Christianity?* is that it belongs to the communities of faith.[3]

> No culture is so advanced and so superior that it can claim exclusive access or advantage to the truth of God, and none so marginal and remote that it can be excluded.[4]

---

[1] Bonk, "Defender of the Good News."
[2] Sanneh, *Translating the Message*.
[3] Sanneh, *Whose Religion Is Christianity?*
[4] Sanneh, *Disciples of all Nations*, 25.

However, it is exceptionally challenging to generate a comprehensible translation of Scripture in tribal languages. Many minority languages

---

83. Walls, *Missionary Movement in Christian History*, 27.

lack abstract terms such as love, holy, hope, kingdom, or faith. So translators and mother-tongue speakers must be resourceful in finding alternatives. In one example, Fortosis relates that the disciples on the road to Emmaus asked each other, "Did not our hearts *cool* within us?"[84] In another example, one translation rendered Luke 4:32, "The crowds were amazed at his teaching, for he taught as a heavy-mouthed one."[85] These "functional equivalents" aren't meant to be avant-garde, (compare the Cotton Patch Bible); they are serious attempts of translators to be faithful in two languages: the source and the receptor language.[86]

Most Christians agree on the need for Bible translation; the missiological debates related to Bible translation have to do with the role of expatriate translators, and the criteria for determining which languages need translation.

## The Role of Expatriate Translators

Bible translation organizations face an internal struggle over the role of expatriate translators. Is it desirable for non-native speakers (often from the West) who are typically highly trained in translation philosophy and exegesis, but may lack an expert command of the vernacular, to have a direct role in translation? Or should indigenous communities bear much of the responsibility, and westerners take on a consulting role?

For the first 1800 years of church history, as the gospel came to a new setting, it was native speakers who brought Scripture to their own people.[87] This method can be traced all the way back to Ulfilas's translation of the Bible into his childhood Gothic language in the fourth century AD. Then, in the age of missionary expansion, pioneer missionaries in the early Protestant era took on translation. Finally, recently sodalities are beginning to engage in translation-as-partnership—a model that combines the expertise of expatriate consultants with the language capacity of expert native speakers.

The debate about the role of expatriate translators has to do with two realities: 1) non-native speakers may not understand the target language well enough to produce an acceptable translation, and 2) post-colonial

---

84. Fortosis, *Multilingual God*, 99.

85. Fortosis, *Multilingual God*, 90.

86. Fortosis, *Multilingual God*, 133. Small portions of this paragraph come from Nehrbass, Review of the Book *Multilingual God*.

87. Smalley, *Translation as Mission*.

## SEMINAL MODELS FOR CROSS-CULTURAL DISCIPLESHIP 261

sentiment suggests that expatriates should take on more of a "facilitator" role in all missionary endeavors, including translation.

William Carey epitomizes, in some ways, the "non-native" model of the Protestant mission era. Admirers of Carey point out that he translated the Bible into six languages and portions into another 29. Is such a feat possible, and if one did attempt to do this, would the quality be any good? What are the chances that Carey's translation philosophy and methods, in 1800, were able to produce the kind of meaning-based vernacular translations we produce today?

Smalley reports that Carey's translation was "seriously flawed. If there had been competent Bible translation consultants in Carey's day, they would not have approved for publication much, if any, of the translation work done by Carey and under his supervision."[88] Culshaw's review of Carey's Bengali translation concludes that Bangla Christians can understand Carey's text, but they don't actually talk that way.[89] Culshaw suggests that this level of comprehensibility, alone, is a remarkable accomplishment for a missionary who was pioneering not only a translation, but also a system of writing for these languages. Drawing on S. K. Das's critique of the Bengali translation, Culshaw provides some examples of issues that Carey faced (which Bible translators still struggle with today):

1. Carey relied heavily on English, and carried over some English-isms like the frequent use of conjunctions (e.g., and); supplying "is/are" when it's unnecessary in the target language, following English word order or using a string of verbs in one sentence. Many of these features don't fit well in the target language. For example, "Jesus hurried and came" doesn't work well in Bengali.

2. Carey wasn't sure who his audience was. The phrasing of the Bengali Bible is too "high speech" for the commoner, but too colloquial for a scholar.

3. Carey's use of "love" was too closely tied to the terms for sexuality.

While it is possible that native speakers would avoid some of Carey's mistakes, mother-tongue translators are just as capable of translation errors as non-native speakers. Native or not, those who are unfamiliar with Bible translation philosophy tend toward producing word-for-word

---

88. Smalley, *Translation as Mission*, 47.
89. Culshaw, "William Carey—Then and Now."

translations that sound unnatural, miss the nuances of the source text, or don't communicate the meaning of implicit information and idioms in the target language.

Also, it is questionable whether Carey actually epitomizes the "non-native" model of translation. He passed the torch to "numerous translations done by Indian assistance. They would translate into their own languages, consulting with each other about problems as they did so."[90] This leads us to the second issue around the debate of "locus of control": Are indigenous communities responsible for their own Bible translations? In addition to being self-multiplying, self-governing, and self-funding, should ecclesial communities be self-translating?

Much of the discourse about indigenous translation projects is linked with the discourse of post-colonialism, as well as an emphasis on "acceleration." Is it paternalistic for western-trained linguists to initiate and manage translation projects? And besides, highly-trained expatriate scholars can take twenty years to complete a translation—at such a rate, how would we ever complete the next 2,500 translations? Could we ever finish the task, if "the number of people training in the West to do Bible translation is on the decline"?[91] A number of linguists in the Bible translation movement agree with Beine that the highest quality Bible translations result with a high level of cooperation between linguists, biblical scholars, native speakers, and indigenous church leaders.[92]

## Who Needs a Translation?

Are all languages capable of communicating God's word? The medieval Roman church believed that Latin was superior to the other languages of Europe, therefore it would be unreasonable to translate the Scripture into more vulgar languages. Ironically, Jerome's Latin translation, from the fifth century AD, was called the Vulgate because it was the vulgar language, not the high ecclesiastical language, at that time. Skeptics in the fourth-century thought Latin was not as capable as Greek or Hebrew of conveying God's word. This sort of debate about suitable church language is repeated throughout the world, as minority languages are sidelined for being too backward for a Bible translation.

In 1918, William Cameron Townsend was selling Spanish Bibles in Guatemala, and a speaker of an Indo-American language challenged

90. Smalley, *Translation as Mission*, 46.
91. Gravelle, "Bible Translation in Historical Context," 13.
92. Beine, "Continuing Role for Western Bible Translators?"

# SEMINAL MODELS FOR CROSS-CULTURAL DISCIPLESHIP 263

"Uncle Cam," "If your God is so powerful, why can't he speak my language?" Townsend was convinced that all languages, regardless of population, size of vocabulary, status of literacy or bilingualism, were deserving of a Bible Translation, and he returned to work on the Cakchiquel New Testament.

Kenneth Pike, an early pioneer in the Summer Institute of Linguistics (SIL), likened the task of Bible translation unto mowing a field: The big work can be done with a tractor.[93] And that's like translating the Bible into Chinese and English. But you are not done mowing the field until you have used the hand mower around the trees and edges—that's like doing smaller national translations. But the real task requires getting on your hands and knees to trim by hand in the flower garden. That's like translating the Bible for speakers of languages in remote areas, sometimes with fewer than a hundred speakers. But God takes delight in completing the field.

Pike was convinced that if people read Scripture in a language other than their "heart language" their understanding would be "highly limited and subject to serious errors."[94] This notion that everyone has a single heart language, and that they understand Scripture best in that language, has significant currency among monolingual supporters of missions; however, some research has called these notions into question. Speakers who grow up in highly multilingual environments may not be limited to a single heart language; and speakers of minority languages may actually comprehend written texts better in their national language (that is, their language of education) than they do in their tribal language.[95]

Regardless of whether multilingual speakers understand the Scripture best in their vernacular or language of wider communication (LWC), many language communities find that the Scripture in the language they use at home has a greater emotional impact than their LWC. For this reason, Wycliffe Bible Translator's philosophy has historically been that all languages deserve a translation.

However, other missionary strategists aim for a quicker route to getting God's word in people's hands, like focusing on a translation of the Gospel of Luke and the Jesus Film. Some advocate a purely oral method of Bible storying in the vernacular, without any written cultural product. These advocates are not typically against Bible translation, but are trying

93. Pike, *With Heart and Mind*.
94. Pike, *With Heart and Mind*, 105.
95. Nehrbass, "Do Multilingual Speakers Understand the Bible Best in Their Heart Language?"

to find strategies that can be bring the gospel to communities in a timely manner, since a translation of a New Testament can take more than 20 years in some regions.

## Vernacular Broadcast Media as a Missionary Strategy

Discipleship, like all culture change, is enacted through communication channels within the context of social groups. Mass media is a highly effective communication channel that is aimed at loosely-tied social groups.[96] Mass media is also the most cost-effective way of reaching large audiences. Audio and video media allow indigenous churches to draw crowds, build curiosity, and to train leaders.[97]

Ever since the invention of radio, disciple makers have capitalized on broadcast media's potential for communicating Christ across cultures. Mission Agencies like Faith Comes by Hearing (FCBH), Global Recordings Network (GRN) and Jungle Aviation and Radio Service (JAARS) distribute media players with Scripture, songs, and Bible stories. Christian engineers have used their ingenuity to create solar powered or hand-crank audio players to get the media into remote villages. One of the most far-reaching vernacular media projects has been the Jesus Film, which has been viewed by more than 5 billion people, and has been translated into 1500 languages.

### Vernacular Media models

#### Why it works:

Vernacular media is a great example of contextualizing the message.

#### What it might miss:

No media is seen as neutral—media missions has to deal with the fact that images can misrepresent the message; and some members of communities even interpret the use of indigenous media (whether on television, dance, music, the internet) as wrong or even demonic.

The difficulty is, unlike most strategies mentioned in this chapter, audio and video discipleship tools are basically one-way conversations.

---

96. Rogers, *Diffusion of Innovations*.
97. Nash, "Part Mass Media Can Play in Mission Strategy."

Preachers' messages, photos, and films can aid in theological education, but they do not respond immediately to their audiences. For example, Far East Broadcasting's station HLKX 1188am, in Seoul, South Korea sends Korean programming to reclusive North Korea; but the conversation is largely one-way, except for the occasional letters that come back across the border. Missiologist Tom Steffen published an article with the controversial title "Don't Show the Jesus Film" to raise awareness that translating Christian media is not enough to ensure that communities will understand the message of Jesus Christ.[98] In many cases, pre-Christian communities need significant background information first.

Media encompasses much more than radio and television in the digital age. Many mission organizations are developing apps with vernacular Scriptures, Bible study tools, devotionals, lectures. Today, digital media has overcome the limitations of radio and TV, and is largely a two-way conversation. Christian ministries use social media to post stories, videos and photos in vernaculars, and receive immediate feedback from their audiences.

## Discipling Across Cultures Through Education

Chapter 7 introduced a number of ways that missiologists use educational theory to further the work of missions. Here I will discuss some specific educational strategies that are being tried.

### Higher Education as a Missionary Strategy

In many restricted access countries, jobs in higher education are a viable way for missionaries to enter the field and act as witnesses for Christ.[99] Christian scholars with advanced degrees are securing positions at secular universities in the former Soviet Union, the Middle East and Asia, where they glorify God by doing exemplary scholarship in their field (such as biology, engineering, history, etc.) and by making relationships with colleagues and students on campus. Their ultimate aim is to make disciples across cultures.

---

98. Steffen, "Don't Show the Jesus Film."
99. Edwards and Nehrbass, "Higher Education as Mission."

## Profile of a Missiologist: Alexander Duff

### 1806–1878

*Education: Theology, St Andrews University (Honorary doctorates from University of Aberdeen and New York University)*

*Occupation: Professor of Missions, New College, Edinburgh*

Alexander Duff's significance in missiology is partly due to the fact that he was the first professor to hold a permanent position of missiology at a university, though C. H. Platt was a private lecturer in missiology in Berlin at the same time. Duff argued that missions is the chief end of the church (note that John Piper would later take issue with this phraseology). "When a church ceases to be evangelistic, it ceases to be evangelical, and when it ceases to be evangelical, it must cease to be a true church of God."[1] Duff concluded, "A church which drops the evangelistic or missionary fervor quickly lapses into superannuation and decay."[2]

Duff was also the first missionary to be sent by the Church of Scotland to India. Like Venn, Duff highlighted the importance of education in India. He noted that most Protestant missionary efforts were aimed at the lower caste, to the neglect of Brahmins. Duff helped found the University of Calcutta, where the eponymous Duff Hall still stands. But unlike Venn and other evangelical missionaries at the time, Duff believed education must be in English to put the Indians on "equal footing." "The English language presents itself as incomparably the best instrument for the noble purposes in view."[3]

> Duff's converts were not numerous: thirty-three are recorded in the eighteen years of his work, but all were of sterling quality, and became the founders of some of the most Christian families in India.[4]

Duff referred to Hinduism as "childish fooleries . . . meaningless rites, . . . atrocious enormities . . . inhuman brutalities . . . licentious abominations . . . ruinous infatuations . . . and monstrous idolatry."[5] Today, many would find Duff's views of Indians to be ethnocentric; though he may have been reflecting the view taken by highly educated atheistic Indians at Calcutta's Hindu College at the time.[6]

Laird concludes, "At one level, therefore, Duff may be seen as a heroic figure who revitalized missionary education in India; at another, as one whose very success bequeathed a somewhat ambiguous legacy to India and its church."[7]

---

[1] Duff, *Missions the Chief End of the Christian Church*, 6, 65, 66, "teach geometry, arithmatic, grammar, history . . . preach in the vernacular" (70).
[2] Duff, *Missions the Chief End of the Christian Church*, 11.
[3] Duff, *Missions the Chief End of the Christian Church*, 78.
[4] Neill, *History of Christian Missions*, 234.
[5] Duff, *Missions the Chief End of the Christian Church*, 49–50.
[6] Anderson, *Biographical Dictionary of Christian Missions*.
[7] Laird, "Legacy of Alexander Duff," 148.

## Teaching English as a Missionary Strategy

One of the most popular forms of education-as-mission is Teaching English as a Second Language (TESOL). TESOL is far more than a "platform" for getting into creative access countries. True, "teaching English feeds a worldwide craving" which has opened the door for more than a hundred mission agencies to enter Asia and the Middle East.[100] But TESOL missionaries do not typically separate their work and witness, teaching English by day, and witnessing by night. Nor is it even necessary, in many restricted regions, to abstain from Christian witness in the classroom.

Teaching English is a fitting discipleship strategy: The curriculum in English classes often involve far more than just the nuts and bolts of the English language. It may be unethical or illegal in certain contexts to turn ESL classroom into an evangelism forum; but often students read stories and essays in English on important issues like "human rights, women's rights, the environment and civic education . . . racism, AIDS, the death penalty."[101] Students can journal about ethical and religious issues, they can debate these issues, and teachers can point students to fiction and non-fiction that was written from a Christian worldview.[102]

### Educational Methods

*Why it works:*

Education is a highly coveted commodity that missionaries can bring to needy parts of the world. Education also serves as a natural pathway for teaching Scripture and discussing spiritual issues.

*What it might miss:*

Education models should not just be platforms for getting visas; missionaries should be committed to the content that they agree to teach, as well as committed to "teaching them to obey all Jesus commanded."

---

100. Baurain, "Teaching English Feeds a Worldwide Craving."
101. Purgason, *Professional Guidelines for Christian English Teachers*, 3, 10.
102. Purgason, *Professional Guidelines for Christian English Teachers*, 3, 10.

Dormer recognizes that Christian English Teachers (CETs) employ various approaches toward ESL as a missionary strategy.[103] On one continuum, the ministry is either on the missionary's own turf, such as a church-run ESL course, or an English class at a Christian university. In this case, the "host" enjoys a great deal of latitude. On the other hand, the missionary may be a guest, for example, at a foreign secular university. In this case, the missionary has less freedom. ESL-as-mission approaches also differ in the end goal. Some are more discipleship-oriented, while other approaches are strictly focused on ESL-as-evangelism.

As with any other missionary work, ESL-as-mission requires the teachers to attain skills in their profession (teaching English); and they must also possess relational, communication, and ministry skills.[104]

## Discipling Across Cultures through Business

Since the production of goods (at the least, food) is essential to life, missionaries have always engaged in commercial activities. Their reason for engaging in business has varied, from business as a way to profit, to business as a "platform" for entering a country, to business as a way to sustain the mission, to business as a way of helping others flourish. I'll discuss and critique each of these strategies below.

### Tentmaking

Before the phrase "business as mission" became popular, most missiologists lumped all economic activities of missionaries into the category of tentmaking. Abraham herded sheep; Nehemiah was a cupbearer; Paul made tents (Acts 18:1–3). Even though Paul was a busy missionary, he engaged in commercial activity because he didn't want to be a burden on the local communities where he was ministering, or on the churches that sent him out. He was happy to receive help (whether food or shelter); but also felt that "if you don't work, you don't eat" (2 Thess 3:10).

Tentmaking, today, is a strategy where missionaries engage in a commercial activity to fund their lives, quite separate from their gospel ministry. An example would be Brian Sanders, who works as a middle level manager for Toyota in Japan, but also hopes to be a light for Christ

---

103. Dormer, *Teaching English in Missions*.
104. Dormer, *Teaching English in Missions*, 46–60.

and in his apartment building. Note that tentmaking is not always entrepreneurship—it may involve working for foreign governments, or even studying internationally for a period of time.

In many ways, this strategy is the most "normal" of all missionary strategies. It reflects the global trends of economic transmigration—people crossing borders for financial reasons, and taking their religious influence with them. Christianity, like Islam and Buddhism, has spread around the world almost inadvertently due to commerce; and globalization has sped up the pace. In fact, Greear, the president of the Southern Baptist Convention, believes that much of Asia will be won to Christ through ordinary Christian businesspeople who immigrate there.[105]

Missiologists are concerned about the efficacy of tentmaking. It can represent the amatuerization of missions, as lay Christians who spend much of their time in business do not have the training or time to study their host culture in depth. Additionally, these entrepreneurs may lack credentials, time, and training, to evangelize, plant churches, and raise up church leaders. So while tentmaking will likely continue (or increase) as a means by which the gospel spreads across cultures, it will always need to be supplemented with other strategies.

Another difficulty with tentmaking is that missionaries may find it extremely difficult, especially in tribal areas, to earn a living. Even if the government ostensibly allows foreign investment, people from cultures with a "limited good" mentality can feel that every dollar the missionary earns is one dollar stolen from the local economy. Additionally, those from patron-client societies may feel strongly that the role of the missionary is to be a self-funded patron, who gives resources, rather than taking them, from the local economy. In these settings, any time a missionary begins to get ahead, economically, her business, her witness (and maybe her life) is in peril.

## Platform Ministries

The Bomgartners,[106] from Iowa, with no experience in running fisheries, moves to Bangladesh to start a Tilapia farm. Even after 20 years, the fishery never makes a profit; and the couple receives nearly 100 percent

---

105. Greear, *Gaining by Losing*.
106. A pseudonym.

of their finances from churches in the USA. But this is not a failure in their eyes, or in the eyes of their supporters—the fishery was just a "platform" for getting a visa into a "restricted access country" (RAC). Teaching English to speakers of other languages (TESOL) has also often been a platform ministry. While expatriates receive salaries in East Asia for teaching English, the salary often does not cover living expenses; and many who engage in TESOL consider evangelism to be their real reason for being in the country.

The main concern missiologists have with platform ministries is they can jeopardize the visas of other expatriates in these RACs. If the Bangladeshi government discovers that Bomgartners are not really doing what they promised, they can lose their visa, and cause the government to be suspicious of other foreigners. Additionally, the biblical virtue of integrity compels Christians to be true to their word. If you plan to run a fishery, run it well. However, others who have a strong sense of urgency about the great commission argue that we should try to gain entry to RACs, and being duplicitous on a visa application justifies the ends.

The difficulties of platform ministries can be addressed. A long veteran of this strategy suggested that learning the language, working with a team, having accountability, and having a strong spiritual life can help missionaries succeed in witness and work.[107]

## Business as Development

In desperately poor settings, some missionaries have tried to increase the standard of living of those around them through commercial activity. For example, Carlie, in Malaysia, has taught some women in her host village how to make bracelets. Carlie sells the bracelets as "fair trade" items to her church friends in the USA. The funds go back to the Malay artisans. Other examples include a coffee plantation in Papua New Guinea, or a coffee houses that was set up in "missionary enclave" in Cambodia. In all cases, the missionaries help transfer talent, resources, and knowledge, to their host communities. The business isn't primarily meant to be self-sustaining; it is meant to give locals skills like accounting or cash cropping, that they can then use on their own.

Befus noted that this strategy is best suited for places where there are no jobs. Economic activities that help with the social uplift of others

---

107. Lai, "Tentmaking Unveiled—The Survey Says."

include: 1) service business such as clinics or bookstores, 2) business incubators (viable business projects that create jobs or income); and 3) offering affordable loans (micro-credit) for small businesses.[108]

The advantage of this model is that it can work in patron-client, limited good societies, because the missionary is not seen to be taking money from the local economy, the way a tentmaker might. The disadvantage is that, as some female entrepreneurs in Indonesia discovered, when the missionary returns to her home country, the customer base dries up.[109]

## Business as Mission

### Business as Mission

*Why it works:*

Entrepreneurial activity has raised the standards of billions. Christians have an easier time getting business visa than a missionary visa.

*What it might miss:*

BAM isn't for every missionary, and isn't for every field. The worker must be savvy about the business model. And the host country must have the sort of economy that can support these business activities without creating high levels of jealousy. The BAM worker must also learn to balance discipleship and entrepreneurship.

Business as mission (BAM) developed organically over the past twenty-five years to mitigate many of the disadvantages listed above. This strategy involves "the utilization of for-profit businesses as instruments for global mission."[110] BAM seeks to send out entrepreneurs who are well trained in both their business model and in spreading the gospel. They are honest with their host governments; and they try to run businesses that will not just pay the bills, but will transfer capital and skills to their

---

108. Befus, *Where There Are No Jobs.*
109. Martin, *Understanding the Perceptions of Indonesian Women.*
110. Johnson and Rundle, "Distinctives and Challenges of Business as Mission," 25.

host communities. These businesses are only considered successful if they can be sustained when the missionary leaves. Rundle and Steffen provide six case studies of how Great Commission Companies can excel at profits and outreach.[111] The companies they studied ranged from three million to tens of millions in gross revenue, and employed between 30 and 1,500. Yet the entrepreneurs also actively discipled their employees.

Yet BAM is not a one-size-fits-all strategy. Rundle and Steffen's case studies inadvertently reinforce the impression that GCCs require extraordinary talent to succeed.[112] These companies were run by men and women with extensive backgrounds in business and theology. And while it is possible to run a business in Asia that grosses millions and employs thousands, it is unlikely that this model can succeed in tribal or exchange-based areas.

## Discipling Across Cultures with Short-term Missions

Churches with a comprehensive outreach ministry often combine three strategies for missions: support long-term missionaries, educate the church about missions, and send out the church on short-term missions (STM). While some churches use their long-term missionaries to host the short-term teams, many parachurch organizations (sodalities) also provide STM experiences for churches. One website helps potential mission-goers select from over 500 short term mission opportunities, with names like Visiting Orphans, Tennis Ambassadors, and Dancelink.[113] Priest calculates that more than 2 million Christians go on a mission trip every year.[114]

Missionary organizations also recognize that short-term missions is a key component of their work. Guthrie argues, "A short term missionary service program is a must. Organizations not providing this option will face a manpower crisis."[115] Guthrie is assuming that STM is the funnel for long-term missionaries.

---

111. Rundle and Steffen, *Great Commission Companies*.
112. Rundle and Steffen, *Great Commission Companies*.
113. See Missionfinder.org.
114. Priest, "Are Short-Term Missions Good Stewardship?"
115. Guthrie, *Missions in the Third Millennium*, 88.

## Critiquing STM

At times, faulty ecclesiology serves as part of the impetus for STM: If Jesus is coming back so soon, sealing the fate of those who have never heard, why take the time to get a Bible degree, learn a trade, then learn another language and culture, then raise a long-term support team, and apply for all the necessary visas and work permits. Why not just go!

Howell's study of two STMs to the Dominican Republic illustrated how the value of STMs can vary greatly. One team had inadequate pre-field preparation, a paternalistic approach to community development, and shallow cross-cultural encounters. They had unrealistic assessments of the value they were providing. The other team worked closely with the national church to set realistic expectations and to ensure the Americans behaved in culturally appropriate ways, and built rapport across cultures.[116]

Taylor noted that short-term missions suffer from some shortcomings. Goers tend to overstate the importance of the trip before and afterward. The STM industry seems to sideline national ministries, can exhaust the long-term missionaries who host those teams, and produce limited results despite the high travel costs involved.[117]

Given some of Taylor's observations, perhaps the name "short term mission" is a misnomer. Are we really making disciples when we spend a couple weeks, as amateur builders or leading vacation Bible studies through an interpreter? Does it weaken the definition of "disciple making" and "mission" to refer to summer sports camps in South America "short term missions?" Howell suggests we re-frame these annual events as "religious pilgrimages." True, some donors will be less enthusiastic about giving funds to a "religious pilgrimage" than they would be about funding missions. However, most participants, trip leaders, host communities, and church leaders, understand that the purpose and value of these trips is the way impact it has on the participant.[118]

---

116. Howell, *Short Term Mission*.
117. Taylor, "Place of Short-Term Missions."
118. Taylor, "Place of Short-Term Missions."

## Short Term Missions

### Why it works:

STMs get people out of their comfortable place and expose them to the world's needs. STMs help churches show the importance of global missions. And many goers report that they experience spiritual benefits.

### What it might miss:

STMs cost a great deal of money for sometimes little measurable impact in the host country. And some research has shown that badly-run STMs actually damage the witness of the church in the host country. It is not clear if people who go on STMs are more likely to become life-long disciple makers across cultures.

But do STMs have a significant impact on participants? One study on participants in STM recorded that goers said they felt closer to God and were more likely to go in to missionary service; however, they were not found to have higher scores for spiritual well-being or self-concept compared to people who chose not to go on STMs.[119] Another study indicated that participants of STMs reported an immediate increase in their interest in missions and cultural intelligence; but these effects waned over time for those who did not have ongoing debriefing, and did not continue to be engaged in cross-cultural discipleship.[120] In a widely circulated and disappointing assessment of STM, Ver Beek followed up on 162 North Americans who built homes in Honduras at an average of $30,000 per home—homes which could have been built by Hondurans for $2,000. The goers indicated the trips significantly impacted them, but their financial giving to missions was not changed long-term. He and also followed up on the thirty families who were recipients of the homes, and noted no positive or negative impact of the STM.[121]

What should churches and parachurch organizations do about these mixed results of STM? So much research has been done lately, hopefully,

---

119. Manitsas, *Short Term Mission Trips*.
120. Friesen, "Long-term Impact of Short -term Missions."
121. Ver Beek, *Impact of Short-term Missions*.

leaders will discard the paternalism, capitalize on the opportunities to build rapport and draw people closer to God.

## Conclusion

Making disciples across cultures involves much more than speaking the propositions of the gospel in foreign languages. Discipleship is a radical reorientation of all spheres of life under the lordship of Christ. Therefore, cross-cultural discipleship engages the arts, education, agriculture, rituals, social relationships, business, politics and everything else we do in culture. Missionaries have typically been drawn to the sphere that suits their calling and gifting, such as evangelism, education, leadership training, or community development. But we must each remember that the methods we embrace are not necessarily the ones that are most appropriate for all missionaries or for all cultural contexts in all time periods.

## Move into Action

Consider your church's missionary outreach. What models does it support? Are there important models that it is neglecting?

## Ideas for Further Research

Much research could be done to understand the effectiveness of various missionary strategies. Some examples include:

1. Do a quantitative study on the correlation between oral Bible storytelling and comprehension of biblical doctrines.
2. Do a quantitative study on the correlation between pastoral training programs and laypeople's comprehension of biblical doctrines.
3. Study the factors that contribute to use and disuse of translated Scriptures.
4. Do ethnographies on how majority world Christians are using their own cultural artforms to share the gospel.

## Review Question

1. What are the advantages and drawbacks of using the various missionary methods listed above for disciple-making?

## Reflection Questions

1. In what way are various missionary methods (community development, TESOL, business as mission, etc.) all aspects of making disciples?

2. Remember Winter's theory of sodalities and modalities (chapter 9). Are there missionary models that more or less require a "guild" like a sodality can provide? What models does your church support (as a modality).

*Chapter 11*

# The Future of Missiology

WHAT WILL FUTURE WORKS by missiologists look like? How do changing global trends in the twenty-first century affect the way we will study missions? In this chapter I explore the trends and issues that will likely shape the future of missiology.

### Chapter Goals

*Knowledge goals:*

- Explain the half-life and long "tail life" of missiological "facts."
- Describe trends that have persistently been in focus in missiology, trends which have gone out of focus, and trends that are emerging in importance.
- Explain how and why missiology is becoming more diverse.

*Action goals:*

- Conduct inquiries in missiology that are timely, credible, and useful.

*Heart goals:*

- Commit to obeying the first commandment (Gen 1:28), the greatest commandments, and the Great Commission (Matt 28:19–20).

Below, I look at the following four realities:

1) Increased diversity among missionaries and missiologists: The slower growth of Christianity in many Western nations, and its more rapid growth in South America, Sub-Saharan Africa, the Pacific and Asia, will influence the issues that missiologists study. Missiologists will come from more diverse backgrounds as Christianity's global voice is increasingly recognized, and as more women with missions-related PhDs are receiving faculty appointments.

2) Globalization: Missiology will address twenty-first-century global trends, such as globalization, diasporas, urbanization, secularism, and the return of animism/spiritism.

3) Interdisciplinarity: Missiology will become even more interdisciplinary as scholars come from more diverse backgrounds, and as research becomes easier in the internet age.

4) Finishing the task: Missiology will need to reexamine closure theology, as "Finishing the task" seems elusive due to the steady growth of Islam.

## Twenty-First-Century Missiology Will Be More Diverse Than Ever

Global Christianity is becoming more diverse.[1] Therefore, the missionary force is becoming more diverse, including not just highly educated long term missionaries from Western nations, but Christians with humble means and less education.[2] This diversity of global Christianity will also shape those who go into missiology, which will in turn likely shape the questions we ask in missiology.

It is difficult to measure ethnic diversity in a field like missiology. Priest and DeGeorge's study of missions-related dissertations determined that between 2002 and 2012, while the majority may have been produced by scholars of European ancestry, nearly 13 percent were by those of African ancestry, 5 percent South Asian, 2.5 percent Hispanic, 4 percent Chinese, and 10 percent Korean.[3] The field of missiology will certainly continue to be more ethnically diverse as missiological degrees become increasingly available to students throughout the world—partly through online education, partly due to increased numbers of international students

---

1. Jenkins, *Next Christendom*; Yeh, *Polycentric Missiology*.
2. Yohannan, *Revolution in World Missions*.
3. Priest and DeGeorge, "Doctoral Dissertations on Mission," 196–97.

in schools of mission, and partly through the establishment of schools of world mission around the globe.

### Profile of a Missiologist: Enoch Wan

*(contemporary)*

Education: PhD and MA (Anthropology, State University of New York); MTS (Gordon-Conwell); BA (Nyack College)

Occupation: Professor of Intercultural Studies and Anthropology at Western Seminary (Oregon) and Reformed Theological Seminary (Jackson, MS)

Enoch Wan grew up in South China and later Hong Kong. After the death of his mother, "Papa Wan" had to place Enoch and his siblings in an orphanage, for a time. The family was united when Papa Wan remarried.

Enoch Wan has authored more than 80 articles and books on missiological topics like diaspora missiology, Asian theology, and contextualization. He co-authors books with his graduate students in order to help them find in-roads for their own academic contributions. Wan founded and directs *Global Missiology*, an online missiology publication. He also serves as an editor for numerous other missiological publications. He was the president of the Evangelical Missiological Society, the founding director for the Centre for Chinese Studies at Canadian Theological Seminary, has been a visiting professor at eight other universities globally, has served on the board of directors of several mission organizations, and has conducted seminars all over the world on intercultural studies, spiritual warfare, and church planting.

One of Wan's contributions to missiological theory is the study of the impact of current demographic trends on missionary strategy. For example, Wan has studied the ramifications of increased immigration to urban centers. Wan contends that mission strategy will involve missions to, through, and beyond these communities that are in diaspora. That is, globalization not only means that churches must become relevant to multiethnic congregations, but must mobilize these diverse Christians to be engaged in missions. As new global trends come along, missiologists should apply the same technique of exegeting those trends in order to tailor relevant missionary strategies.

A more diverse missiological community will likely affect the issues missiologists look at, and how we study those issues. Dissertations in the first decade of the twenty-first century increasingly focused on Asia and Africa, with a slight decline in Latin America, North America, and Oceania. Missiologists from around the globe are studying how the political, theological, social, and educational issues from their home countries affect the way we make disciples across cultures. Just to take one national-level example, hundreds of missiologists from South Korea have studied missiological issues,[4] including church planting in Korea,[5] Korean theologies of mission,[6] Korean attitudes toward missions,[7] community development within a Korean context,[8] Korean mission agencies,[9] issues related to Korean-American churches, among many others.[10] The same types of national-level missiological studies are being done in Africa, Asia, the Pacific and Australia, and South America.

In light of this increasing diversity, is missiology becoming more gender-equitable as well? In 2017, 29 percent of full-time faculty in intercultural studies from 9 universities that offer an MA or PhD in ICS were women.[11] But since the majority (51 percent) of PhD degrees awarded each year are going to women, with more than 60 percent of social science degrees going to women,[12] the faculties will likely continue to incorporate a higher percentage of women as well. As more women enter the field of missiology, they will be publishing more in the field. Currently, between 10 to 30 percent of articles in missiological journals are written by women (see Figure 11).

4. Nehrbass, "Korean Missiology."

5. Choi and Park, *Toward a Basic Theory for Missional Church Planting in Postmodern Korea*; Han, "Christian Mission Environments and Strategies in Che Ju Island."

6. Cho, "Factors Contributing to the Development of the Modern Korean Missions Movement"; Lee, "Necessity of Power Ministry in Korean Evangelical Missionary Training Programs."

7. Jang, "Global Missions Perspective and Attitude Toward Contextual Theology Among Korean Alumni."

8. Jung, "Incarnational Mission and Community Development."

9. Kim, "Internationalization of Three Korean Mission Agencies."

10. Keum, "Grounded Theory Study on The Emerging Negative Perception."

11. The full-time intercultural studies (or similar monikers) faculty at Trinity Evangelical Divinity School (TEDS), Fuller School of Intercultural Studies, Asbury School of Theology, Cook School of Intercultural Studies at Biola University, Dallas Theological Seminary, Western Seminary, Wheaton College, Columbia International University (CIU) and Assemblies of God Theological Seminary (AGTS) revealed 19 females compared 67 males.

12. Allum and Okahana, *Graduate Enrollment Report 2004*.

THE FUTURE OF MISSIOLOGY 281

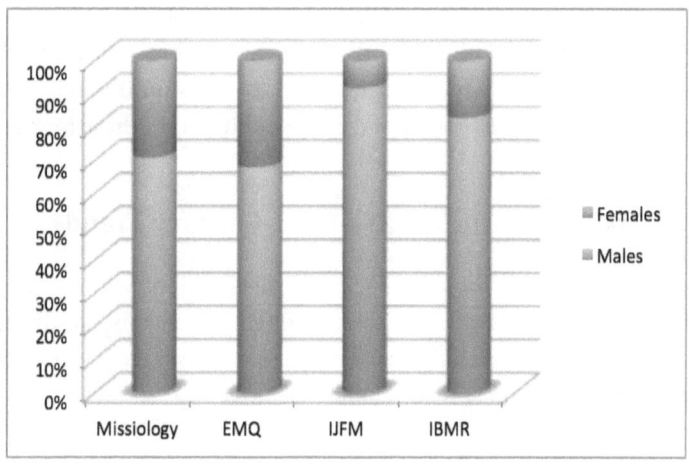

Figure 11: Male to female ratio of published articles 2012-2017[13]

While this ratio is unbalanced; it is more balanced than early missiology journals. Consider the ratio of articles written by men to women in EMQ, IBMR and Missiology (starting 1973) between January 1970 and July 1975 in Figure 12, below (note IJFM's second volume, in 1985, was the first issue to have articles by female authors).

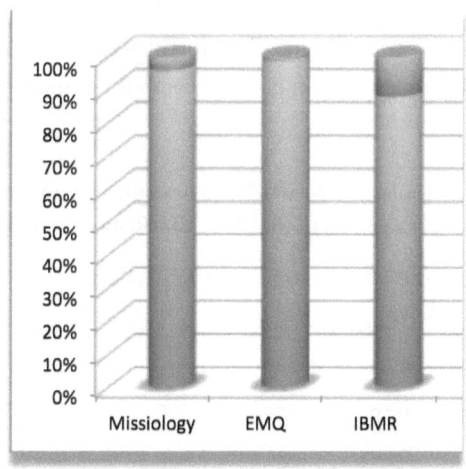

Figure 12: Ratio men:women 1970-1975[14]

13. The data is based on 320 articles where I could identify the author's gender, including all co-authors, assuming the authors' pronouns and pseudonyms accurately reflect the authors' genders. *IJFM* 92 percent male, *EMQ* 68 percent, *Missiology* 71 percent, *IBMR* 80 percent.

14. *Missiology* articles were written by 96 percent males, *EMQ* 99 percent, *IBMR*

It is hard to tell how an increase in published articles by female missiologists will affect the way that missiological studies are researched and written. The extent to which women tend to focus on different themes than men do will shape the topics that are published in these journals.

## Will Focus on Twenty-First-Century Trends

Just as the missionary force is changing, the situations which we would call the "missionary field" are also changing. These changing dynamics shape the types of research that missiologists carry out. We will be changing our strategies to meet those changing needs.

### The Changing Missiological Topics

Just as the prototypical missionary force is changing from expatriate to facilitator,[15] the prototypical missionary field is changing from foreign to diaspora.[16] Traditionally, missions-at-home has focused especially on issues of church growth, evangelism, and multiculturalism. Yet Tennent predicts that missiologists will increasingly need to reckon with issues like the collapse of Christendom, and the rise of postmodernism in the West.[17]

What issues are missiologists looking at today? Table 8 below lists the frequency of articles, by topic, in three major missiological journals from 2014 to 2017.

Table 8: Topics of 150 articles in missiological journals between 2014 and 2017 (in EMQ, IBMR, and Missiology)

| | |
|---|---|
| Religion and conversion (especially Islam) | 20 |
| Mission theology/philosophy | 17 |
| Individual missiologists | 11 |
| Ethics/worldview | 11 |
| Social issues (including refugees) | 9 |

---

88 percent.

15. Steffen, *Facilitator Era*.
16. George, "Diaspora."
17. Tennent, *Invitation to World Missions*.

| | |
|---|---|
| Historical missiological | 8 |
| Teaching missiology | 8 |
| Discipleship/evangelism | 7 |
| Mission/multicultural teams | 7 |
| Missionary life, Third Culture Kids | 7 |
| Orality | 6 |
| Diaspora missiology | 5 |
| Mission organizations | 4 |
| Globalization | 4 |
| Culture learning and culture shock | 4 |
| Partnership/dependency | 3 |
| Biblical missiology | 3 |
| Catholic issues | 3 |
| Language issues | 2 |
| Cultural values (including honor/shame) | 2 |
| Mobilization/training | 2 |
| Specific Missionary methods | 1 |
| Missions and public life | 1 |
| Women's issues | 1 |
| Healing | 1 |
| Spirituality in missions, spiritual formation | 1 |
| Teaching missiology | 1 |
| Business as Mission | 1 |

The topics covered are broad, representing the breadth of missiology as an interdisciplinary field. But note that the topics do not differ that significantly from those covered in three journals from 1960 to 1973 (Table 9 below).

**Table 9: Topics of 150 articles in missiology journals from 1960 to 1973 (in EMQ, IBMR, and Missiology, formerly Practical Anthropology)**

| | |
|---|---|
| Mission philosophy/theology | 16 |
| Missions and indigenous Culture | 13 |
| Religions | 9 |

| | |
|---|---|
| Syncretism, contextualization, ethnotheology | 8 |
| Ecumenism | 8 |
| Church and missions, role of laity | 8 |
| Indigenous church | 8 |
| Missionary anthropology | 7 |
| Social (esp. medical and racism) | 7 |
| Public life, communism, revolutions | 7 |
| Missionary life | 6 |
| History of missions | 6 |
| Missionary vocation | 5 |
| Role of missions | 5 |
| Organizations/denominations | 4 |
| Church growth | 4 |
| Cultural products | 4 |
| Biblical missiology | 3 |
| Missiologists | 3 |
| Communication/language | 3 |
| Conferences | 3 |
| Cultural adjustment | 2 |
| Spirituality | 2 |
| Evangelism | 2 |
| Church life | 2 |
| Missions and money | 1 |
| Conversion | 1 |
| Methods | 1 |
| Letters | 1 |
| Holy Spirit | 1 |

The two lists, separated by five decades, seem to cover many similar issues, with some notable changes: Certain social issues (diaspora, refugees) are more prominent today, whereas issues of communism and revolution were discussed 50 years ago. And it seems the issue of missionary calling was more prominent then. But missiologists in both contexts have spent a good deal of time working out a theology and philosophy of mission, and culturally-specific strategies for heralding the gospel.

## The Expiration Date of Missiological Research[18]

Some themes in missiology are enduring, whereas some are short-lived. Elsewhere, I have documented how in any discipline, ideas have a half-life, as they go out of vogue.[19] Some ideas have a longer tail life, and gain steam over decades. For example, from 1961 to 1970, only two articles were published on "contextualization" among the four missiological journals. From 1971 to 1980, these journals published eleven articles that specifically focused on the subject of contextualization. The trend remained the same in the 1980s. But from 1991 to 2000, the rate increased to 47, and from 2001 to 2010, there were 58 articles published on the topic (see Figure 13).

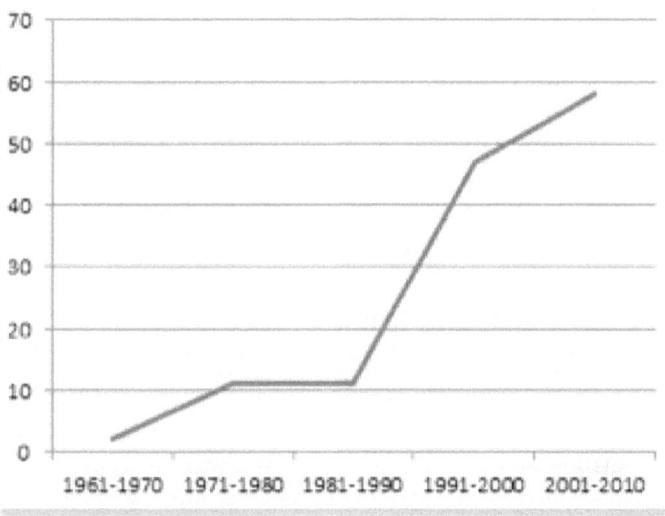

Figure 13: Number of missiological articles published by decade, specifically on "contextualization" 1961–2010 *EMQ, Missiology, IBMR,* and *IJFM*

We can see how quickly the rate of research on the topic has been increasing. Missiologists had published ten articles on contextualization in four prominent missiological journals up to 1980. They were publishing

18. This section is adapted from Nehrbass, "Half-Life of Missiological Facts."
19. Nehrbass, "Half-Life of Missiological Facts."

20 articles per decade on the subject by 1990, and more than 40 by 2000. So the rate of publication on contextualization has been doubling quicker than every ten years.

Yet research on some missiological issues reaches a plateau, and other lines of inquiry even decline. If we plot the research on "member care" by decade, we see a leveling off in the past decade (see Figure 14).

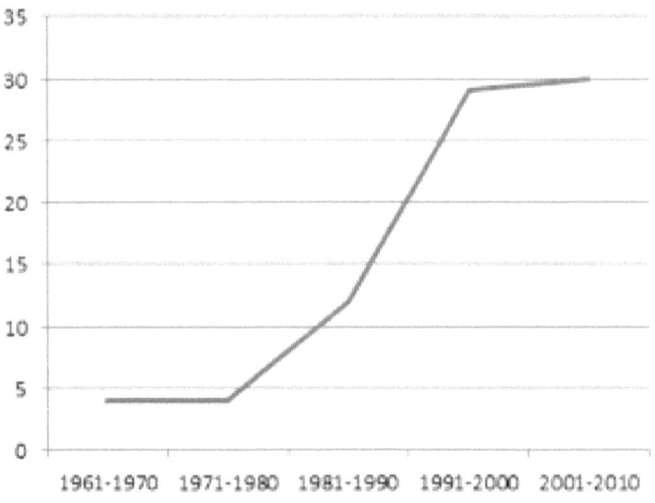

Figure 14: Number of missiological articles published on "member care" by decade from 1961 to 2010 *EMQ, Missiology, IBMR,* and *IJFM*

Why the plateau? This "logistic curve" is expected for the diffusion of knowledge in any field, as information about a topic diffuses through the population. The high, plateaued portion of the line is the asymptote: it becomes increasingly difficult to continue producing at the previous rate, as the population becomes saturated with information on a topic. This is not to suggest that we know all there is to know about member care. This sub-field of missiology may be experiencing a paradigm shift, rendering the term "member care" less relevant. Perhaps experts on member care have found other, more specialized journals in which to publish; perhaps missiologists' energies are being diverted to other fields; maybe there will be a resurgence of interest in the topic later on. Or perhaps there just isn't enough data from these four missiological journals to find a trend at this point.

Regardless of the reason for the plateau, we know that a portion of our missiological knowledge has an expiration date. As national borders open up or close, as communities move into diaspora, as the majority world mobilizes for missions, and as Western interest in missions changes (from long term to short term), our missiological strategies change. Sometimes our theology (or how we write about it) even changes. For example, today, evangelicals no longer need to be shy about engaging in social action—as they were in the last decades of the twentieth century; many evangelicals now see social action as important as proclamation (see chapter 6). These are just some examples which show how the issues we were researching so passionately fifty years ago eventually become less relevant, while other topics that were taboo or dormant (as expected) come to the foreground.

In fact, Arbesman argues, most of what we know in any field has an expiration date. It is especially obvious that as our knowledge of physics and medicine increases exponentially, the earlier research quickly passes out of date. For instance, a hospital in England reported that half of its research on the liver became irrelevant in fifty years. The half-life of research in physics is about 13 years, psychology and history have a half-life of seven years.[20] This doesn't mean that what we used to think in a particular discipline like missiology is necessarily wrong; it just means that we move on to newer concepts as they appear more useful to us.

One useful idea which has lost valence in missiology is that of "functional equivalents" (i.e., Christian substitutes) for autochthonous rites and rituals (see chapter 4). The most recent article, among four missiological journals, to employ the term was published in 1981.[21] Since missiology is dependent on anthropology, when trends like functionalism (on which functional equivalence was based) fall out of fashion in academia, their dependent theories are also mentioned less frequently.

Certain missiological topics become outdated as the world situation changes. A stark example would be the prolific reports of cannibalism in missionary literature before the twentieth century, whereas a search for "cannibals" or "cannibalism" through the archives of the four prominent missiological journals from the twentieth century turns up zero results.

Arbesman refers to the eventual "expiration date" of certain ideas or terms in academic as the "half-life of facts."[22] Church growth is a

---

20. Arbesman, *Half-Life of Facts*, 32.
21. See Grönblom and Thorgaard, "Notion of Functional Equivalence."
22. Arbesman, *Half-Life of Facts*.

missiological sub-discipline that seems to have had a definite half-life. The bulk of research on "church growth" was published from 1980 to 2000, and there has been a drastic decline in the term "church growth" in *EMQ, Missiology, IBMR,* and *IJFM* in the past ten years (see Figure 15). Some church growth specialists would say this is a worrisome sign. But it doesn't mean missiologists are thinking less about church growth. We know that church growth researchers are currently publishing in more specialized journals. So it's not that we've exhausted all there is to say about church growth within missiology; what is more likely is that we're now talking about church planting movements, disciple making movements, church multiplication, partnerships, or insider movements (insider movements, by the way, don't show up in ATLA until 2007).

Figure 15: Number of articles published on "church growth," by decade, in four missiological journals from 1961 to 2010

Yet some sub-disciplines in missiology fit neither Arbesman's exponential doubling model nor his half-life model.[23] For instance, articles which focus on mission agencies (in the four missiological journals in this study) have been published at a rate of 8 to 15 each decade since the 1960s (see Figure 16). Interest is neither waning nor exploding.

---

23. Arbesman, *Half-Life of Facts*.

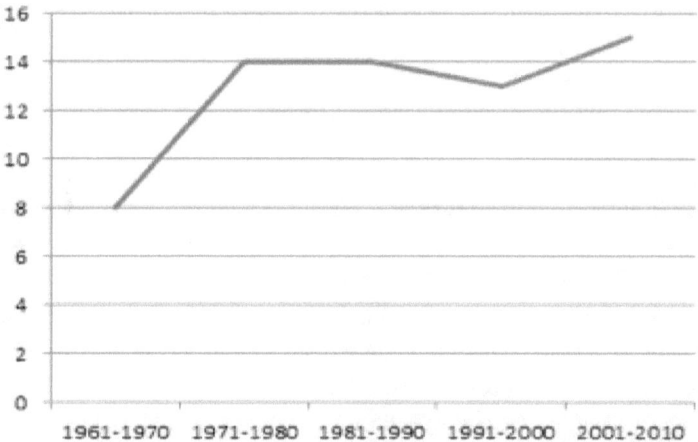

Figure 16: Number of articles published on "mission agencies," by decade, in four missiological journals from 1961 to 2010

This discussion of out-dating may concern or embarrass scholars, as if it puts our credibility on the line. However, the point of recognizing a half-life in research—especially in social science research such as missiology—is to understand that when our strategies are going out of date, this is a good indication that the world is rapidly changing and that we are continually updating our discipline in order to maximize our impact for the kingdom of God.

## Paradigm Shifts in Missiology

Research in any field also shifts dramatically after a major paradigm shift. With the increasing educational levels and economic status of Christians in the majority world, the global missiological discussion has shifted from paternalistic attitudes to partnership. Also, Ralph Winter's contribution of "people groups" forever changed missiological strategy from engaging the world's 200+ "nation-states" as if they were cohesive units (as William Carey did in his *Enquiry*) to reaching specific people groups.

Other recent significant changes in missiology include research on the short-term mission (STM) avalanche.[24] In fact, a search on the American Theological Library Association (ATLA) database for the term

---

24. Slimbauch, "First, Do No Harm."

"short term missions" turned up 131 academic articles, with 121 published in 2000 or later.[25]

### The Long "Tail Life" of Research

Even though our knowledge increases exponentially across the board in missiology, certain ideas have a half-life while other ideas persist. Perhaps (should the Lord tarry) we won't be talking about the 10/40 Window (see chapter 9) in fifty years. Other models will come along to revolutionize our strategy for targeting specific groups—perhaps we won't even talk about "targeting" specific groups. (I hope we're not still arguing about social justice versus proclamation in fifty years, as we were fifty years ago!) If the past is any predictor, and given the unpredictability and mutability of human behavior, we will probably still be strategizing on reconciliation and justice, rather than arriving at comprehensive solutions to such problems. But some missiological ideas have much more staying power. Arbesman describes the persistence of such seminal academic ideas as a long "tail life."[26]

To take an example, Henry Venn's "three self" model for independent indigenous churches (see chapter 9) is a foundational model that continues to be cited by mission strategists every year. Venn has been referenced 49 times in the ATLA database, as recently as 2012. Other missiological contributions with long tail lives undoubtedly include McGavran's "people movements" (also in chapter 9),[27] Niehbur's taxonomy of "Christ in Culture,"[28] as well as Hiebert's ideas of the "excluded middle"[29] and "critical contextualization"[30] which are both mentioned in chapter 9.

This (quite incomplete) list of missiological contributions with long tail lives suggests that concepts and theologies of mission have more staying power than specific strategies for mission. Strategies, as I mentioned earlier in the discussion on half-life, are *supposed* to

---

25. This search was conducted in 2019.
26. Arbesman, *Half-Life of Facts*.
27. McGavran, *Bridges of God*.
28. Niebuhr, *Christ and Culture*.
29. Hiebert, "Flaw of the Excluded Middle."
30. Hiebert, "Critical Contextualization."

go out of date as the world changes. The longest tail lives are conceptual frameworks and theologies which are grounded in data that spans the centuries, often across two or more continents.

## Twenty-First-Century Missiology Will Keep Up with Changing Trends in Academia

On into the future, we will likely continue to deal with world religions, spirituality, missionary life, individual missionaries, and women's issues in missions; but our approaches to writing on these issues may change: Studies may become more interdisciplinary. And in an effort to retain credibility and relevance to other disciplines, our methods should be rigorous, and based on empirical research.

### Missiology Will Be Connected to the Workplace

Academic departments are under increasing pressure by stakeholders (employers, administration, government, parents, and students) to connect their fields to workplace skills. Missiology will need to follow suit if it will remain as part of Christian university curriculum. This doesn't mean that students of missiology expect to earn large paychecks with their degrees, but they (and their mission agencies) need to know how the study of missions history, or the theology of missions, or TESOL, etc., connects to their work. By addressing twenty-first-century realities on the mission field (discussed above) missiology can demonstrate its practical usefulness. That is, by focusing on the sorts of research questions that missionaries are actually interested in, and not just the problems that academicians are interested in, missiology can remain alive and relevant.

### Missiology Will Be More Interdisciplinary

If missiology is to remain relevant to the scholarly community, it cannot be stuck in old paradigms, such as the social functionalist explanation of culture, a west-to-the-rest paradigm for mission, or reductionistic generalizations (stereotypes) of people groups. Missiology in the twenty-first century will need to take the best of learning (from an interdisciplinary perspective).

Missions in the globalized twenty-first century is a political activity; it has economic consequences; it delves into issues of rhetoric, education, identity, culture change, leadership, gender, technology. As I discussed in chapter 1, missiology is performed by bringing in multiple academic fields. Missiology will need to interact with failed states, the rapid economic growth in many nations where we serve, the phenomenon of reverse migration and remittances, and ethnic violence.

## Missiology Will Have to Reckon with Notions about "Finishing the Task"

The year 2000 was a symbolic year for missiology, somehow garnering excitement about "finishing the task" (however that was conceived), just as the Student Volunteer Movement rallied at the dawn of the twentieth century for "evangelization in this generation." Now that Y2K has come and gone, and we are still facing the reality that 3 billion people live in unreached, un-evangelized people groups (UUPGs), missiology must seriously face questions about what it means to finish the task. As Dana Robert mentioned, "A century ago the participants at Edinburgh 1910 complained that only one-third of the world was Christian. Today we rejoice that one-third of the world are followers of Christ."[31]

In 2050, there will be 2.9 billion Christians and 2.8 billion Muslims.[32] Consider the following realities:

- Out of 648 million Great Commission Christians, 70 percent have never been told about the world's 1.6 billion unevangelized individuals.

- The majority of the unreached people groups are in countries that are restricted access. Western missionaries may not even be able to get to them.

- Despite Christ's command to evangelize, 67 percent of all humans from AD 30 to the present day have never even heard of his name.

- 648 million Christians today (called Great Commission Christians) are active in Christ's world mission; 1,352 million Christians are inactive in this mission.

31. Kim and Anderson, *Mission Today and Tomorrow*, 67–68.
32. Burke, D. "The World's Fastest Growing Religion Is . . ."

- Organized Christianity has total contact with 3,590 religions but no contact at all with 353 other religions and their over 500 million adherents.[33]

If "closure theology" is a significant motivator for our missionary efforts, will our missionary forces be discouraged when Islam and Christianity are head-to-head for numbers of adherents? Taylor warns against the following:

- The use of emotive slogans to drive missions, leading to a false understanding of both task and success;
- The temptation to use simplistic thinking, guided by marketing strategies and secular concepts of success;
- The reduction of world evangelization to statistics, objects and outcomes;
- The temptation to limit missions to specific geographic regions;
- An over-emphasis on short term missions; and
- The idea that the church can accomplish the Great Commission through mass media.[34]

The point is, our impulse to make disciples across cultures, our strategies for motivating the church, and our understanding of the task, should be shaped by Scripture (including our eschatology) rather than by global trends. We are called to make disciples in times of awakening and persecution, in urban and rural settings, whether Jesus comes back tomorrow or in a thousand years. Global trends may shape *how* we go about that task; but our missionary theology and impulse is rather timeless, in contrast to trends that will come and go in the next century.

## Conclusion

How can the study of missions be useful and credible? These chapters have argued that missiology is useful when it does the following:

1. Generates theory. It demonstrates how the history of the expansion of Christianity in a missionary field may suggest "best practices" for

33. Johnson and Barrett, *World Christian Trends*, 3.
34. Taylor, "From Iguassu to the Reflective Practitioners," 3–4.

making disciples across cultures—or how it demonstrates pitfalls to avoid.

2. Connects theory to the Great Commission. It describes how theory relates to making disciples across cultures. If not, the study may be interesting, and even credible, but will not be missiological.

3. Contributes to missiological systematic theology. It addresses theological questions that are of importance to the missionary field, such as the nature of God's revelation to humankind, the way that the gospel becomes good news to people of various cultures, the role of the Holy Spirit in sending out missionaries, etc.

4. Integrates other disciplines. It draws on understandings of global politics, sociality, theology, economics, education, etc., to further our understanding of making disciples across cultures.

5. Stays current. It takes into account current global realities, and does not rely on theories (whether educational, anthropological, etc.) that have gone out of date.

6. Is diverse. As the missionary force and the missiological community are both increasingly diverse, missiological questions must reflect and encourage the diversity of thought on how to make disciples across cultures.

7. Is grounded in real data. Many of the missiological works that are mentioned in this text are based on actual field experiences. The exemplary studies explicitly describe the methodology (interviews, surveys, observations, etc.) that helped generate theoretical explanations in anthropology, education, theology, history etc.

8. Is self-critical, rather than naïve. As in every other academic field, missiologists sharply disagree on issues. Robust studies of missions must reflect the controversies and multiple points of view, rather than simply reiterate a position from one side.

This book explored several hundred missiological works from various sub-disciplines in the field, especially noting seminal theories that have been either adopted into missiology, or which were developed by missiologists. Table 10 below lists some of the important people and ideas that have shaped missiology. It is unlikely that anyone could be an expert in all of these fields, but missiologists should be conversant with these seminal ideas:

Table 10: People and Ideas that have shaped missiology

| Theoretical sphere | Theorists and ideas (theories or models) |
| --- | --- |
| Missiological theology | *Missio Dei*; the kingdom of God as mission (van Engen and Glasser); Missionary hermeneutic (Wright); Universalism, inclusivism, exclusivism; Systematic Missiological Theology (Nehrbass); Christian hedonism (Piper) |
| Missiological historiography | Bosch's 6 paradigms of mission; Winter's 3 eras of protestant missions; Latourette's five epochs; The "translatability" of Christianity (Sanneh) |
| Missiological anthropology | Malinowski's permanent vital sequence (biological determinism); Radin's theory of economic determinism; Radcliff-Brown and the British school's theory of social determinism; the theory that culture is genetic; Marvin Harris's theory of environmental determinism; Pierce, Levi-Strauss, and Geertz's theories of how culture is transmitted through symbol (semiotics); Victor Turner and Arnold Van Gennep's theories of ritual and rites of passage; Boaz's particularism; functional substitutes (Tippett) |
| Intercultural studies | Cultural values (Hofstede; Hall); Orientalism (Said); facework (Ting-Toomey); cross-cultural leadership (Lingenfelter and Mayers); contextualization (Moreau); cultural intelligence (Livermore, Earley and Ang); shame/honor (Wu; Georges) |
| Theories unique to missiology | Three selves model (Anderson, Nevius); C1–C6 scale; emic/etic distinction (Pike), homogeneous unit principle; flaw of the excluded middle (Hiebert); critical contextualization (Hiebert); indigenizing and pilgrim principle (Walls); 10/40 Window (Bush); unreached people groups (Winter); redemptive analogies (Richardson); Melchizedek principle (Richardson); sodality/modality model (Winter) |
| Church planting as a missionary strategy | Disciple making movements; church planting movements (Garrison); T4T (Smith) |
| Economic development as a missionary strategy | Transformational development (Myers, Sider, Sterns); prioritism; social gospel (Rauschenbusch); integral mission (Padilla) |
| Orality as missionary strategy | Chronological Bible storying (McIlwain); oral-formulaic theory (Walter Ong) |

Hundreds of others have contributed to missiology; and many others in the future will continue to shape the field.

## Move into Action

You have decided to take on your own studies of missiology, undoubtedly because, as a disciple of Jesus Christ, you are compelled to help others obey all that He commanded. I encourage you to carry out your studies in ways that are credible to the scholarly world, and yet useful to those who are "on the ground" making disciples across cultures.

## Ideas for Further Research

1. Research what missiological topics are being studied in contexts outside of the West.

2. Explore the tail life and expiration date of an idea that has shaped missiology.

## Review Questions

1. How will changes in the "mission field" shape missiology in the near future?

2. How will changes in the missionary force shape missiology in the near future?

## Reflection Questions

1. Why do missiological theories and models go out of date?

2. The purpose of this book is to help scholars study missions in a way that is useful, timely and credible. How has the book accomplished that goal?

3. What are key elements for studying missions in a way that is useful, timely, and credible?

# Contributors' Biographies

Rebeca de la Torre Burnett (PhD in Intercultural Education from Biola University) is an adjunct professor of history at Biola University. She has worked in the field of higher education for over 14 years, working with college students in recruitment, student development, and teaching. She has a BA in History and an MA in Latin American History from the University of South Florida, in Tampa. She has lived in three Latin American countries and has had the privilege of serving overseas in long and short-term missions. Her research has focused on the intersectionality of education and missions. Other research interests include college students and various topics in history.

Leanne Dzubinski (PhD in Adult Education and HROD from the University of Georgia) is Associate Professor of Intercultural Education in the Cook School of Intercultural Studies at Biola University. She teaches doctoral courses on education, leadership, and research methods for students working in multicultural settings. Her PhD dissertation examined how women lead in evangelical missions organizations. Her publications include studies of adult learning, online learning, qualitative research, women in mission work, women in Christian higher education, and women in leadership. Prior to starting her second career in academia, she spent 20 years as a missionary, working in evangelism, church planting, and education. She also has a BA from Emory University, a ThM from Dallas Theological Seminary, and a DMin from Gordon-Conwell Theological Seminary.

Julie Martinez, PhD, has spent 25 years overseas as a missionary working in Honduras, Chile, Zambia, and Cambodia and specializes in transformational development. She is currently an Assistant Professor and the Director of the Intercultural Studies Program at Lee University in Cleveland, Tennessee.

# Bibliography

Aasland, Erik. "The Narrativization of Kazakh Proverbs: College Students' Language Ideologies Concerning 'Community.'" Unpublished doctoral diss., Fuller Theological Seminary, 2013.

Abbott, Walter M. *Documents of Vatican II*. New York: Guild, 1966.

Addison, James Thayer. *The Medieval Missionary: a Study of the Conversion of Northern Europe, A.D. 500–1300*. Philadelphia: Porcupine, 1976.

Adeney, Miriam. "Esther Across Cultures: Indigenous Leadership Roles for Women." *Missiology: An International Review* 15 (1987) 323–37.

———. "Review of Eternity in their Hearts." *Missiology: An International Review* 10 (1982) 123–27.

———. "Telling Stories: Contextualization and American Missiology." In *Global Missiology for the 21st Century: The Iguassu Dialogue*, edited by W. Taylor, 377–88. Grand Rapids: Baker Academic, 2000.

Adogame, Afe, ed. "Mapping Globalization with the Lens of Religion: African Migrant Churches in Germany." In *New Religions and Globalization*, edited by Armin Geertz and Margit Warburg, 189–214. Aarhus: Aarhus University Press, 2008.

———. *Who Is Afraid of the Holy Ghost?: Pentecostalism and Globalization in Africa and Beyond*. Trenton, NJ: Africa World, 2011.

Ahanotu, Austin M. "The Nigerian Military and the Issue of State Control of Mission Schools." *Church History* 52 (1983) 333–44.

Ahrens, Theodor. "On Grace and Reciprocity: A Fresh Approach to Contextualization with Reference to Christianity in Melanesia." *International Review of Mission* 89 (2000) 515–28.

Allen, Catherine B. "Charlotte (Lottie) Moon 1840–1912: Demonstrating 'No Greater Love.'" In *Mission Legacies: Biographical Studies of Leaders of the Modern Missionary Movement*, edited by G. Anderson, 205–15. Maryknoll, NY: Orbis, 1994.

———. "The Legacy of Lottie Moon." *International Bulletin of Missionary Research* 17 (1993) 146–52.

Allen, R. *Missionary Methods: St. Paul's or Ours?* Grand Rapids: Eerdmans, 1962.

———. *The Spontaneous Expansion of the Church: And the Causes Which Hinder It*. London: World Dominion, 1927.

Allison, Norman E. "The Contribution of Cultural Anthropology to Missiology." In *Missiology and the Social Sciences: Contributions, Cautions and Conclusions*, edited by E. Rommen and G. Corwin, 30–46. Pasadena: William Carey Library, 1996.

———. "An Evaluation of Emerging Churches on the Basis of the Contextualization Spectrum (C1–C6)." Evangelical Theological Society. Washington, DC, 2006.

Allum, Jeff, and Hironao Okahana. *Graduate Enrollment Report 2004 to 2014*. Washington, DC, 2015. http://www.cgsnet.org/ckfinder/userfiles/files/E_and_D_2014_report_final.pdf.

Anderson, Gerald H. *Biographical Dictionary of Christian Missions*. New York: Macmillan, 1999.

———. "Introducing Missiology." *Missiology: An International Review* 1 (1973) 3–4.

Anderson, J. "An Overview of Mission." In *Missiology: An Introduction to the Foundations, History and Strategies of World Missions*, edited by J. M. Terry et al., 1–17. Nashville: Broadman and Holman, 1998.

Anderson, Neil. *In Search of the Source*. Portland, OR: Multnomah, 1992.

Anderson, V. D. "Implicit Rhetorical Theory of Preachers in Wolaitta Ethiopia with Implications for Homiletics Instruction in Theological Education." PhD diss., Biola University, 2008.

Andresen, William. "Evaluating an Asset-Based Effort to Attract and Retain Young People." *Community Development* 43 (2012) 49–62.

Andrews, Edward. *Native Apostles: Black and Indian Missionaries in the British Atlantic World*. Cambridge, MA: Harvard University Press, 2013.

Ang, Soon, and Linn Van Dyne. *Handbook of Cultural Intelligence: Theory Measurement and Application*. New York: Routledge, 2009.

Arbesman, Samuel. *The Half-Life of Facts: Why Everything We Know has an Expiration Date*. New York: Current, 2012.

Armstrong, Cameron D. "The Efficiency of Storying." *Evangelical Missions Quarterly* 49 (2013) 322–28.

Arrington, Aminta. "Christian Hymns as Theological Mediator: The Lisu of South-west China and Their Music." *Studies in World Christianity* 21 (2015) 140–60.

———. "Hymns of the Everlasting Hills: The Written Word in an Oral Culture in Southwest China." PhD diss., Biola University, 2014.

———. "Recasting the Image: Celso Constantini and the Role of Sacred Art and Architecture in the Indigenization of the Chinese Catholic Church, 1922–1933." *Missiology: An International Review* 41 (2013) 438–51.

Asaju, Dapo. "Colonial Politicization of Religion: Residual Effects on the Ministry of African Led Churches in Britain in Christianity." In *Africa and the African Diaspora*, edited by A. Adogame et al., 279–92. New York: Continuum International, 2008.

Atallah, Ramez. "A Tribute to René Padilla and Samuel Escobar." *Journal of Latin American Theology* 5 (2010) 12–18.

Austring, G. K. "The Analysis of the Role of Adult Learning Theory in Understanding AGWM Missionaries' Cultural Adaptation to Latin America." PhD diss., Biola University, 2011.

Baker, Dwight P. "Missiology as an Interested Discipline—and Where Is It Happening." *International Bulletin of Missionary Research* 38 (2014) 17–20.

Bakke, Raymond J. "Urban Evangelization: a Lausanne Strategy since 1980." *International Bulletin of Missionary Research* 8 (1984) 149–54.

Bar, Christel. "The Development of a Contextualized Indigenous Education System." Unpublished diss., Biola University, 1989.

Barnes, Peter. *Aneityum: Missionary Methods and the Theology of Mission*. Eugene, OR: Wipf & Stock, 2015.

Barney, G. Linwood. "The Challenge of Anthropology to Current Missiology." *International Bulletin of Missionary Research* 5 (1981) 172–77.

Barram, M. "'Occupying' Genesis 1–3: Missionally Located Reflections on Biblical Values and Economic Justice." *Missiology: An International Review* 42 (2014) 386–98.

Barton, J. "Confusion and Communion: Christian Mission and Ethnic Identities in Postgenecide Rwanda." *Missiology: An International Review*, 40 (2012) 229–48.

Baurain, B. "Teaching English Feeds a Worldwide Craving." *Evangelical Missions Quarterly* 28 (1992) 164–73.

Bavinck, J. H. *An Introduction to the Science of Missions.* Philadelphia: Presbyterian and Reformed, 1960.

Beach, Edgar S. "Urbana: An Ongoing Experience." In *Confessing Christ as Lord: The Urbana '81 Compendium*, edited by J. Alexander, 21–31. Downers Grove, IL: InterVarsity, 1982.

Beattie, Warren R., ed. *Ministry Across Cultures: Sharing the Christian Faith in Asia.* Oxford: Regnum, 2016.

Beckner, W. Benjamin. "Eugene Casalis and the French Mission to Basutoland (1833–1856): A Case Study of Lamin Sanneh's Mission-By-Translation Paradigm in Nineteenth-Century Southern Africa." *Missiology: An International Review* 43 (2015) 73–86.

Befus, D. *Where There Are No Jobs: Enterprise Solutions for Employment and "Public Goods" for the Poor.* Miami: Latin America Mission, 2005.

Beine, David. "A Continuing Role for Western Bible Translators?" In *Controversies in Mission: Theology, People and Practice of Mission in the 21st Century*, edited by R. Scheuermann and E. Smither, 165–86. Pasadena: William Carey Library, 2016.

Bell, Rob. *Love Wins: At the Heart of Life's Big Questions.* New York: Collins, 2011.

Bendassolli, Pedro F. "Theory Building in Qualitative Research: Reconsidering the Problem of Induction." *Forum Qualitative Sozialforschung / Forum: Qualitative Social Research* 14 (2013) 1–20.

Benedict, Ruth. *The Chrysanthemum and the Sword.* New York: Houghton Mifflin Harcourt, 1946.

Bennett, Milton J. "Towards Ethnorelativism: A Developmental Model of Intercultural Sensitivity." In *Cross-cultural Orientation: New Conceptualizations and Applications,* edited by M. Paige, 27–70. New York: University Press of America, 1986.

———. "Towards a Developmental Model of Intercultural Sensitivity." In *Education for the Intercultural Experience*, edited by R. M. Paige. Yarmouth, ME: Intercultural, 1993.

Berding, Kenneth. "At the Intersection of Mission and Spiritual Formation in the Letters of Paul." *Journal of Spiritual Formation and Soul Care* 6 (2013) 18–37.

Best, Harold M. "God's Creation and Human Creativity: Seven Affirmations." In *Worship and Mission for the Global Church: An Ethnodoxology Handbook*, edited by J. Krabill. Pasadena: William Carey Library, 2013.

Bialecki, Jon. "The Third Wave and the Third World: C. Peter Wagner, John Wimber, and the Pedagogy of Global Renewal in the Late Twentieth Century." *Pneuma* 37 (2015) 177–200.

Blomberg, Craig L. "Mission in the Bible: Non-Existent in the Old Testament but Ubiquitous in the New?" *Themelios* 32 (2007) 62–74.

Bonk, Jonathan J. "Christian Mission: Lengthened Shadow of a Great Man." *International Bulletin of Missionary Research* 29 (2005) 57–58.

———. "The Defender of the Good News: Questioning Lamin Sanneh." http://www.christianitytoday.com/ct/2003/october/35.112.html.

———. *The Theory and Practice of Missionary Identification 1860–1920*. Lewiston, NY: Mellen, 1989.
Bosch, D. J. *Transforming Mission*. New York: Orbis, 1991.
Bowen, Earle, and Dorothy Bowen. "Contextualizing Teaching Methods in Africa." *Evangelical Missions Quarterly* 25 (1989) 270–75.
Bradley, Anthony B. *Liberating Black Theology: The Bible and the Black Experience in America*. Wheaton, IL: Crossway, 2010.
Bradley, James E., and Richard A. Muller. *Church History: An Introduction to Research, Reference Works, and Methods*. Grand Rapids: Eerdmans, 1995.
Bragg, Wayne G. "Beyond Development to Transformation." *International Review of Mission* 73 (1984) 153–65.
Brewer, K. W. "Rob Bell and John Wesley on the Fate of the Lost and Those Who Never Heard the Gospel." *Wesleyan Theological Journal* 48 (2013) 117–34.
Bulatao, Jaime. *Split-level Christianity*. Manila, Philippines: Anteneo University, 1966.
Burgess, Alan. *The Small Woman: The Heroic Story of Gladys Aylward*. New York: Dutton, 1957.
Burgess, Stanley M. "The South Indian Pentecostal Movement in the Twentieth Century." *The Journal of Ecclesiastical History* 61 (2010) 433–34.
Burke, Daniel. "The World's Fastest Growing Religion Is. . ." *CNN*, April 2, 2015. http://www.cnn.com/2015/04/02/living/pew-study-religion/.
Burke, Trevor J. "The Holy Spirit as the Controlling Dynamic in Paul's Role as Missionary to the Thessalonians." In *Paul as Missionary: Identity, Activity, Theology, and Practice*, edited by T. Burke and B. Rosner, 142–57. London: T. & T. Clark, 2011.
Burnett, Rebecca. "It's a Major Decision: The Process of Choosing a Major by First Generation College Students in a Scholarship Program." Unpublished diss., Biola University, 2017.
Bush, L. "A Brief Historical Overview of the AD2000 and Beyond Movement and Joshua Project." Presented at the North East Asia AD2000/Joshua Project 2000 Consultation. Seoul, South Korea, 1996.
———. "Getting to the Core of the Core: The 10/40 Window." from www.ad2000.org/1040broc.htm.
Caldwell, Larry. "Selected Missiological Works of Alan R. Tippett." *Missiology: An International Review* 17 (1989) 283–92.
Calhoun, Craig, and Diana Rhoten. "Integrating the Social Sciences: Theoretical Knowledge, Methodological Tools, an Practical Applications." In *Oxford Handbook of Interdisciplinarity*, edited by R. Frodeman, 104–19. London: Oxford University Press, 2010.
Campbell, Marla June. "An Experiential Learning Approach to Faculty Training in Asia-Pacific Education." Unpublished doctoral diss., Biola University, 2000.
Carlyle, Thomas. *On Heroes, Hero Worship and the Heroic in History*. Boston: James Fraser, 1841.
Carriker, C. Timothy. "Missiological Hermeneutic and Pauline Apocalyptic Eschatology." In *Good News of the Kingdom: Mission Theology for the Third Millennium*, edited by C. van Engen and D. Gilliland, 45–55. Maryknoll, NY: Orbis, 1991.
Carson, D. A. *The Gospel According to John*. The Pillar New Testament Commentary. Grand Rapids: Eerdmans, 1990.
Casey, Anthony. "Identifying and Reaching Ethnic Groups in the City." *Great Commission Research Journal* 4 (2012) 60–75.

Castro, E. "Moratorium." *International Review of Mission* 64 (1975) 117–217.
Cerny, P. "The Relationship Between Theology and Missiology: The Missiological Hermeneutics." *European Journal of Theology* 19 (2010) 104–9.
Chamberlain, Michael. "Factors Impacting Openness To Christianity Among Graduate Students Who Attended A Christian University In the US." Unpublished doctoral diss., Biola University, 2000.
Chambers, Robert. "Poverty and Livelihoods: Whose Reality Counts?" *Environment and Urbanization* 71 (1995) 173–204.
———. *Rural Development: Putting the Last First*. New York: Routledge, 1983.
Chapman, Alister. "Evangelical International Relations in the Post-Colonial World: The Lausanne Movement and the Challenge of Diversity, 1974–89." *Missiology: An International Review* 37 (2009) 355–68.
Chen, G. M. "Relationships of the Dimensions of Intercultural Communication Competence." *Communication Quarterly* 37 (1989) 118–33.
Chinchen, Delbert. "The Patron-Client Relationship Concept: A Case Study from the African Bible Colleges in Liberia and Malawi." Unpublished doctoral diss., Biola University, 1994.
———. "The Return of The Fourth 'R' to Education: Relationships." *Missiology: An International Review* 25 (1997) 321–35.
Cho, James. "Understanding Leadership: Conceptions of Leadership from both First and Second-Generation Korean-American Pastors' Perspectives." Unpublished doctoral diss., Biola University, 2010.
Cho, J. Y. "Factors Contributing to the Development of the Modern Korean Missions Movement: A Historical Analysis." Unpublished doctoral diss., The Southern Baptist Theological Seminary, 2002.
Choi, Dong-Kyu, and T. K. Park. *Toward a Basic Theory for Missional Church Planting in Postmodern Korea*. ProQuest Dissertations and Theses. Pasadena: Fuller Theological Seminary, 2006.
Chow, Alexander. "Protestant Ecumenism and Theology in China since Edinburgh 1910." *Missiology: An International Review* 42 (2014) 167–80.
Christian, Jayakumar. *The God of the Empty-handed: Poverty, Power and the Kingdom of God*. Monrovia, CA: MARC, 2011.
Ciampa, Roy E. "Paul's Theology of the Gospel." In *Paul as Missionary: Identity, Activity, Theology, and Practice*, edited by T. Burke and B. Rosner, 180–91. London: T. & T. Clark, 2011.
Cobb, John B. *Beyond Dialog: Toward a Mutual Transformation of Christianity and Buddhism*. Philadelphia: Fortress, 1982.
Coe, Shoki. "Contextualizing Theology." In *Mission Trends No. 3*, edited by G. Anderson and T. Stransky. Grand Rapids: Eerdmans, 1976.
Cohen, Shaye J. D. *The Significance of Yavneh and Other Essays in Jewish Hellenism*. Tübingen, Germany: Mohr Siebeck, 2010.
Coker, Adam. "Review Essay: A Strange Sort of Orthodoxy: An Analysis of the T4T and CMP Approach to Missions." *Southwestern Journal of Theology* 59 (2016) 78–87.
Colby, B. "Indian Attitudes Towards Education and Inter-ethnic Contact in Mexico." In *Readings in Missionary Anthropology II*, edited by W. Smalley, 190–98. South Pasadena: William Carey Library, 1978.
Coleman, Robert. *The Masterplan of Evangelism*. Grand Rapids: Baker, 2006.
Cone, James H. *The Cross and the Lynching Tree*. Maryknoll, NY: Orbis, 2011.

Conn, Harvey. *Eternal Word and Changing Worlds: Theology, Anthropology, and Mission in Trialogue*. Grand Rapids: Zondervan, 1984.

Cook, Harold R. *An Introduction to the Study of Christian Missions*. Chicago: Moody, 1970.

Coote, Robert T. "'AD 2000' and the '10/40 Window:' A Preliminary Assessment." *International Bulletin of Missionary Research* 24 (2000) 160.

———. "Lausanne II and World Evangelization." *International Bulletin of Missionary Research* 14 (1990) 10.

Corbett, Steve, et al. *When Helping Hurts*. Chicago: Moody, 2014.

Corrigan, Gregory M. "Paul's Shame for the Gospel." *Biblical Theology Bulletin* 16 (1986) 23–27.

Cortez, Felix H. "The Mission-Charity Dilemme: Fresh Perspectives from Paul's Practice." *Journal of the Adventist Theological Society* 26 (2015) 160–73.

Corwin, Gary R. "Sociology and Missiology: Reflections on Mission Research." In *Missiology and the Social Sciences: Contributions, Cautions and Conclusions*, edited by E. Rommen and G. Corwin, 19–29. Pasadena: William Carey Library, 1996.

———. "Unpacking Cape Town 2010." *Evangelical Missions Quarterly* 47 (2011) 136–37.

Craffert, P. F. "Is the Emic-Etic Distinction a Useful Tool for Cross-Cultural Interpretation of the New Testament." *Religion and Theology* 2 (1995) 14–37.

Crockett, William V. "Will God Save Everyone in the End?" In *Through No Fault of Their Own: the Fate of Those Who Have Never Heard*, edited by W. Crockett and J. Sigountos, 159–66. Grand Rapids: Baker, 1991.

Cross, Terry, et al. *Towards a Culturally Competent System of Care*. Washington, DC: Georgetown University Center for Child and Human Development, 1989.

Crossan, John Dominic. *The Historical Jesus: The Life of a Mediterranean Jewish Peasan*. San Francisco: HarperSanFrancisco, 1991.

Crouch, Andy. *Culture Making: Recovering Our Creative Calling*. Downers Grove, IL: InterVarsity, 2008.

Crush, Jonathan. *Power of Development*. New York: Psychology, 1995.

Culshaw, Wesley J. "William Carey—Then and Now." *The Bible Translator* 18 (1967) 53–60.

Daniels, Gene, and Pam Arlund. "Fruitful Near-culture Church Planters: A Qualitative Study." *Evangelical Missions Quarterly* 52 (2016) 21–27.

Daugherty, B. J. "Praying for the Lost in the 10/40 Window." *International Journal of Frontier Missions* 15 (1998) 219.

Davidson, Theresa, and Carlos Garcia. "Welcoming the Stranger: Religion and Attitudes Toward Social Justice for Immigrants in the U.S." *Journal of Religion and Society* 16 (2014) 1–16.

Davies, Daniel M. *The Life and Thought of Henry Gerhard Appenzeller (1858–1902), Missionary to Korea*. Lewiston, NY: Edwin Mellen, 1988.

Davis, Charles. *Making Disciples Across Cultures: Missional Principles for a Diverse World*. Downers Grove, IL: InterVarsity, 2015.

Davis, R. J. "From Effervescence to Knowledge: The Role of Power in the Evolution of a Christian Church." Unpublished doctoral diss., University of Wisconsin, 1989.

Dawson, David G. "The Church and the Edinburgh Missionary Conference." *Missiology: An International Review* 39 (2011) 157–74.

De Nui, Paul H., and David S. Lim. *Communicating Christ in the Buddhist World.* Pasadena: William Carey Library, 2006.

Demarest, Bruce A., and Richard J. Harpel. "Don Richardson's 'Redemptive Analogies' and the Biblical Idea of Revelation." *Bibliotheca Sacra* 146 (1989) 330–43.

Dennis, James S. *Christian Missions and Social Progress.* New York: Revell, 1897.

Deyoung, Kevin, and Greg Gilbert. *What Is the Mission of the Church?: Making Sense of Social Justice, Shalom and the Great Commission.* Wheaton, IL: Crossway, 2011.

Dierck, Lorraine Wendy. "Teams that Work: Leadership, Power, and Decision-Making in Multicultural Teams in Thailand." Unpublished doctoral diss., Biola University, 2007.

Dinani, Thandiwe T. "The Impact of Ethnic Identity Stage Development on the Intercultural Sensitivity of African American Students During Study Abroad." Unpublished doctoral diss., Biola University, 2016.

Dormer, Jan. *Teaching English in Missions: Effectiveness and Integrity.* Pasadena: William Carey Library, 2011.

Douglas, Mary. *Cultural Bias.* London: Royal Anthropological Institute, 1978.

———. *Natural Symbols: Explorations in Cosmology.* London: Barrie & Rockliff, 1970.

Dries, A. Review of *American Women in Mission: Social History of Their Thought and Practice. Missiology: An International Review* 26 (1998) 214–16.

Duff, Alexander. *Missions the Chief End of the Christian Church.* Edinburg: Andrew Elliott, 1877.

Dyrness, William A. *Learning about Theology from the Third World.* Grand Rapids: Zondervan, 1990.

Dzubinski, L. "Playing by the Rules: How Women Lead in Evangelical Mission Organizations." Unpublished doctoral diss., University of Georgia, 2013.

Edmund, Charlotte. "84% of Refugees Living in Developing Countries." *World Economic Forum.* (June 2017). https://www.weforum.org/agenda/2017/06/eighty-four-percent-of-refugees-live-in-developing-countries/.

Edwards, L., and Kenneth Nehrbass. "Higher Education as Mission." *Great Commission Research Journal* 9 (2017) 71–80.

Elizondo, Virgil, and Ignacio Castuera. "Responses to the Article by C. Peter Wagner." *International Bulletin of Missionary Research* 10 (1986) 65–66.

Elliot, Elisabeth. "Amy Carmichael of India." In *Bright Legacy: Portraits of Ten Outstanding Christian Women*, edited by A. Spangler, 23–43. Ann Arbor, MI: Servant, 1983.

Elmer, Duane. *Cross-cultural Connections: Stepping Out and Fitting In Around the World.* Downers Grove, IL: IVP Academic, 2002.

———. *Cross-cultural Servanthood.* Downers Grove, IL: InterVarsity, 2006.

Engelsviken, Tormod. "Mission, Evangelism and Evangelization—From the Perspective of the Lausanne Movement." *International Review of Mission* 96 (2007) 204–9.

Erickson, Millard. "The State of the Question." In *Through No Fault of Their Own: The Fate of Those Who Have Never Heard*, edited by W. Crockett and J. Sigountos, 23–34. Grand Rapids: Baker, 1991.

Eriksen, Annelin. *Gender, Christianity and Change in Vanuatu.* Burlington, VT: Ashgate, 2008.

Escobar, Samuel, et al. "A Latin America Critique of Latin American Theology." *Evangelical Review of Theology* 7 (1983) 48–62.

———. "Urbana '90—a student missionary convention and missiological event." *Missiology* 19 (1991) 333–46.
Escobar, Samuel, and J. Driver. *Christian Mission and Social Justice*. Scottdale, PA: Herald, 1978.
Fields, Bruce. *Introducing Black Theology*. Grand Rapids: Baker Academic, 2001.
Flemming, Dean E. *Contextualization in the New Testament: Patterns for Theology and Mission*. Downer's Grove, IL: Intervarsity, 2005.
Flinn, Juliana. *Mary, the Devil, and Taro: Catholicism and Women's Work in a Micronesian Society*. Honolulu: University of Hawai'i Press, 2010.
Flowers, E. H. "The Contested Legacy of Lottie Moon: Southern Baptists, Women, and Partisan Protestantism." *Fides et Historia* 43 (2011) 15–40.
Forman, Charles W. "South Pacific Style in the Christian Ministry." *Missiology: An International Review* 2 (1974) 421–35.
Fortosis, Steve. *The Multilingual God: Stories of Translation*. Pasadena: William Carey Library, 2012.
Fox, Frampton F. "Money as Water: A Patron-Client Approach to Mission Dependency in India." Unpublished doctoral diss., Trinity Evangelical Divinity School, 2003.
Friedman, John. *Empowerment: The Politics of Alternative Development*. New York: Wiley-Blackwell, 1992.
Friedman, Milton. *Capitalism and Freedom*. Chicago: University of Chicago Press, 1962.
Friesen, J. Stanley. *Missionary Responses to Tribal Religions at Edinburgh, 1910*. New York: P. Lang, 1996.
Friesen, R. G. "The Long-term Impact of Short-term Missions on the Beliefs, Attitudes and Behaviours of Young Adults." Unpublished doctoral diss., University of South Africa, 2005.
Frodeman, Robert, ed. *The Oxford Handbook on Interdisciplinarity*. London: Oxford University Press, 2010.
Frykenberg, Robert Eric. "The Legacy of Pandita Ramabai: Mahatma of Mukti." *International Bulletin of Missionary Research* 40 (2016) 60–70.
Gallagher, Robert L. "Missionary Methods: St. Paul's, St. Roland's or Ours." In *Missionary Methods: Research, Reflections and Realities*, edited by C. Ott and J. Payne, 3–22. Pasadena: William Carey Library, 2013.
Garrison, David. "10 Church Planting Movement FAQs." *Mission Frontiers* (March-April 2010) 9–10.
———. *Church Planting Movements*. Midlothian, VA: WIGTake Resources, 2004.
Gaventa, B. R. "The Mission of God in Paul's Letter to the Romans." In *Paul as Missionary: Identity, Activity, Theology, and Practice*, edited by T. J. Burke and B. S. Rosner, 65–75. London: T. & T. Clark, 2011.
Geertz, C. *The Interpretation of Cultures*. New York: Basic, 1973.
Geisler, N. "A Response to Paul G. Hiebert: The Gospel in Human Contexts: Changing Perceptions of Contextualization and to Darrell Whiteman and Michael Pocock." In *Mission Shift: Global Mission Issues in the Third Millennium*, edited by D. Hesselgrave and E. Stetzer, 129–43. Nashville: B&H Academic, 2010.
George, Sherron. "Constructing Latin American Missiology." *International Bulletin of Missionary Research* 40 (2016) 30–41.
———. "Diaspora: a Hidden Link to 'From Everywhere to Everywhere' Missiology." *Missiology* 39 (2011) 45–56.

George, T. "John R. W. Stott and C. René Padilla Critiqued: A Response to Their Views on Evangelism/Social Responsiblity." *Crux* 28 (1992) 34–41.

Georges, Jayson. "From Shame to Honor: A Theological Reading of Romans for Honor-Shame Contexts." *Missiology: An International Review* 38 (2010) 295–307.

Gieschen, C. A. "Christ's Coming and the Church's Mission in 1 Thessalonians." *Concordia Theological Quarterly* 76 (2012) 37–55.

Glasser, Arthur. "Missiology—What Is It All About?" *Missiology: An International Review* 6 (1978) 3–10.

"Global Statistics." https://joshuaproject.net/people_groups/statistics.

Goheen, Michael. *Introducing Christian Mission Today: Scripture, History and Issues.* Downers Grove, IL: IVP Academic, 2014.

Gong, Wenhui, and Kenneth Nehrbass. "Reaching Out to Diaspora Chinese in East Africa: Barriers and Bridges." *Missiology* 45 (2017) 236–51.

Goodman, Martin. *Mission and Conversion: Proselytizing in the Religious History of the Roman Empire.* Oxford: Clarendon, 1994.

Gorlorwulu, John, and Tim Rahschulte. "Organizational and Leadership Implications for Transformational Development." *Transformation* 27 (2010) 199–208.

Graham, Billy. "Why Lausanne?" In *Let the Earth Hear His Voice*, edited by G. Scharf, 26–27. Minneapolis: World Wide, 1974.

Granados, Alexander. "Academic and Spiritual Impact of a Semester Abroad Program in Israel on Its Undergraduate Participants." Unpublished doctoral diss., Biola University, 2008.

Grant, A. E. "Theological Education in India: Leadership Development for the Indian or Western Church?" Unpublished doctoral diss., Biola University, 1999.

Gration, John. "The Homogeneous Unit Principle: Another Perspective." *Evangelical Missions Quarterly* 17 (1981) 197–204.

Gravelle, Gilles. "Bible Translation in Historical Context: The Changing Role of Cross-cultural Workers." *International Journal of Frontier Missiology* 27 (2010) 11–20.

Greear, J. D. *Gaining By Losing: Why the Future Belongs to Churches That Send.* Grand Rapids: Zondervan, 2016.

Green, Stanley W. "Report on Cape Town 2010." *International Bulletin of Missionary Research* 35 (2011) 7.

Gregerson, Marilyn B. "Rengao Myths: A Window on the Culture." In *Readings in Missionary Anthropology II*, edited by W. Smalley, 348–62. South Pasadena: William Carey Library, 1978.

Grenfell, Anne, and Katie Spalding. *Le petit nord, or annals of a Labrador harbor.* Boston: Houghton Mifflin, 1920.

Grenham, Thomas G. "Reconstructing Christian Culture toward the Globalization of Gospel Vision: Identity, Empowerment, and Transformation in an African Context." *Missiology: An International Review* 31 (2003) 223–38.

Grönblom, Gunnar, and Jørgen Thorgaard. "The Notion of Functional Equivalence with Special Regard to Its Usage in Empirical Sociology of Religion." *Annual Review of the Social Sciences of Religion Utrecht* 5 (1981) 133–65.

Gudykunst, W. B. "An Anxiety/Uncertainty Management (AUM) Theory of Effective Communication." In *Theorizing About Intercultural Communication*, edited by W. Gudykunst, 281–322. Thousand Oaks, CA: Sage, 2004.

Gullahorn, J. T., and J. E. Gullahorn. "An Extension of the U-Curve Hypothesis." *Journal of Social Issues* 19 (1963) 33–47.

Guthrie, Stan. *Missions in the Third Millennium*. Waynesboro, GA: Paternoster, 2005.
Gutierrez, Gustavo. *A Theology of Liberation: History, Politics and Salvation*. Maryknoll, NY: Orbis, 1973.
Hall, Dave. "10 Reasons Why Every Church-planting Team Needs a Worship Leader." *Evangelical Missions Quarterly* 36 (2000) 50–53.
Hall, Edward T. *Beyond Culture*. New York: Anchor, 1976.
———. *The Hidden Dimension*. New York: Anchor, 1990.
———. *The Silent Language*. New York: Doubleday, 1959.
Hamilton, Roy W., ed. *The Art of Rice: Spirit and Sustenance in Asia*. Los Angeles: UCLA Flower Museum of Cultural History, 2003.
Han, K.-Y. "Christian Mission Environments and Strategies in Che Ju Island, with Special Reference to Mission Strategies of the Sam Yang Church (Korea)." Unpublished doctoral diss., Fuller Theological Seminary, 1987.
Hanciles, Jehu J. "Migration and Mission: Some Implications for the Twenty-First-Century Church." *International Bulletin of Missionary Research* 27 (2003) 146–53.
Hardage, Jeanette. *Mary Slessor—Everybody's Mother: The Era and Impact of a Victorian Missionary*. Eugene, OR: Wipf & Stock, 2008.
Harnack, Adolf von. *Die Mission und Ausbreitung des Christentums in den ersten drei Jahrhunderten*. Leipzig, Germany: J. C. Hinrichs, 1924.
Harper, K. *Send the Light: Lottie Moon's Letters and Other Writings*. Macon, GA: Mercer University, 2002.
Harr, Gerrie ter, ed. *Imagining Evil: Witchcraft Beliefs and Accusations in Contemporary Africa*. Trenton, NJ: Africa World, 2006.
Harris, Marvin. "The Cultural Ecology of India's Sacred Cattle." *Current Anthropology* 7 (1966) 51–54, 66.
Hastings, Adrian. *The Construction of Nationhood: Ethnicity, Religion and Nationalism*. Cambridge: Cambridge University Press, 1997.
Haushofer, Johannes, and Jeremy Shapiro. "The Short-term Impact of Unconditional Cash Transfers to the Poor: Experimental Evidence from Kenya." *The Quarterly Journal of Economics* 131 (2016) 1973–2042.
Hawks, Francis Lister, and William Stevens Perry. *Journal of the General Conventions of the Protestant Episcopal Church, Vol 6*. Philadelphia: King and Baird, 1860.
Headland, Thomas N., et al., eds. *Emics and Etics: The Insider/Outsider Debate*. Newbury Park, CA: Sage, 1990.
Henry, Carl F. H. "The Cultural Relativizing of Revelation." *Trinity Journal* 1 (1980) 153–64.
Hesselgrave, David J. *Communicating Christ Cross-culturally*. Grand Rapids: Zondervan, 1979.
———. "Did Cape Town 2010 Correct the 'Edinburgh Error?': A Preliminary Analysis." *Southwestern Journal of Theology* 55 (2012) 77–89.
———. "The Millennium and Missions." *Evangelical Missions Quarterly* 24 (1988) 70–77.
———. *Paradigms in Conflict: 10 Key Questions in Christian Missions Today*. Grand Rapids: Kregel Academic, 2005.
———. "Paul's Missions Strategy." In *Paul's Missionary Method: In His Time and Ours*, edited by R. Plummer and I. M. Teny, 127–45. Downers Grove, IL: IVP Academic, 2012.

———. "Preface." In *Missiology and the Social Sciences: Contributions, Cautions and Conclusion*, edited by E. Rommen and G. Corwin, 1–3. Pasadena: William Carey Library, 1996.

———. "Will We Correct the Edinburgh Error? Future Mission in Historical Perspective." *Southwestern Journal of Theology* 2 49 (2007) 142.

Hettne, Bjorn. *Development Theory and the Three Worlds: Towards an International Political Economy of Developmen*. 2nd ed. Harlow, NY: Longman, 1995.

Hibbert, Evelyn. "Considering a Gendered Approach to Church Planting in Muslim-Background Contexts." *Missiology: An International Review* 43 (2015) 286–96.

Hibbert, Evelyn, and Richard Y. Hibbert. *Walking Together on the Jesus Road: Discipling in Intercultural Contexts*. Littleton, CO: WIlliam Carey, 2018.

Hiebert, Paul G. *Anthropological Insights for Missionaries*. Grand Rapids: Baker, 1985.

———. *Anthropological Reflections on Missiological Issues*. Grand Rapids: Baker, 1994.

———. "Critical Contextualization." *International Bulletin of Missionary Research* (1987) 104–11.

———. "The Flaw of the Excluded Middle." *Missiology: An International Review* 10 (1982) 35–47.

———. *The Gospel in Human Contexts*. Grand Rapids: Baker, 2009.

———. "Missions and Anthropology: A Love/Hate Relationship." *Missiology: An International Review* 6 (1978) 165–80.

———. "Missions and the Understanding of Culture." In *The Church in Mission*, edited by A. J. Klassen, 251–65. Fresno, CA: Board of Christian Literature, Mennonite Brethren Church, 1967.

———."The Social Sciences and Missions: Applying the Message." In *Missiology and the Social Sciences: Contributions, Cautions and Conclusions*, edited by E. Rommen and G. Corwin. Pasadena: Wiliam Carey Library, 1996.

———. *Transforming Worldviews*. Grand Rapids: Baker, 2008.

Hiebert, Paul G., et al. *Understanding Folk Religion*. Grand Rapids: Baker, 1999.

Hoefer, Herbert. *Churchless Christianity*. Pasadena: William Carey Library, 2001.

Hofstede, G. *Culture's Consequences: Comparing Values, Behaviors, Institutions and Organizations Across Nations*. Beverly Hills: Sage, 1980.

Holmes, Brian, ed. *Educational Policy and the Mission Schools: Case Studies from the British Empire*. London: Routledge & K. Paul, 1967.

Hong, E. "Church Splits in Korean-American Churches." Unpublished doctoral diss., Biola University, 2010.

Hood, George. "A History of the English Presbyterian Mission in East Guangdong Province." *International Bulletin of Missionary Research* 9 (1985) 77.

Hood, Jason B. *The Messiah, His Brothers, and the Nations: Matthew 1:1–17*. Library of New Testament Studies 441. London: T. & T. Clark, 2011.

Hooker, Richard. *Of the Lawes of Ecclesiasticall Politie. Eyght Bookes*. London: John Windet, 1597.

Houger, B. R. "Instructors' Pedagogies as the Frame of Influence for East Asian Assemblies of God Bible Schools." Unpublished doctoral diss., Biola University, 2011.

Houger, W. B. "A Recipient Driven Curriculum for Asian Assemblies of God Bible Schools." Unpublished doctoral diss., Biola University, 2009.

Howard, David M. "The Road to Urbana and Beyond." *Evangelical Missions Quarterly* 21 (1985) 6–21.

Howell, Brian M. *Short Term Mission*. Downers Grove, IL: IVP Academic, 2012.
Hrangkhuma, F. "How Redemptive Analogies Can Help Churches Grow." *Evangelical Missions Quarterly* 28 (1992) 182–87.
Hua, Zhu. *Exploring Intercultural Communication*. New York: Routledge, 2014.
Huizing, R. "In Search of the Healthy Church: A Meta-Ethnographic Study." *Great Commission Research Journal* 4 (2012) 3–59.
Hultgren, A. J. "Paul's Christology and His Mission to the Gentiles." In *Paul as Missionary: Identity, Activity, Theology, and Practice*, edited by T. Burke and B. Rosner, 115–27. London: T. & T. Clark, 2011.
Hunt, R. A. "The History of the Lausanne Movement, 1974–2010." *International Bulletin of Missionary Research* 35 (2011) 81–84.
Hunter, George G, III. "The Legacy of Donald A. McGavran." *International Bulletin of Missionary Research* 16 (1992) 158–62.
Hyatt, Erik. "From Homogeneous to a Heterogeneous Unit Principle." *Evangelical Missions Quarterly* 50 (2014) 226–32.
Im, H. "The Desired African Teacher for Contemporary Urban Multicultural Christian Schools in East Africa." Unpublished doctoral diss., Biola University, 2015.
Inglehart, Ronald, ed. *Human Values and Social Change: Findings from the Values Survey*. Boston: Brill, 2003.
Inglehart, Ronald, et al. *Human Values and Beliefs: A Cross-cultural Sourcebook*. Ann Arbor, MI: University of Michigan, 1998.
Irvin, Dale T., and Scott W. Sunquist. *History of the World Christian Movement. V. II*. Maryknoll, NY: Orbis, 2017.
Irwin, Barry. "The Liability Complex Among the Chimbu Peoples of New Guinea." In *Readings in Missionary Anthropology II*, edited by W. Smalley, 219–26. South Pasadena: William Carey Library, 1978.
Jaccard, James, and Jacob Jacoby. *Theory Construction and Model-Building Skills: A Practical Guide for Social Scientists*. Methodology in the Social Sciences. New York: Guilford, 2009.
Jackson, Jane. *Introducing Language and Intercultural Communication*. New York: Routledge, 2014.
Jang, Young-Ho. "Global Missions Perspective and Attitude Toward Contextual Theology Among Korean Alumni of Chongshin University and Theological Seminary in Seoul, Korea, and Reformed Theological Seminary in Jackson, Mississippi, United States of America." Unpublished doctoral diss., Reformed Theological Seminary, 2000.
Jebadu, Alexander. "Ancestral Veneration and the Possiblity of its Incorporation into the Christian Faith." *Exchange2* 36 (2007) 246–80.
Jenkins, Philip. *Dream Catchers: How Mainstream America Discovered Native American Spirituality*. Oxford: Oxford University Press, 2004.
———. *The Lost History of Christianity: The Thousand-Year Golden Age of the Church in the Middle East, Africa, and Asia-and How It Died*. New York: HarperOne, 2009.
———. *The Next Christendom: The Coming of Global Christianity*. Oxford: Oxford University Press, 2002.
Jenkins, Willis. "Missiology in Environmental Context: Tasks for an Ecology of Mission." *International Bulletin of Missionary Research* 32 (2008) 176–82.
Jeyakumar, Arthur. "Amy Carmichael of Dohnavur 1867-1951." *Indian Church History Review* 36 (2002) 5–11.

Jeyaraj, Daniel. "Amy Carmichael: the Child-Rescuing 'Amma.'" *American Baptist Quarterly*, 24 (2005) 220–41.

John Paul II. *Lumen Gentium*. https://www.vatican.va/archive/hist_councils/ii_vatican_council/documents/vat-ii_const_19641121_lumen-gentium_en.html.

Johnson, Andy. "Ecclesiology, Election, and the Life of God: A Missional Reading of the Thessalonian Correspondence." *Journal of Theological Interpretation* 9 (2015) 247–65.

Johnson, C. N., and Steve Rundle. "The Distinctives and Challenges of Business as Mission." In *Business as Mission: From Impoverished to Empowered*, edited by T. Barnett and M. Barnett, 19–36. Pasadena: William Carey Library, 2006

Johnson, Tom M., and David B. Barrett. *World Christian Trends*. Pasadena: William Carey Library, 2013.

Johnstone, Patrick, and Jason Mandryk. *Operation World*. 6th ed. Waynesboro, GA: Paternoster, 2001.

Jones, William R. *Is God a White Racist?: A Preamble to Black Theology*. Boston: Beacon, 1997.

Joshi, Vibha. *A Matter of Belief: Christian Conversion and Healing in North-East India*. New York: Berghahn, 2012.

Jung, Il Nam. "Incarnational Mission and Community Development: Three Korean Case Studies." Unpublished doctoral diss., United Theological Seminary, 2002.

Junod, H. P. "Anthropology and Missionary Education." *International Review of Missions* 24 (1935) 213–28.

Kaemingk, Matthew. *Christian Hospitality and Muslim Immigration in an Age of Fear*. Grand Rapids: Eerdmans, 2018.

Kähler, Martin. *Schriften zur Christologie und Mission: esmtausgabe der Schriften zur Mission Mit einer Bibliographie*. Munich, Germany: Kaiser, 1908.

Kaiser, Walter. *Mission in the Old Testament: Israel as a Light to the Nations*. Grand Rapids: Baker Academic, 2000.

Kamath, Neetha, and N. Udayakiran. "Effectiveness of Participatory Learning Activity (PLA) and Lecture Method on Knowledge in HIV/AIDS among Nursing Students." *International Journal of Nursing Education* 7 (2015) 223–28.

Kane, Herbert J. *A Concise History of the Christian World Mission: A Panoramic View of Missions from Pentecost to the Present*. Grand Rapids: Baker, 1982.

Kant, Immanuel. *Critique of Judgment: Including the First Introduction*. London: Macmillan, 1914.

Kaplan, Sidney. *The Black Presence in the Era of the American Revolution*, Amherst, MA: University of Massachusetts, 1989.

Kasdorf, Hans. "The Legacy of Gustav Warneck." *Occasional Bulletin of Missionary Research* 4 (1980) 102–7.

Kaye, Alan S. "An Interview with Kenneth Pike." http://www-01.sil.org/klp/kayeint.htm.

Kealey, Daniel J. "A Study of Cross-cultural Effectiveness: Theoretical Issues, Practical Applications." *International Journal of Intercultural Relations* 13 (1989) 387–428.

Keener, Craig S. "Sent Like Jesus: Johannine Missiology (John 20:21–22)." *Asian Journal of Pentecostal Studies* 12 (2009) 21–45.

Kennedy, C., and R. Emerson. "Building Schools for Girls in Afghanistan: A Debt of Gratitude." *Journal of Applied Christian Leadership* 6 (2012) 108–19.

Keum, K. "A Grounded Theory Study on The Emerging Negative Perception and Public Criticism of the Korean Protestant Church by Non-Christian Koreans." Unpublished doctoral diss., Biola University, 2011.

Kidwell, Clara Sue, et al. *A Native American Theology*. Maryknoll, NY: Orbis, 2001.

Kim, Hansung. "The Internationalization of Three Korean Mission Agencies." ProQuest Dissertations and Theses. Unpublished doctoral diss., Biola University, 2011.

———. "Myungdongchon: A People Movement Among Diaspora Koreans in the Early 20th Century." *Missiology: An International Review* 43 (2015) 270–85.

Kim, H. H. "A Study of the Relationship Between Academic Mentoring and the Development of Intercultural Competence in a Multicultural Higher Educational Context." Unpublished doctoral diss., Biola University, 2007.

Kim, Mantae. "A Comparative Missiological Study of Sinhalese Buddhist and Sinhalese Christian Attitudes Toward the Puberty Ritual." *Missiology: An International Review* 38 (2012) 411–30.

Kim, S. Y. "Theological Education Among Dominican Republic Pastors in Corona, New York: A Study of Motivational Factors and Barriers that Influence Their Participation." Unpublished doctoral diss., Biola University, 2004.

Kim, Sebastian. *Christianity as a World Religion*. New York: Bloomsbury, 2008.

Kim, Young Yun. *Becoming Intercultural: An Integrative Theory of Communication and Cross-Cultural Adaptation*. Thousand Oaks, CA: Sage, 2001.

Kim, Kirsteen, and Andrew Anderson, eds. *Mission Today and Tomorrow*. Oxford: Regnum, 2011.

King, Roberta R. *Pathways in Christian Music Communication: The Case of the Senufo of Côte d'Ivoire*. Eugene, OR: Pickwick, 2009.

Kinney, John W. "The Theology of John Mbiti: His Sources, Norms, and Method." *Occasional Bulletin of Missionary Research* 3 (1979) 65–68.

Klauber, Martin I., and Scott M. Manetsch. *The Great Commission: Evangelicals and the History of World Missions*. Nashville: Broadman and Holman, 2008.

Klem, Herbert. "Dependence on Literacy Strategy: Taking a Hard Second Look." *International Journal of Frontier Missiology* 12 (1995) 59–64.

Kluckhohn, Florence Rockwood, and Fred L. Strodtbeck. *Variations in Value Orientations*. Evanston, IL: Row & Peterson, 1961.

Knutsson, Beniamin. "The Intellectual History of Development: Towards a Widening Potential Repertoire." *Perspectives* 13 (2009) 1–46.

Koeshall, Anita. "Toward a Theory of Dynamic Asymmetry and Redeemed Power: A Case Study of Reflexive Agents in German Pentecostal Churches." Unpublished doctoral diss., Fuller Theological Seminary, 2008.

Koggie, Amos, et al. "'That Was the Beginning of Great Things at Miango': Brra Kwe Tingwe and the Origins of Christianity in Miango, Nigeria, 1913-1936." *International Bulletin of Missionary Research* 39 (2015) 133–36.

Köstenberger, Andreas J. "The Challenge of a Systematized Biblical Theology of Mission: Missiological Insights from the Gospel of John." *Missiology: An International Review* 23 (1995) 445–64.

Köstenberger, Andreas J., and Peter T. O'Brien. *Salvation to the Ends of the Earth*. Downers Grove, IL: InterVarsity, 2001.

Kovács, Abrahám. *The History of the Free Church of Scotland's Mission to the Jews in Budapest and Its Impact on the Reformed Church of Hungary, 1841–1914*. Frankfurt am Main: Peter Lang, 2006.

Koyama, Kōsuke. *Water Buffalo Theology*. Maryknoll, NY: Orbis, 1999.
Kraft, Charles H. *Anthropology for Christian Witness*. Maryknoll, NY: Orbis, 1996.
———. "Anthropological Apologetic for the Homogeneous Unit Principle in Missiology." *Occasional Bulletin of Missionary Research* 2 (1978) 121–26.
———. *Communication Theory for Christian Witness*. Rev. ed. Maryknoll, NY: Orbis, 1991.
———. *Culture, Communication and Christianity*. Pasadena: William Carey Library, 2001.
———. "Tippett, Alan Richard (1911–1988)." In *Australian Dictionary of Evangelical Biography*, edited by B. Dickey, 364. Sydney, Australia: Evangelical Historical Association, 1994.
Kraft, Charles H., and Douglas D. Priest. "Who Was This Man? A Tribute to Alan R. Tippett." *Missiology: An International Review* 17 (1989) 269–81.
Krishnaswamy, R. "Postcolonial and Globalization Studies: Connections, Conflicts, Complicities." In *The Postcolonial and the Global*, edited by R. Krishnaswamy and J. Hawley, 2–21. Minneapolis: University of Minnesota Press, 2008.
Krohn, Wolfgang. "Interdisciplinary Cases and Disciplinary Knowledge." In *The Oxford Handbook of Interdisciplinarity*, edited by R. Frodeman, 31–38. London: Oxford University Press, 2010.
Kuhn, Thomas S. *The Structure of Scientific Revolutions*. Chicago: University of Chicago Press, 1962.
Kwast, Lloyd E. "Understanding Culture." In *Perspectives on the World Christian Movement*, edited by R. Winter and S. Hawthorne, C3–C6. Pasadena: William Carey Library, 1992.
La George, Lisa. "Short-term Missions at the Master's College: An Experiential Education." Unpublished doctoral diss., Biola University, 2009.
LaBreche, Pamela. "Missionary Performance Evaluation: Surfacing Issues." *Missiology: An International Review* 42 (2014) 425–37.
LaClare, D. "Wearing Different Hats: The Attitudes, Behaviors and Experiences of 6 Transcultural Workers." Unpublished doctoral diss., Biola University, 2018.
Lai, Patrick. "Tentmaking Unveiled—The Survey Says." *EMQ* 43 (2007) 168–75.
Laird, Michael A. "The Legacy of Alexander Duff." *Occasional Bulletin of Missionary Research* 3 (1979) 146–49.
Landau, Martin, et al. "The Interdisciplinary Approach and the Concept of Behavioral Sciences." In *The Interdisciplinary Approach and the Concept of Behavioral Sciences*, edited by N. Washburne, 7–25. New York: Pergamon, 1962.
Langmead, Ross. "What is Missiology?" *Missiology: An International Review* 42 (2014) 67–79.
Laniak, Timothy S. *Shame and Honor in the Book of Esther*. Atlanta: Scholars, 1998.
Larsen, Timothy. *The Slain God*. New York: Oxford University Press, 2014.
Latourette, Kenneth Scott. *The Great Century in the Americas, Australasia and Africa*. New York: Harper, 1953.
———. *A History of Christianity*. San Francisco: HarperOne, 1975.
———. *A History of the Expansion of Christianity*. New York: Harper, 1945.
Lee, Amberly Doss. "Teaching and Learning Around the Cycle: An Experiential Model for Intercultural Training for Cross-cultural Kids." Unpublished doctoral diss., Biola Univeristy, 2008.

Lee, E. M. "Holistic Curriculum Development for Theological Education in Malaysia." Unpublished doctoral diss., Biola University, 2003.
Lee, K. H. "The Necessity of Power Ministry in Korean Evangelical Missionary Training Programs." Unpublished doctoral diss., Fuller Theological Seminary, 1994.
Lee, M. "Benefits and Challenges in Globalization in Christian Higher Education: A Comparative Case Study of English Medium Instruction of Two Universities in South Korea." PhD diss., Azusa Pacific University, 2017.
Lee, Yeongook. "Factors Affecting the Well-being of Korean Missionary Kids Studying at American Universities." Unpublished doctoral diss., Biola University, 2016.
Legrand, Lucien. *Unity and Plurality: Mission in the Bible*. Maryknoll, NY: Orbis, 1990.
Levi-Strauss, Claude. *Structural Anthropology*. Garden City, NY: Anchor, 1963.
Lewis, Donald M., ed. *Christianity Reborn: The Global Expansion of Evangelicalism in the Twentieth Century*. Grand Rapids: Eerdmans, 2004.
Lewis, M. Paul, et al. *Ethnologue: Languages of the World*. 17th ed. Dallas, TX: Summer Institute of Linguistics, 2013.
Lim, K. Y. "Generosity from Pauline Perspective: Insights from Paul's Letters to the Corinthians." *Evangelical Review of Theology* 37 (2013) 20–33.
Lin, R.-H. J. "The Jewish Identity Crisis Posed by Paul's Gentile Mission." *Taiwan Journal of Theology* 35 (2012) 91–112.
Lingenfelter, Judith. "Why Do We Argue Over How to Help the Poor?" *Missiology: An International Review* 26 (1998) 155–66.
Lingenfelter, Judith, and Sherwood Lingenfelter. *Teaching Cross-culturally: An Incarnational Model for Learning and Teaching*. Grand Rapids: Baker Academic, 2003.
Lingenfelter, Sherwood. "The DNA of the Church: Anthropological Reflections on the Missionary Structure of the Church." *Svensk Missionstidskrift* 93 (2005) 433–47.
———. *Leading Cross-culturally: Covenant Relationships for Effective Christian Leadership*. Grand Rapids: Baker Academic, 2008.
———. "Possessions, Wealth, and the Cultural Identities of Persons: Anthropological Reflections." *International Bulletin of Missionary Research* 31 (2007) 176.
Lingenfelter, Sherwood, and Marvin K. Mayers. *Ministering Cross-culturally*. Grand Rapids: Baker, 1986.
Little, Don. *Effective Discipline in Muslim Communities*. Downers Grove, IL: InterVarsity, 2015.
Liubinskas, Susann. "The Body of Christ in Mission: Paul's Ecclesiology and the Role of the Church in Mission." *Missiology* 41 (2013) 402–15.
Livermore, David A. *Cultural Intelligence: Improving Your CQ to Engage Our Multicultural World*. Grand Rapids: Baker Academic, 2009.
———. *Leading with Cultural Intelligence*. New York: AMACOM, 2010.
———. *Serving Jesus with Eyes Wide Open*. Grand Rapids: Baker, 2006.
Livingston, J. K. "The Legacy of David J. Bosch." *International Bulletin of Missionary Research* 21 (1999) 26–32.
Loewen, Jacob A. "Leadership in the Choco Church." *Missiology: An International Review* 1 (1973) 73–90.
———. "Myth and Mission: Should a Missionary Study Tribal Myths." In *Readings in Missionary Anthropology II*, edited by W. Smalley, 287–332. South Pasadena: William Carey Library, 1978.

Loewen, R. J. "The Faith Vineyard Christian Fellowship." ProQuest Dissertations and Theses. Unpublished doctoral diss., University of Calgary, 1997.

Long, Charles H., and Anne Rowthorn. "The Legacy of Roland Allen." *International Bulletin of Missionary Research* 13 (1989) 65–70.

Lonborg, Susan D., and Neal Bowen. "Counselors, Communities, and Spirituality: Ethical and Multicultural Considerations." *Professional School Counseling* 7 (2004) 318–25.

Lorance, Cody C. "The Holy Spirit and the Pace of Mission." *Evangelical Missions Quarterly* 42 (2006) 326–32.

Lowell, J. M. "Educational Contributions of Assemblies of God Women Missionary Educators in the Formation of Leadership in Tamil Nadu, India." Unpublished doctoral diss., Biola University, 2001.

Lupton, Robert. *Toxic Charity: How Churches and Charities Hurt Those They Help, And How to Reverse It*. San Francisco: HarperOne, 2012.

Luzbetak, Louis J. "Applied Missionary Anthropology." *Anthropological Quarterly* 34 (1961) 165–76.

———. *The Church and Cultures*. Pasadena: William Carey Library, 1988.

Ma, Julie. "Touching Lives of People Through the Holistic Mission Work of the Buntains in Calcutta, India." *International Bulletin of Missionary Research* 40 (2016) 2–83.

MacArthur, John. "Contextualization and the Corruption of the Church." https://www.gty.org/library/Blog/B110922.

Madinger, Charles. "Coming to Terms with Orality: A Holistic Model." *Missiology: An International Review* 38 (2010) 201–13.

Malinowski, Bronislaw. *Argonauts of the Western Pacific*. New York: E.P. Dutton, 1922.

———. *A Scientific Theory of Culture and Other Essays, Volume 9*. Chapel Hill: University of North Carolina, 1944.

Manna, Mike. A. "The Indigenous Contextualization Model: Ukrainian Youth Ministers' Adaptation of Practical Theological Education." Unpublished doctoral diss., Biola University, 2015.

Manitsas, D. "Short Term Mission Trips: A Vehicle for Developing Personal and Spiritual Wellbeing." Unpublished doctoral diss., George Fox University, 2000.

Marantika, Saria Iswari. "The Use of a Culturally Sensitive Song Form, Macapat, to Teach the Bible in Rural Java." Unpublished doctoral diss., Biola University, 2002.

Martin, C. "Understanding the Perceptions of Indonesian Women Employed by International Female Christian Entrepreneurs." Unpublished doctoral diss., Biola University, 2018.

Martinez, J. "Transformational Development Outcomes in Cambodia." Unpublished doctoral diss., Biola University, 2018.

Mathew, J. K. "A Study of the Effects of a University Education Upon the Ministerial Behaviors of Indian Pentecostal Church of God Pastors in the State of Kerala, India." Unpublished doctoral diss., Biola University, 2010.

Matsumoto, David, et al. "Development and Validation of a Measure of Intercultural Adjustment Potential in Japanese Sojourners: the Intercultural Adjustment Potential Scale (ICAPS)." *International Journal of Intercultural Relations* 25 (2001) 483–510.

Mauss, Marcel. *The Gift: The Form and Reason for Exchange in Archaic Societies*. New York: W. W. Norton, 1990.

Maxwell, John C. *The 21 Irrefutable Laws of Leadership: Follow Them and People Will Follow You.* Nashville: Thomas Nelson, 1998.

Mayers, Marvin Keene. *Christianity Confronts Culture: A Strategy for Cross-cultural Evangelism.* Grand Rapids: Zondervan, 1974.

Mbiti, John. "Theological Impotence and the Universality of the Church." In *Mission Trends No. 3: Third World Theologies*, edited by G. Anderson and T. Stransky, 7–18. New York: Paulist, 1976.

Mbuva, James Muli. "A Comparative Study of Two Religious Training Schools in Kenya and California." Unpublished doctoral diss., Biola University, 1998.

McClintock, Wayne. "Sociological Critique of the Homogeneous Unit Principle." *International Review of Mission* 77 (1988) 107–16.

McCollum, Frank, and Endemina Ifamut. "Liana-Seti Origin Myths Corrected and Answered by Biblical Myths." *Missiology: An International Review* 31 (2003) 289–302.

McDermott, Gerald R., and Harold A. Netland. *A Trinitarian Theology of Religions: An Evangelical Proposal.* New York: Oxford University Press, 2014.

McDowell, Sean, et al. "The Bible and Immigration." *Think Biblically* (June 2018). https://www.biola.edu/blogs/think-biblically/2018/the-bible-and-immigration.

McEwan, Cheryl. "Postcolonialism, Feminism and Development: Intersections and Dilemmas." *Progress in Development Studies* 1 (2001) 93–111.

McGavran, Donald. *The Bridges of God: A Study in the Strategy of Missions.* New York: World Dominion, 1955.

———. "My Pilgrimage in Mission." *International Bulletin of Missionary Research* 10 (1986) 53–58.

———. *Understanding Church Growth.* Grand Rapids: Eerdmans, 1990.

McGee, R. Jon, and Richard L. Warms, eds. *Anthropological Theory: An Introductory History.* 6th ed. Lanham, MD: Rowman & Littlefield, 2017.

McGeechan, G. J., et al. "A Coproduction Community Based Approach to Reducing Smoking Prevalence in a Local Community Setting." *Journal of Environmental and Public Health* (2016).

McIlwain, T. *Building on Firm Foundations.* Rev. ed. Sanford, FL: New Tribes Mission, 2005.

McIntosh, G. L. "McGavran's Family Heritage." *Great Commission Research Journal* 6 (2014) 115–34.

McQuilkin, Robertson. "Use and Misuse of the Social Sciences: Interpreting the Biblical Text." In *Missiology and the Social Sciences: Contributions, Cautions and Conclusions,* edited by E. Rommen and G. Corwin, 165–83. Pasadena: William Carey Library, 1996.

Mead, Margaret. *Coming of Age in Samoa.* New York: William Morrow & Co, 1928.

Meeks, Wayne A. *The First Urban Christians: The Social World of the Apostle Paul.* 2nd ed. New Haven, CT: Yale, 2003.

Metzger, Paul Louis. "The Halfway House of Hedonism: Potential and Problems in John Piper's Desiring God." *Crux* 41 (2005) 21–27.

Meyers, Megan. "Contextualization Is Complicated: A Case Study of Contextualized Worship Arts in Mozambique." *Missiology: An International Review* 44 (2016) 257–68.

Micah Network. "The Micah Network Declaration on Integral Mission." http://www.micahnetwork.org/sites/default/files/doc/page/mn_integral_mission_declaration_en.pdf.
Migration Data Portal. "International Students." https://migrationdataportal.org/themes/international-students.
Miller, Raymond C. "Varieties of Interdisciplinary Approaches in the Social Sciences." *Issues in Integrative Studies* 1 (1982) 1–37.
Montgomery, Helen Barrett. *Western Women in Eastern Lands.* New York, NY: MacMillan, 1910.
Montgomery, James A. "Hebrew Hesed and Greek Charis." *Harvard Theological Review* 32 (1939) 97–102.
Montgomery, Robert L. *The Lopsided Spread of Christianity: Toward an Understanding of the Diffusion of Religions.* Westport, CT: Praeger, 2002.
Moon, W. Jay. *African Proverbs Reveal Christianity in Culture: A Narrative Portrayal of Builsa Proverbs Contextualizing Christianity in Ghana.* Eugene, OR: Wipf & Stock, 2009.
———. *Intercultural Discipleship.* Grand Rapids: Baker Academic, 2017.
Moore, Edward Caldwell. *The Spread of Christianity in the Modern World.* Chicago: University of Chicago Press, 1919.
Moreau, A. Scott. *Contextualization: Mapping and Assessing Evangelical Models.* Grand Rapids: Kregel, 2012.
———. "A Critique of John Mbiti's Understanding of the African Concept of Time." *East Africa Journal of Theology* 5 (1986) 36–48.
Moreau, A. Scott, et al. *Effective Intercultural Communication: A Christian Perspective.* Grand Rapids: Baker Academic, 2014.
———. *Introducing World Missions.* 2nd ed. Grand Rapids: Baker Academic, 2015.
Morrison, Kenneth M. "Discourse and the Accommodation of Values: Toward a Revision of Mission History." *Journal of the American Academy of Religion* 53 (1985) 365–82.
Mostowlansky, Till, and Andrea Rota. "A Matter of Perspective?: Disentangling the Emic—Etic Debate in the Scientific Study of Religions." *Method and Theory in the Study of Religion* 28 (2016) 317–36.
Moyo, Anderson. *The Audacity of Diaspora Missions.* The Antioch Multiethnic Church-Planting Model for African Reverse Missionaries in Post-Christendom Britain By Moyo Anderson. Saarbrücken, Germany: Lap LAMBERT Academic, 2015.
Muller, Roland. *Honor and Shame: Unlocking the Door.* XLibris, 2001.
———. "The 'Indigenizing' and 'Pilgrim' Principles of Andrew F. Walls Reassessed from a South African Perspective." *Theology Today* 70 (2013) 311–22.
Murray, Iain H. *Amy Carmichael: Beauty for Ashes.* Carlisle, PA: Banner of Truth, 2015.
Myers, Bryant L. "Progressive Pentecostalism, Development, and Christian Development NGOs: A Challenge and an Opportunity." *International Bulletin of Missionary Research* 39 (2015) 115–20.
———. *Walking with the Poor: Principles and Practices of Transformational Development.* Maryknoll, NY: Orbis, 2011.
Nacpil, Marian. "The Church in the Twenty-first Century Diaspora." *International Bulletin of Mission Research* 2 (2018) 68–75.

Nash, Tom. "The Part Mass Media Can Play in Mission Strategy." *Evangelical Missions Quarterly* 46 (2010) 336–42.
Neely, Alan. "Saints Who Sometimes Were: Utilizing Missionary Hagiography." *Missiology* 27 (1999) 441–57.
Nehrbass, Kenneth. *Christianity and Animism in Melanesia: Four Approaches to Gospel and Culture*. Pasadena: William Carey Library, 2012.
———. "The Controversial Image of the US American in Missions." In *Controversies in Mission: Theology, People and Practice of Mission in the 21st Century*, edited by R. Scheuermann and E. Smither, 143–64. Pasadena: William Carey, 2016.
———. "Do Multilingual Speakers Understand the Bible Best in Their Heart Language? A Tool for Comparing Comprehension of Translations in Vernacular Langauges and Languages of Wider Communication." *The Bible Translator* 65 (2014) 88–103.
———. "Does Missiology Have Three Legs to Stand On? The Upsurge of Interdisciplinarity." *Missiology: An International Review* 44 (2016) 50–65.
———. "Formal Theological Education in Vanuatu: Hopes, Challenges and Solutions." *Melanesian Journal of Theology* 27 (2011) 54–72.
———. *God's Image and Global Cultures: Integrating Faith and Culture in the 21st Century*. Eugene, OR: Cascade, 2016.
———. "The Half-Life of Missiological Facts." *Missiology: An International Review* 42 (2014) 284–94.
———. "The Haystack Revival." In *Popular Encyclopedia of Christian History*, edited by D. Mitchell and E. Hindson, 170–71. Eugene, OR: Harvest House, 2013.
———. "Korean Missiology: A Survey of Dissertations and Theses from Western Institutions." *Reformed Theology and Mission* 2 (2012) 149–73.
———. Review of the Book *Multilingual God*. *Missiology* 41 (2013) 359–60.
———. "Profile of a Missiologist: Tom Steffen." *Occasional Bulletin* 33 (2019) 1–10.
Neill, Stephen. *Creative Tension: The Duff Lectures, 1958*. Edinburgh: Edinburgh House, 1959.
———. *A History of Christian Missions*. New York: Penguin, 1964.
Newbigin, Lesslie. *The Gospel in a Pluralist Society*. Grand Rapids: Eerdmans, 1989.
———. *The Household of God*. London: SCM, 1953.
———. "Mission and Missions." *Christianity Today* 4 (1960) 911.
———. "What Is 'A Local Church Truly United'?" *The Ecumenical Review* 29 (1977) 124.
Newell, Peggy, ed. *North American Mission Handbook: US and Canadian Protestant Ministries Overses 2017–2019*. 22nd ed. Pasadena: William Carey Library, 2017.
Ng, K.-Y., et al. *Cultural Intelligence: A Review, Reflections, and Recommendations for Future Research. Conducting Multinational Research: Applying Organizational Psychology in the Workplace*. Washington, DC: American Psychological Association, 2012.
Ng, T. D. "A Study on Community at a Theological Institution in Manila Using Victor Turner's Theory." Unpublished doctoral diss., Biola University, 2000.
Nicklas, Tobias, and Herbert Schlögel. "Mission to the Gentiles, Construction of Christian Identity, and Its Relation to Ethics According to Paul." In *Sensitivity Towards Outsiders: Exploring the Dynamic Relationship Between Mission and Ethics in the New Testament and Early Christianity*, edited by J. Kok, T. Nicklas, D. T. Roth, and Christopher M. Hays, 324–39. Tubingen, Germany: Mohr, 2014.

Nida, Eugene A. *Customs and Cultures: Anthropology for Christian Missions*. New York: Harper and Row, 1954.
Niebuhr, H. Richard. *Christ and Culture*. New York: Harper & Brothers, 1975.
Nishioka, Billy Yoshiyuki. "Worldview Methodology in Mission Theology: A Comparison Between Kraft's and Hiebert's Approaches." *Missiology: An International Review* 26 (1998) 457–76.
Nkonge, Dickson K. "The Church Missionary Society's Burden: Theological Education for a Self-supporting, Self-governing, and Self-propagating African Anglican Church in Keyna 1844–1930." *Anglican and Episcopal History*, 83 (2014) 20–41.
Norton, H. Wilbert. "Urbana: Thirty Years Growing." *Christianity Today* 21 (1976) 16–17.
Novak, Michael. *Will It Liberate?* Mahwah, NJ: Paulist, 1987.
Nwaka, Jacinta Chiamaka. "The Early Missionary Groups and the Context for Igboland: A Reappraisal of Their Evangelization Strategies." *Missiology: An International Review* 40 (2012) 409–24.
Oberg, K. "Cultural Shock: Adjustment to New Cultural Environments." *Practical Anthropology* 7 (1960) 177–82.
Oborji, Francis Anekwe. "Edinburgh 1910 and Christian Identity Today: An African Perspective." *Missiology: An International Review* 41 (2013) 300–314.
Ogereau, Julien M. "Paul's κοινωνία with the Philippians: Societas as a Missionary Funding Strategy." *New Testament Studies* 60 (2014) 360–78.
Olsen, Stephen E. "Czech Social Relations and Czech Academic Mentoring: With Implications for Christian Mentoring." Unpublished doctoral diss., Biola University, 1996.
Olson, C. Gordon, and Don C. Fanning. *What in the World is God Doing? Essentials of Global Missions*. Lynchburg, VA: Branches, 2011.
Ong, Walter J. *Orality and Literacy*. New Accents. New York: Routledge, 1982.
Oswalt, John N. "The Mission of Israel to the Nations." In *Through No Fault of Their Own: The Fate of Those Who Have Never Heard*, edited by W. Crockett and J. Sigountos, 85–97. Grand Rapids: Baker, 1991.
Ott, Craig. "The Power of Biblical Metaphors for the Contextualized Communication of the Gospel." *Missiology* 42 (2014) 357–74.
Ott, Craig, et al. *Encountering Theology of Mission: Biblical Foundations, Historical Developments, and Contemporary Issues*. Grand Rapids: Baker Academic, 2010.
Ott, Craig, and Gene Wilson. *Global Church Planting: Biblical Principles and Best Practices for Multiplication*. Grand Rapids: Baker Academic, 2011.
Padilla, C. René. "From Lausanne I to Lausanne III." *Journal of Latin American Theology* 5 (2010) 19–50.
———. "The Globalization of Greed." *Journal of Latin American Theology* 9 (2014) 43–67.
———. "Integral Mission and Its Historical Development." In *Justice, Mercy and Humility: Integral Mission and the Poor*, edited by T. Chester, 42–58. Milton Keynes, UK: Paternoster, 2002.
———. "My Theological Pilgrimage." *Journal of Latin American Theology* 4 (2009) 91–111.
———. "The Unity of the Church and the Homogeneous Unit Principle." *International Bulletin of Missionary Research* 6 (1982) 23–30.

Parsons, N. T. "The Impact of a Contextualized Narrative Curriculum on Gospel Understanding Among Homeless Adult Male Mission Students." PhD diss., Biola University, 2006.

Pattison, Stephen. "Shame and the Unwanted Self." In *The Shame Factor: How Shame Shapes Society*, edited by R. Jewett, 9–29. Eugene, OR: Cascade, 2011.

Pentecost, Edward C. *Issues in Missiology*. Grand Rapids: Baker, 1982.

Peters, George W. *A Biblical Theology of Missions*. Chicago: Moody, 1984.

Pickett, Mark. "Caste-Sensitive Church Planting: Revisiting the Homogeneous Unit Principle." *Transformation* 32 (2015) 177–87.

Pierson, Arthur T. *The Modern Mission Century Viewed as a Cycle of Divine Working: A Review of the Missions of the Nineteenth Century with Reference to the Superintending Providence of God*. London: James Nisbet & Co, 1901.

Pieterse, Jan Nederveen. "After Post-Development." *Third World Quarterly* 21 (2000) 175–91.

Pike, Kenneth L. *Language in Relation to a Unified Theory of the Structure of Human Behavior. Volume 1*. Glendale, CA: Summer Institute of Linguistics, 1954.

———. *With Heart and Mind: A Personal Synthesis of Scholarship and Devotion*. Grand Rapids: Eerdmans, 1962.

Piper, John. *Filling Up the Afflictions of Christ*. Wheaton, IL: Crossway, 2014.

———. "John Piper's Personal Tribute to the Late Ralph Winter." http://www.desiringgod.org/articles/john-pipers-personal-tribute-to-the-late-ralph-winter.

———. *Let the Nations Be Glad: The Supremacy of God in Missions*. Grand Rapids: Baker, 1993.

———. "Missions, Orality, and the Bible." https://www.desiringgod.org/articles/missions-orality-and-the-bible.

Pitarch, Pedro. *The Jaguar and the Priest: An Ethnography of Tzeltal Souls*. Austin, TX: University of Texas, 2010.

Plueddemann, J. E. "Needed: An Enlarged View of Church Growth." *Evangelical Missions Quarterly* 23 (1987) 32–38.

Pocock, M. "Introduction: An Appeal for Balance." In *Missiology and the Social Sciences: Contributions, Causations and Conclusions*, edited by E. Rommen and G. Corwin, 7–18. Pasadena: William Carey Library, 1996.

Pocol, C., and M. McDonough. "Women, Apiculture and Development: Evaluating the Impact of a Beekeeping Project on Rural Women's Livelihoods." *Bulletin of University of Agricultural Sciences and Veterinary Medicine Cluj-Napoca. Horticulture* 72 (2015) 487–92.

Pope, R., et al. "Multicultural Competence in Student Affairs." *Journal of Higher Education* 77 (2006) 1110–12.

Porter, Stanley E. "Reconciliation as the Heart of Paul's Missionary Theology." In *Paul as Missionary: Identity, Activity, Theology, and Practice*, edited by T. J. Burke and B. S. Rosner, 169–79. London: T. & T. Clark., 2011.

Priest, Robert J. "Are Short-Term Missions Good Stewardship?" *Christianity Today*. (July, 2005). https://www.christianitytoday.com/ct/2005/julyweb-only/22.0.html.

———. "Missionary Positions: Christian, Modernist, Postmodernist." *Current Anthropology* 42 (2001) 29–68.

———. "Paul G. Hiebert: A Life Remembered." *Trinity Journal* 30 (2009) 171–75.

———. "The Value of Anthropology for Missiological Engagements with Context: The Case of Witch Accusations." *Missiology: An International Review* 43 (2015) 27–42.

Priest, Robert J., and Robert DeGeorge. "Doctoral Dissertations on Mission: Ten-year Update, 2002–2011 (revised)." *International Bulletin of Missionary Research* 37 (2013) 195–202.
Prilleltensky, Isaac. "Poverty and Power." In *Poverty and Psychology: From Global Perspective to Local Practice*, edited by S. C. Carr and T. S. Sloan. New York: Plenum, 2003.
Prior, Randall. *Gospel and Culture in Vanuatu 4: Local Voices on Jesus Christ and Mission*. Wattle Park, Australia: Gospel Vanuatu, 2005.
Purgason, Kitty B. *Professional Guidelines for Christian English Teachers: How to Be a Teacher with Convictions While Respecting Those of Your Students*. Pasadena: William Carey Library, 2016.
Radcliffe, Sarah. "Popular and State Discourses of Power." In *Human Geography Today*, edited by D. Massey et al., 219–42. Cambridge, England: Polity, 1999.
Rainer, Thom S. *The Book of Church Growth: History, Theology and Principles*. Nashville: B&H, 1993.
Ramanayake, D. "Evangelizing International Students in the United States by Understanding Worldview." Unpublished doctoral diss., Oral Roberts University, 2002.
Ramsay, William. *The Imperial Peace: An Ideal in European History*. London: Oxford University Press, 1913.
Ranis, Gustav. "Human Development and Economic Growth." *Yale University Economic Growth Center Discussion Paper No. 887*. New Haven, CT: Yale University, 2004.
Rauschenbusch, Walter. *A Theology for the Social Gospel*. New York: Abingdon, 1917.
Rawson, Katie Jean. "Evangelizing East Asian Students in the United States with Special Reference to Media Tools." Unpublished doctoral diss., Fuller Theological Seminary, 1999.
Reed, Lyman E. *Preparing Missionaries for Intercultural Communication: A Bicultural Approach*. Pasadena: William Carey Library, 1985.
Reid, J. M. *Missions and Missionary Society of the Methodist Episcopal Church*. New York: Hunt and Eaton, 1879.
Reid-Henry, Simon. *The Political Origins of Inequality*. Chicago: University of Chicago, 2015.
Reyburn, William D. "Polygamy, Economy, and Christianity in the Eastern Cameroun." In *Readings in Missionary Anthropology II*, edited by W. Smalley, 255–73. South Pasadena: William Carey Library, 1978.
Rice, Delbert. "Evangelism and Decision-making Processes." In *Readings in Missionary Anthropology II*, edited by W. Smalley, 530–539. South Pasadena: William Carey Library, 1978.
Richardson, Don. *Eternity in Their Hearts*. Ventura, CA: Regal 1981.
———. *Peace Child*. Ventura, CA: Regal, 1975.
Ricks, David A. *Big Business Blunders: Mistakes in Multinational Marketing*. Homewood, IL: Dow Jones-Irwin, 1983
Rist, Gilbert. *The History of Development: From Western Origins to Global Faith*. London: Zed, 1977.
Robert, Dana L. *American Women in Mission: A Social History of Their Thought and Practice*.
———. *The Catholic Historical Review*. Macon, GA: Mercer University, 1996.

---. *Christian Mission: How Christianity Became a World Religion.* Malden, MA: Wiley-Blackwell, 2009.

---. "Cross-cultural Friendship in the Creation of Twentieth-Century World Christianity." *International Bulletin of Missionary Research* 35 (2011) 100–107.

---. "Global Friendship as Incarnational Missional Practice." *International Bulletin of Missionary Research* 39 (2015) 180–82, 184.

---. "What Happened to the Christian Home? The Missing Component of Mission Theory." *Missiology: An International Review* 33 (2005) 325–40.

---. "World Christianity as a Woman's Movement." *International Bulletin of Missionary Research* 30 (2006) 180–88.

Robinson, Charles Henry. *How the Gospel Spread through Europe.* New York: Macmillan, 1919.

Rogers, Everett M. *Diffusion of Innovations.* New York: Free, 2003.

Rosner, Brian S. "The Glory of God in Paul's Missionary Theology and Practice." In *Paul as Missionary: Identity, Activity, the Ology, and Practice*, edited by T. J. Burke and B. S. Rosner, 158–68. London: T. & T. Clark, 2011.

Rostow, W. W. *The Stages of Economic Growth: A Non-Communist Manifesto.* New York: Cambridge University Press, 1960.

Ruben, Brent D. "Guidelines for Cross-Cultural Communication Effectiveness." *Group and Organization Studies* 2 (1977) 470–79.

Ruder, Romney. "Competencies and the Changing World of Work: The Need to Add Cultural Adaptability and Cultural Intelligence to the Mix When Working with Urban Missionary Candidates." Unpublished doctoral diss., Pepperdine University, 2017.

Rundle, Steven, and Tom A. Steffen. *Great Commission Companies: The Emerging Role of Business in Missions.* Downer's Grove, IL: InterVarsity, 2013.

Rupp, Daniel. "Sherpas and Shepherds: A Qualitative Exploration of Ministry Models Held by American Millennial Missionaries and the Chinese House Church Pastors They Serve." Unpublished doctoral diss., Biola University, 2019.

Russell, Sue, et al. "Suits or Sandals: Making Business as Mission Work." In *Business as Mission: From Impoverished to Empowered*, edited by T. Steffen and M. Barnett, 291–304. Pasadena: William Carey Library, 2006.

RWSN. *Sustainable Rural Water Supplies.* St Gallen, Switzerland, 2012.

Rynkiewich, Michael A. "Corporate Metaphors and Strategic Thinking: 'The 10/40 Window' in the American Evangelical Worldview." *Missiology* 35 (2007) 217–41.

---. "Mission in 'The Present Time': What About the People in Diaspora?" *International Journal of Frontier Missiology* 30 (2013) 103–14.

Said, Edward W. *Orientalism.* New York: Vintage, 1979.

Salamone, Frank A. "Missionaries and Anthropologists: An Inquiry into Their Ambivalent Relationship." *Missiology: An International Review* 14 (1986) 55–70.

Salisbury, Kevin. "Paul's First Letter to Timothy: An Example of Missonal Contextualization." *Colloquium* 44 (2012) 78–101.

Samuel, Vinay, and Chris Sugden, eds. *The Church in Response to Human Need.* Grand Rapids: Eerdmans, 1987.

Sanneh, Lamin. *Disciples of All Nations: Pillars of World Christianity.* Oxford: Oxford University Press, 2008.

---. *Translating the Message: The Missionary Impact on Culture.* Maryknoll, NY: Orbis, 1989.

———. *Whose Religion Is Christianity? The Gospel beyond the West*. Grand Rapids: Eerdmans, 2003.
Schaff, Philip. *Church History*. 8 vols. Peabody, MA: Hendrickson, 2006.
Schafroth, Verena. "Female Genital Mutilation in Africa: An Analysis of the Church's Response and Proposals for Change." *Missiology: An International Review* 37 4 (2009) 527–42.
Scherer, James A. "Missiology as a Discipline and What It Includes." *Missiology: An International Review* 15 (1987) 507–22.
Schmidt, Wilhelm. *The Origin and Growth of Religion: Facts and Theories*. London: Methuen, 1931.
Schnabel, Eckhard J. *Early Christian Mission*. Downers Grove, IL: InterVarsity, 2004.
———. "Paul the Missionary." In *Paul's Missionary Methods: In His Time and Ours*, edited by R. Plummer and J. M. Terry, 29–43. Downers Grove, IL: IVP Academic, 2012.
Schreiter, Robert J. "Anthropology and Faith: Challenges to Missiology." *Missiology* 19 (1991) 283–94.
———. *Constructing Local Theologies*. Maryknoll, NY: Orbis, 1985.
Scotchmer, David. "Symbols of Salvation: A Local Mayan Protestant Theology." *Missiology: An International Review* 17 (1989) 293–308.
Selka, Stephen. *Religion and the Politics of Ethnic Identity in Bahia, Brazil*. Gainsville, FL: University of Florida, 2007.
Sen, Amartya. *Development as Freedom*. New York: Anchor, 2000.
———. "Well-Being, Agency and Freedom: The Dewey Lectures 1984." *The Journal of Philosophy* 82 (1985) 169.
Seton, Rosemary. *Western Daughters in Eastern Lands: British Missionary Women in Asia*. Santa Barbara, CA: Praeger, 2013.
Seward, Nadine, et al. "Effects of Women's Groups Practising Participatory Learning and Action on Preventive and Care-Seeking Behaviours to Reduce Neonatal Mortality: A Meta-Analysis of Cluster-Randomised Trials." *PLOS Medicine* 14 (2017) 1–22.
Shank, Nathan. *Four Fields of Kingdom Growth*. 3rd ed. Self-published, 2015.
Sharp, Lauriston. "Steel Axes for Stone-Age Australians." *Human Organization* 11 (1952) 17–22.
Sharpe, Eric J. "The Legacy of Amy Carmichael." *International Bulletin of Missionary Research* 20 (1996) 121–25.
———. "Reflections on Missionary Historiography." *International Bulletin of Missionary Research* 13 (1989) 76–81.
Shenk, Wilbert R. "Dr. Ralph Winter and the American Society of Missiology." *Missiology: An International Review* 38 (2010) 92–93.
———. "Henry Venn's Instructions to Missionaries." *Missiology: An International Review* 5 (1977) 467–85.
———. "Henry Venn's Legacy." *Occasional Bulletin of Missionary Research* 1 (1977) 16–19.
———. "The Origins and Evolution of the Three-Selfs in Relation to China." *International Bulletin of Missionary Research* 14 (1990) 28–35.
Short, Mabel Dickson. "Lottie Moon: Sacrificed All for Her Beloved China." *Fundamentalist Journal* 6 (1987) 33.

Sider, Ronald J. *Rich Christians in an Age of Hunger: Moving from Affluence to Generosity.* Nashville: Thomas Nelson, 1977.

Sigountons, J. "Did Early Christians Believe Pagan Religions Could Save?" In *Through No Fault of Their Own: The Fate of Those Who Have Never Heard*, edited by W. Crocket and J. Sigountos, 229–41. Grand Rapids: Baker, 1991.

Sinha, R., et al. "Economic Evaluation of Participatory Learning and Action with Women's Groups Facilitated by Accredited Social Health Activists to Improve Birth Outcomes in Rural Eastern India." *Cost Effectiveness and Resource Allocation* 15 (2017) 1–9.

Skreslet, Stanley H. "Thinking Missiologically About the History of Mission." *International Bulletin of Missionary Research* 31 (2007) 58–62.

Slack, J. "Just How Many Church Planting Movements Are There?" *Mission Frontiers* (March-April 2011) 12–13.

Slimbauch, Richard. "First, Do No Harm: Short-Term Missions at the Dawn of a New Millennium." *Evangelical Missions Quarterly* 36 (2000) 428–41.

Smalley, William A. "The Gospel and the Cultures of Laos." *Practical Anthropology* 3 (1956) 47–57.

———. *Translation as Mission: Bible Translation in the Modern Missionary Movement.* Macon, GA: Mercer, 1991.

Smith, Henry Boynton. "The Nature and Worth of the Science of Church History." *Bibliotheca Sacra* 8 (1851) 415–26.

Smith, Lucius E. *Heroes and Martyrs of the Modern Missionary Enterprise: A Record of Their Lives and Labors.* Providence, RI: Potter, 1856.

Smith, Steve. *T4T: A Discipleship ReRevolution.* Monument, CO: WIGTake Resources, 2011.

Smither, Edward L. "When the Church was the Mission Organization: Rethinking Winter's Two Structures of Redemption Paradigm." In *Churches on Mission: God's Grace Abound to the Nations*, edited by G. Hart et al., 25–46. Pasadena: William Carey Library, 2017.

Spencer, Aída Besançon. "Romans 1: Finding God in Creation." In *Through No Fault of Their Own: The Fate of Those Who Have Never Heard*, edited by W. Crocket and J. Sigountos, 125–35. Grand Rapids: Baker, 1991.

Spickard, James V. "A Guide to Mary Douglas' Three Versions of Grid/Group Theory." *Sociological Analysis* 50 (1989) 151–70.

Stafford, Tim. "Ralph Winter: An Unlikely Revolutionary." *Christianity Today* 6 (1984) 14–18.

Stanley, B. "1974—Redefining the Great Commission: the Lausanne Congress." *Hill Road* 15 (2012) 37–57.

———. "Lausanne 1974: The Challenge From the Majority World to Northern-Hemisphere Evangelicalism." *The Journal of Ecclesiastical History* (2013) 533–51.

Stark, Rodney. *The Rise of Christianity.* Princeton: Princeton University Press, 1996.

Starkes, M. T. *God's Commissioned People: A Fresh History of Christian Missions. Broadman.* Nashville: Broadman, 1984.

Stearns, Richard. *The Hole in Our Gospel Special Edition: What Does God Expect of Us? The Answer That Changed My Life and Might Just Change the World.* Nashville: Thomas Nelson, 2014.

Steffan, Melissa. "The Surprising Countries Most Missionaries Are Sent From and Go To." *Christianity Today*. (July 2013). https://www.christianitytoday.com/news/2013/july/missionaries-countries-sent-received-csgc-gordon-conwell.html.
Steffen, Tom. *Business as Usual in the Missions Enterprise*. La Habra, CA: Center for Organizational Ministry and Development, 1999.
———. "A Clothesline Theology for the World: How a Value-Driven Grand Narrative of Scripture Can Frame the Gospel." *Great Commission Research Journal* 9 (2018) 235–72.
———. "Don't Show the Jesus Film." *Evangelical Missions Quarterly* 29 (1993) 272–75.
———. *The Facilitator Era*. Eugene, OR: Wipf & Stock, 2011.
———. "Minimizing Crosscultural Evangelism Noise." *Missiology* 43 (2015) 413–28.
———. "Missiological Education for the 21st Century." *Evangelical Missions Quarterly* 29 (1993) 172–83.
———. "Missiology's Journey for Acceptance in the Educational World." *Missiology: An International Review* 21 (2011) 131–53.
———. "Orality Comes of Age: The Maturation of a Movement." *International Journal of Frontier Missiology* 31 (2014) 139–47.
———. *Passing the Baton*. Rev. ed. Pasadena: Center for Organization & Ministry, 1997.
———. *Reconnecting God's Story to Ministry: Cross-cultural Storytelling at Home and Abroad*. La Habra, CA: Center for Organizational Ministry & Development, 1996.
Steinbronn, A. J. "Missiological Bridge-Building Based Upon an Emic and Etic Understanding of Culture As Derived From Music." *Missio Apostolica* 7 (1999) 34–41.
Stetzer, Ed. "C. Peter Wagner (1930–2016), Some Thoughts on His Life and Passing." http://www.christianitytoday.com/edstetzer/2016/october/in-memory-of-c-peter-wagner.html.
Steuernagel, Valdir R. "Social Concern and Evangelization: The Journey of the Lausanne Movement." *International Bulletin of Missionary Research* 15 (1991) 53–56.
Stinton, Di. *Jesus of Africa: Voices of Contemporary African Christology*. Maryknoll, NY: Orbis, 2004.
Stipe, Claude E., et al. "Anthropologists Versus Missionaries: The Influence of Presuppositions [and Comments and Reply]." *Current Anthropology* 12 (1980) 165–79.
Storti, Craig. *The Art of Crossing Cultures*. Boston: Intercultural, 2001.
Stott, John R. "Evangelism and Social Responsibility: An Evangelical Commitment." *Lausanne Occasional Paper* 21 (1982).
———. "Twenty Years After Lausanne: Some Personal Reflections." *International Bulletin of Missionary Research* 19 (1995) 50–55.
Stuttaford, M., and C. Coe. "The 'Learning' Component of Participatory Learning and Action in Health Research: Reflections From a Local Sure Start Evaluation." *Qualitative Health Research* 17 (2007) 1351–60.
Strauss, R. M. "The Design and Delivery of Intentional and Integral Missionary Training: A Case Study of New Tribes Mission." Unpublished doctoral diss., Biola University, 2008.
Strelan, John G. *The Search for Salvation: Studies in the History and Theology of Cargo Cults*. Adelaide, Australia: Lutheran, 1977.
Strom, Donna. "Christianity and Culture Change Among the Mizoram." *Missiology: An International Review* 8 (1980) 307–17.

Suarez, Gustavo V. "Donald McGavran's Understanding of Conversion." *Great Commission Research Journal* 4 (2013) 182–201.

Sugden, C. *Gospel, Culture and Transformation*. Oxford: Regnum, 2000.

———. "Transformational Development: Current State of Understanding and Practice." *Transformation* 20 (2003) 71–77.

Suh, G. S. "Exploring a Contextualized Leadership Development Model Built on Spiritual Formation for Emerging Christian Leaders in Urban Cambodia." Unpublished doctoral diss., Biola University, 2017.

Sullivan, Regina D. *Lottie Moon: a Southern Baptist Missionary to China in History and Legend*. Baton Rouge: Louisiana State University, 2011.

Sumule, Leonard. "The Impact of Informal Mentoring: Perceptions of Alumni of Evangelical Theological Schools in Indonesia." Unpublished doctoral diss., Biola University, 2016.

Tasie, Godwin, et al. "History of Mission: Urgent Research Fields; Role of Women in Mission." *Missiology: An International Review* 7 (1979) 92–96.

Taylor, Bill. "The Place of Short-Term Missions." https://urbana.org/blog/place-short-term-missions.

Taylor, J. "Goods and Gods: A Follow-up Study of 'Steel axes for Stone Age Australians.'" In *Aboriginal Australians and Christian Missions: Ethnographic and Historical Studies*, edited by T. Swain and D. Rose, 438–51. Bedford Park, South Australia: Australian Association for the Study of Religions, 1988.

Taylor, William David. "From Iguassu to the Reflective Practitioners of the Global Family of Christ." In *Global Missiology for the 21st Century: The Iguassu Dialogue*, edited by W. Taylor, 3–14. Grand Rapids: Baker Academic, 2000.

Tennent, Timothy. *Invitation to World Missions: A Trinitarian Missiology for the Twenty-first Century*. Grand Rapids: Kregel, 2010.

———. *Theology in the Context of World Christianity: How the Global Church is Influencing the Way We Think About and Discuss Theology*. Grand Rapids: Zondervan, 2007.

Terry, George A. "A Missiology of Excluded Middles: An Analysis of the T4T Scheme for Evangelism and Discipleship." *Themelios* 42 (2017) 335–52.

Terry, J. O. "Chronological Bible Storying to Tribal and Nomadic Peoples." *International Journal of Frontier Missiology* 14 (1997) 167–72.

Terry, J. O., et al. *Missiology: An Introduction to the Foundations, History, and Strategies of World Missions*. Nashville: B&H, 1998.

Thigpen, L. Lynn. "Connected Learning: A Grounded Theory Study of How Cambodian Adults with Limited Formal Education Learn." Unpublished doctoral diss., Biola University, 2016.

Thomas, Norman E. "Springboards for 21st Century Mission: Celebrating Edinburgh 1910." *Missiology: An International Review* 39 (2010) 141–56.

Thorbecke, Erik. "The Evolution of the Development Doctrine and the Role of Foreign Aid, 1950–2000." In *Advancing Development. Studies in Development Economics and Policy*, edited by G. Mavrotas and A. Shorrocks, 3–37. London: Palgrave, 2007.

Ting-Toomey, S. "Identity Negotiation Theory." In *Theorizing About Intercultural communication*, edited by W. Gudykunst, 11–23. Thousand Oaks, CA: Sage, 2005.

Tippett, Alan R. *Deep Sea Canoe: The Story of Third World Missionaries in the South Pacific*. Pasadena: William Carey Library, 2005.

———. "Indigenous Principles in Mission Today." In *Verdict Theology in Missionary Theory*, edited by A. Tippett, 126–41. Pasadena: William Carey Library, 1973.
———. *Introduction to Missiology*. Pasadena: William Carey Library, 1987.
———. "Missiology, a New Discipline." In *The Means of World Evangelization: Missiological Education at the Fuller School of World Missions*, edited by A. Martin, 25–31. Pasadena: William Carey Library, 1974.
———. *People Movements in South Polynesia*. Chicago: Moody, 1971.
———. *Solomon Islands Christianity*. Pasadena: William Carey Library, 1967.
Travis, J. "The C1–C6 Spectrum after Fifteen Years." *Evangelical Missions Quarterly* 51 (2015) 358–65.
Trobisch, Walter. "Congregational Responsibility for the Christian Individual." In *Readings in Missionary Anthropology II*, edited by W. Smalley, 227–40. South Pasadena: William Carey Library, 1978.
Trompf, G. W. "Missiology and Anthropology: a Viable Relationship?" *Oceania* 55 (1984) 148–53.
Truman, Harry S. "Inaugural Address." 1949. https://avalon.law.yale.edu/20th_century/truman.asp.
Tucker, Ruth A. *From Jerusalem to Irian Jaya: A Biographical History of Christian Missions*. Grand Rapids: Zondervan, 2004.
———. *Guardians of the Great Commission: The Story of Women in Modern Missions*. Grand Rapids: Zondervan, 1994.
Tucker, Ruth A., and Walter Liefeld. *Daughters of the Church: Women and Ministry from New Testament Times to the Present*. Grand Rapids: Baker Academic. 1987.
Twiss, Richard. *Rescuing the Gospel from the Cowboys: A Native American Reflection on the Jesus Way*. Downers Grove, IL: InterVarsity, 2015.
Tylor, Edward B. *Anthropology: An Introduction to the Study of Man and Civilization*. London: Macmillan, 1881.
Umer, H. "The Relational Theory of the Leadership-Followership Process: Perceptions of Leaders and Followers in the Ethiopian Kale Heywet Church." Unpublished doctoral diss., Biola University, 2019.
Uys, Jamie. *The Gods Must Be Crazy*. South Africa: C. A. T. Films, 1981.
Van der Zee, Karen I., and Jan Pieter Van Oudenhoven. "The Multicultural Personality Questionnaire: A Multidimensional Instrument of Multicultural Effectiveness." *European Journal of Personality* 14 (2000) 291–309.
Van Engen, Charles E. "Bridges of God: The Mission Legacy of Donald Anderson McGavran." *Great Commission Research Journal* 1 (2009) 27–32.
———. *Mission on the Way: Issues in Mission Theology*. Grand Rapids: Baker Academic, 1996.
Van Engen, Charles E., et al. *Announcing the Kingdom*. Grand Rapids: Baker Academic, 2003.
van Gennep, Arnold. *The Rites of Passage*. Chicago: University of Chicago Press, 1961.
van Wyk, J. J. "Mbiti, John Samuel." http://www.dacb.org/stories/kenya/mbiti_john.html.
Vara, J. J. "Academic Success Among Hispanic Students in Christian Higher Education." Unpublished doctoral diss., Biola University, 2004.
Varughese, John. "A Sense of History and Apologetics in a Hindu Context." *Missiology: An International Review* 36 (2008) 219–26.

Ver Beek, Kurt Alan. "The Impact of Short-term Missions: A Case Study of House Construction in Honduras after Hurricane Mitch." *Missiology: An International Review* 34 (2006) 477–95.

Verkuyl, Johannes. "The Biblical Foundation for the Worldwide Mission Mandate." In *Perspectives on the World Christian Movement*, edited by S. Hawthorne and R. Winter, 27–33. Pasadena: William Carey Library, 1998.

———. *Contemporary Missiology*. Grand Rapids: Eerdmans, 1978.

Verstraelen, Frans J., et al., eds. *Missiology: An Ecumenical Introduction*. Grand Rapids: Eerdmans, 1995.

Vinay, Samuel, and Chris Sugden, eds. *Missions as Transformation: A Theology of the Whole Gospel*. Eugene, OR: Regnum, 2009.

Voekel, Jack. "21 Missionaries You Should Know." https://urbana.org/blog/21-missionaries-you-should-know.

Wagner, C. Peter. "How Ethical is the Homogeneous Unit Principle." *Occasional Bulletin of Missionary Research* 2 (1978) 12–19.

———. "What Is 'Making Disciples'?" *Evangelical Missions Quarterly* 9 (1973) 285–93.

Wagner, C. Peter, et al., eds. *Praying through the 100 Gateway Cities of the 10/40 Window*. Seattle: YWAM, 1995.

Wallace, Anthony F. C. "Movements Revitalization." *Stress: The International Journal on the Biology of Stress* 58 (2009) 264–28.

Walls, Andrew F. *Crossing Cultural Frontiers: Studies in the History of World Christianity*. Maryknoll, NY: Orbis, 2017.

———. *The Missionary Movement in Christian History: Studies in the Transmission of Faith*. Maryknoll, NY: Orbis, 1996.

———. "The Rise of Global Theologies." In *Global Theology in Evangelical Perspective*, edited by J. Greenman and G. Green, 19–34. Downers Grove, IL: IVP Academic, 2010.

Walters, J. "Donald McGavran and the City." *Great Commission Research Journal* 4 (2013) 202–15.

———. "Donald McGavran's Theological Foundations for 'Effective Evangelism.'" *Great Commission Research Journal* 2 (2010) 50–61.

Walton, Steve. "Paul, Patronage and Pay: What Do We Know About the Apostle's Financial Support?" In *Paul as Missionary: Identity, Activity, Theology, and Practice*, edited by T. Burke and B. Rosner, 220–33. London: T. & T. Clark, 2011.

Wan, Enoch. "Diaspora Missiology and Beyond." *CreateSpace*, 2014.

Wang, Yuting, and Fenggang Yang. "More than Evangelical and Ethnic." *Sociology of Religion* 67 (2006) 179–92.

Ward, Colleen and Antony Kennedy. "Psychological and Socio-Cultural Adjustment During Cross-Cultural Transitions: A Comparison of Secondary Students Overseas and at Home." *International Journal of Psychology* 28 (1993) 129–47.

Warneck, Gustav. *Outline of a History of Protestant Missions from the Reformation to the Present Time: A Contribution to Modern Church History*. New York: Fleming H. Revell, 1901.

Watkins, Morris G. *Literacy, Bible Reading, and Church Growth Through the Ages*. Pasadena: William Carey Library, 1978.

Weaver, A. R. "Toward a Cross-cultural Theory of Leadership Emergence: The Hungarian Case." Unpublished doctoral diss., Fuller Theological Seminary, 2004.

Wheeler, Ray. "The Legacy of Shoki Coe." *International Bulletin of Missionary Research* 26 (2002) 77–80.

White, Ben L. "The Eschatological Conversion of 'All the Nations' in Matthew 28.19-20: (Mis)reading Matthew through Paul." *Journal for the Study of the New Testament (Online)* 36 (2014) 353–82.

Whiteman, Darrell L. "Anthropology and Mission: the Incarnational Connection." *Missiology: An International Review* 31 (2003) 397–415.

———. "The Legacy of Alan R Tippett." *International Bulletin of Missionary Research.* 16 (1992) 163–66.

———. "Anthropology and Mission: the Incarnational Connection." *International Journal of Frontier Missiology* 20 (2003) 35–44.

Whitfield, Keith. "The Triune God; The God of Mission." In *Theology and Practice of Mission: God, the Church and the Nations*, edited by B. Ashford, 1–35. Nashville: B&H, 2011.

Wiest, Jean-Paul. "The Maryknoll China History Project." *International Bulletin of Missionary Research* 9 (1985) 50–56.

Wilcox, M. M. "Of Markets and Missions: the Early History of the Universal Fellowship of Metropolitan Community Churches." *Religion and American Culture* 11 (2001) 83–108.

Williams, M. S. "Revisiting the C1-C6 spectrum in Muslim contextualization." *Missiology: An International Review* 39 (2011) 335–51.

Wilson, J. "The Search for Salvation: Millenarianism and Cargo Cults." *Occasional Bulletin* (2010) 6–7.

Wiltgen, Ralph M. *Gold Coast Mission History, 1471–1880*. Techny, IL: Divine Word, 1957.

Wimber, John, and Kevin Springer. *Power Evangelism*. New York: HarperCollins, 1986.

Winney, G. "The Impact of Strategic Planning Training on the Organizational Culture of Latino churches in Southern California." Unpublished doctoral diss., Biola University

Winter, Ralph D. "Three Mission Eras; And the Loss and Recovery of Kingdom Mission, 1800–2000." In *Perspectives on the World Christian Movement*, edited by R. Winter and S. Hawthorne, 263–78. Pasadena: William Carey Library, 2009.

———. "Two Structures of God's Redemptive Mission." *Missiology: An International Review* 2 (1974) 121–39.

Winter, Ralph D., and Steven C. Hawthorne, eds. *Perspectives on the World Christian Movement*. 4th ed. Pasadena: William Carey Library, 2013.

Woodberry, Robert D. "The Missionary Roots of Liberal Democracy." *American Political Science Review* 106 (2012) 244–74.

Woodhouse, B. Neil. "'You are Jesus, and I Am Your Bird': Christ, Persian Poetry, and Theological Imagination in the Iranian Diaspora." *Missiology: An International Review* 44 (2016) 416–29.

Woodmansee, Naomi L. "Haitian Educational Leaders' Perceptions of the Impact and Use of a Master of Education Degree in Developing Teachers." Unpublished doctoral diss., Columbia International University, 2017.

Woolnough, Brian E. "Christian NGOs in Relief and Development: One of the Church's Arms for Holistic Mission." *Transformation* 28 (2011) 195–205.

"World Missionary Conference, 1910. (Vol. 5)." New York: Fleming H Revell, 1910.

Wright, Christopher J. H. *The Mission of God: Unlocking the Bible's Grand Narrative*. Downers Grove, IL: IVP Academic, 2006.

Wu, Jackson. "How Christ Saves God's Face ... and Ours: A Soteriology of Honor and Shame." *Missiology: An International Review* 44 (2016) 375–87.

Wydick, Bruce. "Cost-Effective Compassion." *Christianity Today* (February 2012) 24–29.

Wydick, Bruce, et al. "Does International Child Sponsorship Work? A Six-Country Study of Impacts on Adult Life Outcomes." *Journal of Political Economy* 121 (2013) 393–436.

Yang, E. S. "An Experiential Approach to Korean Family Ministry Leaders' Training." Unpublished doctoral diss., Biola University, 1999.

Yeh, Allen. *Polycentric Missiology: Twenty-first Century Mission from Everyone to Everywhere*. Downer's Grove, IL: IVP Academic, 2016.

Yeneabat, Mulu, and Alice Butterfield. "'We Can't Eat a Road:' Asset-Based Community Development and The Gedam Sefer Community Partnership in Ethiopia." *Journal of Community Practice* 20 (2012) 134–53.

Yinger, Kent. "Paul and Evangelism: A Missiological Challenge from New Testament Specialists." *Missiology* 37 (2009) 385–96.

Yohannan, K. P. *Revolution in World Missions*. Carrolton, TX: GFA, 2004.

Yount, William, and Mike Barnett. *Called to Reach*. Nashville: B& H Academic, 2007.

Yusuf, Shahid, and Joseph E. Stiglitz. "Development Issues: Settled and Open." In *Frontiers of Development Economics*, edited by G. Meier and J. Stiglitz, 227–68. Washington, DC: Oxford University Press, 2001.

Zhang, Bin. "The Global-Local Dialectic in Postcolonial Approaches in Communication Studies." *Pennsylvania Communication Annual* 70 (2014) 91–116.

Zocca, Franco. *Sanguma in Paradise: Sorcery, Witchcraft and Christianity in Papua New Guinea*. Goroka, PNG: Melanesian Institute, 2009.

Zscheile, D. "Forming and Restoring Community in a Nomadic World: A Next Generation Perspective on the Future of the Discipline of Missiology." *Missiology: An International Review* 42 (2013) 1–13.

Zvobgo, C. J. M. *A History of Christian Missions in Zimbabwe, 1890–1939*. Gweru, Zimbabwe: Mambo, 1996.

www.ingramcontent.com/pod-product-compliance
Lightning Source LLC
Chambersburg PA
CBHW030433300426
44112CB00009B/977